European Union Case Law on the Birds and Habitats Directives

Energy and Environmental Law and Policy Series

VOLUME 43

Editor

General Editor: Professor Kurt Deketelaere, Professor of Law, University of Leuven, Belgium; Honorary Professor of Law, University of Dundee, UK; Honorary Chief of Staff, Flemish Government; Secretary-General, League of European Research Universities (LERU), Belgium. Kurt's CV – see www.kurtdeketelaere/en/kurt.

Introduction

Environmental protection and energy efficiency/security are important societal challenges. In order to tackle them, policy and legal frameworks are developed at national, regional and global level. Through study and best practices development, the challenges will prove to be solvable.

Contents/Subjects

Environment/Nature/Energy/Climate.

Objective

The aim of this series is to publish works of excellent quality that focus on the study of energy and environmental policy. Through this series the editors:

- contribute to the improvement of the quality of energy/environmental law and policy in general and environmental quality and energy efficiency in particular; increase the access to environmental and energy information for academics, non-governmental organizations, government institutions, and business; and
- facilitate cooperation between academic and non-academic communities in the field of energy and environmental law and policy throughout the world.

Readership

Academics and practitioners in environmental and energy matters.

The titles published in this series are listed at the end of this volume.

European Union Case Law on the Birds and Habitats Directives

Nina Claudia Miron

&

Liam Cashman

Wolters Kluwer

Published by:
Kluwer Law International B.V.
PO Box 316
2400 AH Alphen aan den Rijn
The Netherlands
E-mail: lrs-sales@wolterskluwer.com
Website: www.wolterskluwer.com/en/solutions/kluwerlawinternational

Sold and distributed by:
Wolters Kluwer Legal & Regulatory U.S.
920 Links Avenue
Landisville, PA 17538
United States of America
E-mail: customer.service@wolterskluwer.com

ISBN 978-94-035-2557-0

e-Book: ISBN 978-94-035-2567-9
web-PDF: ISBN 978-94-035-2577-8

Wallace Stegner, 'Wilderness Letter':

> *We simply need that wild country available to us, even if we never do more than drive to its edge and look in. For it can be a means of reassuring ourselves of our sanity as creatures, a part of the geography of hope.*

Nina:

> *I would like to refer to the words of Robert Macfarlane to describe a process that brought the idea of this text to life: 'My own map was filling out, moving to a state not of completion – it would never achieve that – but of coherence. I did not want it to be definitive, only to have caught and absorbed something of the places I had passed through, and something of how they had changed me, brought me to think differently.' 'The Wild Places', page 232.*

Advocate General Sharpston in Case C-664/15, *Protect:*

> *Neither water nor the fish swimming in it can go to court. Trees likewise have no legal standing.*

Liam:

> *As a case-handler, I developed a kind of dread, discovering how easy it is to cause species and habitats to decline and disappear, and how difficult it is to act to protect them.*

Table of Contents

Foreword[*]

As directors responsible, respectively, for nature conservation and for compliance and enforcement in the Directorate-General for the Environment of the European Commission, we were very conscious of the key role of the Court of Justice in delivering the European Union's objectives for nature conservation.

The nature case-law is at once a historic and a living phenomenon. Past judgments continue to exert their positive influence and new decisions respond to new or evolving challenges. In 2017, for instance, the Court issued landmark interim orders to halt logging operations in the ancient Białowieża forest in Poland and made clear, for the first time, that it was ready, if necessary, to impose financial penalties to uphold such orders. Furthermore, by strengthening access to justice, the Court has enabled civil society to make future interventions on nature's behalf.

When, getting on for forty years ago, the Court handed down its first rulings on the 1979 Birds Directive, Europe was still divided into East and West and the EU had only a third of its present membership. From the beginning, the Court stressed the need to safeguard a 'common heritage', through rigorous habitat conservation and protection of species. Completeness of protection became an abiding theme.

Thanks to the 1992 Habitats Directive and successive waves of EU enlargement, the common heritage has since vastly expanded. It embraces – and is embraced by – the largest coordinated network of protected sites on the planet, Natura 2000. This was the result in no small part of the nature case-law that emerged in response to disputes about the directives.

Much has been achieved, and the contribution of the nature directives has been recognised in their detailed 'fitness check' completed in 2016.

Red lights have been flashing for nature and biodiversity decline since well before the nature directives were adopted, however, not only in Europe but globally. Recent initiatives under the European Green Deal, such as the ambitious Biodiversity Strategy for 2030 and the Nature Restoration Proposal, underscore the scale of action needed to

* This Foreword was written in the personal capacity of the authors and does not necessarily reflect the views of the European Commission or its position.

halt and reverse the decline of nature, including and beyond what derives from the nature directives. So do global initiatives, noticeably the historic 2022 agreement on the Kunming-Montreal Global Biodiversity Framework under the UN Convention on Biological Diversity. At the level of individual Member States, the Commission's Environmental Implementation Review highlights the steps required to fully implement the Birds Directive and the Habitats Directive.

While these directives do not define the entire scope of the action now needed in the EU, they remain at its core, as does the nature case-law that underpins them.

We would like to congratulate and thank the authors for the efforts made to put all the relevant information together in order to make this book available to all those who want to understand better the scope of the legal protection of biodiversity within the EU, including the rights and means available to those who want to defend it in practice. This book is intended as a help for decision-makers and civil servants, judges and other law enforcement officials, environmental defenders and citizens at large.

Humberto Delgado Rosa, Director, Biodiversity, (2015 – present)
Aurel Ciobanu-Dordea, Director, Implementation and Support to Member States (2014-2022)

Directorate-General Environment,
European Commission

Acknowledgements

We both thank our respective spouses, Daniel and Martina, for their patience and support. We also thank Irina and Catalina for kindly reading and commenting on the text.

We pay tribute to all the European Commission colleagues who, in the period since the mid-1980s, worked on cases described in this book.

The text was written in the personal capacity of the authors and does not necessarily reflect the views of the European Commission or its position.

CHAPTER 1
Introduction

§1.01 LOSS OF NATURE IN EUROPE

In the last four decades, global wildlife populations fell by 60% as a result of human activities.[1] Almost three-quarters of the Earth's surface has been altered, squeezing nature into an ever-smaller corner of the planet.[2]

In the European Union (EU), a report on the state of nature covering the period 2013-2018 showed that, of 463 bird species that naturally occur in the EU, the proportion with poor and bad conservation status had increased by 7% over the reporting period to reach a total of 39%.[3]

The report also addressed 1,389 non-avian protected species and showed that, of these, only around a quarter had a good conservation status, although this represented a slight improvement (4%) compared to the previous reporting period, 2008-2012.[4]

As for natural habitats, the picture is even worse. Between the two reporting periods mentioned, the share of 233 protected habitat types with bad conservation status increased by 6%. According to the latest report, only 15% of habitat types are assessed as having a good conservation status, with 81% having poor or bad conservation status at the EU level and 4% reported as unknown.[5]

---

1. World Wildlife Fund (2018), Living Planet Report – 2018: Aiming Higher, quoted by the EU Biodiversity Strategy for 2030 (COM/2020/380 final), https://eur-lex.europa.eu/legal-content/EN/TXT/?qid=1590574123338&uri=CELEX:52020DC0380.
2. Intergovernmental Science-Policy Platform on Biodiversity and Ecosystem Services (IPBES) (2019), Summary for policymakers, p. 4, A4, quoted by the EU Biodiversity Strategy for 2030 (COM/2020/380 final), https://eur-lex.europa.eu/legal-content/EN/TXT/?qid=1590574123338&uri=CELEX:52020DC0380.
3. European Environment Agency, *State of Nature in the EU, Results from reporting under the nature directives 2013-2018*, p. 5, EEA Report No. 10/2020, https://www.eea.europa.eu/publications/state-of-nature-in-the-eu-2020.
4. *Ibid.*, p. 6.
5. *Ibid.*, pp. 5 and 6.

The key pressures vary by habitat type, species and region but reflect a very wide range of human activities or human-related intrusions and changes. The most frequently reported pressures for both habitats and species stem from agricultural activities and urbanisation.[6] The latter includes sports, tourism and leisure activities, with sensitive coastal areas especially vulnerable. Forestry activities are the second largest pressure category for species generally. For wintering and passage birds, exploitation through hunting and illegal killing is reported as having the greatest impact.

In terms of outlook, the report states that nature in the EU 'continues to decline and faces deteriorating trends from changes in land and sea use, overexploitation and unsustainable management practices, as well as water regime modification, pollution, invasive alien species and climate change'.[7]

If nature is to have any hope of recovering and prospering, strict application of existing nature conservation rules is of utmost importance, especially as 'recent evaluations show that although legislation is fit for purpose, implementation on the ground is lagging behind'.[8]

§1.02 NATURE DIRECTIVES, THE BEDROCK OF EU NATURE CONSERVATION POLICY

Two main pieces of legislation adopted at the EU level address nature conservation: the Birds Directive[9] and the Habitats Directive.[10] Together, they represent the bedrock of the EU's nature conservation policy[11] and 'coordinate conservation efforts for more than 2,000 species and habitats across the EU Member States with the aim of maintaining them at or restoring them to a favourable conservation status'.[12]

The nature directives do not exist in isolation. They are governed by an EU Treaty framework that influences their interpretation, and they sit alongside other EU environmental legislation pursuing complementary goals. They are part of wider

6. The report identifies 15 overarching pressure categories: agriculture; forestry; extraction of resources; energy production; transport; urbanisation; exportation of species; other human intrusions; invasive alien species; pollution; modification of water regimes; natural processes; geological events; climate change; other. *See* European Environment Agency, *State of Nature in the EU, Results from reporting under the nature directives 2013-2018*, pp. 73 and 74, EEA Report No. 10/2020, https://www.eea.europa.eu/publications/state-of-nature-in-the-eu-2020.
7. EEA Report No. 10/2020, State of Nature in the EU, p. 7, https://www.eea.europa.eu/publications/state-of-nature-in-the-eu-2020.
8. EU Biodiversity Strategy for 2030 Bringing nature back into our lives, COM/2020/380 final, https://eur-lex.europa.eu/legal-content/EN/TXT/?qid=1590574123338&uri=CELEX:52020DC0380#footnoteref79.
9. Directive 2009/147/EC of the European Parliament and of the Council of 30 November 2009 on the conservation of wild birds codifying Council Directive 79/409/EEC of 2 April 1979 on the conservation of wild birds, OJ L 20, 26.1.2010, p. 7-25.
10. Council Directive 92/43/EEC of 21 May 1992 on the conservation of natural habitats and of wild fauna and flora, OJ L 206, 22.7.1992, p. 7-50.
11. https://ec.europa.eu/environment/nature/legislation/habitatsdirective/index_en.htm.
12. EEA Report No. 10/2020, State of Nature in the EU, p. 5, https://www.eea.europa.eu/publications/state-of-nature-in-the-eu-2020.

multilateral efforts to conserve nature and are linked to regional, international and global conventions and agreements to safeguard biodiversity. They have also interacted with other international frameworks.

§1.03 BIRDS DIRECTIVE

Adopted over four decades ago, in 1979,[13] following considerable public pressure in favour of such a measure,[14] the Birds Directive is one of the earliest EU environmental laws and one of the most enduring.[15]

At the time, the European Economic Community (EEC) lacked explicit environmental powers under the Treaty governing it. That is why, initially, the Birds Directive was adopted under a general-purpose legal basis, namely Article 235 of the EEC Treaty, which provided that:

> If action by the Community should prove necessary to attain, in the course of the operation of the common market, one of the objectives of the Community, and this Treaty has not provided the necessary powers, the Council shall, acting unanimously on a proposal from the Commission and after consulting the European Parliament, take the appropriate measures.

Its later codified version, Directive 2009/147/EC,[16] was adopted on an environment-legal basis, i.e., under Article 175(1) of the Treaty establishing the European Community.[17]

The Birds Directive is remarkable in its scope, aiming at the 'conservation of all species of naturally occurring birds in the wild state in the European territory of the Member States to which the Treaty applies'.[18] As a result, over 460 wild bird species naturally occurring in the EU benefit from its provisions.

In structure, the directive comprises a preamble 18 recitals which, *inter alia*, set out the reasons for the content of its legal requirements; 20 articles which set out legal requirements for Member States to fulfil and 7 annexes, 5 of which set out lists of bird species and other matters referred to in the main text.

In content, it has two principal categories of conservation provision.

The first covers the protection of bird habitats.[19] Member States must formally 'classify', i.e., designate Special Protection Areas (SPAs), and inside those areas, adopt conservation measures for 194 particularly threatened species[20] as well as, more

13. Council Directive 79/409/EEC of 2 April 1979 on the conservation of wild birds, OJ L 103, 25.4.1979, p. 1.
14. Ludwig Kramer, *EC Environmental Law, Sixth Edition*, 202 (Sweet and Maxwell, 2007).
15. Most other environmental laws of that decade have since been repealed or greatly modified.
16. Directive 2009/147/EC of the European Parliament and of the Council of 30 November 2009 on the conservation of wild birds, OJ L 20, 26.01.2010, p. 7-25.
17. Following further Treaty revisions, the current 'Environment' Chapter is under Title XX, Articles 191 to 193 of the Treaty on the Functioning of the European Union (TFEU).
18. Article 1(1) of the Birds Directive.
19. Articles 3 and 4 of the Birds Directive.
20. Article 4(1), in combination with Annex I, of the directive. *See* https://ec.europa.eu/environment/nature/legislation/birdsdirective/index_en.htm.

generally, for migratory species.[21] For these species, they must also strive to avoid pollution and habitat deterioration outside the SPAs.[22] This category of provision is addressed in detail in Chapters 2, 3 and 5.

The second category aims at safeguarding wild birds from direct threats. Within this category are general prohibitions on the killing or capture of wild birds and the destruction of their nests;[23] prohibitions and restrictions on the sale, keeping or marketing of wild birds;[24] restrictions on hunting, which limit the wild bird species which may be hunted and the season when hunting is lawful;[25] a prohibition on non-selective and large-scale means of killing birds;[26] and allowance, under strict conditions, for exceptions known as 'derogations'.[27] This category is sometimes referred to as 'species protection' and is addressed in detail in Chapter 4.

These principal categories are bracketed between opening provisions covering the directive's scope and objectives[28] and subsequent provisions covering scientific research[29] and introductions,[30] as well as periodic Member State reporting to the Commission,[31] adaptation to technical and scientific progress,[32] appointment of a committee,[33] and transposition into national law. There is a stand-still clause[34] and provision for Member States to take stricter protective measures.[35] The reporting provision is very important for establishing the state of nature at the European level.

Under its original version, Member States were given two years to adopt the necessary measures to implement the Directive.

§1.04 HABITATS DIRECTIVE

Adopted 13 years after the Birds Directive, the 1992 Habitats Directive[36] aims, according to its Article 1, to 'contribute towards ensuring bio-diversity through the conservation of natural habitats and of wild fauna and flora in the European territory of the Member States'. Over 1,000 animal and plant species, as well as 200 habitat types listed in the directive's annexes, are protected by various legal provisions.

21. Article 4(2).
22. Article 4(4), second sentence.
23. Article 5.
24. Article 6.
25. Article 7.
26. Under Article 8, all forms of non-selective and large-scale killing of birds, in particular those listed in Annex IV of the Directive, are banned.
27. Article 9.
28. Articles 1 and 2.
29. Article 10. *See* Agustín García Ureta, *EU Biodiversity Law: Wild Birds and Habitats Directives*, Chapter 6, X (Europa Law Publishing 2020).
30. Article 11. *See* Agustín García Ureta, *EU Biodiversity Law: Wild Birds and Habitats Directives*, Chapter 6, X (Europa Law Publishing 2020).
31. Article 12.
32. Article 15.
33. Article 16.
34. Article 13.
35. Article 14.
36. Council Directive 92/43/EEC of 21 May 1992 on the conservation of natural habitats and of wild fauna and flora, OJ L 206, 22.7.1992, p. 7-50.

In structure, the directive comprises a preamble; 21 recitals which set out the reasons for the content of its legal requirements; 24 articles which set out legal requirements for Member States to fulfil; and 6 annexes which set out lists of habitat types, species and other matters referred to in the main text.

Its provisions, like those of the Birds Directive, can be divided into two broad categories.

The first is made up of provisions concerning the establishment and conservation of a network of protected sites, known as 'Natura 2000'. Natura 2000 is made up of, first, special areas of conservation (SACs) designated under the Habitats Directive for over 200 habitat types[37] and 900 animal species,[38] and, second, SPAs classified under the Birds Directive.[39] Member States must adopt conservation measures for SACs,[40] protect all Natura 2000 sites from habitat deterioration,[41] and ensure that plans and projects likely to significantly affect them are made subject to strict assessment and decision-making requirements.[42] There is also a provision on the wider landscape aimed at improving the ecological coherence of Natura 2000.[43] This category of provision is covered in Chapters 2, 3 and 5.

As with the Birds Directive, the second category comprises species protection provisions. For about 400 species,[44] a very strict legal protection regime applies, composed of general prohibitions concerning activities that would threaten or harm those species.[45] For about 90 species, their exploitation and live capture must be compatible with and not hamper their maintenance in favourable conservation status.[46] Allowance is made for derogations under strict conditions.[47] This category of provision is addressed in Chapter 4.

Again, like the Birds Directive, these provisions are followed by a provision on reporting. Together with the corresponding reporting provision in the Birds Directive, this enables European state-of-nature reports to be prepared – and an overall picture to be presented of the condition of what is recognised as a 'common heritage'. There is provision for amendment of annexes[48] and for a committee,[49] as well as provisions on surveillance[50] and research,[51] and on re-introductions and introductions.[52]

---

37. These are listed in Annex I.
38. These are listed in Annex II.
39. For a detailed account of the origins and implementation of the Natura 2000 network and a history of the nature directives, *see* Andrew L.R. Jackson, *Conserving Europe's Wildlife: Law and Policy of the Natura 2000 Network of Protected Areas* (Routledge 2018).
40. Article 6(1).
41. Article 6(2).
42. Article 6(3) and (4).
43. Article 10.
44. Listed in Annex IV to the directive.
45. Articles 12 and 13.
46. Article 14, and also Article 15.
47. Article 16.
48. Article 19.
49. Article 20.
50. Article 11. *See also* Chapter 5.
51. Article 18.
52. Article 22. *See* Agustín García Ureta, *EU Biodiversity Law: Wild Birds and Habitats Directives*, Chapter 11, V (Europa Law Publishing 2020).

The transposition time limit was two years. There was a separate time frame for designation of SACs, to run until 1998.

§1.05 ACTION ON NATURE AT GLOBAL AND INTERNATIONAL LEVELS

[A] Period Leading up to Adoption of the Birds Directive

[1] Stockholm Conference

Notable international conservation initiatives were emerging in the decade when the Birds Directive was adopted. The first United Nations Conference on the Human Environment was held in Stockholm, Sweden, in 1972. The Stockholm Declaration contained a set of 26 'common principles to inspire and guide the peoples of the world in the preservation and enhancement of the human environment'.[53] The Conference's outputs included the decision to establish the United Nations Environment Programme (UNEP) and 109 recommendations on actions to be taken for the human environment at international level. Recommendation 32, for instance, exhorted Governments to 'give attention to the need to enact international conventions and treaties to protect species inhabiting international waters or those which migrate from one country to another'.

The Stockholm Declaration helped lay the basis for the first EU action programme on the environment, which was adopted in 1973.[54] This action programme itself helped lay the basis for the Birds Directive and figures in the first recital of the directive's original 1979 version.

[2] Convention on International Trade in Endangered Species of Wild Fauna and Flora

Signed in 1973, the Convention on International Trade in Endangered Species of Wild Fauna and Flora (CITES) entered into force in 1975. It covers roughly 6,610 species of animals and 34,310 species of plants and aims to ensure that international trade in specimens of wild animals and plants does not threaten the survival of the species. It is currently implemented in the EU through a 1997 regulation.[55] Trade in certain species is strictly prohibited; for others, it is regulated. There is some limited overlap with the nature directives, with some CITES species also covered by the Birds and Habitats Directive. The legal approach of prohibiting or regulating trade is also found

53. Declaration of the United Nations Conference on the Human Environment, https://www.un.org/en/conferences/environment/stockholm1972
54. *See* para. 6 of Title II of the Declaration of the Council of the European Communities and of the representatives of the Governments of the Member States meeting in the Council of 22 November 1973 on the programme of action of the European Communities on the environment, OJ C 112, 20/12/1973 P. 0001-0002.
55. Council Regulation (EC) No. 338/97 of 9 December 1996 on the protection of species of wild fauna and flora by regulating trade therein, OJ L 61, 3.3.1997, p. 1-69.

in the nature directives – and there are some comparable enforcement challenges when it comes to respect dealing with illegal trade in species.

[3] Ramsar Convention on the Conservation of Wetlands

In 1975, shortly before the adoption of the Birds Directive, an important international nature convention – the Ramsar Convention on the Conservation of Wetlands[56] – came into force.[57] The EU has never formally become a party to this, but the convention's influence can be seen in the drafting of the Birds Directive.[58] Furthermore, many of the Ramsar sites in the EU benefit from the protective provisions of the Birds Directive, the Habitats Directive and the Water Framework Directive.[59] For instance, '83.3% of the area of the 659 Ramsar sites in the EU for which digital boundaries are available falls inside Natura 2000'.[60]

[4] Bern Convention on the Conservation of European Wildlife and Natural Habitats

The Council of Europe's Bern Convention on the Conservation of European Wildlife and Natural Habitats is the nature conservation convention with the closest relationship to the nature directives. Adopted in 1979, it entered into force in 1982. The Council of Europe 'aimed to create the first pan-European conservation instrument',[61] and the convention was groundbreaking.[62] Like the nature directives, it has provisions

56. https://www.ramsar.org/fr.
57. 'The Birds Directive: 40 years conserving our shared natural heritage', https://ec.europa.eu/environment/nature/conservation/wildbirds/40%20yrs%20Birds%20Brochure%20WEB.pdf.
58. According to John Temple Lang, one of the lawyers who drafted the Birds Directive, 'The key habitat provision of the directive was Article 4, which required EU Member States to establish a network of specially protected areas (SPAs) for the conservation of certain endangered and migratory bird species. This was the extension of the concept of "areas of international importance" in the Ramsar Convention on wetlands, as defined by the conference in Cagliari of the parties to the Ramsar Convention'. *See* John Temple Lang, *The Requirements for an Effective International Nature Conservation System, and the EU Birds and Habitats Directives*, 33, in *Nature Law and Policy in Europe*, Chapter 3 (Andrew L.R. Jackson ed., Routledge 2023).
59. Directive 2000/60/EC of the European Parliament and of the Council of 23 October 2000 establishing a framework for Community action in the field of water policy.
60. Alison E. Beresford, Graeme M. Buchanan, Fiona J. Sanderson, Rebecca Jefferson & Paul F. Donald, *The Contributions of the EU Nature Directives to the CBD and Other Multilateral Environmental Agreements, in Conservation Letters*, A Journal for the Society for Conservation Biology, DOI: 10.1111/conl.12259. https://conbio.onlinelibrary.wiley.com/doi/pdf/10.1111/conl.12259.
61. Yaffa Epstein, *The Habitats Directive and Bern Convention: Synergy and Dysfunction in Public International and EU Law*, 26(2) Georgetown International Environmental Law Review (GIELR) 145-173 (2014), quoting Jean Pierre-Ribaut, *How the Bern Convention came into Being*, Naturopa, 101/2004 https://rm.coe.int/090000168093e8a8.
62. According to Eladio Fernández-Galiano 'In the field of biological diversity, the Bern Convention was the first international European text to try to cover all aspects of nature conservation, and not just a particular group of species or a certain type of habitat. This approach was bold and innovative and paved the way for the most influential treaty in this field, the Convention on

dedicated to the protection of habitats[63] and provisions dedicated to the protection of species.[64] The EU has been a contracting party since 1982.[65]

The convention has been important in at least four respects.

First, conceptually and in terms of European cooperation, it helped pave the way for the Habitats Directive.

Second, in providing a common framework for nature conservation, it helps ensure a broadly common approach between the EU and other European countries. In particular, the establishment of the Natura 2000 network under the Habitats Directive is complemented by the Emerald Network under the Bern Convention.[66] The latest updated Emerald Network list comprises sites in Andorra, Belarus, Georgia, Norway, Moldova, Switzerland, Ukraine and the United Kingdom.[67] There is also a list of officially nominated candidate Emerald Network sites.[68] Through its Neighbourhood Policy instruments, including funding, the EU has supported this Emerald network and the creation of new Emerald sites.[69]

Third, the Convention uses a case-file system as a monitoring tool. Dating back to 1984, this is based on complaints about possible breaches of the Convention that can be submitted by environmental associations or even private citizens. Complaints are processed by the Secretariat, the Bureau and, when particularly relevant, also by the Standing Committee, according to their merits and on the basis of the information submitted. When the Standing Committee or its Bureau considers that further information is needed, they can arrange for on-the-spot visits by independent experts, who report to the Standing Committee. The case-file system stems from decisions taken by the Standing Committee itself. The latest register of complaints lists 218 complaints dating from between 1982 and 2023.[70] Amongst these are complaints about topics and places that are prominent in the EU nature case-law.[71]

Biological Diversity of 1992'. *See* Eladio Fernández-Galiano, *A Laboratory of Ideas: The 25 Years of the Bern Convention, Naturopa, 101/2004.*

63. Chapter II.
64. Chapter III. Chapter IV covers migratory species.
65. Council Decision 82/72/EEC of 3 December 1981 on the conclusion on behalf of the Community of the Convention on the Conservation of European Wildlife and Natural Habitats, OJ L 38, 10.2.1982, p. 1.
66. Yaffa Epstein, *The Habitats Directive and Bern Convention: Synergy and Dysfunction in Public International and EU Law*, 26(2) Georgetown International Environmental Law Review (GIELR) 145-173 (2014).
67. 1680a93ca5 (coe.int).
68. *Ibid.*
69. Briefing – Protected areas in the Eastern Partnership countries, https://www.eea.europa.eu/highlights/europes-eastern-partnership-countries-make; European Environment Agency (EEA)'s website, https://www.eea.europa.eu/themes/biodiversity/europe-protected-areas/protected-areas-in-the-eastern.
70. Methods (coe.int); Case-files – Convention on the Conservation of European Wildlife and Natural Habitats (coe.int).
71. *See* complaint 20 about *Caretta caretta*, the sea turtle, in Laganas Bay in Greece; complaint 23 about the Santona Marshes; complaint 66 about the Bielowiesa Forest; Complaint 68 about habitats for the survival of the common hamster (Cricetus cricetus) in Alsace, France; complaint 70 about the Donana National Park; complaint 92 about wind farms in Balchik and Kaliakra, Bulgaria; and complaint 114 about threats to marine turtles in Thines Kiparissias, Greece.

Fourth, the convention has provided a structure for bringing expertise to bear on particular topics and problems. Under its auspices, for instance, a series of valuable recommendations have been adopted on the eradication of illegal killing, trapping and trade of wild birds.

[5] Bonn Convention on Migratory Species and the African-Eurasian Migratory Waterbird Agreement

The Bonn Convention on Migratory Species[72] was signed in Bonn, Germany, in 1979 and came into force in 1983.[73] It is an example of the international cooperation encouraged by the Stockholm Conference in 1972 and was concluded under the aegis of the UNEP. The EU has been a contracting party since 1983.[74]

The Bonn Convention has served as a parent convention for a separate international instrument, the African-Eurasian Migratory Waterbird Agreement (AEWA). This was signed in 1995 and entered into force in 1999. The EU has been a contracting party to this Agreement since 2005.[75] The Birds Directive includes within its scope bird species which migrate to or from places outside the EU and to and from Africa. AEWA is a means of establishing coordinated conservation and management of migratory waterbirds throughout their entire migratory range. In this way, it complements the Birds Directive.

[B] Period Since the Adoption of the Birds Directive

[1] Convention on Biological Diversity

The signing of the Convention on Biological Diversity at the 1992 Rio Earth Summit gave a further impetus to nature conservation. The convention entered into force in 1993. Its three pillars pursue the following objectives: conservation of biological diversity, sustainable use of the components of biological diversity, and fair and equitable sharing of the benefits arising out of the utilisation of genetic resources.

---

72. www.cms.int/en/convention-text.
73. https://www.cms.int/fr/node/17492.
74. Council Decision 82/461/EEC of 24 June 1982 on the conclusion of the Convention on the conservation of migratory species of wild animals, OJ L 210, 24.6.1982, p. 10. Parties and Range States | CMS ., https://urldefense.com/v3/__https:/u11928460.ct.sendgrid.net/ls/click?upn=IdqGng1vvZXj5mjWQhsh7xUg7UO-2F79-2BZX-2BzdXLpeLM3xf1pG4BfsBMh3NxIHLxB2OIn-2FVoYiywh7PbkNx-2B2vrA-3D-3DluMA_-2BxjSk3grIHdnE4vQMcxd-2B-2FaTCqF8e-2F7uF9STDH2w91eu7Dcqh8rYZ3KTSwrl9gPM-2BORjLiRHYCHv3S2RX5DRXh8-2Fc-2BYrJGpEaAC-2FMBo0hUAQ1RRtE6ZqdEsJ8JsrnspJER6ku5H9X-2BYHidi-2BajRCNjH9-2BqgrjHSIvnuAY1jQDNHyPPLUA2bJ1gztqRI5zkZQUYkXQIvsfDCi7P07FOYMVIQ2GfSCpqasvzy-2B6F7Mq3A-3D__;!!DOxrgLBm!FpVjPK1cb19znqAVQU9HP47ptv9Dz0VDEQjQHH-AhctwUi0AfzJnEA-BpQ19Pq5oPRXsHnx-IRmfpFgDV0RSyxyMp6n8$.
75. Council Decision 2006/871/EC of 18 July 2005 on the conclusion on behalf of the European Community of the Agreement on the Conservation of African-Eurasian Migratory Waterbirds, OJ L 345, 8.12.2006, p. 24.

The EU ratified the convention in 1993 and became a party in 1994.[76] The nature directives are 'also part of the implementation' of the convention.[77]

At the global level, the convention has served as the main forum for addressing threats to biodiversity. Regular conferences of the parties (COPs) have sought to strengthen action. COP 15, the most recent, saw the adoption in 2022 of the Kunming-Montreal Global Biodiversity Framework,[78] which includes a global target that, by 2030, at least 30% of the world's 'terrestrial and inland water areas, and of marine and coastal areas' are effectively conserved and managed',[79] with emphasis on areas of particular importance for biodiversity and ecosystem functioning and services. A further target is that, by 2030, at least 30% of areas of degraded terrestrial, inland water, and marine and coastal ecosystems are under effective restoration.[80] There is a monitoring framework[81] to measure and report on progress.

Currently, 17% of the world's terrestrial and 10% of the world's marine areas are under protection.[82] The nature directives provide a globally important contribution through Natura 2000, the 'largest coordinated network of protected sites in the world'.[83]

§1.06 OTHER RELEVANT INTERNATIONAL FRAMEWORKS

Two other international frameworks deserve mention.

[A] Aarhus Convention

The Aarhus Convention on Access to Information, Public Participation in Decision-making and Access to Justice in Environmental Matters has been described as 'the international instrument that establishes environmental rights as human rights, and that guarantees the respect of those rights through good governance mechanisms and through enforcement procedures open to the public'.[84] It has bolstered the nature directives by creating rights for the public and environmental associations, in particular, to participate in environmental decision-making, and to obtain judicial reviews. In important respects, the nature case-law reflects the requirements of the convention.[85]

76. List of Parties (cbd.int).
77. *See* Jan Darpö, *Can Nature Get It Right? A Study on Rights of Nature in the European Context*, 38 (European Parliament, Policy Department for Citizens' Rights and Constitutional Affairs Directorate-General for Internal Policies PE 689.328, March 2021).
78. COP15: Nations Adopt Four Goals, 23 Targets for 2030 In Landmark UN Biodiversity Agreement | Convention on Biological Diversity (cbd.int).
79. COP 15 Decision 15/4, Target 3, 15/4. Kunming-Montreal Global Biodiversity Framework (cbd.int).
80. Target 2 (cbd.int).
81. COP 15 Decision 15/5, 15/5. Monitoring framework for the Kunming-Montreal Global Biodiversity Framework (cbd.int).
82. COP15: Nations Adopt Four Goals, 23 Targets for 2030 In Landmark UN Biodiversity Agreement | Convention on Biological Diversity (cbd.int).
83. The Natura 2000 protected areas network – European Environment Agency (europa.eu).
84. Jean-François Brakeland, *Access to Justice in Environmental Matters: Developments at EU Level* (published in the Gyoseiho-kenkyu 2014, No. 5), untitled (osaka-u.ac.jp).
85. *See* Chapters 3, 4 and 8.

Furthermore, like the Bern Convention, the Aarhus Convention operates a complaint system which is open to individuals and environmental associations. The findings of the Aarhus Convention Compliance Committee (ACCC) have proved very important in securing rights given under the Convention. As with the Bern Convention, it is possible for there to be an overlap with cases featuring in the nature case-law – although ACCC cases will focus on procedural rights rather than substantive compliance with nature conservation requirements.[86]

[B] European Convention on Human Rights and Fundamental Freedoms

There has also been interaction between the nature directives and the European Convention on Human Rights and Fundamental Freedoms (ECHR), although this has not involved the nature case-law directly since the EU has still not acceded to this Convention. In particular, the implications for convention-related rights of measures to comply with the nature directives have been examined in the context of the convention. No contravention of the convention has been found, however.[87]

§1.07 EVOLUTION OF EU LAW AND POLICY RELEVANT TO THE NATURE DIRECTIVES SINCE 1979

[A] EU Treaty Changes

As indicated above, in 1979, the EEC lacked explicit environmental powers under the Treaty governing it. In 1987, the Single European Act conferred express powers on the Community to take environmental action by introducing a new title VI 'Environment'.[88] The Treaty of Maastricht (1993) included specific references to environmental policy. The Treaty of Amsterdam (1999) established the duty to integrate environmental protection into all EU sectoral policies with a view to promoting sustainable development. The Treaty of Lisbon (2009) embedded the Charter of Fundamental rights in the Treaty framework.

86. As JF Brakeland notes, the ACCC had a file (Case ACCC/C/2008/31) on the issues addressed in Case C-115/09, *Trianel. See* Jean-François Brakeland, *Access to Justice in Environmental Matters: Developments at EU Level* (published in the Gyoseiho-kenkyu 2014, No. 5), untitled (osaka-u.ac.jp).
87. *O'Sullivan McCarthy Mussel Development Ltd. v. Ireland,* 44460/16, discussed in Agustín García Ureta, *EU Biodiversity Law: Wild Birds and Habitats Directives,* 269 (Europa Law Publishing, Zutphen 2020). The European Court of Human Rights dismissed the plaintiff's claim that measures taken to comply with the Court of Justice judgment in Case C-418/04, *Commission v. Ireland,* had infringed their right to earn a livelihood. Compliance with the Habitats Directive represented a legitimate general-interest obligation. For the relevance of the convention to the environment, *see also* Jan Darpö, *Can Nature Get It Right? A Study on Rights of Nature in the European Context,* 26-32 (European Parliament, Policy Department for Citizens' Rights and Constitutional Affairs Directorate-General for Internal Policies PE 689.328, March 2021).
88. Articles 130r, 130s and 130t of the Single European Act, OJ L 169, 29.6.1987, pp. 1-28.

Treaty changes, in particular the inclusion of the precautionary principle and the Charter of Fundamental Rights, have exerted an important influence on the interpretation of the nature directives.[89]

[B] Nature Directives

[1] EU Enlargement, 1981, 1986, 1995, 2004, 2007, 2013

Apart from the amendments to the Birds Directive mentioned below, the bodies of the nature directives have not changed in content or structure. As the EU has steadily enlarged, however, successive accession treaties have changed the directives' material scope by adding species and/or habitat types – thus changing the coverage of relevant annexes. The process started in respect of the Birds Directive as early as 1981, with the accession of Greece, and continued in 1986 with the accession of Spain and Portugal. The coverage of both directives increased in 1995 with the accession of Austria, Finland, and Sweden; in 2004 with the accession of the Czech Republic, Estonia, Cyprus, Latvia, Lithuania, Hungary, Malta, Poland, Slovenia, and Slovakia; in 2007 with the accession of Romania and Bulgaria; and finally in 2013 with the accession of Croatia.

The 1995 enlargement led to the addition of a Boreal biogeographical region; the 2004 one to the addition of the Pannonian biogeographical region; and the 2007 one to the addition of the Black Sea and Steppic regions.

By way of example, the 1995 accessions added 28 new habitat types to Annex I, 68 species to Annex II of the Habitats Directive, and 7 bird species to Annex I of the Birds Directive.

[2] Amendment of the Birds Directive in 1992 by the Habitats Directive

In 1992, the Habitats Directive amended the Birds Directive in respect of the preventive regime applicable to SPAs.[90] The new directive also added the SPA site network to a new unified network of protected sites, Natura 2000.[91]

[3] 1994 Proposal to Change the Birds Directive

Following strict interpretations by the Court of Justice of the directive's hunting provisions, the Commission made a proposal to introduce greater flexibility.[92] In an early indication of the strength of political support for the content of the nature directives, the European Parliament rejected the proposal, and the Commission withdrew it.[93]

89. *See* Chapters 3, 4 and 8.
90. *See* Chapter 3.
91. *See* Chapter 2.
92. Proposal for a Council Directive amending Directive 79/409/EEC on the conservation of wild birds, OJ C 100, 9.4.1994, p. 12-13.
93. *See* Mícheál Ó Bríain, *Recent Developments in Implementation of EU Nature Legislation*, 12, in *Nature Law and Policy in Europe*, Chapter 2 (Andrew L.R. Jackson ed., Routledge 2023).

[4] *2009 Codification of the Birds Directive*

As already noted, through its codification, Directive 2009/147/EC,[94] the Birds Directive was expressly brought under an environmental legal basis.

[5] *2014-2016 Fitness Check*

In 2016, the Commission published the results of a comprehensive evaluation or 'fitness check' on both nature directives.[95] The exercise, which began in 2014, was carried out within the framework of the Commission's Regulatory Fitness and Performance Programme (REFIT). Fitness checks are *ex post* evaluations complementing the *ex ante* impact assessments, which now precede Commission legislative proposals. They evaluate existing legislation for effectiveness, efficiency, coherence, relevance, and EU added value. The public consultation phase of the nature fitness check attracted a huge response, revealing strong support for the nature directives and opposition to changing them. The fitness check concluded that the nature directives were fit for purpose but, to achieve their objectives, needed substantial improvement in their implementation in relation to both effectiveness and efficiency.

With regard to effectiveness, the evaluation found that, notwithstanding the ongoing decline of nature, the status and trends of species and habitats protected by the nature directives would be significantly worse in their absence. Nevertheless, effectiveness had been hindered by delays in establishing Natura 2000 and in putting in place the necessary conservation measures.[96]

[C] Adoption of Other Relevant Environmental Legislation

While the provisions of the nature directives have remained essentially unchanged, their implementation is influenced by a number of other environmental directives adopted since 1979. To date, the most important are the Environmental Impact Assessment (EIA) Directive[97] and the Strategic Environmental Assessment (SEA) Directive,[98] for reasons explained in Chapters 3 and 6. Also significant are the Water

---

94. Directive 2009/147/EC of the European Parliament and of the Council of 30 November 2009 on the conservation of wild birds, OJ L 20, 26.01.2010, p. 7-25.
95. European Commission, *Fitness Check of the EU Nature Legislation (Birds and Habitats Directives)*, SWD(2016) 472 final.
96. For a detailed account of the nature fitness check and its sequel, *see* Mícheál Ó Bríain, *Recent Developments in Implementation of EU Nature Legislation*, in *Nature Law and Policy in Europe*, Chapter 2 (Andrew L.R. Jackson ed., Routledge 2023).
97. Directive 2011/92/EU of the European Parliament and of the Council of 13 December 2011 on the assessment of the effects of certain public and private projects on the environment (codification) Text with EEA relevance, OJ L 26, 28.1.2012, p. 1-21. This is a codification of the original EIA Directive, 85/337/EEC.
98. Directive 2001/42/EC of the European Parliament and of the Council of 27 June 2001 on the assessment of the effects of certain plans and programmes on the environment, OJ L 197, 21.7.2001, p. 30-37.

Framework Directive[99] and the Environmental Liability Directive, for reasons explained in Chapter 6.[100]

Other instruments deserving of mention are the Environmental Crime Directive,[101] the Invasive Species Regulation[102] and the Marine Strategy Framework Directive.[103]

[D] Addressing the Biodiversity Crisis

[1] The Global Threat

According to the 2020 Global Risk Report of the World Economic Forum,[104] biodiversity loss will be one of the biggest threats facing humanity in the next ten years. Loss of biodiversity affects crop yields and fish harvests and leads to more flooding and other disasters. From 1997 to 2011, for instance, there was an estimated loss of around EUR 3.5-18.5 trillion per year expressed in ecosystem services, owing to land-cover change, and an estimated EUR 5.5-10.5 trillion per year from land degradation.[105] As mentioned, the Convention on Biological Diversity provides a global framework for addressing the crisis.

[2] Biodiversity Strategy for 2030 and the Nature Restoration Proposal

A core part of the European Green Deal, the Commission's communication on an EU Biodiversity Strategy for 2030,[106] amongst other things, stresses the importance of stepping up the efforts to implement and enforce the nature directives.[107] It outlines the Commission's enforcement objectives[108] and commits the Commission to working

99. Directive 2000/60/EC of the European Parliament and of the Council of 23 October 2000 establishing a framework for Community action in the field of water policy, OJ L 327, 22.12.2000, p. 1-73.
100. In relation to the Environmental Liability Directive, *see also* Chapter 7.
101. *See* Chapter 7. Directive 2008/99/EC of the European Parliament and of the Council of 19 November 2008 on the protection of the environment through criminal law, OJ L 328, 6.12.2008, p. 28-3.
102. Regulation (EU) No. 1143/2014 of the European Parliament and of the Council of 22 October 2014 on the prevention and management of the introduction and spread of invasive alien species, OJ L 317, 4.11.2014, p. 35-55.
103. Directive 2008/56/EC of the European Parliament and of the Council of 17 June 2008 establishing a framework for community action in the field of marine environmental policy, OJ L 164, 25.6.2008, p. 19-40.
104. The Global Risks Report 2020, p. 7, http://www3.weforum.org/docs/WEF_Global_Risk_Report_2020.pdf, visited on 15 March 2021.
105. Organisation for Economic Co-operation and Development (OECD) (2019), Biodiversity: Finance and the Economic and Business Case for Action, https://www.oecd.org/environment/resources/biodiversity/G7-report-Biodiversity-Finance-and-the-Economic-and-Business-Case-for-Action.pdf, visited on 15 March 2021.
106. EU Biodiversity Strategy for 2030 (COM/2020/380 final), https://eur-lex.europa.eu/legal-content/EN/TXT/?qid=1590574123338&uri=CELEX:52020DC0380.
107. *Ibid.*, section 3.2 of the Communication.
108. *See* Chapter 8.

with Member States on compliance assurance[109] and access to justice, thereby supporting 'civil society's role as a compliance watchdog'.

Clearly, the fulfilment of these goals will involve applying the nature case-law presented in the chapters which follow.

The Biodiversity Strategy also aims to extend protected areas, including under Natura 2000, driven by the conclusion that 'we need to protect more nature' and that 'at least 30% of the land and 30% of the sea should be protected in the EU'.[110]

Furthermore, as part of a wider set of ambitions, the Strategy announced a Commission intention to propose a nature restoration law, an intention fulfilled with the tabling in 2022 of a Proposal for a Regulation of the European Parliament and of the Council on Nature Restoration.[111] This sets 'multiple binding restoration targets and obligations across a broad range of ecosystems'[112] to cover at least 20% of the EU's land and sea areas by 2030 and all ecosystems in need of restoration by 2050.[113] The proposal generated intense political debate during 2023, and the final outcome of the legislative process remained unknown at the time of writing.

As can be seen, the objectives of improving implementation of the nature directives and extending protected areas and restoration efforts should contribute to the Kunming-Montreal Global Biodiversity Framework mentioned above.

§1.08 ROLE OF THE EUROPEAN COMMISSION IN RELATION TO THE NATURE DIRECTIVES

[A] Enforcement and Involvement in Preliminary References

In the context of the present book, the exercise of the Commission's enforcement role is paramount since it has generated a large part of the case-law addressed. This role is covered in detail in Chapter 8. Also important is the Commission's role in preparing and submitting observations on preliminary references made by national courts. Again, this is covered in Chapter 8.

[B] Supportive Administrative Role

The Commission exercises a crucial administrative role in support of the nature directives. Formal Commission decisions are needed during the process of establishing Natura 2000, for instance. To ensure that the network is treated cohesively, the Commission needs to manage a mass of information transmitted by Member States on individual Natura 2000 sites. The institution holds regular multilateral and bilateral meetings with Member States, the committees created under each nature directive providing a forum for regular multilateral exchanges.

109. *See* Chapter 7.
110. EU Biodiversity Strategy for 2030, section 2.1.
111. COM/2022/304 final.
112. EUR-Lex - 52022PC0304 - EN - EUR-Lex (europa.eu).
113. Article 1.

Based on the periodic reports submitted by Member States pursuant to each directive, the Commission submits a formal report to the Commission and Parliament.[114] It is now assisted by the European Environment Agency, which processes the detailed data submitted by Member States in order to compile state-of-nature reports for the whole EU. These reports have been referred to in the opening of this chapter.

The Commission has tried to help Member States implement the nature directives by preparing guidance and technical documents on important topics such as the management of Natura 2000 sites and the content of the Bird's Directive hunting provisions. These documents reflect the case-law as it stood at the time of their preparation. As will be seen in Chapters 3 and 4, they have also sometimes influenced subsequent case-law.

In addition to use of its enforcement powers, since 2016, the Commission has employed the Environmental Implementation Review (EIR) to provide Member States with periodic feedback on what it views as the most important implementation challenges they face in relation to, amongst other EU environmental legislation, the nature directives. The EIR largely consists of individual country reports.[115] A 2022 Commission communication, which forms part of the latest EIR,[116] notes that, although the provisions of the nature directives are long established and well-known, many Member States still fail to designate SACs and to establish conservation objectives and measures.[117] As a priority action, it identifies steps required of these Member States to address the shortcomings. Another priority action addresses the need to improve the quality of appropriate assessments, develop and promote smart and streamlined implementation approaches, in particular, for appropriate assessment procedures and species permitting procedures.[118] A further priority action covers the need to ensure the necessary regulatory framework for protected species, collect reliable data on the conservation status of protected habitats and species and carry out a sound monitoring system.[119] There is also a priority action that covers the need of several Member States to ensure the appropriate enforcement of hunting and/or trapping bans for protected bird species, illegal forest logging and turf cutting.[120]

114. The most recent report is entitled 'The state of nature in the European Union Report on the status and trends in 2013 – 2018 of species and habitat types protected by the Birds and Habitats Directives', COM/2020/635 final.
115. European Commission: https://environment.ec.europa.eu/law-and-governance/environmental-implementation-review_en#background.
116. Communication on the Environmental Implementation Review 2022, Turning the tide through environmental compliance, COM/2022/438 final.
117. The EIR Communication notes that designation of SACs is incomplete for Bulgaria, Cyprus, Ireland and Portugal. In the case of Spain, Belgium, the Czech Republic, Greece, Germany, Italy, Poland, Lithuania, Latvia, Malta, Slovakia and Estonia, conservation objectives are not correctly established. For Austria, Denmark, France, Hungary, Finland, Latvia, the Netherlands and Slovenia, additional site protection measures are needed.
118. This concerns Belgium, Bulgaria, Cyprus, Estonia, Hungary and Greece.
119. This concerns Greece, Finland, Hungary and Romania.
120. The Member States concerned are Cyprus, Greece, Ireland, Malta and Romania.

EU funding plays a crucial role in supporting the nature directives, in particular, through the LIFE Regulation[121] but also through the Common Agricultural Policy (CAP). The Commission plays a key role in administering this funding.

The Commission represents the EU in relevant international conventions and agreements, complementing its work on the nature directives.

Finally, in developing EU biodiversity policy, the Commission takes account of the nature directives, as the content of the Biodiversity Strategy for 2030 shows.

§1.09 ROLE OF THE COURT OF JUSTICE OF THE EUROPEAN UNION

EU case-law on the nature directives comprises judgments of the Court of Justice of the European Union (CJEU), which interpret those directives and related points of EU law.

The CJEU was established in 1952 and is currently divided into two courts: the Court of Justice and the General Court. Its mission is to ensure that 'the law is observed' 'in the interpretation and application' of the EU Treaties. That mission extends to reviewing the legality of acts of the EU institutions, including the Commission; ensuring that Member States comply with their obligations under the Treaties (which includes the fulfilment of the requirements of secondary EU legislation such as the nature directives); and interpreting EU law at the request of national courts.

The case-law includes judgments relating to the exercise of all of these functions. Overwhelmingly, however, it consists of judgments concerning Member States' compliance with the nature directives and judgments on questions of interpretation of the nature directives presented by national courts. These judgments have come from the Court of Justice rather than the General Court, and so this book generally refers to the Court of Justice or simply 'the Court' rather than the CJEU. The complete case-law does, nevertheless, include some decisions of the General Court.[122]

§1.10 IMPORTANCE OF THE EU NATURE CASE-LAW

Why does the nature case-law matter, and why does it deserve a book devoted to it?

In a nutshell, the case-law is both consequential and extensive – and, at the same time and paradoxically, not consequential enough.

It is consequential for multiple reasons. The nature case-law forms part of the body of EU law and is therefore governed by the principle of the primacy of EU law. All Member States and Member State authorities are obliged to adhere to the interpretations set out in the case-law. As indicated, there are other potentially relevant supra-national frameworks, but, in relation to nature, nothing matches the scope and reach of the Court's jurisdiction. Furthermore, the nature case-law includes interpretations relevant to addressing the many pressures that the nature directives require

121. Regulation (EU) 2021/783 of the European Parliament and of the Council of 29 April 2021 establishing a Programme for the Environment and Climate Action (LIFE), and repealing Regulation (EU) No. 1293/2013, OJ L 172, 17.5.2021, p. 53-78.

122. *See* Chapters 2 and 8.

Member States to address. The interpretations are applicable to multiple decision-making processes within Member States, as well as to the administrative arrangements for conserving nature. The interpretations have helped achieve important outcomes, such as the establishment of the largest coordinated network of protected sites in the world, Natura 2000. Court rulings – and the interpretations that underpin them – have limited the damaging impacts of infrastructure projects and other interventions and contributed to species protection and site conservation.

The nature case-law has also helped to ensure its own consequentiality by facilitating the watchdog role of civil society. This is in response to the Aarhus Convention and the Charter of Fundamental Rights, but there is a historic echo from one of the Court's famous foundational rulings, Case C-26/62, *Van Gend en Loos*,[123] which recognised the effective supervision that results from the vigilance of individuals in protecting their rights.[124]

In terms of the case-law's extent, relevant judgments are numerous. The case-law also addresses a great many specific points. It is therefore useful to present the cases systematically in order to show the links between them. The presentation reflects the authors' previous experience as case-handlers, which involved focusing on very precise legal issues. This experience also prompted the coverage in Chapter 8 of the mechanics of the procedures through which cases reach and are decided by the Court.

It may seem paradoxical to suggest that the case-law is insufficiently consequential. What is meant is that, notwithstanding the case-law, the nature directives continue to suffer from important implementation gaps – as is evident from the priority actions identified in the last EIR. As the state-of-nature reporting shows, nature badly needs improved implementation.

The authors hope that, by setting out the case-law systematically, they may make a small contribution towards extending its positive influence.

123. C-26/62, *Van Gen den Loos*. As JF Brakeland notes, the Court stated that 'the vigilance of individuals concerned to protect their rights amounts to an effective supervision in addition to the supervision entrusted by Articles 169 and 170 [now Articles 258 and 260 of the TFEU] to the diligence of the Commission and of the Member States (p. 13)'.

124. As JF Brakeland notes, in Case *Van Gend en Loos*, the Court 'stressed that the public was also the guardian of the correct application of EU law, through access to the national court systems'; Jean-François Brakeland, Access to justice in environmental matters – developments at EU level (published in the Gyoseiho-kenkyu, 2014, No. 5), untitled (osaka-u.ac.jp), p. 6.

CHAPTER 2
Formal Recognition of Natura 2000 Sites

§2.01 NATURA 2000

'Natura 2000' is the name given to a network of areas which benefit from a special protection regime and which have been established and are regulated pursuant to two EU legal instruments, the Birds Directive and the Habitats Directive. These areas have to be identified and formally recognised within the '*European* territory of the Member States to which the Treaty applies' (emphasis added).[125]

The Court of Justice has stated that the Habitats Directive also applies beyond the Member States' territorial waters and must be implemented in the exclusive economic zone and on the continental shelf over which the Member States exercise sovereign rights.[126]

The concept of Natura 2000 was introduced by the Habitats Directive and it encompasses both SACs, designated under the Habitats Directive and SPAs, classified by the Member States pursuant to the Birds Directive.

Thus, according to Article 3(1) of the Habitats Directive:

> A coherent European ecological network of special areas of conservation shall be set up under the title Natura 2000. This network, composed of sites hosting the natural habitat types listed in Annex I and habitats of the species listed in Annex II, shall enable the natural habitat types and the species' habitats concerned to be maintained or, where appropriate, restored at a favourable conservation status in their natural range.

Furthermore, as laid down under Article 3(1) second paragraph of the Habitats Directive:

---

125. Article 2(1) of the Habitats Directive sets its geographical scope and Article 1(1) of the Birds Directive sets its geographical scope.
126. C-6/04, *Commission v. United Kingdom*, para. 117.

> The Natura 2000 network shall include the special protection areas classified by the Member States pursuant to Directive 79/409/EEC.

To be precise, 'designation' is a term introduced by the Habitats Directive, and formally, it refers to the last step in the process of site-identification, listing and recognition required under that directive. The Birds Directive uses the term 'classify'. More informally, 'designation' is often used to describe the stage at which sites are given formal legal protection as part of Natura 2000. In the case of the Birds Directive, the Court itself sometimes uses 'designation' rather than 'classification'.

Natura 2000 is the largest coordinated network of protected areas in the world. It stretches over almost one-fifth of the EU's land area and approximately 10% of its marine territory[127] and is still set to be extended. It is designed to preserve and protect Europe's most valuable and threatened species and habitats. It aims at the conservation of 463 bird species that naturally occur in the EU, 233 habitats and 1,389 species other than birds.[128]

But this is an evolving process. Large though it is, Natura 2000 may not represent the ultimate coverage of areas protected for nature. According to the EU Biodiversity Strategy for 2030,[129] 'at least 30% of the land and 30% of the sea should be protected in the EU'. This was 'a minimum of an extra 4% for land and 19% for sea areas as compared to' the time when the Strategy was adopted.[130] This key commitment of the EU Biodiversity Strategy to propose legally binding targets to restore degraded EU ecosystems, notably those with a carbon sink potential, led to the Nature Restoration Law Proposal, adopted by the European Commission on 22 June 2022.[131] Proposed in the form of a Regulation, the Nature Restoration Law would aim at establishing a framework for 'area-based restoration measures' which would cover at least 20% of the Union's land and sea areas by 2030 and all ecosystems that need restoration by 2050.[132]

Article 4(1) and (2) of the Birds Directive regulate the process of classification of SPAs, while Article 4 of the Habitats Directive regulates a four-stage process with the final aim of designating SACs.

The next sections describe the steps provided for under both legal instruments and the extensive case-law governing the process of formal recognition of Natura 2000 sites.

---

127. EEA Report No. 10/2020, State of Nature in the EU, p. 6, https://www.eea.europa.eu/publications/state-of-nature-in-the-eu-2020.
128. *Ibid.*, p. 5.
129. Communication from the Commission to the European Parliament, the Council, the European Economic and Social Committee and the Committee of the Regions – EU Biodiversity Strategy for 2030, Bringing nature back into our lives, 20 May 2020, COM/2020/380 final, https://op.europa.eu/en/publication-detail/-/publication/a3c806a6-9ab3-11ea-9d2d-01aa75ed71a1/language-en.
130. *Ibid.*, p. 4.
131. Proposal for a Regulation of the European Parliament and of the Council on nature restoration, 22 June 2022, COM/2022/304 final.
132. *See* Article 1(2) of the Proposal. For a Regulation of the European Parliament and of the Council on nature restoration, 22 June 2022, COM/2022/304 final.

It is important to note that, while the Birds Directive and the Habitats Directive pursue entwined protection objectives and complement each other, they remain nevertheless two separate legal regimes,[133] laying down distinct duties on Member States. A Member State cannot relieve itself from complying with the obligations under Article 4(1) and (2) of the Birds Directive, by relying, for instance, on measures foreseen by the Habitats Directive.[134]

§2.02 CLASSIFICATION OF SPAS UNDER THE BIRDS DIRECTIVE

[A] References to Protected Areas in Both Articles 3 and 4

Adopted in 1979, Directive 79/409/EEC on the conservation of wild birds[135] aimed at the conservation of all species of naturally occurring birds in the wild state in the European territory of the Member States.[136]

The ninth recital in the preamble to the directive notes that for bird conservation, it is essential to preserve, maintain or restore a sufficient diversity and area of habitats and 'that certain species of birds should be the subject of special conservation measures concerning their habitats in order to ensure their survival and reproduction in their area of distribution', also taking account of migratory species.

Article 3 of the Birds Directive requires Member States to take the necessary measures 'to preserve, maintain or re-establish a sufficient diversity and area of habitats for all the species of birds'[137] naturally occurring and provides that this shall include the creation of protected areas and/or biotopes, upkeep and management inside and outside protected zones and re-establishment of destroyed biotopes.[138]

This obligation exists 'before any reduction is observed in the number of birds or any risk of a protected species becoming extinct has materialized'.[139]

Article 4(1) of the Birds Directive reads as follows:

> The species mentioned in Annex I shall be the subject of special conservation measures concerning their habitat in order to ensure their survival and reproduction in their area of distribution.
>
> In this connection, account shall be taken of:
>
> (a) species in danger of extinction;
> (b) species vulnerable to specific changes in their habitat;
> (c) species considered rare because of small populations or restricted local distribution;

133. C-374/98, *Commission v. France*, paras 50-56.
134. C-235/04, *Commission v. Spain*, para. 79.
135. OJ L 103, 25.4.1979, p. 1. The original directive has in the meantime been codified and renumbered as Directive 2009/147/EC of the European Parliament and of the Council of 30 November 2009 on the conservation of wild birds, OJ L 20, 26.1.2010, p. 7-25.
136. Article 1 of Directive 79/409/EEC.
137. Article 3(1) of Directive 79/409/EEC.
138. Article 3(2) of Directive 79/409/EEC.
139. C-355/90, *Commission v. Spain*, para. 15.

(d) other species requiring particular attention for reasons of the specific nature of their habitat.

Trends and variations in population levels shall be taken into account as a background for evaluations.

Member States shall classify, in particular, the most suitable territories in number and size as SPAs for the conservation of these species in the geographical sea and land area where this Directive applies.

Article 4(2) of the Birds Directive provides as follows:

> Member States shall take similar measures for regularly occurring migratory species not listed in Annex I, bearing in mind their need for protection in the geographical sea and land area where this Directive applies, as regards their breeding, moulting and wintering areas and staging posts along their migration routes. To this end, Member States shall pay particular attention to the protection of wetlands and particularly to wetlands of international importance.

The relationship between Articles 3 and 4 is also addressed in Chapter 5. Suffice it to say here that the case-law describes Article 3 as imposing obligations of a *general* nature, while Article 4 sets out *specific obligations* with regard to the species of birds listed in Annex I and migratory species not listed in that annex.[140] Thus, Article 4 takes primacy in respect of Annex I and migratory species, but Article 3 has residual importance for resident species not listed in Annex I.

While Article 3 of the Birds Directive allows Member States to take account of economic and recreational requirements mentioned in Article 2[141] for the implementation of general conservation measures, including the creation of protection areas, the Court made it clear in Case C-44/95, *Lappel Bank* that 'Article 4 makes no such reference for the implementation of special conservation measures, in particular the creation of SPAs.'[142] The Article 2 considerations cannot therefore be invoked to justify less SPA classification than is scientifically required. The nature case-law envisages a classification process based uniquely on scientific data.[143]

Furthermore, the first sentence of Article 4(4) of the Birds Directive provides that, within SPAs, Member States are required to take appropriate measures 'to avoid pollution or deterioration of habitats or any disturbances affecting the birds, in so far as these would be significant having regard to the objectives of that article'. The Habitats Directive amended this provision by introducing a more detailed regime consisting of a similar duty of avoidance combined with an obligation to assess the impact of plans and projects on SPAs. The relevant provisions are addressed in Chapter 3.

140. *Ibid.*, para. 23.
141. Article 2 of the Birds Directive reads as follows: 'Member States shall take the requisite measures to maintain the population of the species referred to in Article 1 at a level which corresponds in particular to ecological, scientific and cultural requirements, while taking account of economic and recreational requirements, or to adapt the population of these species to that level.'
142. C-44/95, *Lappel Bank*, para. 24.
143. *Ibid.*, para. 26.

[B] Obligation to Classify SPAs for Both Annex I and Migratory Bird Species

[1] Obligation on Member States to Adopt Measures and Notify the Commission

The Court has clarified that not only are Member States under an obligation to adopt special conservation measures under Article 4(1) of the Birds Directive [which includes classifications] but they are also obliged to notify the Commission of these.

This is evident from the judgment in Case C-334/89, *Commission v. Italy*, one of the earliest concerning Article 4(1) of the Birds Directive. The Commission brought the proceedings because Italy had not notified it of Article 4(1) measures taken to implement Commission Directive 85/411/EEC, which amended Annex 1 to the Birds Directive 'to take account of the latest information on the situation as regards avifauna'.[144]

The Italian Government argued that since not all of the species listed in the new Annex 1 occur on the Italian territory, it expected the Commission to indicate which species must be the subject of special conservation measures in Italy.

The Court held that:

> It is clear from that allocation of responsibilities that it is for the Member States to identify the species which must be the subject of the special protective and conservation measures required by Article 4(1) of the directive. Moreover, the Member States are better placed than the Commission to ascertain which of the species listed in Annex I to the directive occur in their territory.[145]

[2] Classification Obligation Covers Both Annex I Species and Migratory Species

The classification obligation covers *both* Annex I species and migratory species.

In Case C-191/05, *Commission v. Portugal*, a case concerning the completeness of classification of a Portuguese SPA, the Court observed that 'Article 4 of Directive 79/409 lays down a system which is specifically targeted and reinforced both for the species listed in Annex I to that directive and for migratory species not included in that annex, an approach justified by the fact that they are, respectively, the most endangered species and the species constituting a common heritage of the Community.'[146]

Where a bird species is both migratory and listed in Annex I, the duty to classify will arise under Article 4(1) rather than Article 4(2). In Case C-374/98, *Commission v. France* (*'Basses Corbières'*), the Court observed that:

144. Commission Directive 85/411/EEC of 25 July 1985 amending Council Directive 79/409/EEC on the conservation of wild birds, OJ L 233, 30.08.1985, p. 0033-0041.
145. C-334/89, *Commission v. Italy*, para. 9.
146. C-191/05, *Commission v. Portugal*, para. 9.

> It has not been shown that there are migratory species justifying the classification of the Basses Corbières site as an SPA by virtue of Article 4(2) of the birds directive. All the species mentioned for that purpose by the Commission as migratory species, such as the honey buzzard, the black kite, the kite, the Egyptian vulture, the short-toed eagle, the marsh harrier, the hen harrier and Montagu's harrier are listed in Annex I to the birds directive, whereas *Article 4(2) of that directive applies only to migratory species not listed in Annex I* (emphasis added).[147]

[C] Deadline for Classifying SPAs

The Birds Directive is not explicit as regards the deadline[148] for classifying SPAs and this gave rise to an argument that the obligation could be fulfilled only gradually.[149] In Case C-355/90, *Commission v. Spain* ('*Santoña Marshes*'),[150] however, the Court clarified that, in the absence of any specific derogation in its accession conditions, a [new] Member State had to put into effect the measures necessary to comply with the Birds Directive by the date of its accession. It may be noted that Spain had not been a Member State at the time of the Bird's Directive's adoption. More generally, the Court ruled that the obligations of Article 4 needed to be fulfilled by the two-year deadline prescribed in the directive for the adoption of transposition measures - a finding relevant to the nine countries that were Member States in 1979.[151] The number of EU Member States has tripled since the adoption of the Birds Directive. No accession treaty has postponed the deadline for fulfilling classification duties beyond the accession date. As C-355/90, *Santoña Marshes* indicates, the accession date is therefore the date on which new Member States are expected to have completed their SPA classifications.[152]

[D] Selection of 'Most Suitable Territories': Margin of Discretion Limited by Ornithological Criteria

In the process of recognising and delineating SPAs, Member States are bound by the criteria contained in paragraphs (1) and (2) of Article 4. In Case C-44/95, *Lappel Bank*,

147. C-374/98, '*Basses Corbières*', para. 16.
148. Marc Clément, Droit européen de l'environnement, Jurisprudence commentée, Editions Larcier, p. 336.
149. C-355/90, *Commission v. Spain*, para. 10.
150. C-355/90, *Santoña Marshes*, para. 11.
151. *See also* C-334/04, *Commission v. Greece*, para. 32.
152. *See*, for instance, Article 53(1) of the Act concerning the conditions of accession of the Republic of Bulgaria and Romania and the adjustments to the Treaties on which the European Union is founded: 'Bulgaria and Romania shall put into effect the measures necessary for them to comply, from the date of accession, with the provisions of directives and decisions within the meaning of Article 249 of the EC Treaty and of Article 161 of the EAEC Treaty, unless another time limit is provided for this Act. They shall communicate those measures to the Commission at the latest by the date of accession or, where appropriate, by the time limit provided for in this Act'.

the Court was clear that 'the criteria in question are ornithological criteria'.[153] As noted above, the Court specifically pointed out that, unlike Article 3, Article 4 does not make reference to Article 2 of the Birds Directive.

Moreover, although, in the process of classification, Member States enjoy a certain margin of discretion with regard to the choice of the areas concerned, this margin is significantly circumscribed by the obligation to take account of scientific data. In Case C-355/90, *Santoña Marshes*, the Court held that the classification of areas is 'subject to certain ornithological criteria determined by the directive, such as the presence of birds listed in Annex I, on the one hand, and the designation of a habitat as a wetland area, on the other'.[154] Furthermore, while the Directive's reference in Article 4(1) to suitable territories in number and size relates to Annex I species, a comparable ornithological reasoning applies to migratory species under Article 4(2).[155]

[E] Economic Interests Cannot Be Taken into Account

As noted, in the process of classifying an SPA and defining its boundaries, Member States are not authorised to take account of the economic requirements mentioned in Article 2 of the Birds Directive.[156]

In Case C-235/04, *Commission v. Spain*, Spain argued that it could not classify an SPA for the species, lesser kestrel because that species is found within urban areas, which could not be classified as SPAs. The Court rejected this objection and indicated that if the area in question, be it urban, represents a specific nesting area for that species, it has to be classified. Naturally, this may generate complications concerning projects or activities which are normally developed in urban areas. But in case 'measures of urban development were to override the interest in protecting that species, they would have to be implemented under Article 6(4) of Directive 92/43'.[157]

[F] Need for Classification to Be Complete at Site Level and Network Level

[1] Site Level

Case C-44/95, *Lappel Bank* confirms that the obligation to classify also applies to territories which do not necessarily host any Annex I species but are important for migratory species. Furthermore, it underscores the importance of completeness when classifying territories. The Lappel Bank had been excluded from the classification of a coastal wetland, although it supported a great number of bird species, represented an

153. C-44/95, *Lappel Bank*, para. 26.
154. C-355/90, *Commission v. Spain*, para. 26.
155. Graham Machin, *Protecting Bird Habitat of European Importance: The View from Basses Corbières*, 6 Environmental Law Review 175-189 (2004) DOI: 10.1350/enlr.6.3.174.60201; *see also* Case C-334/04, *Commission v. Greece*, para. 24.
156. C-44/95, *Lappel Bank*, para. 27.
157. C-235/04, *Commission v. Spain*, para. 73.

'important component of the overall estuarine ecosystem',[158] and its loss was likely to result in a reduction in the water and wildfowl populations in adjacent territories classified as an SPA. The Court considered that, in terms of the classification obligation, the Lappel Bank's exclusion was unjustified.

[2] Network Level

Completeness in classification is not only important at the level of individual sites but also at the level of the SPA network.

The need for network completeness was made evident in Case C-3/96, *Commission v. Netherlands*. In that case, the Court held that the Member States' margin of discretion in choosing the most suitable territories for classification as SPAs does not concern the appropriateness of classifying as SPAs the territories which appear the most suitable according to ornithological criteria, but only *the application* of those criteria for identifying the most suitable territories for conservation of the species listed in Annex I to the Directive.[159] 'Consequently, Member States are obliged to classify as SPAs *all* the sites which, applying ornithological criteria, appear to be the most suitable for conservation of the species in question (emphasis added).'[160]

In Case C-202/01, *Commission v. France*, a finding of failure to meet the obligations under Article 4(1) and (2) of the Directive was based, *inter alia*, on the fact that six species of wild birds listed in Annex I to the Directive, which are found on French territory, were not protected by any SPA classification.[161]

In Case C-334/04, *Commission v. Greece*, the Court assessed whether Greece had classified SPAs sufficient in number and size 'to offer protection to all the species of birds listed in Annex I to Directive 79/409 and also to the migratory species not included in that annex'.[162] It found that the Commission's arguments on incompleteness were well founded and that Greece had failed to classify SPAs in respect of certain species of birds included in Annex I to the Birds Directive, migratory species not included in that annex, and certain Annex I species insufficiently represented within classified SPAs.

[G] Inventory of Important Bird Areas: A Reference for Assessing the Sufficiency or Completeness of Classification

In Case C-3/96, *Commission v. Netherlands*, the Commission, for the first time, sought to address at a national scale the non-classification of SPAs by Member States. It argued that, at the scale of its overall network, the Netherlands had failed sufficiently to classify SPAs in accordance with Article 4(1) of the Birds Directive. Classification of SPAs under Article 4(2) of the Birds Directive did not feature in the case.

158. C-44/95, *Lappel Bank*, para. 12.
159. C-3/96, *Commission v. Netherlands*, para. 61.
160. *Ibid.*, para. 62.
161. C-201/01, *Commission v. France*, para. 20.
162. C-334/04, *Commission v. Greece*, para. 28.

To substantiate its claim, the Commission relied on a Europe-wide inventory of important bird areas IBAs in the European Community, originally published in 1989 ('IBA 89') and periodically updated since then. The IBA inventory was initially prepared for the competent directorate-general of the Commission by the Eurogroup for the Conservation of Birds and Habitats in conjunction with the International Council of Bird Preservation and in cooperation with Commission experts.[163]

The latest iteration of the IBA inventory has been described as constituting 'a comprehensive network of areas for breeding, wintering, feeding, moulting and roosting, and is intended to provide habitat protection at staging areas along migration routes. It is also intended to provide protection in places where birds are vulnerable to being shot at "bottle-necks" such as mountain passes and straits where migratory birds come together. This network has a purely scientific basis: it is not based on the national frontiers of States'.[164] The inventory was based on a set of objective criteria[165] and was compiled using a mass of ornithological data collected by professional and amateur ornithologists.

The Commission pointed out that, whereas IBA 89 identified, on the basis of ornithological criteria, 70 territories in the Netherlands with a total area of 797,920 hectares suitable for classification, the Netherlands had classified 23 territories with a total area of 327,602 hectares, i.e., less than half the sites listed by IBA 89, with respect to both the number of sites and their total area.[166] In the Commission's view, this was manifestly insufficient.

The Court upheld the Commission's reliance on the IBA inventory, stating that, although not legally binding, the inventory 'can, by reason of its acknowledged scientific value'[167] and in the absence of contrary scientific evidence, be used by the Court as a basis of reference when assessing the extent to which the Member States have fulfilled their classification obligations.

Indeed, in terms of the duty of completeness in classification, the Court went further than the Commission had sought to plead [*see* section [F][2] above].

In Case C-378/01, *Commission v. Italy*, a large number and area of the sites listed in the IBA 89 inventory had not been classified as SPAs and while the Italian Government argued, at the hearing, that that inventory required revision, it also admitted that it 'had not been in a position to challenge it with a more persuasive document'. Quoting, *inter alia*, Case C-3/96, *Commission v. Netherlands*, the Court reiterated that in the absence of any scientific evidence to show that the obligations flowing from Article 4(1) and (2) of the Directive could be satisfied by classifying as

163. C-3/96, *Commission v. Netherlands*, para. 68.
164. John Temple Lang, *The Requirements for an Effective International Nature Conservation System, and the EU Birds and Habitats Directives*, 35, in *Nature Law and Policy in Europe*, Chapter 2 (Andrew L.R. Jackson ed., Routledge 2023).As a lawyer in the Commission Legal Service, John Temple Lang worked on the drafting of the Birds Directive; as an eminent ornithologist, he has also played a key role in the creation of the inventory.
165. For further details of the criteria and of how specific criteria have featured in the case-law, *see* Agustín García Ureta, *EU Biodiversity Law: Wild Birds and Habitats Directives*, 104-106 (Europa Law Publishing 2020).
166. C-3/96, *Commission v. Netherlands*, paras 40 to 44.
167. *Ibid.*, para. 70.

SPAs sites other than those appearing in that inventory and covering a smaller total area, that inventory, although not legally binding on the Member State concerned, can be used by the Court as a basis of reference.[168]

[1] An Evolving Process: Use of Updated Versions of the IBA Inventory

The ruling in Case C-3/96, *Commission v. Netherlands*, opened the way for similar Commission direct actions against other Member States: Case C-240/00, *Commission v. Finland*, Case C-202/01, *Commission v. France*, Case C-378/01, *Commission v. Italy*, Case C-235/04, *Commission v. Spain*, Case C-334/04, *Commission v. Greece*, Case C-418/04, *Commission v. Ireland*.

In Case 235/04, *Commission v. Spain*, the Court upheld the Commission's use of an updated version of the IBA 89 inventory and stressed the importance of up-to-date scientific information.

In that case, the Commission pleaded that Spain had not classified as SPAs territories sufficient in size and number having regard to the areas of importance for the conservation of birds identified in the ornithological list published in 1998 ('IBA 98'). The Spanish Government objected to the use of IBA 98, arguing that, unlike IBA 89, it had not been commissioned or supervised by the Commission. It had been drawn up exclusively on the initiative of the Spanish Ornithological Society, 'SEA/BirdLife'.

In rejecting the arguments of the Spanish Government, the Court stressed that the updating of scientific data is necessary to determine the situation of the most endangered species and the species constituting the common heritage of the Community, in order to classify the most suitable areas as SPAs. It was therefore necessary to use the most up-to-date scientific data available.[169] The Court recognised that IBA 98 constituted a basis of reference for assessing whether a Member State had fulfilled its classification duty.[170]

In Case C-334/04, *Commission v. Greece*, the Court held that a further updated IBA inventory, IBA 2000, constituted, in the absence of scientific evidence to the contrary, 'a basis of reference for assessing whether that Member State has classified as SPAs areas sufficient in number and size to offer protection to all the species of birds listed in Annex I to Directive 79/409 and also to the migratory species not included in that annex'.[171] In contrast to Case C-3/96, *Commission v. Netherlands*, Article 4(2) of the Birds Directive featured in this case.

The Court found that the Greek Government had not submitted any evidence capable of disproving the results of IBA 2000.[172] The Court added that this finding could not be called into question by the argument that it is necessary to allow Member States a reasonable period of time to carry out long-term observation and cartographical

168. C-378/01, *Commission v. Italy*, para. 18.
169. C-235/04, *Commission v. Spain*, para. 24.
170. *Ibid.*, para. 27.
171. C-334/04, *Commission v. Greece*, para. 28.
172. *Ibid.*, para. 30.

studies for the purpose of establishing the areas of importance for the conservation of birds.[173] It went on to observe that:

> although the Member States bear sole responsibility for the classification of SPAs and must base that classification on the best scientific knowledge available, that does not mean that such an obligation does not apply as long as the competent authorities have not evaluated and verified the new scientific knowledge. Such an obligation to classify has existed since the expiry of the period for transposition of Directive 79/409, that is to say, since 6 April 1981, so far as concerns the Hellenic Republic.[174]

Therefore, in the presence of updated scientific data pointing to the need to extend SPA coverage, Member States cannot justify inaction and hide behind the need to evaluate and verify the new scientific data.

[2] Obligation to Classify Even Where Ornithological Interest Seems Lost

In Case C-418/04, *Commission v. Ireland,*[175] another direct action based on IBA 2000, Ireland contested the need to classify the Cross Lough IBA. Up to a recent period before the court case, the Cross Lough IBA had been an important breeding ground for the sandwich tern, but the bird had disappeared because of the predatory activity of American mink (an introduced species that had escaped into the wild). No measures had ever been put in place to protect the colony. The Court rejected an argument from Ireland that it should not be required to classify the IBA since the site had lost its interest for the bird species concerned.

The Court noted that, having failed to take such measures for that area, Ireland had not provided proof that the area would no longer be suitable even if protection measures had been taken. The Court was convinced by Commission evidence that protection measures were still possible. This evidence showed that trapping of mink could reduce the pressure on sandwich terns and that there was a genuine chance that the tern might resettle in the area.[176]

[H] Other Ornithological Evidence May Support Classification

In Case C-418/04, *Commission v. Ireland,* the Commission argued that, while it constituted a reliable reference, IBA 2000 was not exhaustive, and it also adduced other evidence to show that classification was incomplete. It should be noted that the Court confirmed that the fact that IBA 2000 was not exhaustive did not undermine the probative value of the inventory.[177]

More specifically, the Commission argued that:

173. *Ibid.*, para. 31.
174. *Ibid.*, para. 32.
175. C-418/04, *Commission v. Ireland,* para. 80.
176. *Ibid.*, paras 86 to 88.
177. *Ibid.*, para. 51.

for the red-throated diver (*Gavia stellata*), the hen harrier (*Circus cyaneus*), the merlin (*Falco columbarius*), the peregrine falcon (*Falco peregrinus*), the golden plover (*Pluvialis apricaria*), the corncrake, the kingfisher, the white-fronted goose (Greenland race) (*Anser albifrons flavirostris*) and the short-eared owl (*Asio flammeus*), protected species referred to in Annex I, and also for the lapwing (*Vanellus vanellus*), the redshank (*Tringa totanus*), the snipe (*Callinago galli nago*), the curlew (*Numenius arquata*) and the dunlin (*Calidris alpina*), regularly occurring migratory species, the areas of importance for the conservation of birds identified in IBA 2000 clearly *do not offer a sufficient set of sites* in number and in size to satisfy the conservation needs of those species (emphasis added at end).[178]

The Court upheld the Commission's complaint for several of these species, although not all.[179]

[I] Classification: A Formal Act Which Implies Site Management and a Legal Protection Regime

Classification under the Birds Directive 'is a formal, dateable act by a Member State executed under and by virtue of the following words of Article 4(1) or (2) of the Birds Directive'.[180] It involves adopting the requisite legislative and regulatory measures at national level.

[1] Need for Classification to Be Definitive

In Case C-240/00, *Commission v. Finland*, the Court held that a contingent classification of SPAs, which might be amended following national court judgments in legal actions brought against it, cannot be held to constitute proper fulfilment of the classification obligation under Article 4(1) and (2) of the Birds Directive.[181] The background was that, while the Finnish Council of Ministers had adopted a list of sites to be classified as SPAs, this list was not definitive, pending the outcome of appeals to the Finnish Supreme Administrative Court.

[2] Legally Enforceable SPA Delineation

In Case C-415/01, *Commission v. Belgium*, the Court held that the maps demarcating SPAs must 'be invested with unquestionable binding force. If not, the boundaries of SPAs could be challenged at any time'.[182] It also held that the classification must be such that it 'automatically and simultaneously entails the application of a system of protection and conservation complying with Community law'.[183] In this case, Belgium

178. *Ibid.*, para. 103.
179. *Ibid.*, paras 105 and 106.
180. Graham Machin, *Protecting Bird Habitat of European Importance: The View from Basses Corbières*, 6 Environmental Law Review 175-189 (2004) DOI: 10.1350/enlr.6.3.174.60201.
181. C-240/00, *Commission v. Finland*, para. 19.
182. C-415/01, *Commission v. Belgium*, para. 22.
183. *Ibid.*, para. 26.

was condemned by the Court because it failed to demarcate SPAs within its territory in such a manner that they could be relied upon against third parties. Thus, the maps had simply been lodged in municipal offices to enable the population to become acquainted with them, while in Belgian law, measures adopted by the regional authorities must be published in the Belgian Official Journal ('Moniteur Belge') in order to have binding force.

It is important to note, however, that in Case C-535/07, *Commission v. Austria,* the Court ruled that cartographic representation is not the only possible and reliable form of delimitation of a site.[184]

[3] Identification of Species Protected by an SPA

In Case C-535/07, *Commission v. Austria,* the Court held that, apart from the delimitation of an SPA, which must be invested with unquestionable binding force, 'the identification of the species which have warranted classification of that SPA must satisfy the same requirement'.[185]

[4] Legal Protection Regime

[a] Substance

Classification is not a 'formalistic' act only: it must institute a legal protection regime for the areas classified. With regard to such a regime, measures need to be defined and finalised; they should not be temporary but provide a lasting guarantee with regard to the conservation status of the species concerned and their habitats. The measures should not only be adopted but also implemented. The measures may also need to be of a positive nature.

It is important to state, however, that the legal protection regime required by Article 4(1) and (2) of the Birds Directive must also be seen in light of the protective measures required by the first sentence of Article 4(4) of the Birds Directive - or the protective and compensatory requirements of Article 6(2) to (4) of the Habitats Directive.

In Case C-350/90, *Santoña Marshes,* the Court looked at the fulfilment of the classification duty in relation to both Article 4(1) and 4(2) of the Birds Directive. It did not consider the classification of part of the marshes as a nature reserve as having satisfied these provisions.[186] The nature reserve did not cover all of the marshes, and, even for the parts it did cover, Spain had not defined the necessary protection measures. In this case, the national law required a plan for the management of nature reserves, but such a plan had not been approved by the competent authorities. The Court noted that the requirements around the legal status as a protected area cannot be

184. C-535/07, *Commission v. Austria,* para. 82.
185. *Ibid.,* para. 64.
186. C-355/90, *Commission v. Spain,* para. 28.

deemed fulfilled if 'measures as essential as those determining the management of the area or governing the use of the marshes and the activities carried out there have not been adopted'.[187] The Court underlined the utmost importance for the protection of wild birds of such a plan, intended to identify activities which will give rise to a change in the ecosystems of the area.

In Case C-166/97, *Commission v. France*, concerning a site in the Seine Estuary, the Court held that 'Article 4(1) and (2) of the directive on birds requires the Member States to provide SPAs with a legal protection regime that is capable, in particular, of ensuring both the survival and reproduction of the bird species listed in Annex I to the directive and the breeding, moulting and wintering of migratory species not listed in that annex which are regular visitors.'[188] The Court noted that at the relevant time [the expiry of the Commission's Reasoned Opinion], the 'only status of the SPA created in 1990 was that of State-owned land and of a maritime game reserve'.[189] It held that 'for want of any specific substantive measures, except in relation to hunting, such a regime is incapable of providing adequate protection for the purposes of Article 4(1) and (2) of the Wild Birds Directive'.[190]

In Cases C-334/04, *Commission v. Greece* and C-235/04, *Commission v. Spain,* the Court noted that it is clear from the ninth recital in the preamble of the Birds Directive that the preservation, maintenance or restoration of a sufficient diversity and area of habitats is essential to the conservation of all species of birds. It went on to state that 'Member States are therefore required to adopt the measures necessary for the conservation of those species.'[191]

In Case C-418/04, *Commission v. Ireland,* the Court held that, as regards the legal protection regime required by Article 4(1) and (2) of the Birds Directive, 'the protection of SPAs may not be limited to avoiding harmful human effects but must also include *positive measures* to preserve or improve the state of the area, as the case may be (emphasis added)'.[192]

In Case C-661/20, *Commission v. Slovakia*, the Commission successfully pleaded that Slovakia had failed to fulfil its obligations under Article 4(1) by failing to adopt the special conservation measures applicable to the habitat of the capercaillie in the SPAs classified for its conservation in order to ensure its survival and reproduction in its area of distribution.[193] The Court cited its own decision in Case C-164/17, *Grace and Sweetman*, to the effect that the classification of an area as an SPA 'entails the *lasting* preservation of the constitutive characteristics of the habitat in that area, the survival of the species in question and its reproduction being the objective justifying the designation of that area (emphasis added)'.[194] In Case C-661/20, *Commission v. Slovakia,* it pronounced itself especially strongly on the obligation of Article 4(1),

187. *Ibid.*, para. 31.
188. C-166/97, *Commission v. France,* para. 21.
189. *Ibid.*, para. 24.
190. *Ibid.*, para. 25.
191. C-334/04, *Commission v. Greece,* para. 24; C-235/04, *Commission v. Spain,* para. 23.
192. C-418/04, *Commission v. Ireland,* para. 154.
193. C-661/20, *Commission v. Slovakia,* para. 112 and paras 127 to 135.
194. C-164/17, *Grace and Sweetman*, para. 35.

stating: 'that provision requires, if it is not to be rendered redundant, that the conservation measures necessary for maintaining a favourable conservation status of the protected habitats and species within the site concerned not only be adopted, but also, and above all, be *actually implemented* (emphasis added)'.[195] The Court noted that, for seven SPAs classified for the species, maintenance programmes for its habitat had neither been adopted nor implemented;[196] while the authorities had prepared certain conservation projects, such as the creation of a nature reserve, these had not been finalised or implemented;[197] other measures were temporary and needed to be extended through subsequent decisions, with the result that the protection provided 'cannot provide a *lasting* guarantee' (emphasis added) that the conservation status of the capercaillie and its habitats would remain favourable within the SPAs concerned.[198]

[b] Form

The legal protection regime can take the form of a single instrument or of a number of instruments. In this regard, there are no specific requirements in the Birds Directive. In Case C-304/05, *Commission v. Italy*, the Court considered that the existence of a regulatory framework consisting of a number of instruments of Italian law was potentially sufficient if the legal framework determined by those various instruments conferred an appropriate protective status on the respective area.[199]

In Case C-418/04, *Commission v. Ireland*, the Court accepted the possibility of an integrated approach to the fulfilment of Article 4(1) and 4(2) of the Birds Directive and Article 6(1) of the Habitats Directive.[200] In that case, Ireland successfully argued that, for purposes of transposition, it had fulfilled the requirements of Article 4(1) and 4(2) of the Birds Directive via its transposing legislation for Article 6 of the Habitats Directive, since that transposition had also referred to the Birds Directive. Thus, requirements to fulfil Article 6(1) of the Habitats Directive could also fulfil those of Article 4(1) and (2) of the Birds Directive.

[J] Modification of SPA Boundaries or Size, and Declassification of SPAs

Once classified, SPAs 'are almost inviolate as regards their extent'.[201] Thus, in Case C-350/90, *Santoña Marshes*, the Court held that:

> although Member States do have a certain discretion with regard to the choice of the territories which are most suitable for classification as special protection areas,

195. C-661/20, *Commission v. Slovakia*, para. 128.
196. *Ibid.*, para. 130.
197. *Ibid.*, para. 132 and para. 133.
198. *Ibid.*, para. 134.
199. C-304/05, *Commission v. Italy*, paras 106 and 107.
200. C-418/04, *Commission v. Ireland*, paras 153 to 168.
201. Graham Machin, *Protecting Bird Habitat of European Importance: The View from Basses Corbières*, 6 Environmental Law Review 175-189 (2004) DOI: 10.1350/enlr.6.3.174.60201.

they do not have the same discretion under Article 4(4) of the directive in modifying or reducing the extent of those areas.[202]

In Case C-44/95, *Lappel Bank,* the Court referred to the fact that, in Case C-57/89, *Leybucht Dykes*, it had held that the power of a Member State to reduce the extent of an SPA could be justified only on 'exceptional grounds, being grounds corresponding to a general interest superior to the general interest represented by the ecological objective of the directive'.[203] Case C-44/95, *Lappel Bank,* arose from a decision of the UK Government to exclude from the classification of a coastal wetland 22 hectares of intertidal mudflat known as 'Lappel Bank'. The Port of Sheerness envisaged developing this area. The Court's judgment made it clear that, in terms of the classification duty, the exclusion of Lappel Bank could not be justified in order to facilitate the port.

In Case C-191/05, *Commission v. Portugal,* the Commission successfully argued that Portugal had infringed Article 4(1) of the Birds Directive by altering the demarcation of the 'Moura, Mourão, Barrancos' SPA, thereby excluding from it areas providing a habitat for species of bird for which the SPA had been classified. The boundaries of the SPA concerned were altered on the ground that the SPA included areas which were not important habitats for steppe-land birds.[204] The Court noted, however, that:

> although the areas excluded from the SPA concerned by that Decree-Law do not provide a habitat for steppe-land birds, they did provide a habitat for other species of wild birds listed in Annex I to the Directive for whose protection that SPA had been designated, namely the crane (*Grus grus*), the eagle owl (*Bubo bubo*), the black vulture (*Aegypius monachus*), the booted eagle (*Hieraaetus pennatus*) and the griffon vulture (*Gyps fulvus*).[205]

Against this background, the Court held that a Member State may not reduce the surface area of an SPA or alter its boundaries 'unless the areas excluded from the SPA are no longer the most suitable territories for the conservation of species of wild birds within the meaning of Article 4(1) of the Directive'.[206]

It is possible, nevertheless, that an error may occur. In Case C-96/98, *Commission v. France ('Marais-Poitevin')*, the Court accepted that the removal of part of an SPA represented the rectification of an error rather than a declassification. It was satisfied that the area concerned was not intended to form part of the SPA.[207]

[K] Obligation to Send Site Information to the Commission

Article 4(3) of the Birds Directive provides as follows:

> Member States shall send the Commission all relevant information so that it may take appropriate initiatives with a view to the coordination necessary to ensure

202. C-355/90, *Commission v. Spain,* para. 35.
203. C-44/95, *Lappel Bank,* para. 29.
204. C-191/05, *Commission v. Portugal,* para. 11.
205. *Ibid.*, para. 12.
206. *Ibid.*, para. 13.
207. C-96/98, *Marais-Poitevin,* paras 48-56.

> that the areas provided for in paragraphs 1 and 2 form a coherent whole which meets the protection requirements of these species in the geographical sea and land area where this Directive applies.

In Case C-378/01, *Commission v. Italy,* the Court upheld a Commission complaint that by not sending it full and precise ornithological data and sufficiently detailed maps, the Italian authorities had infringed Article 4(3) of the Birds Directive. The breach was not contested by Italy.[208]

Although the Commission did not plead a breach of Article 4(3) in Case C-240/00, *Commission v. Finland,* the Court considered that the lack of definitive classification as SPAs of the sites at issue in that case prevented the Commission from taking the appropriate initiatives, in accordance with Article 4(3) of the Birds Directive, for the purpose of the coordination necessary to ensure that the SPAs form a coherent network[209] [*see* section §2.02[I][1] above].

§2.03 DESIGNATION PROCESS UNDER ARTICLES 4 AND 5 OF THE HABITATS DIRECTIVE

[A] Four-Stage Procedure

Designation under the Habitats Directive is primarily regulated by Article 4, which reads as follows:

> 1. On the basis of the criteria set out in Annex III (Stage 1) and relevant scientific information, each Member State shall propose a list of sites indicating which natural habitat types in Annex I and which species in Annex II that are native to its territory the sites host. For animal species ranging over wide areas these sites shall correspond to the places within the natural range of such species which present the physical or biological factors essential to their life and reproduction. For aquatic species which range over wide areas, such sites will be proposed only where there is a clearly identifiable area representing the physical and biological factors essential to their life and reproduction. Where appropriate, Member States shall propose adaptation of the list in the light of the results of the surveillance referred to in Article 11.
>
>   The list shall be transmitted to the Commission, within three years of the notification of this Directive, together with information on each site. That information shall include a map of the site, its name, location, extent and the data resulting from application of the criteria specified in Annex III (Stage 1) provided in a format established by the Commission in accordance with the procedure laid down in Article 21.
> 2. On the basis of the criteria set out in Annex III (Stage 2) and in the framework both of each of the five biogeographical regions referred to in Article 1 (c) (iii) and of the whole of the territory referred to in Article 2 (1), the Commission shall establish, in agreement with each Member State, a draft list of sites of Community importance drawn from the Member States' lists identifying those which lost one or more priority natural habitat types or priority species.

208. C-378/01, *Commission v. Italy,* paras 20-22.
209. C-240/00, *Commission v. Finland,* para. 20.

> Member States whose sites hosting one or more priority natural habitat types and priority species represent more than 5% of their national territory may, in agreement with the Commission, request that the criteria listed in Annex III (Stage 2) be applied more flexibly in selecting all the sites of Community importance in their territory.
>
> The list of sites selected as sites of Community importance, identifying those which host one or more priority natural habitat types or priority species, shall be adopted by the Commission in accordance with the procedure laid down in Article 21.
>
> 3. The list referred to in paragraph 2 shall be established within six years of the notification of this Directive.
> 4. Once a site of Community importance has been adopted in accordance with the procedure laid down in paragraph 2, the Member State concerned shall designate that site as a special area of conservation as soon as possible and within six years at most, establishing priorities in the light of the importance of the sites for the maintenance or restoration, at a favourable conservation status, of a natural habitat type in Annex I or a species in Annex II and for the coherence of Natura 2000, and in the light of the threats of degradation or destruction to which those sites are exposed.
> 5. As soon as a site is placed on the list referred to in the third subparagraph of paragraph 2 it shall be subject to Article 6 (2), (3) and (4).

In Case C-444/21, *Commission v. Ireland*, the Court described this as a four-stage procedure:

> The procedure governing the designation of sites as special areas of conservation, as provided for in Article 4 of the Habitats Directive, consists of four stages. Under Article 4(1) of that directive, each Member State proposes a list of sites indicating the natural habitat types and native species they host and that list is transmitted to the Commission (first stage). Under Article 4(2), the Commission establishes, in agreement with each Member State, a draft list of sites of Community importance drawn from the Member States' lists (second stage). On the basis of that draft list, the Commission adopts the list of selected sites (third stage). Under Article 4(4), once a site of Community importance has been adopted, the Member State concerned designates it as a special area of conservation as soon as possible and within six years at most, establishing priorities in the light of the importance of the sites for the maintenance or restoration, at a favourable conservation status, of a natural habitat type or species and for the coherence of Natura 2000 (fourth stage) (see, to that effect, judgment of 12 June 2019, *CFE*, C-43/18, EU:C:2019:483, paragraph 37).[210]

Article 4 is supplemented by Article 5, which provides for a bilateral consultation procedure, under certain circumstances, in relation to sites missing from the Member State's proposal in Stage I.

210. C-444/21, *Commission v. Ireland*, para. 45.

[B] Stage I of the Designation Process: Proposal by Member States of Sites of Community Importance (Proposed SCIs)

[1] Requirement of an Exhaustive List

In Stage I of the designation process, on the basis of the criteria set out in Annex III, together with relevant scientific information, Member States must propose and transmit to the Commission a list of sites, indicating which natural habitat types in Annex I and native species in Annex II are to be found there. Member States' contributions depend on the representation on their territory of the natural habitat types and species' habitats listed in Annexes I and II to the Directive.

In Case C-371/98, *First Corporate Shipping*, a United Kingdom court made a preliminary reference to the Court, asking whether, when deciding which sites to propose to the Commission pursuant to Article 4(1) of that Directive and/or in defining the boundaries of such sites, Member States are entitled or obliged to take account of the considerations laid down in Article 2(3) of the Habitats Directive, namely, economic, social and cultural requirements and regional and local characteristics. In this case, the plaintiff, First Corporate Shipping Ltd, had challenged an announced intention of the UK Government to propose the Severn Estuary as part of Stage I of the designation process. Unsurprisingly, and in the same vein as its case-law on the Birds Directive, the Court indicated that a Member State cannot, 'of its own accord, whether because of economic, social or cultural requirements or because of regional or local characteristics',[211] delete such sites of ecological relevance from the list which they must draw up and transmit to the Commission. Indeed, if Member States had been accorded such discretion when selecting sites and defining their boundaries, this could deprive the Commission of having *an exhaustive list* of sites eligible as SACs, with the risk of undermining the Directive's objective of creating a coherent European ecological network of SACs.

The Court's judgment in C-371/98, *First Corporate Shipping* was followed by judgments in relation to Commission's direct actions over the failure of certain Member States to submit a compliant national list. The Court held that although 'it follows from the rules governing the procedure for identifying sites eligible for designation as SACs, set out in Article 4(1) of the Habitats Directive, that Member States have a margin of discretion when making their site proposals',[212] they must do so in compliance with the criteria set by the Directive in Annex III.[213]

The Court again stressed the importance of the Commission receiving *exhaustive* national lists in order to enable the Commission to fulfil its role in Stages II and III. In Case C-220/99, *Commission v. France*, the Court emphasised the pan-EU context as follows:

211. C-371/98, *First Corporate Shipping*, para. 23.
212. C-67/99, *Commission v. Ireland*, para. 33.
213. C-220/99, *Commission v. France*, para. 30.

> Only in that way, moreover, is it possible to realise the objective, set out in the first subparagraph of Article 3(1) of the directive, of maintaining or restoring the natural habitat types and the species' habitats concerned at a favourable conservation status in their natural range, which may lie across one or more frontiers inside the Community. It follows from Article 1(e) and (i) of the directive, read in conjunction with Article 2(1) thereof, that the favourable conservation status of a natural habitat or a species must be assessed in relation to the entire European territory of the Member States to which the Treaty applies.[214]

Predictably, the Court did not accept that domestic difficulties or the necessity of ample public consultations could exonerate Member States from the obligation to draw up and communicate on time the complete list of sites and the accompanying information, to the Commission.[215] Nor did the Court accept that a delay in a Commission decision on the format to be used to transmit the national list and accompanying information exonerated the Member States concerned. In the pre-litigation procedure, the Commission had given these Member States a reasonable time to comply.[216]

[2] Consultation Foreseen under Article 5

Article 5 of the Habitats Directive reads as follows:

> 1. In exceptional cases where the Commission finds that a national list as referred to in Article 4(1) fails to mention a site hosting a priority natural habitat type or priority species which, on the basis of relevant and reliable scientific information, it considers to be essential for the maintenance of that priority natural habitat type or for the survival of that priority species, a bilateral consultation procedure shall be initiated between that Member State and the Commission for the purpose of comparing the scientific data used by each.
> 2. If, on expiry of a consultation period not exceeding six months, the dispute remains unresolved, the Commission shall forward to the Council a proposal relating to the selection of the site as a site of Community importance.
> 3. The Council, acting unanimously, shall take a decision within three months of the date of referral.
> 4. During the consultation period and pending a Council decision, the site concerned shall be subject to Article 6(2).

Case C-340/10, *Commission v. Cyprus*, sheds an interesting light on Article 5. The Commission brought the action against Cyprus for, *inter alia*, not having included the site of Paralimni Lake in the national list of proposed Sites of Community Interest (SCIs). The site was important for the Cypriot grass snake. Cyprus argued that, to address the matter, the Commission should have used the bilateral consultation procedure under Article 5(1) of the Habitats Directive rather than an infringement

214. *Ibid.*, para. 32.
215. C-67/99, *Commission v. Ireland*. paras 32 and 38.
216. *Ibid.*, paras 39 to 44; C-71/99; *Commission v. Germany*, paras 27, 30 and 38.

procedure under what is now Article 258 TFEU (Treaty on the Functioning of the European Union).

The Court observed that, in fact, it had not been disputed that the site should have been included in the list of proposed SCIs. It followed the Commission's argument that the use of Article 5 presupposes the existence of a scientific disagreement with the Member State concerned, whereas in this case, both parties had used the same scientific information. Moreover, Cyprus had actually listed the site, but after the expiry of the deadline set in the Commission's Reasoned Opinion. The Court held that the conditions for the application of Article 5 of the Habitats Directive were not met.[217]

[C] Stages II and III of the Designation Process: Adoption by the Commission of a List of SCIs

As laid down in Article 4(2) of the Directive in Stage II of the classification procedure, the Commission establishes, in agreement with each Member State, a draft list of SCIs drawn from the proposals previously submitted by the Member States. According to the text of the Habitats Directive, the Annex III criteria must be taken into account in the framework of each of the five biogeographical regions,[218] – i.e., Alpine, Atlantic, Continental, Macaronesian and Mediterranean – existing in the EU and for the whole European territory of the EU.[219] It is important to note that EU enlargement has increased the number of biogeographical regions (and their characteristic habitats and species). The Boreal region was added with the accession of Sweden and Finland; the Pannonian region was added with the accession of Hungary, Czech Republic and Slovakia; the Steppic region with the accession of Romania; and the Black Sea Region with the accession of Bulgaria and Romania.

A certain degree of flexibility can be allowed, in agreement with the Commission, for Member States whose sites hosting one or more priority natural habitat types and priority species represent more than 5% of their national territory.

The lists of sites selected as SCIs are then adopted by the Commission (Stage III).[220] The lists must identify SCIs which host one or more priority natural habitat types or priority species.

[1] Limits on the Member States' Role in List Adoption

The extent to which a Member State can refuse to consent to a list proposed for adoption by the Commission was examined in Case C-226/08, *Stadt Papenburg*. In this case, a German court asked the Court whether Article 4(2) allows a Member State to

217. C-340/10, *Commission v. Cyprus*, para. 25.
218. Referred to in Article 1(c)(iii) of the Habitats Directive.
219. Referred to in Article 2(1) of the Habitats Directive, which provides that: 'The aim of this Directive shall be to contribute towards ensuring bio-diversity through the conservation of natural habitats and of wild fauna and flora in the European territory of the Member States to which the Treaty applies.'
220. In accordance with the procedure laid down in Article 21 of the Habitats Directive.

refuse to agree to the Commission's draft list of SCIs on grounds other than nature conservation ones.[221] The national court also asked if those grounds may include the interests of municipalities, including in the context of planning intentions. The Court's reply was negative. It ruled that the achievement of the objective referred to in Article 3(1) of the Habitats Directive, namely the setting up of the Natura 2000 network, 'would be put in danger' if the Member States 'were permitted to refuse to give their agreement on grounds other than environmental protection'.[222]

The Court further reinforced its position by adding:

> That would, in particular, be the case were the Member States able to refuse to give their agreement on the basis of economic, social and cultural grounds and regional and local characteristics as referred to in Article 2(3) of the Habitats Directive, a provision which, moreover, as was stated by the Advocate General in point 38 of her Opinion, does not constitute an autonomous derogation from the general system of protection put in place by that directive.[223]

[2] Derecognition or Modification of Boundaries of SCIs

The leading case on this, Case C-301/12, *Cascina Tre Pini,* confirms that the legal possibility to de-recognise an SCI,[224] reduce its size or modify its boundaries is strictly limited to situations where the site no longer corresponds to the criteria that justified its selection, and the deterioration is not imputable to inactions or actions of the Member State concerned. When these conditions are met, the Member State is actually under an obligation to take steps to have the site removed from the Habitats Directive's scope.

Thus, when a site on the list of SCIs is definitively no longer capable of contributing to the achievement of the objectives of the Habitats Directive, the Member State concerned 'is required to propose to the Commission that the site be declassified'.[225] This can be the case when the results of the surveillance undertaken by the Member States pursuant to Article 11 of the directive lead to the conclusion that the Annex III criteria, which initially led to the classification of the site, 'can irretrievably no longer be met'.[226]

In reaching this conclusion, the Court drew on relevant objectives of the Directive. It would be useless, in such circumstances, for the Member State concerned

221. C-226/08, *Stadt Papenburg*, para. 18.
222. *Ibid.*, para. 31.
223. *Ibid.*, para. 32.
224. For a valuable analysis of this case in the context of Article 9 of the Habitats Directive, *see* Agustín García Ureta, *EU Biodiversity Law: Wild Birds and Habitats Directives*, 247-254 (Europa Law Publishing 2020). Article 9 of the Habitats Directive provides that: 'The Commission, acting in accordance with the procedure laid down in Article 21, shall periodically review the contribution of Natura 2000 towards achievement of the objectives set out in Article 2 and 3. In this context, a special area of conservation may be considered for declassification where this is warranted by natural developments noted as a result of the surveillance provided for in Article 11'. As García Ureta notes, the Court's decision in Case C-301/12, *Cascina Tre Pini*, is not based on Article 9, since Article 9 only applies to SACs.
225. C-301/12, *Cascina Tre Pini*, para. 28.
226. *Ibid.*, para. 27.

to continue to use resources 'in vain'[227] to manage a site which is no longer of use and no longer contributes to objectives related to the Natura 2000 network.

The Court also invoked property rights, observing that 'the obligation on the Member States to propose to the Commission the declassification of a site on the list of SCIs which has become irretrievably unsuitable to achieve the objectives of the Habitats Directive, is all the greater when that site includes land belonging to an owner whose exercise of his right to property is restricted as a result of that listing'.[228] Such restrictions of the right to property are only justified by the objective of protecting the environment[229] laid down in that directive, so where the required qualities of the site are no longer present, 'continuing to restrict the use of that site might be an infringement of the right to property'.[230]

The Court stressed, however, that the factual basis for declassification needed to rest on solid and reliable evidence. 'Not all degradation of a site on the list of SCIs justifies its declassification',[231] and 'a mere allegation of environmental degradation'[232] made by owners of property on the respective sites is not sufficient. 'It is essential that that degradation should make the site irretrievably unsuitable to ensure the conservation of natural habitats and of the wild fauna and flora or the setting up of the Natura 2000 network, so that that site can definitively no longer contribute to the achievement of the objectives of the directive set out in Articles 2 and 3 thereof.'[233]

In this context, an account must be taken of the obligation flowing from Article 6(2) of the Habitats Directive that Member States take the requisite protection measures to avoid deterioration of the natural habitats and the habitats of species in the areas concerned (SCIs or SACs). Therefore, Member States cannot justify declassification where the deterioration is the result of their own failure to fulfil the protection obligations prescribed by the Directive. On the contrary, they must 'take the measures necessary to safeguard that site'.[234] The Court thus subjects any possibility of derecognition to a condition of initial compliance with the protection provisions of Article 6(2) to (4) of the Habitats Directive.

The Court brought these different strands of reasoning together in the following formulation:

> Member States are required to propose to the Commission the declassification of a site on the list of SCIs, where those authorities have received a request from the owner of land included in that site, alleging an environmental degradation of the site, provided that that request is based on the fact that, despite compliance with the provisions of Article 6(2) to (4) of that directive, that site can definitively no

227. *Ibid.*, para. 28.
228. *Ibid.*, para. 29.
229. C-416/10, *Križan*, paras 113 and 114.
230. C-301/12, *Cascina Tre Pini*, para. 29.
231. *Ibid.*, para. 31.
232. *Ibid.*, para. 30.
233. *Ibid.*, para. 30.
234. *Ibid.*, para. 32.

longer contribute to the conservation of natural habitats and of the wild fauna and flora or the setting up of the Natura 2000 network.[235]

A subsequent case, C-281/16, *Vereniging Hoekschewaards Landschap*, underscores the importance of the evidence base used to justify the removal of an area from SCI coverage. The proceedings involved a legal challenge to the validity of a European Commission Decision to place the Haringvliet site in the Netherlands on the list of SCIs without including a specific area, the Leenheerenpolder, which had previously formed part of the proposed SCI. During the process of adoption of the impugned list, the Netherlands made a proposal to reduce the size of the Haringvliet site. The Commission responded positively on the grounds that the Netherlands had made a 'scientific error'[236] in its initial proposal to include the Leenheerenpolder. The Dutch Council of State asked the Court of Justice to rule on the validity of the resulting Commission Decision. Both the Commission and the Dutch authorities had agreed that the other areas comprised in the SCI sufficed to achieve the conservation objectives for the Haringvliet site. The Court, nevertheless, declared that the Commission's Decision to adopt the SCI in a reduced size was invalid because the Commission had failed to provide conclusive scientific evidence capable of proving that a scientific error had vitiated the initial proposal. It noted that the Netherlands had not invoked any scientific error when requesting the Commission to reduce the SCI. The Court concluded as follows:

> As the inclusion of an area in the list gives rise to the presumption that it is relevant in its entirety from the point of view of the directive's objective of conserving natural habitats and wild fauna and flora, a proposal by a Member State to remove certain sites from the list or to reduce their size requires proof that the areas in question do not have a relevant ecological interest at national level. In addition, the Commission may accept and implement the proposal only if it concludes that those areas are also not necessary from the perspective of the entire European Union.[237]

[3] Direct Challenges Before the CJEU by Natural or Legal Persons to the Commission List of SCIs

Placing an area within Natura 2000 can lead to restrictions and obligations for the owners of the land concerned; likewise, removing an area from it can result in the removal of these site safeguards.

Case C-301/12, *Cascina Tre Pini* and Case C-281/16, *Vereniging Hoekschewaards Landschap*, illustrate how it is possible, via national courts, for landowners or

235. *Ibid.*, para. 36.
236. C-281/16, *Vereniging Hoekschewaards Landschap*, para. 27.
237. *Ibid.*, para. 36.

environmental associations to raise questions of interpretation or validity before the Court of Justice in relation to sites on the Commission list.

The CJEU case-law shows, however, that it is not possible for landowners to directly challenge the Commission list before the General Court[238] on the basis of the procedure now set out in Article 263(4) of the TFEU.

In particular, in Case T-150/05, *Markku Sahlsted*, the Court of First Instance (now the General Court) rejected as inadmissible an application submitted by Finnish landowners and a Finnish association of farmers and foresters for annulment of Commission Decision 2005/101 adopting, pursuant to the Habitats Directive, the list of SCIs for the Boreal biogeographical region, which designated areas in Finland as SCIs. As far as the Court of First Instance was concerned, the plaintiffs did not satisfy the procedural criterion [of what is now Article 263(4)] that the Commission Decision must be of direct and individual concern to them.

The Court of First Instance noted that the Commission's Decision imposed no obligation on economic operators or private persons and contained no specific provision in relation to the system of protection of the SCIs, such as conservation measures or authorisation procedures. 'It affects neither the rights or obligations of the landowners nor the exercise of those rights.'[239]

The Court of First Instance also found that Articles 4 to 6 of the Habitats Directive, although binding on the Member States from the moment of the designation of a site as an SCI, are not directly applicable to legal operators since they necessitate a measure on the part of the Member State concerned, in order to specify how it intends to implement them.

Although it dismissed the action, the Court of First Instance did refer to the EU's complete system of legal redress, noting that 'the applicants may still challenge the measures adopted in implementation of Article 6 of the Habitats Directive which affect them and, in that context, they retain the possibility of relying on its illegality before the national courts, adjudicating in accordance with Article 234 EC [now Article 267 TFEU]'.[240]

It may be noted that, in Finland, landowners could and did make extensive use of the national court system to challenge decisions concerning the establishment of Natura 2000. The Court judgment in Case C-240/00, *Commission v. Finland*, mentions that 850 applications had been made to the Finnish Supreme Court for the amendment of a Finnish government decision on a list of SPAs.[241]

238. Prior to the coming into force of the Lisbon Treaty on 1 December 2009, the Court of First Instance.
239. Order of the Court of First Instance of 22 June 2006, *Markku Sahlstedt and Others v. Commission*, T-150/05, para. 54.
240. T-150/05, *Markku Sahlsted*, para. 63; *see also* Judgment of 17 November 1998, *Kruidvat BVBA v. Commission of the European Communities*, C-70/97, EU:C:1998:545, para. 48 and 49.
241. C-240/00, *Commission v. Finland*, para. 7.

[D] Stage IV of the Designation Process: Formal Designation of SACs by the Member States and Establishment of Priorities and Conservation Objectives

The final stage of formal recognition is the designation of SCIs as SACs by Member States. Designation must be done as soon as possible and within six years at the latest, and, for those areas, Member States must establish priorities in light of the importance of the sites for the maintenance or restoration, at a favourable conservation status, of a natural habitat type in Annex I or a species in Annex II and for the coherence of Natura 2000, and in light of the threats of degradation or destruction to which those sites are exposed. This implies that conservation objectives must be established.

[1] Formal Designation, a Distinct Obligation

In Case C-290/18, *Commission v. Portugal* and again in Cases C-444/21, *Commission v. Ireland* and C-116/22, *Commission v. Germany*, the Court had to address an argument by Portugal, Ireland and Germany that existing national conservation measures and programmes applied already to these countries' SCIs, and that the obligations of Article 4(4) were thereby satisfied even if the process of formal SAC designation was not finalised. The Court was clear, however, that the obligation to designate SACs is 'a mandatory stage in the system of protection of habitats and species provided for'[242] by the Habitats Directive. The Court was also clear that the obligation to adopt the necessary conservation measures for SACs was a distinct obligation and not to be conflated with the formal obligation of designation.[243]

[2] Establishment of Priorities and Conservation Objectives

With regard to the reference to establishment of priorities in Article 4(4) of the Habitats Directive, in Case C-90/10, *Commission v. Spain*, the Commission successfully argued that Spain had failed to establish these.[244] Given that Spain had only submitted a relevant ministerial decree after the expiry of the deadline set in the Reasoned Opinion, the Court upheld the Commission's plea.[245]

In Case C-849/19, *Commission v. Greece*, the Court derived a requirement in Article 4(4) for Member States to set conservation objectives.[246] In deriving this requirement, the Court observed that 'conservation objectives' were referred to in the Habitats Directive's eighth and tenth recitals[247] and in its Article 6(3).[248]

242. C-444/21, *Commission v. Ireland*, para. 52.
243. *Ibid.*, para. 54; C-116/22, *Commission v. Germany*, paras 33 to 36.
244. C-90/10, *Commission v. Spain*, para. 17.
245. *Ibid.*, para. 26.
246. C-849/19, *Commission v. Greece*, para. 46.
247. The eighth recital reads: 'Whereas it is appropriate, in each area designated, to implement the necessary measures having regard to the conservation objectives pursued'. The tenth recital

As it stated in Case C-444/21, *Commission v. Ireland*:

> With regard to the wording of Article 4(4) of the Habitats Directive, it should be pointed out that, although it does not explicitly mention the obligation to set conservation objectives, that provision nevertheless requires the competent authorities of the Member State concerned, when designating the special area of conservation, to establish priorities in light of the importance of the sites for the maintenance or restoration, at a favourable conservation status, of a habitat type. Establishing those priorities implies that those conservation objectives have already been set.[249]

The case-law on conservation objectives, in particular that found in Case C-116/22, *Commission v. Germany*, indicates the importance of not considering conservation objectives in isolation but of viewing them in conjunction with the conservation measures required under Article 6(1) of the Habitats Directive and the procedural steps required under Article 6(3) of the Habitats Directive.

[a] *Time Frame for Setting Conservation Objectives*

In terms of timing, the conservation objectives must be set within the six-year time frame allowed for SAC designation and the establishment of priorities. In Case C-444/21, *Commission v. Ireland*, the Court explained the reason for this: 'that period applies also to the establishment of the conservation objectives, given that they are necessary for the setting of those priorities and must, therefore, precede it'.[250] As will be seen in Chapter 3, however, it does not follow that site conservation objectives must be set before the establishment of conservation measures under Article 6(1) of the Habitats Directive.[251]

[b] *Requirement for Conservation Objectives to Be Specific and Precise*

In Cases C-849/19, *Commission v. Greece*, C-444/21, *Commission v. Ireland*, and C-116/22, *Commission v. Germany*, the Court stressed that only *specific and precise* objectives may be regarded as 'conservation objectives' within the meaning of the Habitats Directive.[252]

In Case C-849/19, *Commission v. Greece*, the Court rejected a submission that appropriate objectives had been fixed for SACs comprised within two national parks, 'Schinia – Marathona' and 'Koronia – Volvi'. The Court held that the objectives were not specific to the SACs concerned and did not take into account their specific interests. Objectives such as 'the conservation of the Schinia wetland' or the 'conservation of the

---

reads: 'Whereas an appropriate assessment must be made of any plan or programme likely to have a significant effect on the conservation objectives of a site which has been designated or is designated in future'.

248. C-849/19, *Commission v. Greece*, para. 47.
249. C-444/21, *Commission v. Ireland*, para. 64.
250. *Ibid.*, para. 65.
251. *See* Chapter 3, §3.04[B][4].
252. C-444/21, *Commission v. Ireland*, para. 66.

ecosystems of the region' were too general and imprecise to constitute 'conservation objectives' within the meaning of the Habitats Directive. Furthermore, Greece had not provided for objectives in respect of the main habitat types and species present in the SACs.[253]

[c] *Conservation Objectives Do Not Necessarily Need to Be Quantified, However*

While confirming that conservation objectives need to be specific and precise, the Court in Case C-116/22, Commission v. Germany, rejected a Commission argument that there was a general obligation to formulate objectives in quantitative and measurable terms. The Court took a nuanced position, stating that 'the need to formulate those objectives in quantitative and measurable terms must be examined in each specific case and cannot be considered to be a general obligation on the part of the Member States'.[254] It endorsed an argument by Germany that 'the quantitative and measurable approach to determining conservation objectives can prove ill-suited to some complex habitats and some conservation areas with a dynamic character, whose features vary considerably depending on external environmental factors or interact significantly with other habitats and areas of conservation'.[255]

[d] *Nor Do Conservation Objectives Necessarily Need to Distinguish Between Maintenance and Restoration*

In Case C-116/22, Commission v. Germany, the Court also rejected a Commission argument that conservation objectives needed to distinguish between restoration and maintenance of assets, holding that:

> There is nothing in the Habitats Directive to permit the inference that Member States are required, in all cases, to distinguish between the restoration of the assets to be protected, on the one hand, and the maintenance thereof, on the other, already at the stage when those objectives are being formulated.

Once again, the Court's position was nuanced. It accepted that 'that distinction may be relevant at the stage when specific conservation measures are being set, without there being a need for it to be drawn in the context of the determination of conservation objectives'.[256]

253. C-849/19, *Commission v. Greece*, paras 58 and 59.
254. C-116/22, *Commission v. Germany*, para. 116.
255. *Ibid.*, para. 117.
256. *Ibid.*, para. 130.

[e] *Nor Do Conservation Objectives Need to Be Binding Vis-à-vis Third Parties*

In Case C-116/22, Commission v. Germany, the Court rejected a Commission argument that conservation objectives must be legally binding vis-à-vis third parties. It noted that 'conservation objectives are, by nature, intended to be implemented by way of concrete conservation measures'[257] and that the latter must be adopted by the Member States as legal instruments with binding force, if necessary in particular vis-à-vis third parties.[258] There was nothing in the Habitats Directive, however, 'to permit the inference that, in order to ensure the effectiveness of conservation measures, the objectives on which those measures are based must themselves be legally binding vis-à-vis third parties'.[259] The Court went on to observe that 'the absence of such binding force in no way precludes those objectives from indirectly producing binding effects vis-à-vis third parties, in particular inasmuch as they serve as an assessment criterion, pursuant to Article 6(3) of the Habitats Directive, for assessing the implications that a plan or project may have for a protected site, as such an assessment may in fact lead to the prohibition of that plan or project'.[260]

257. *Ibid.*, para. 133.
258. *Ibid.*, para. 134.
259. *Ibid.*, para. 135.
260. *Ibid.*, para. 135.

CHAPTER 3
Protection of Natura 2000 Sites

§3.01 OBLIGATIONS PENDING FORMAL RECOGNITION

[A] Obligations under Both Nature Directives to Safeguard the Ecological Interest of Sites

The nature case-law confirms that there is an obligation on Member States to safeguard the ecological interest of sites which are eligible for formal recognition under EU law, *even before the classification or designation procedure is finalised.* Moreover, this obligation extends to sites which, on the best available evidence, qualify for recognition but whose eligibility is disputed or recognition resisted by the Member States concerned.

As Chapter 2 explains, the Birds and the Habitats Directive provide for different procedures (and, in the case of the Habitats Directive, different stages) for the formal recognition of the areas that are most important for the protection of species and habitats, i.e., SPAs under the Birds Directive and SCIs and SACs under the Habitats Directive. Notwithstanding these differences, similar considerations, arising from the site protection objectives of both instruments, justify the approach enshrined in the case-law.

[B] Obligation to Protect Bird Sites Eligible for Classification under the Birds Directive

The question of whether sites which are not formally recognised should be given interim protection first arose in respect of the Birds Directive. The question was linked to delays and problems of incompleteness in SPA classifications.

[1] Non-regression Obligation

In effect, in interpreting the first sentence of Article 4(4) of the Birds Directive,[261] the Court derived a non-regression obligation.[262] Thus, as long as sites are proven to have all the characteristics to be classified as SPAs but have not yet (fully) undergone the classification procedure, the case-law confirms that the non-deterioration requirements of the first sentence of Article 4(4) apply.

[2] Rationale for the Obligation

In the first important decision, Case C-355/90, *Santoña Marshes*, the Court rejected an argument, put forward by the Spanish Government, that Member States cannot put protection measures in place as long as a site has not been defined as an SPA [*see also* Chapter 2]. It held that:

> The objectives of protection set out in the directive, as expressed in the ninth recital in its preamble, could not be achieved if Member States had to comply with the obligations arising under Article 4(4) only in cases where a special protection area had previously been established.[263]

Similarly, in Case C-96/98, *Commission v. France* ('*Marais-Poitevin*'), the Court noted that Article 4(4) 'requires Member States to take appropriate steps to avoid, *inter alia*, deterioration of habitats in the areas which are most suitable for the conservation of wild birds, *even where the areas in question have not been classified as SPAs*, provided that they should have been so classified (emphasis added)'.[264]

[C] Obligation to Protect Sites Eligible for Listing as SCIs under the Habitats Directive

Similar questions – i.e., of whether sites which are not formally recognised should be given interim protection – have arisen under the Habitats Directive.

As already noted, Article 4 of the Habitats Directive provides for a multi-stage procedure leading to final designation of SACs. SACs represent the finalisation of the designation process and inaugurate the most complete set of conservation requirements under the Directive. To briefly recall the designation procedure, according to

261. The first sentence of Article 4(4) of the Birds Directive reads as follows: 'In respect of the protection areas referred to in paragraphs 1 and 2 above, Member States shall take appropriate steps to avoid pollution or deterioration of habitats or any disturbances affecting the birds, in so far as these would be significant having regard to the objectives of this Article.'
262. The Birds Directive actually has a 'stand-still' clause, applicable to Annex I species. Article 13 provides as follows: 'Application of the measures taken pursuant to this Directive may not lead to deterioration in the present situation as regards the conservation of the species of birds referred to in Article 1.' *See* Agustín García Ureta, *EU Biodiversity Law: Wild Birds and Habitats Directives*, 88-89 (Europa Law Publishing 2020).
263. C-355/90, *Santoña Marshes*, para. 22.
264. C-96/98, *Marais-Poitevin*, para. 41. *See also* C-355/90, *Commission v. Spain*, para. 22 and C-166/97, *Commission v. France*, para. 38.

Article 4(1), Member States must first propose their own list of sites 'indicating which natural habitat types in Annex I and which species in Annex II that are native to its territory the sites host'. They must then communicate this list to the European Commission which, under Article 4(2), is required to establish, in agreement with Member States and, on the basis of criteria set out in Annex III of the Directive, a draft list of SCIs, drawn from the Member States' lists. The list of sites selected as SCIs at European level is required to be formally adopted by the Commission (by way of a Commission decision). Finally, once an SCI has been placed on the adopted list, the Member State concerned is obliged under Article 4(5) to designate that site as an SAC.

According to Article 4(5) of the Habitats Directive:

> As soon as a site is placed on the list referred to in the third subparagraph of paragraph 2, it shall be subject to Article 6(2), (3) and (4).

This means that, on a literal interpretation, Article 6(2), (3) and (4) obligations apply only once the sites are identified by the Member States and agreed with the European Commission as SCIs.

Having regard to potential problems of delays and incompleteness in the process of listing SCIs, what obligations, if any, do Member States have with regard to the eligible sites that have not yet acquired the status of formally listed SCIs at European level (to which Article 6(1), (2) and (3) of the Habitats Directive apply)?

[1] Rationale for the Obligation

The Court provided clarification on this question in Case C-117/03, *Dragaggi*, following a preliminary reference from an Italian court.[265] It confirmed, first of all, that the obligations under Article 6(2), (3) and (4) are only incumbent upon Member States once a site is listed as an SCI, observing as follows:

> On a proper construction of Article 4(5) of the Directive, the protective measures prescribed in Article 6(2), (3) and (4) of the Directive are required only as regards sites which, in accordance with the third subparagraph of Article 4(2) of the Directive, are on the list of sites selected as Sites of Community Importance adopted by the Commission in accordance with the procedure laid down in Article 21 of the Directive.[266]

Nevertheless, this does not mean that, at the incipient stage of identification and proposal by Member States under Article 4(1) of the Habitats Directive, sites do not benefit from any legal protection under EU law. On the contrary, by virtue of the conservation objectives of the Habitats Directive, Member States are obliged to provide sites with a measure of interim protection.

265. In a dispute between Societa Italiana Dragaggi SpA and Ministero delle Infrastrutture e dei Trasporti and Regione Autonoma del Friuli Venezia Giulia, an Italian court requested an interpretation of Articles 4(5), 6(3) and 21 of the Habitats Directive.
266. C-117/03, *Dragaggi*, para. 25.

Thus, as concerns sites eligible for identification as SCIs which are included in the national lists transmitted to the Commission and, in particular, sites hosting priority natural habitat types or priority species, Member States are required to take the appropriate protective measures from the point of view of the Habitats Directive's conservation objectives, for the purpose of safeguarding the relevant ecological interest which those sites have at national level.[267]

Indeed, as the Court states:

> If those sites are not appropriately protected from that moment, achievement of the objectives seeking the conservation of natural habitats and wild fauna and flora, as set out in particular in the sixth recital in the preamble to the Directive and Article 3(1) thereof, could well be jeopardised. Such a situation would be particularly serious as priority natural habitat types or priority species would be affected, for which, because of the threats to them, early implementation of conservation measures would be appropriate, as recommended in the fifth recital in the preamble to the Directive.[268]

In a subsequent preliminary reference, Case C-244/05, *Bund Naturschutz,* the Court further developed its teleological interpretation, providing additional details on what is to be expected from the national authorities in such situations.

The referring court asked for clarification with regard to the protection scheme that is applicable to sites which have been listed as proposed SCIs by the competent national authorities with a view to their recognition as formally listed SCIs but whose inclusion on the European list is still awaiting a decision by the Commission.

The Court confirmed that until a site which appears on the national list transmitted to the Commission under Article 4(1) of the Habitats Directive is placed on the list of SCIs adopted by the Commission in accordance with Article 4(2) of the Directive, it must benefit from an appropriate protection scheme in order to maintain its ecological characteristics. That appropriate protection scheme not only requires Member States not to authorise interventions which incur the risk of seriously compromising the ecological characteristics of those sites but also to take, in accordance with the provisions of national law, all the measures necessary to avoid such interventions.[269]

In so far as, in accordance with the first part of Annex III to the Directive, the ecological characteristics of a site identified by the competent national authorities must reflect a number of assessment criteria which are expressly listed there, Member States 'cannot authorise interventions which may pose the risk of seriously compromising the ecological characteristics of a site, as defined by those criteria. This is particularly the case when an intervention poses the risk either of significantly reducing the area of a site, or of leading to the disappearance of priority species present on the site, or, finally, of having as an outcome the destruction of the site or the destruction of its representative characteristics'.[270]

---

267. *Ibid.*, para. 30.
268. *Ibid.*, para. 27.
269. C-244/05, *Bund Naturschutz*, paras 47 and 51.
270. *Ibid.*, para. 46.

The Commission must 'be sure of having available to it an exhaustive list of sites eligible as special areas of conservation, the drawing up of which aims at forming a coherent European ecological network'.[271] It follows that, at the time of the decision which the Commission is called upon to take, the sites identified by the Member States must reflect the situation on the basis of which the scientific evaluations of potential SCIs have been carried out.[272] If that were not the case, the European decision-making process which is not only based on the integrity of the sites as notified by the Member States but is also characterised by the ecological comparisons between the different sites proposed by the Member States, would run the risk of being distorted and the Commission would no longer be in a position to fulfil its duties in the area concerned.[273]

The *Dragaggi* and *Bund Naturschutz* case-law helped lay the basis for a number of Commission direct actions against Member States.

[2] Commission Direct Actions to Enforce the Obligation

[a] Tourism Complex in Italy

In Case C-491/08, *Commission v. Italy,* which concerned the construction of a tourism complex 'Is Arenas', in a site proposed for SCI listed status, the Court reaffirmed the stance taken in the *Dragaggi* case. It upheld the action brought by the Commission and declared that Italy had failed to take the necessary protection measures before the site's formal listing and, as the situation of breach persisted, Italy had also violated Article 6(2) of the Habitats Directive which had become applicable after the inscription of the site on the SCI list.[274] In this case, Italy actually intended to remove from the proposed SCI the area where the project was to be constructed, since that area would, it was claimed, not have maintained the characteristics required for such a formal listing.[275] However, that area was essential as it was serving the function of an ecological corridor between two parts of the site, and the draft management plan for the site specified that the project needed revision as the impact on the habitats would be excessive.[276] The project had nevertheless continued without the revision required by the draft management plan. These elements combined to lead the Court to conclude that obligations had been infringed.

[b] Open-Cast Mining in Spain

The Commission was less successful in Case C-404/09, *Commission v. Spain,* which related to the conservation of the brown bear in the Cantabrian region of Spain. One of

271. *Ibid.*, para. 41.
272. *Ibid.*
273. *Ibid.*, para. 42.
274. C-491/08, *Commission v. Italy,* para. 43.
275. *Ibid.*, para. 16.
276. *Ibid.*, paras 32, 33 and 34.

the complaints put forward by the Commission referred to open-cast mining activities taking place between the time of proposal of a site as an SCI and its formal European listing. The Commission claimed that the Spanish authorities had not taken the necessary measures to protect the ecological interest of the site concerned, as required pursuant to the *Dragaggi* and *Bund Naturschutz* case-law. More specifically, it argued that the mining activities had aggravated a 'barrier effect', rendering it more difficult for Cantabrian brown bears to use the Leitariegos pass, which is of great importance for the north-south migration of this bear population. The Court rejected the Commission's complaint as, according to scientific studies presented by Spain, the number of individual bears had actually increased without interruption, including in the interval when the open-cast mining activities took place. Thus, the mining activities were not proven to seriously compromise the ecological characteristics of the site nor to lead to the disappearance of Cantabrian brown bears from it.[277]

[c] Multiple Threats to Habitats of the Cypriot Grass Snake

In Case C-340/10, *Commission v. Cyprus*, the Court found a breach of Article 4(1) of the Habitats Directive as Cyprus had not proposed, for SCI listed status, the site of Paralimni Lake, which was important for the preservation of the Cypriot grass snake and its habitats. In addition, the Court found a breach of Article 4(1) in respect of the tolerance by Cyprus of activities 'which seriously compromise the ecological characteristics of Paralimni Lake' and in respect of the failure by Cyprus to take 'the protective measures necessary to maintain the population of Natrix natrix cypriaca (Cypriot grass snake), the species which constitutes the ecological interest of the lake and Xyliatos Dam'.[278] The tolerated activities were moto-cross racing, excessive extraction of water on the site and property developments in or near the site.

The Court also found a parallel breach of Article 12 of the Habitats Directive, the Cypriot grass snake being protected under that provision.[279] This shows that activities that contravene Article 4(1) of the Habitats Directive can, at the same time, contravene Article 12.

§3.02 OVERVIEW OF PROTECTION REGIMES UNDER THE NATURE DIRECTIVES

First, it is useful to clarify here what is meant by 'protection regime'. In its widest sense, it means provisions that aim at preventing damage, compensating for damage and taking positive conservation measures.

277. C-404/09, *Commision v. Spain*, paras 169 and 170.
278. C-340/10, *Commission v. Cyprus*, operative part of judgment.
279. *See* Chapter 4, §4.03[B][3][b].

For SPAs, the position can be especially complex for three reasons:

(1) In its original form, the Birds Directive required a legal protection regime by virtue of the classification provisions of its Article 4(1) and 4(2). Since it represents an aspect of classification, the requirement for such a legal protection regime has already been outlined in Chapter 2. At the same time, the Birds Directive also required the application of preventive measures under the first sentence of its Article 4(4). Thus, the protection regime in its widest sense derived from a combination of Article 4(1) and 4(2) and the first sentence of Article 4(4).
(2) By virtue of Article 7 of the Habitats Directive, classified SPAs are no longer subject to the first sentence of Article 4(4) but to the provisions of Article 6(2) to (4) of the Habitats Directive. The requirements of Article 4(1) and (2) remain applicable, however. As the Court noted in Case C-304/05, *Commission v. Italy*, 'the obligations flowing from Article 4(1) and (2) of Directive 79/409 remain fully applicable'.[280] Obligations contained under Article 4(1) and (2) are 'autonomous in nature and pursue objectives different from those envisaged in Article 6(2) to (4) of Directive 92/43'.[281]
(3) The nature case-law establishes that, for important bird sites which are unclassified but ought to have been classified, the requirements of the first sentence of Article 4(4) of the Birds Directive continue to apply.

For Natura 2000 sites recognised or designated under the Habitats Directive, the protection regime comprises, for SCIs, the preventive and compensatory obligations of Article 6(2), (3) and (4) of the Habitats Directive and, for SACs, these obligations together with the conservation obligations of Article 6(1) of the Habitats Directive.

§3.03 PROTECTION REGIMES APPLYING TO SPAs OR SITES ELIGIBLE AS SPAs UNDER THE BIRDS DIRECTIVE

[A] Legal Protection Regime Required by Article 4(1) and 4(2) of the Birds Directive

The substantive requirements of the legal protection regime required by Article 4(1) and 4(2) of the Birds Directive have already been outlined in Chapter 2.

In this context, it is useful to recall that this legal protection regime can serve similar objectives to those of Article 6(1) of the Habitats Directive. Indeed, in Case C-418/04, *Commission v. Ireland*, the Court confirmed that 'the protection of SPAs may not be limited to avoiding harmful human effects but must also include positive measures to preserve or improve the state of the area, as the case may be'[282] and that

280. C-304/05, *Commission v. Italy*, para. 104.
281. *Ibid.*
282. C-418/04, *Commission v. Ireland*, para. 154.

the national transposing legislation for Article 6(1) of the Habitats Directive could also serve the requirements of Article 4(1) and 4(2) of the Birds Directive.

Furthermore, as already established in Chapter 2, it is not sufficient to adopt a legal protection regime under Article 4(1) and 4(2). It is also necessary to actually implement it.[283]

Finally, as Case C-432/21, *Commission v. Poland* shows, it is not permissible for a Member State to adopt provisions which override the legal protection regime required by Article 4(1) and 4(2) – *see* §3.04[C][3][e] below.

[B] Initial Preventive Regime under the First Sentence of Article 4(4) of the Birds Directive

The first sentence of Article 4(4) of the Birds Directive provides for a stricter protection regime than the regime provided for under Article 6(2), (3) and (4) of the Habitats Directive. Indeed, the Habitats Directive had as one of its objectives to bring about a relaxation of some of the strict requirements of the first sentence of Article 4(4) of the Birds Directive as interpreted by the Court in Case C-57/89, *Leybucht Dykes*. The effect of Article 7 of the Habitats Directive was that, with the entry into force of the Habitats Directive, the stricter regime of the first sentence of Article 4(4) gave way to the regime of Article 6(2), (3) and (4) of the Habitats Directive. The earlier regime did not entirely disappear, however. As will be seen, it remains relevant to sites eligible to be classified as SPAs before their classification.

The first sentence of Article 4(4) of the Birds Directive reads as follows:

> In respect of the protection areas referred to in paragraphs 1 and 2 above, Member States shall take appropriate steps to avoid pollution or deterioration of habitats or any disturbances affecting the birds, in so far as these would be significant having regard to the objectives of this Article.

The ambit of this obligation is defined by the case-law of the Court, which has followed a strict interpretation.

[1] Only Limited Interests Can Override the Preventive Regime

The approach the Court followed in the recent cases, C-141/14, *Commission v. Bulgaria* and C-461/14, *Commission v. Spain*, was first set out in the judgment it delivered in Case C-57/89, *Leybucht Dykes*, before the adoption of the Habitats Directive. In this earlier case, the Commission brought an action against Germany for planning or undertaking works detrimental to the habitat of protected birds in SPAs, contrary to Article 4 of the Birds Directive.[284] The works in question involved the extension of a sea-dyke as part of a coastal defence project. The extension departed from the line of the existing dyke and protruded into a protected area. The Court took note of the

283. C-661/20, *Commission v. Slovakia*, para. 112.
284. C-57/89, *Leybucht Dykes*, para. 1.

objective of the works, stating that 'the danger of flooding and the protection of the coast constitute sufficiently serious reasons to justify the dyke works and the strengthening of coastal structures as long as those measures are confined to a strict minimum and involve only the smallest possible reduction of the special protection area'.[285] Thus, while recognising the legitimacy of the objective being pursued, the Court set strict limits on what could be justified by reference to it. In referring to the fact that the project also enabled the access of fishing vessels to a local harbour, the Court stated clearly that the pursuit of such an interest is, in principle, incompatible with the requirements of the provision.

In the specific circumstances, the works were considered acceptable by the Court. It took note of positive consequences for the habitats of birds and given the 'offsetting ecological benefits',[286] the project successfully passed the scrutiny of the Court. Moreover, the disturbance arising from the construction work itself had not exceeded what was necessary as there was no significant change in the number of avocets in that sector as a result of the works.

However, the Court did not follow the line proposed by the German Government that Member States must have discretionary power to strike a balance between the various public interests at stake. Nor did it follow the interpretation put forward by the United Kingdom that 'deterioration of a special protection area must be such as to threaten the survival or reproduction of protected species within their area of distribution'.[287]

[2] *Examples of Breaches of the First Sentence of Article 4(4)*

[a] *Pollution in and Deterioration of the Santoña Marshes*

All sorts of activities can be found to be harmful and may constitute a breach of the non-deterioration obligation of the first sentence of Article 4(4). In Case C-355/90, *Santoña Marshes*, the Court found that the discharge of wastewater containing dangerous toxic substances was highly detrimental to the ecological conditions in the wetland concerned.[288] It also condemned the operation of a quarry and the tipping of unused material into the marshes, which had reduced the extent of the protected area.[289] The Court considered that Spain was under the duty, 'where necessary, to provide systems for treating waste in order to prevent pollution of those habitats'.[290]

[b] *Reclamation of Wetlands for Agriculture in the Marais Poitevin*

In Case C-96/98, *Marais Poitevin*, the Court ruled that France had infringed the first sentence of Article 4(4) of the Birds Directive because it did not take measures to avoid

285. *Ibid.*, para. 23.
286. *Ibid.*, para. 26.
287. *Ibid.*, para. 13.
288. C-355/90, *Santoña Marshes*, para. 52.
289. *Ibid.*, para. 54.
290. *Ibid.*, para. 53.

the deterioration of parts of the Poitevin marshes that were either classified or ought to have been classified. In its application, the Commission maintained that the natural meadows, which form the most important habitat for the conservation of wild birds in the Poitevin Marsh and which covered an area of 55,450 hectares in 1973, had an area of some 26,750 hectares in 1990, with approximately 28,700 hectares being placed under cultivation during the intervening period. With a view to facilitating agricultural activity, drainage was carried out, wetlands were reclaimed and ditches were filled in.[291] Wetland reduction had led to a fall in bird populations such as those of wintering ducks and black-tailed godwits.[292] France acknowledged that the protection regime for the area had not always been effective, but it argued that the responsibility for the reduction in the wetlands rested primarily with the CAP and not solely with the French authorities.[293]

The Court was satisfied that evidence, including evidence of a very steep decline in the numbers of wintering ducks, established a breach of the first sentence of Article 4(4) of the Birds Directive in respect of areas of the Marsh that had actually been classified, and dismissed the argument of France concerning the CAP:

> As for the French Government's argument that Community aid measures for agriculture are disadvantageous to agriculture compatible with the conservation requirements laid down by the Birds Directive, it should be pointed out that, even assuming that this were the case and a certain lack of consistency between the various Community policies were thus shown to exist, this still could not authorise a Member State to avoid its obligations under that directive, in particular under the first sentence of Article 4(4) thereof.[294]

As for the part of the Poitevin Marsh that had not been classified but ought to have been, the Court did not consider the extent of wetland loss cited by the Commission to be conclusive evidence, but it was satisfied that a number of areas suitable for classification had been destroyed.[295]

[c] *Deterioration of Habitats of Steppic Birds in Spain*

In C-186/06 *Commission v. Spain*, which concerned an irrigation project in the irrigable area of the Segarra-Garrigues Canal, the Court was clear that the Member State was bound to ensure that no deterioration occurred, irrespective of the 'considerable importance' of the project concerned to the economic and social development of the area affected.[296] 'The Member States' ability significantly to harm areas which ought to have been classified as SPAs and which … fall within the scheme laid down in the first sentence of Article 4(4) of the Birds Directive cannot, in any event, be justified by

291. C-96/98, *Marais Poitevin*, para. 29.
292. *Ibid.*, para. 30.
293. *Ibid.*, para. 32.
294. *Ibid.*, para. 40.
295. *Ibid.*, para. 45.
296. C-186/06, *Commission v. Spain*, para. 37.

economic and social requirements.'[297] In terms of burden of proof, a Member State may be found in breach of the non-deterioration obligation 'before any reduction is observed in the number of birds or any risk of a protected species becoming extinct has materialised'.[298] It should be mentioned, nevertheless, that in this particular case, there was evidence of a damaging impact, stemming from official sources. The environmental impact statement, published in the Official Journal of Generalitat de Catalogne, indicated that the project was 'seriously harmful, particularly with regard to the habitats of steppe-land birds, despite the preventive, corrective and compensatory measures proposed in the environmental impact assessment and despite the additional measures set out in the statement itself'.[299]

[3] Comparison and Relationship with Article 6(2) of the Habitats Directive

In more recent case-law, in particular, Case C-141/14, *Commission v. Bulgaria,* and Case C-461/14, *Commission v. Spain*, in order to establish whether a failure to comply with Article 4(4) has occurred, the Court refers 'by analogy, to the case-law of the Court relating to the failure to fulfil obligations under Article 6(2) of the Habitats Directive, since the content of the latter provision is largely the same as that of the first sentence of Article 4(4) of the Birds Directive'.[300] It is enough to indicate a probability or risk that the project will cause deterioration to the habitats of protected species of birds or cause significant disturbance to those species, as 'the obligations to protect exist before any reduction in the number of birds has been observed or before the risk of a protected species becoming extinct has materialised'.[301]

In Case C-141/14 *Commission v. Bulgaria*, the operation of wind-power installations in an unclassified site was identified as likely to lead to such deterioration or disturbance. Bulgaria's argument that red-breasted geese still used the areas in question was not sufficient to reverse the conclusion of deterioration, as data indicated a loss of attractiveness (red-breasted geese used the site less often than when peak values were recorded before the building of the turbines).[302]

In Case C-461/14, *Commission v. Spain*, the Court found that Spain infringed Article 4(4) of the Birds Directive by failing to take appropriate steps to avoid, in the 'Campiñas de Sevilla' SPA while it was unclassified, the deterioration of natural habitats and the habitats of species, as well as disturbance of the species for which that area was established. It found a similar breach of Article 6(2) of the Habitats Directive after the SPA was classified. Each infringement had the same cause: the authorisation of a high-speed rail line crossing the SPA.

297. *Ibid.*, para. 37.
298. *Ibid.*, para. 36.
299. *Ibid.*, para. 33.
300. C-461/14, *Commission v. Spain,* para. 76; C-141/14, *Commission v. Bulgaria,* para. 69.
301. C-461/14, *Commission v. Spain,* para. 83; C-141/14, *Commission v. Bulgaria,* para. 76; C-186/06, *Commission v. Spain,* para. 36.
302. C-141/14, *Commission v. Bulgaria,* paras 76 and 77.

While the first sentence of Article 4(4) of the Birds Directive and Article 6(2) of the Habitats Directive have been interpreted in a like manner, Case C-461/14, *Commission v. Spain* and other case-law show that, formally speaking, the first sentence of Article 4(4) will apply for as long as a site has not been classified. The Court's formulation is clear on this point of temporal applicability: 'Member States must comply with the obligations arising under the first sentence of Article 4(4) of the Birds Directive, even where the areas in question have not been classified as SPAs, provided that they should have been so classified'.[303]

[4] Breach of the First Sentence of Article 4(4) Will Not Remove the Obligation to Classify

A final point, already mentioned in Chapter 2, is that, should a Member State cause an unclassified site to lose its suitability for a species because of its failure to apply the first sentence of Article 4(4) of the Birds Directive, it will not thereby be absolved of the need to classify that site. This is illustrated by the example of the Moy Valley in Case C-418/04, *Commission v. Ireland.* The Moy Valley had been an important site for the Corncrake but the bird had disappeared from the area. As the Court noted, 'the case-file shows that, in the Moy Valley, which should have been classified as an SPA, the loss of corncrake was the result of changes in agricultural practices which Ireland took no steps to remedy'. The Court concluded that the site ought to be classified.[304]

[C] New Preventive and Compensatory Provisions Applicable to SPAs by Virtue of Article 7 of the Habitats Directive

Article 7 provides that:

> Obligations arising under Article 6(2), (3) and (4) of this Directive shall replace any obligations arising under the first sentence of Article 4(4) of Directive 79/409/EEC in respect of areas classified pursuant to Article 4(1) or similarly recognized under Article 4(2) thereof, as from the date of implementation of this Directive or the date of classification or recognition by a Member State under Directive 79/409/EEC, where the latter date is later.

Once areas are classified as SPAs, the preventive and compensatory provisions prescribed under Article 6(2) to (4) of the Habitats Directive thus become applicable, in substitution for the preventive regime laid down under the first sentence of Article 4(4) of the Birds Directive.

---

303. C-186/06, *Commission v. Spain,* para. 27; *see also* C-166/97, *Commission v. France,* para. 38; and C-388/05, *Commission v. Italy,* para. 18.
304. C-418/04, *Commission v. Ireland,* para. 120.

The framework of the Habitats Directive was 'relaxed, as compared with that under the Birds Directive, by the introduction of a conditional derogatory regime, to be found in Article 6'.[305]

With a view to coherence with the Birds Directive and in light of often potential overlapping of protected sites and their respective protection regimes, the Habitats Directive harmonised the impact assessment and non-deterioration obligations so that the two directives' relevant provisions mirror each other. Moreover, while 'within Article 6 of the Habitats Directive, Article 6(2) is generally similar to Article 4(4) of the Birds Directive',[306] by the introduction of Article 7 in the Habitats Directive, the opportunity of derogations arising from Article 6(3) and (4) of the Habitats Directive was extended to apply also to SPAs classified under the Birds Directive.

[1] Temporal Application of Article 7 of the Habitats Directive

Questions arose with regard to the temporal applicability of Article 7 of the Habitats Directive, and, in particular, the question of whether, for sites which ought to have been classified as SPAs but weren't, Member States could take advantage of the more flexible approach introduced by Article 6(3) and (4) of the Habitats Directive during the pre-classification period.

The Birds' Directive had not included any derogation provisions with respect to projects or plans that might be damaging to sites. Could Member States avail themselves of the more flexible regime introduced by Article 7 if they had not classified an SPA?

In Case C-374/98, *Commission v. France* ('*Basses Corbières*'), the Court clarified the matter, confirming that, as long as an SPA has not been classified, the more flexible approach introduced by Article 7 of the Habitats Directive cannot apply. The Commission brought the case to ensure that the Basses Corbières site would be classified as an SPA for the endangered Bonelli's eagle and also safeguarded from potentially damaging quarry developments. The Commission assumed (wrongly as it turned out) that Article 6(2) to (4) of the Habitats Directive was applicable.

The outcome was dictated by the literal interpretation of Article 7 which refers to its temporal application being from 'the date of classification' when this is later than the transposition date of the Habitats Directive.[307]

But there were also underlying 'policy considerations':[308] had the more flexible regime introduced by Article 7 applied, this could have been perceived as an incentive for Member States not to fulfil their classification obligations in a timely manner. As the original regime of Article 4(4) of the Birds Directive is stricter, Member States can have an incentive to 'carry out classifications, in so far as they thereby acquire the possibility

305. Graham Machin, *Protecting Bird Habitat of European Importance: The View from Basses Corbières*, 6 Environmental Law Review 175-189 (2004) DOI: 10.1350/enlr.6.3.174.60201.
306. *Ibid.*
307. C-374/98, *Basses Corbières*, paras 44 and 45.
308. Graham Machin, *Protecting Bird Habitat of European Importance: The View from Basses Corbières*, 6 Environmental Law Review 175-189 (2004) DOI: 10.1350/enlr.6.3.174.60201.

of using a procedure which allows them, for imperative reasons of overriding public interest, including those of a social or economic nature, and subject to certain conditions, to adopt a plan or project adversely affecting a SPA'.[309] The Court saw a significantly increased risk that 'plans or projects not directly connected with or necessary to the management of the site, and affecting its integrity, may be accepted by the national authorities in breach of that procedure, escape the Commission's monitoring and cause serious, or irreparable ecological damage, contrary to the conservation requirements of that site'.[310] The Court also stated that 'a Member State cannot derive an advantage from its failure to comply with its Community obligations'.[311]

Case C-388/05, *Commission v. Italy,* concerned the carrying out, within the context of a 'zonal agreement', of an industrial development which involved the destruction of part of the 'Valloni e steppe pedegarganiche' area. This had previously been in a well-conserved state, and the ecological damage caused to it imperilled the conservation of several species of protected birds which used that area.[312] The Court ruled that Italy had failed to fulfil its obligations under the first sentence of Article 4(4) of the Birds Directive up to the moment of the classification of the SPA. As the site's deterioration continued after the SPA's classification, the Court also found Italy to be in breach of Article 6(2) of the Habitats Directive, which had become applicable by virtue of Article 7.

[2] Application of Article 6(2) to (4) of the Habitats Directive to Ornithological Interests

While Article 6(2) to (4) of the Habitats Directive provide the possibility of greater flexibility than that allowed under the first sentence of Article 4(4) of the Birds Directive, it is worth stressing that the Court's interpretation of Article 6(2) of the Habitats Directive – a provision which in wording closely mirrors the wording of the first sentence of Article 4(4) of the Birds Directive – has been strict, with the Court treating it as giving rise to an 'obligation of result'.[313]

Case C-535/07, *Commission v. Austria,* provides useful clarification on how Article 6(2) protects ornithological interests. The Court stated that:

> By virtue of Article 6(2) of the Habitats Directive, the obligations under which replace those arising under the first sentence of Article 4(4) of the Birds Directive in respect of classified areas, the protective legal status of SPAs must also guarantee the avoidance therein of the deterioration of natural habitats and the habitats of species as well as significant disturbance of the species for which those areas have been classified.[314]

309. C-374/98, *Basses Corbières,* para. 56.
310. *Ibid.,* para. 53.
311. *Ibid.,* para. 51.
312. C-388/05, *Commission v. Italy,* para. 22.
313. Hendrik Schoukens, *Ongoing Activities and Natura 2000 Biodiversity Protection vs Legitimate Expectations?,* 11 Journal for European Environmental & Planning Law 1-30 (2014) DOI: 10.1163/18760104-01101001.
314. C-535/07, *Commission v. Austria,* para. 58.

Furthermore, as already noted, the obligations of Article 6(2) to (4) of the Habitats Directive sit alongside obligations under Article 4(1) or 4(2) of the Birds Directive and, so, the protection of SPAs must not be limited to 'measures intended to avoid external anthropogenic impairment and disturbance but must also, according to the situation that presents itself, include positive measures to preserve or improve the state of the site'.[315] Section §3.04[C][4] below provides examples of breaches of Article 6(2) in relation to ornithological interests.

§3.04 PROTECTION REGIME UNDER ARTICLE 6 OF THE HABITATS DIRECTIVE

[A] Provisions of Article 6 Form a Coherent Whole

In Case C-387/15, *Orleans*, the Court observed that 'Article 6 of the Habitats Directive divides the measures into three categories, namely *conservation measures*, *preventive measures and compensatory measures*, provided for in Article 6(1), (2) and (4), respectively (emphasis added).'[316]

Furthermore, in this case, it stated:

> The provisions of Article 6 of the Habitats Directive must be construed as *a coherent whole* in the light of the conservation objectives pursued by that directive. Thus, Article 6(2) and (3) are designed to ensure the same level of protection of natural habitats and habitats of species, whilst Article 6(4) constitutes merely a provision derogating from the second sentence of Article 6(3).[317]

It may again be recalled that, by virtue of Article 4(5) of the Habitats Directive, the provisions of Article 6(2), (3) and (4) become applicable as soon the site is placed on the list of SCIs adopted by the Commission. In addition, Article 6(1) of the Habitats Directive makes SACs subject to 'the necessary conservation measures'.

[B] Conservation Measures under Article 6(1)

Article 6(1) of the Habitats Directive provides that:

> For special areas of conservation, Member States shall establish the necessary conservation measures involving, if need be, appropriate management plans specifically designed for the sites or integrated into other development plans, and appropriate statutory, administrative or contractual measures which correspond to the ecological requirements of the natural habitat types in Annex I and the species in Annex II present on the sites.

While the Habitats Directive grants a certain margin of discretion to Member States to define the *form* of conservation measures (i.e., management plans, statutory,

315. C-418/04, *Commission v. Ireland*, para. 154.
316. C-387/15, *Orleans*, para. 33.
317. *Ibid.*, para. 32.

administrative or contractual measures), appropriate measures do need to be in place to protect the habitat types referred to in Annex I and the species referred to in Annex II.[318]

[1] *The Requirement for Conservation Measures Is Mandatory and Must Be Strictly Transposed*

In Case C-508/04, *Commission v. Austria*, the Court held that the Habitats Directive 'requires the adoption of necessary conservation measures, a fact which excludes any discretion in this regard on the part of the Member States and restricts any latitude of the national authorities when laying down rules or taking decisions to the means to be applied and the technical choices to be made in connection with those measures'.[319] This case, amongst other things, concerned the transposition of Article 6(1) of the Habitats Directive in Lower Austria. The Commission complained that the transposing legislation had qualified the requirement for conservation measures with the expression 'if need be'. The Court confirmed that this expression – found in the text of Article 6(1) – related to the choices for achieving conservation and not to the requirement for conservation measures, stating:

> In Article 6(1) of the Directive, on the other hand, the same words relate only to particular cases, that is to say to certain means or technical choices for achieving conservation which are defined as 'appropriate management plans specifically designed for the sites or integrated into other development plans'.[320]
>
> Thus, the Directive requires the adoption of necessary conservation measures, a fact which excludes any discretion, in this regard, on the part of the Member States and restricts any latitude of the national authorities when laying down rules or taking decisions to the means to be applied and the technical choices to be made in connection with those measures.[321]

The Court also rejected an argument by Austria that the domestic legislation concerned was interpreted in a manner consistent with the Habitats Directive, stating:

> Such interpretation of provisions of domestic law in a manner consistent with a directive cannot in itself achieve the clarity and precision needed to meet the requirement of legal certainty.[322]
>
> Moreover, mere administrative practices, which by their nature are alterable at will by the authorities and are not given the appropriate publicity, cannot be regarded as constituting fulfilment of the obligations owed by the Member States in the context of transposition of a directive.[323]

318. 'Managing Natura 2000 Sites – The provisions of Article 6 of the "Habitats" Directive 92/43/EEC', section 2.4.2. Statutory, administrative or contractual measures, p. 21, https://ec.europa.eu/environment/nature/natura2000/management/docs/art6/provision_of_art6_en.pdf.
319. C-508/04, *Commission v. Austria*, para. 76.
320. *Ibid.*, para. 75.
321. *Ibid.*, para. 76.
322. *Ibid.*, para. 79.
323. *Ibid.*, para. 80.

[2] Requirement for Conservation Measures to Cover Each SAC in Its Entirety and to Cover the Entire SAC Network

Clearly, necessary conservation measures must be in place for the relevant SACs in their entirety.[324] Where Member States use pre-existing measures (established for national parks, for instance), they need to make sure that these completely overlap with SAC boundaries and interests so that no portions of protected habitats or species are left out. In Case C-90/10, *Commission v. Spain*, the Court condemned Spain for failing to take measures for SACs which did not coincide with protected natural spaces from the Canary Islands and therefore, could not enjoy the protection regime already in place.[325]

Case C-90/10, *Commission v. Spain* was the first of a series of Commission direct actions addressing Member States' lack of fulfilment of the requirement for conservation measures under Article 6(1) of the Habitats Directive.

In Case C-849/19, *Commission v. Greece*, the Commission addressed the insufficiency of Greek conservation measures. Via 24 legislative instruments, Greece purported to have established conservation measures for approximately 18.5% of the total SAC network addressed by the Commission's action.[326] A large part of the network was therefore not covered by the required measures. Moreover, the Court found that the measures established for 18.5% of the network were also insufficient, since they were too general and needed further concrete steps to ensure their effective implementation.[327]

Similarly, in Case C-444/21, *Commission v. Ireland*, the Court upheld a Commission complaint that there were sites with no conservation measures or incomplete conservation measures. In particular, of 423 SCIs, it held that Ireland had breached Article 6(1) by failing to adopt conservation measures for 230 and by failing to adopt *complete* conservation measures for 149 of the remaining 193 sites.[328]

[3] Requirement for Conservation Measures to Be Complete, Clear and Precise

In Case C-290/18, *Commission v. Portugal*, the Court held that, just like the other obligations prescribed under Article 6, the obligation to adopt conservation measures provided in Article 6(1) 'must be implemented effectively and by complete, clear and precise measures'.[329] In that case, the Court found that the Portuguese measures were incomplete.

In Case C-444/21, *Commission v. Ireland*, the Court held that conservation measures cannot 'be limited to measures intended to avoid external man-caused

324. C-90/10, *Commission v. Spain*, para. 49.
325. *Ibid.*, para. 62.
326. C-849/19, *Commission v. Greece*, para. 81.
327. *Ibid.*, para. 82.
328. C-444/21, *Commission v. Ireland*, para. 154.
329. C-290/18, *Commission v. Portugal*, para. 53.

impairment and disturbance and should include, if necessary, positive proactive measures to maintain the site or restore it to a state of conservation'.[330] In this case, national regulations requiring prior consent for activities that may have an adverse impact on a site were not deemed sufficient in themselves to meet Article 6(1) requirements.

In its finding of incomplete conservation measures in Case C-444/21, *Commission v. Ireland*, the Court used the following formulation:

> It is not possible to establish from the information submitted to the Court by Ireland that the measures adopted by that Member State include systematic conservation measures established in the light of the ecological requirements of each species and habitat type present on those sites. Article 6(1) of the Habitats Directive requires conservation measures to be established in the light of *the ecological requirements of each species and habitat type present on each of the sites* of Community importance at issue (emphasis added).[331]

This formulation underscores the importance of Member States providing sufficient information to demonstrate that their conservation measures are complete.

In Case C-849/19, Commission v. Greece, the Court stressed that, if Article 6(1) was not to be deprived of useful effect, Member States must not only adopt the necessary and appropriate conservation measures but also ensure *the actual implementation* of these through complete, clear and precise measures.[332] As in the other cases mentioned, moreover, the Court found that the Greek measures were incomplete by reference to the ecological requirements of each species and habitat type present in the respective sites.[333] For instance, while some measures would target water birds or lake habitats, no measures were in place to address marine species and habitats.[334]

[4] Relationship Between Conservation Objectives and Conservation Measures

[a] Timing

As already explained in Chapter 2, failure to adopt specific and precise conservation objectives constitutes a violation of Article 4(4) of the Habitats Directive.[335]

It does not follow that conservation objectives must be set in advance of conservation measures, however. In Case C-444/21, *Commission v. Ireland*, the Court stated that Article 6(1) of the Habitats Directive does not require conservation

330. C-444/21, *Commission v. Ireland*, para. 150.
331. *Ibid.*, para. 153.
332. C-849/19, *Commission v. Greece*, para. 77.
333. *Ibid.*, para. 86.
334. *Ibid.*
335. *Ibid.*, paras 42 to 61.

measures to be adopted imperatively *after* the adoption of the conservation objectives.[336] It did stress, however, that conservation measures must still satisfy conservation objectives:

> The fact remains that, even if those objectives are defined after the adoption of the conservation measures, it is necessary for those measures to meet those objectives.[337]

[b] *Need for Binding Force, Including Vis-à-Vis Third Parties*

As Chapter 2 has made clear, the Court's interpretation of 'conservation objectives' in Case C-116/22, Commission v. Germany, also throws light on conservation measures. Thus 'conservation objectives are, by nature, intended to be implemented by way of concrete conservation measures'[338] and 'conservation measures must be adopted by the Member States as legal instruments with binding force, if necessary in particular vis-à-vis third parties.[339]

[5] Temporal Application of Article 6(1)

In Case C-444/21, *Commission v. Ireland,* the Court confirmed that the lack of designation of SCIs as SACs, as required under Article 4(4), does not relieve Member States from the obligation to establish the necessary conservation measures under Article 6(1) of the Habitats Directive.[340]

[6] Compatibility with Article 6(1) of Plans Which Combine Development and Ecological Objectives

What of plans which pursue dual objectives, for example, plans which aim at both development and conservation? Can these be considered compatible with Article 6(1)?

This question arose in Joined Cases C-387/15 and C-388/15, Orleans which concerned a development plan for a large part of the port of Antwerp in Belgium on the left bank of the River Scheldt. This would have affected the Natura 2000 site known as 'Scheldt and Durme estuary from the Dutch border to Ghent'.

The plan proposed, in ecological core areas, the establishment of habitats and habitats of species to offset the negative impacts of the plan. The Flemish Government argued that, since these actions would contribute to the integrity of the Natura 2000 site in question, they did not constitute compensatory measures but rather conservation measures within the meaning of Article 6(1) of the Habitats Directive.[341] In this regard,

336. C-444/21, *Commission v. Ireland,* para. 159.
337. *Ibid.,* para. 160.
338. C-116/22, *Commission v. Germany,* para. 133.
339. Ibid, para. 134.
340. *Ibid.,* para. 140.
341. C-387/15, *Orleans,* para. 21.

the referring court had found that the plan would result in the disappearance of a body of 20 hectares of tidal mudflats and tidal marshes of the Natura 2000 site. The Court observed that, as the measures in issue in the main proceedings envisaged, amongst other things, the disappearance of a part of that site, 'such measures cannot constitute measures ensuring the conservation of that site'.[342]

[7] Incompatibility with Article 6(1) of Presumptive Provisions That Favour Certain Activities

In Case C-432/21, *Commission v. Poland*, the Court considered a wide-ranging national provision introducing a presumption of compliance with nature conservation legislation when forest management operations are implemented according to the requirements of *good forest management practices*. The Court found that this contravened Article 6(1) of the Habitats Directive, as well as Article 4(1) of the Birds Directive and Article 6(2) of the Habitats Directive.[343] Further details of the Court's reasoning are provided below in section §3.04[C][3][e] below.

[C] Preventive Measures: Obligation of General Protection under Article 6(2)

Article 6(2) reads as follows:

> Member States shall take appropriate steps to avoid, in the special areas of conservation, the deterioration of natural habitats and the habitats of species as well as disturbance of the species for which the areas have been designated, in so far as such disturbance could be significant in relation to the objectives of this Directive.

As a preliminary remark, the case-law of the Court has clearly linked the non-deterioration clause contained in Article 6(2) of the Habitats Directive with the objective formulated in the Directive's seventh recital that 'each special area of conservation must form part of a coherent European ecological network'.

The Court has stated that the provision of Article 6(2) establishes an 'obligation to take appropriate protective measures, consisting in avoiding deterioration and disturbance which could be significant in light of the objectives of Directive 92/43'[344] and that 'Article 6(2) of the Habitats Directive establishes an *obligation of general protection* consisting in avoiding deterioration and disturbances which could have significant effects in the light of the Directive's objectives (emphasis added).'[345]

342. *Ibid.*, para. 38.
343. C-432/21, *Commission v. Poland*, paras 109 and 110.
344. C-304/05, *Commission v. Italy*, para. 92.
345. C-127/02, *Waddenzee*, para. 38.

[1] Applicability of Article 6(2): SCIs and SACs under the Habitats Directive and Classified SPAs under the Birds Directive

Chapter 2 has addressed legal obligations flowing from the multi-stage procedure set out in Article 4 of the Habitats aimed at eventually designating sites as SACs. As previously noted, as part of this procedure, sites acquire an interim status as listed SCIs.

At what point does Article 6(2) become applicable?

[a] *Recognised SCIs*

According to Article 4(5) of the Directive, 'as soon as a site is placed on the list referred to in the third subparagraph of paragraph 2 it shall be subject to Article 6(2), (3) and (4)'. Therefore, the obligations of Article 6(2) apply only once the sites are identified by Member States and agreed with the European Commission as SCIs.

The Court has confirmed that the provisions of Article 6(2) become applicable as soon as the area in question gains the status of an SCI, listed in a decision adopted by the Commission, under Article 4(2) of the Habitats Directive. In Case C-117/03, *Draggagi*, the Court stated that 'on a proper construction of Article 4(5) of the Directive, the protective measures prescribed in Article 6(2), (3) and (4) of the Directive are required only as regards sites which, in accordance with the third subparagraph of Article 4(2) of the Directive, are on the list of sites selected as sites of Community importance adopted by the Commission in accordance with the procedure laid down in Article 21 of the Directive'.[346]

Nevertheless, it is worth recalling that Member States have obligations to provide legal protection prior to a site acquiring the status of a listed SCI. As already explained in section §3.01[C] above, in Case C-117/03, *Draggagi* and Case C-244/05, *Bund Naturschutz*, the Court confirmed that, in the case of sites eligible for identification as SCIs and, in particular, sites hosting priority natural habitat types or priority species, the Member States are required to take protective measures for the purpose of safeguarding the relevant ecological interest which those sites have at national level.

[b] *Classified SPAs*

By virtue of Article 7 of the Habitats Directive, the provisions contained in its Article 6(2), (3) and (4) are also applicable to SPAs classified under the Birds Directive. In the case of areas protected under the Birds Directive, applicability starts from the date of a site's classification as an SPA.

Again it is worth recalling that, prior to formal SPA classification, IBAs requiring classification benefit from the protective provisions of the first sentence of Article 4(4) of the Birds Directive – *see* section §3.03[C][1] above.

346. C-117/03, *Dragaggi*, para. 25.

[2] Scope of the Article 6(2) Obligation

The objects of the required protection are natural habitats as well as habitats of species that are protected under the Habitats Directive: 'it should first be noted that Article 6(2) of the Habitats Directive obliges the Member States to avoid the deterioration of natural habitats and the habitats of species'.[347]

As concerns SPAs classified under the Birds Directive, Article 6(2) of the Habitats Directive, in conjunction with Article 7 thereof, requires Member States to take appropriate steps to avoid the deterioration of habitats and significant disturbance of the bird species for which the areas have been classified.

In terms of the actual content of Article 6(2) requirements, prohibitive measures are necessary. Member States are bound by an obligation to refrain from permitting activities likely to lead to habitat deterioration. In Cases C-141/14, *Commission v. Bulgaria* and C-461/14, *Commission v. Spain,* the Court stated that:

> An *activity* complies with Article 6(2) of the Habitats Directive only if it is guaranteed that it will not cause any disturbance likely significantly to affect the objectives of that directive, particularly its conservation objectives (emphasis added).[348]

In Case C-387/15 and Joined Case C-388/15 *Orleans*, the Court held that:

> A *preventive measure* complies with Article 6(2) of the Habitats Directive only if it is guaranteed that it will not cause any disturbance likely significantly to affect the objectives of that directive, particularly its conservation objectives (emphasis added).[349]

The Court has also held that procedures for intervention by the competent authorities that are merely reactive and not preventive disregard the scope of the obligation stemming from Article 6(2).[350]

The obligation laid down under Article 6(2) goes beyond preventive and prohibitive measures targeting human interventions. In Case C-6/04, *Commission v. United Kingdom,* the Court stated:

> It is clear that, in implementing Article 6(2) of the Habitats Directive, it may be necessary to adopt both measures intended to avoid external man-caused impairment and disturbance and *measures to prevent natural developments* that may cause the conservation status of species and habitats in SACs to deteriorate (emphasis added).[351]

In this case, the Court followed the Commission's interpretation and the Opinion of the Advocate General that 'both protective measures – for example prohibitions – against external *man-caused impairment* and disturbance may be necessary and

347. C-6/04, *Commission v. United Kingdom,* para. 33.
348. C-141/14, *Commission v. Bulgaria,* para. 56; C-461/14, *Commission v. Spain,* para. 94.
349. C-387/15, *Orleans,* para. 40.
350. C-293/17, *PAS,* para. 134.
351. C-6/04, *Commission v. United Kingdom,* para. 34.

measures to prevent *natural developments* that may cause the conservation status of species and habitats to deteriorate (emphasis added)'.[352]

The Opinion of the Advocate General provides useful clarification on why the prevention of natural developments may be necessary:

> This also results from the requirements of individual protected habitat types. Thus, open-land habitats frequently lose their special characteristics through scrub growth if this is not prevented by human intervention. In the case of the habitat types 'Lowland hay meadows (*Alopecurus pratensis, Sanguisorba officinalis*)' (Natura 2000 Code 6510) and 'Mountain hay meadows' (Natura 2000 Code 6520), the need for human intervention – in this instance mowing – is already apparent directly or indirectly from their appellation.[353]

The Opinion of the Advocate General also distinguishes such natural developments from structural environmental changes, such as climate change and sea-level rise that jeopardise the conditions for the continued existence of the protected habitats and species in the Natura 2000 sites concerned.[354]

In a nutshell, Article 6(2) of the Habitats Directive requires Member States *not only to adopt prohibitive measures but also to adopt positive measures*. These positive measures have to satisfy, on one hand, the standards of legal certainty and, on the other, they must not be purely voluntary.

Finally, as section §3.04[E] below will show, Article 6(2) provides for powerful residual safeguards when the requirements of Article 6(3) or (4) of the Habitats Directive are not applicable or have not been fully or correctly applied.

[3] Transposition Requirements

[a] Transposing Measures Must Include an Obligation for Competent Authorities to Avoid Deterioration

In terms of transposition requirements for this provision, the case-law is clear: there has to be an express provision that incorporates in the domestic legal system concerned an obligation on the competent authorities to avoid habitat deterioration.

In Case C-6/04, *Commission v. United Kingdom*, the Court upheld a Commission complaint that the transposition of Article 6(2) in respect of Gibraltar was deficient because it was limited to a provision allowing the competent authorities to enter into site management agreements with the owners or occupiers of sites. The Court observed that:

> It is clear that this provision confers only a non-mandatory power on those authorities and that it is not such as to avoid deterioration, contrary to the requirements of Article 6(2) of the Habitats Directive.

352. Opinion of Advocate General in C-6/04, *Commission v. United Kingdom*, para. 19.
353. Opinion of the Advocate General in C-6/04, *Commission v. United Kingdom*, para. 20.
354. *Ibid.*, para. 21.

> Accordingly, inasmuch as domestic law contains no express provision obliging the competent authorities to avoid the deterioration of natural habitats and the habitats of species, it involves an element of legal uncertainty as to the obligations with which those authorities must comply.[355]

The Court thus followed the Advocate General who criticised the absence in the law of 'adequate powers for intervention by the competent authorities where there is a lack of cooperation on the part of owners or occupiers'.[356]

The Court concluded that Article 6(2) of the Habitats Directive had not been transposed clearly, precisely and completely in Gibraltar.

[b] Need to Have Effective Provisions for Preventing Damaging Natural Developments

As already noted, in Case C-6/04, *Commission v. United Kingdom*, the Court confirmed that the implementation of Article 6(2) may require measures to prevent damaging natural developments. Since it made this point in relation to its analysis of the transposition of Article 6(2) in Gibraltar, its finding of deficient transposition also covers this aspect.

[c] Transposing Measures Must Be Preventive and Not Simply Reactive

In Case C-418/04, *Commission v. Ireland*, the Commission successfully argued that Ireland did not comply with Article 6(2) because, amongst other things, it's implementing legislation depended on restrictive notices being served on landowners – and such notices had not been served in respect of all SPAs.[357] In its defence, Ireland cited a possibility under Irish regulations for a minister to seek injunctive relief to stop damaging activities. The Court rejected this line of defence, stating that:

> It is clear that those provisions necessarily can come into play only after the activities in question have already commenced and thus only after any deterioration has already occurred. Moreover, the competent minister is not entitled to prohibit a harmful activity unilaterally and the abovementioned powers presuppose that an appropriate assessment of the environmental impact of that activity has been carried out before any judicial relief is sought. The reactive protection of SPAs may be delayed considerably by those procedural steps. Moreover, those provisions do not ensure protection of SPAs against the activities of individuals, as such protection requires that individuals be prevented in advance from engaging in potentially harmful activities.[358]

In Case C-298/17, *PAS*, the Court further clarified its position in response to a question from the referring court as to whether Article 6(2) of the Habitats Directive must be interpreted as meaning that measures introduced by national legislation, such

355. C-6/04, *Commission v. United Kingdom*, paras 36 and 37.
356. Opinion of Advocate General in C-6/04, *Commission v. United Kingdom*, para. 23.
357. C-418/04, *Commission v. Ireland*, paras 205 and 206.
358. *Ibid.*, para. 208.

as that at issue in the main proceedings, including procedures for the surveillance and monitoring of farms whose activities cause nitrogen deposition and the possibility of imposing penalties, up to and including the closure of those farms are sufficient for the purposes of complying with that provision.

The Court reiterated its position that measures that were merely reactive and not preventive could not satisfy Article 6(2).[359] The Dutch legislation, however, allowed the authorities:

> Having regard to conservation objectives, first, to impose *measures both preventive and corrective*. Secondly, that legislation also includes *a power of coercion*, also including the possibility of adopting urgent measures (emphasis added).[360]

The Court concluded that, such legislation, in so far as it makes it possible to *prevent* the occurrence of a certain number of risks linked to the activities at issue constitutes an appropriate step within the meaning of Article 6(2) of the Habitats Directive.[361]

[d] Impermissible for Transposing Legislation to Presume That Certain Activities Comply with Article 6(2)

Case C-241/08, *Commission v. France*, sheds light on a Member State's margin of discretion when transposing Article 6(2). According to the French transposing measures, fishing, aquaculture, hunting and other hunting-related activities practised under the conditions and in the areas authorised by the laws and regulations in force were considered not to constitute activities causing disturbance or having such an effect. France sought to justify these on the basis that the activities concerned were subject to general rules. The Court observed that:

> While those rules can admittedly reduce the risk of significant disturbance, they can however remove that risk altogether only if they provide for mandatory compliance with Article 6(2) of the Habitats Directive. The French Republic does not claim that that is the situation in this case.[362]

The Court concluded that France had failed to fulfil its obligations under Article 6(2).[363]

[e] A Broad Presumptive Derogation May Contravene Article 6(2)

In Case C-432/21, *Commission v. Poland,* the Court again looked at a presumptive provision, this time, a wide-ranging national provision introducing a presumption of compliance with nature conservation legislation when forest management operations

359. C-298/17, *PAS,* para. 134.
360. *Ibid.,* para. 135.
361. *Ibid.,* para. 136.
362. C-241/08, *Commission v. France,* para. 38.
363. *Ibid.,* para. 39.

are implemented according to the requirements of *good forest management practices*. Poland, amongst other things, argued that, under another national provision, it was prohibited to undertake any activity which is likely to cause deterioration in the state of natural habitats or the habitats of plant and animal species for the protection of which a Natura 2000 site has been designated or to harm species for the protection of which a Natura 2000 site has been designated.[364]

The Court considered that the presumptive provision was drafted in general terms, was very broad in scope, and was therefore capable of being interpreted and applied by the national authorities as constituting a derogation from all the Polish provisions transposing the provisions of the Habitats and Birds Directives. Even if there was other Polish legislation implementing Article 6(2), the presumptive provision did not ensure the necessary clarity and precision in the transposition and implementation of Article 6(2).[365] Using the same reasoning, it found that the Polish presumptive provision also contravened Article 6(1) of the Habitats Directive and Article 4(1) of the Birds Directive.

[4] Examples of Breaches in the Implementation of Article 6(2)

The case-law provides extensive examples of breaches of Article 6(2) in relation to agriculture, forestry, the extractive and energy sectors and urbanistic and touristic developments and activities. The following is a selection.

[a] Failure to Control Sheep Overgrazing in Ireland

In Case C-117/00, *Commission v. Ireland*, the Court found a breach of Article 6(2) in relation to the habitat damage caused by high stocking levels of sheep. The case, amongst other matters, related to habitat deterioration within an SPA classified under the Birds Directive (to which, as has previously been noted, Article 6(2) applies by virtue of Article 7 of the Habitats Directive). Parts of the Owenduff-Nephin Beg Complex SPA had been 'seriously damaged'[366] due to overgrazing by sheep. According to the Conservation Plan of the SPA:

> Some blanket bog and heath areas within the site are heavily eroded caused by the excessive numbers of sheep. In places there is mobile peat with associated hags and gullies that have eroded to the underlying bedrock. On the higher ground, the heath is severely degraded due to the grazing pressure on ericaceous (heath) species. In the recent past, large tracts of the peatland system adjacent to the site have been planted with conifers, resulting in the destruction of vast tracts of both lowland and upland blanket bog.[367]

364. C-432/21, *Commission v. Poland*, para. 103.
365. *Ibid.*, paras 109 and 110.
366. C-117/00, *Commission v. Ireland*, para. 27.
367. *Ibid.*, para. 28.

Ireland had admitted that access by large flocks of sheep in the area and overgrazing caused, particularly, severe damage to slopes. It also recognised the causal link between the degradation of the slopes and a recent decline in the numbers of Greenland White-fronted Geese which feed there. Ireland was condemned by the Court for not having adopted the measures needed to prevent deterioration of the habitats. The Irish Government itself had recognised in its rejoinder that it was necessary not only to take measures to stabilise the problem of overgrazing but also to ensure that damaged habitats are allowed to recover.

[b] Negative Effects of Forestry Activities in Slovakia

In Case *Commission v. Slovakia*, the Court upheld a Commission plea that Slovakia had infringed Article 6(2) of the Habitats Directive by failing to take appropriate steps to prevent the deterioration of habitats and significant disturbance in the SPAs classified for the conservation of the capercaillie. The Commission's concerns were focused on intensive logging, the clear-cutting of large areas and the use of pesticides.[368]

The Court found that intensive felling of timber across large areas and the use of pesticides to combat subcortical insects, including during the capercaillie breeding period, contributed to a significant decline in the population of that species in the 12 SPAs classified for its conservation, namely a decrease of 49.4% between 2004 and 2019.[369]

It also found that Slovakia continued to 'fail to establish that it has taken appropriate steps in order to prevent such forest management activities from causing significant disturbance for the capercaillie'.[370] Forestry control measures that Slovakia invoked in its defence were:

> Incomplete in that they do not include conservation measures established systematically, depending on the ecological requirements of that species and each habitat type present in each of the 12 SPAs designated for its conservation. As the Commission observes, those measures are limited to isolated cases and were adopted, most often, only following complaints from individuals or NGOs, so that they are incomplete and attest to the lack of a structural system designed to ensure the conservation of the capercaillie (*Tetrao urogallus*) by putting an end to the deterioration of its habitat.[371]

[c] Negative Effects of Mining in Spain

In Case C-404/09, *Commission v. Spain*, the Court upheld a Commission complaint that Spain had infringed Article 6(2) by failing to take the necessary measures to prevent the

368. C-661/20, *Commission v. Slovakia*, para. 79.
369. *Ibid.*, para. 103.
370. *Ibid.*, para. 105.
371. *Ibid.*, para. 107.

operation of certain open-cast mines from affecting the 'Alto Sil' SPA and, in particular, the capercaillie species protected there.

The Spanish authorities had indicated that the area in dispute was no longer suitable as it did not contain any breeding ground.[372] The Court did not accept this argument because, while the area in question was not a breeding ground, it 'could conceivably be used by that species as a habitat for other purposes, such as a living or hibernating area'.[373] The Court also cited the potential of the area to have become also usable as a breeding ground, following measures taken by the authorities, to that purpose.[374] The Court recalled that:

> The protection of SPAs is not to be limited to measures intended to avoid external anthropogenic impairment and disturbance but must also, according to the situation that presents itself, include positive measures to preserve or improve the state of the site.[375]

Against this background, the Court found that open-cast mining operations were contrary to Article 6(2) of the Habitats Directive by reason of the noises and vibrations which they produce and which were capable of significantly affecting the conservation of the capercaillie.[376] Some of the operations were capable of producing a barrier effect likely to contribute to the fragmentation of the habitat of the capercaillie and the isolation of certain sub-populations of that species.[377]

[d] Disturbance Caused by Wind Farm in Bulgaria

In Case C-141/14, *Commission v. Bulgaria*, the Court found that the Commission did not have 'to establish the existence of a cause-effect relationship between the operation of installations resulting from a project and the significant disturbance caused to the species concerned'.[378] Where there is a probability or risk that an operation might cause such disturbances, the Member State is likely to have breached the provisions of Article 6(2).[379] The scrutiny applied is strict. The Court did not, however, find any breach of EU law in respect of the destruction of ponto-sarmatic steppes priority habitat as part of ground-preparation works for the wind farm project at the centre of the case, as the destruction had occurred before the Directive became applicable. The Court considered that the subsequent installation of wind turbines had not further impaired the habitat.[380]

372. C-404/09, *Commission v. Spain*, para. 132.
373. *Ibid.*, para. 133.
374. *Ibid.*, para. 134.
375. *Ibid.*, para. 135.
376. *Ibid.*, para. 145.
377. *Ibid.*, para. 148.
378. *See also* C-461/14, para. 97.
379. C-141/14, *Commission v. Bulgaria*, para. 58; *see* similar statement in C-404/09, *Commission v. Spain*, para. 142.
380. C-141/14, *Commission v. Bulgaria*, para. 62.

[e] *Multiple Urbanistic and Touristic Developments and Activities in Greece*

In Case C-504/14, *Commission v. Greece,* the Court found multiple breaches by Greece of Article 6(2) in respect of a protected dune system and habitats of the sea turtle at a tourist location in Kyparissia. The breaches covered the construction of houses, house-building works, opening of roads, failure to enforce a prohibition on wild camping, failure to restrict the operation of beach bars, failure to reduce to presence of beach furniture on beaches protected for the sea turtles, failure to curtail light pollution, and failure to curtail fishing. Further details of the case are set out below in section §3.04[H], since it is especially instructive on the application of Article 6(2) to illegal developments and activities.

[D] Assessment Requirement under Article 6(3)

Article 6(3) reads as follows:

> Any plan or project not directly connected with or necessary to the management of the site but likely to have a significant effect thereon, either individually or in combination with other plans or projects, shall be subject to appropriate assessment of its implications for the site in view of the site's conservation objectives. In the light of the conclusions of the assessment of the implications for the site and subject to the provisions of paragraph 4, the competent national authorities shall agree to the plan or project only after having ascertained that it will not adversely affect the integrity of the site concerned and, if appropriate, after having obtained the opinion of the general public.

[1] *Overarching Importance of the Precautionary Principle*

Rulings of the Court of Justice, with regard to the assessment requirements, under Article 6(3) of the Habitats Directive stand out for the emphasis they place on the strict observance of the precautionary principle enshrined in Article 191 of the TFEU. This principle constitutes a general thread in the reasoning of the Court with regard to different aspects of the application of this provision – and of Article 6 more generally. It influences the wide interpretation that the Court has given to the notion of 'project', the Court's strict position on how competent authorities should approach the risks associated with activities and its position on the relationship between Article 6(2) and 6(3) of the Directive, which may result in activities already authorised having to undergo subsequent scrutiny in terms of their potential to cause habitat deterioration.

[2] *Applicability of Article 6(3): SCIs and SACs, under the Habitats Directive and SPAs under the Birds Directive*

At what point does Article 6(3) become applicable?

[a] *Recognised SCIs*

As section §3.03[B][1] has already noted in relation to Article 6(2) of the Habitats Directive, according to Article 4(5) of the Directive, 'as soon as a site is placed on the list referred to in the third subparagraph of paragraph 2 it shall be subject to Article 6(2), (3) and (4)'. Therefore, like those of Article 6(2), the obligations of Article 6(3) apply only once the sites are identified by Member States and agreed with the European Commission as SCIs.

Once again, it is worth recalling that Member States have obligations to provide legal protection *prior* to a site acquiring the status of a listed SCI – *see* section §3.01[B] above on the case-law in Case C-117/03, *Draggagi* and Case C-244/05, *Bund Naturschutz*.

[b] *Classified SPAs*

By virtue of Article 7 of the Habitats Directive, the provisions contained in its Article 6(2), (3) and (4) are also applicable to SPAs classified under the Birds Directive. In the case of areas protected under the Birds Directive, applicability starts from the date of a site's classification as an SPA.

Again it is worth recalling that, prior to formal SPA classification, IBAs requiring classification benefit from the protective provisions of the first sentence of Article 4(4) of the Birds Directive – *see* section §3.03[C][1] above.

[3] *Non-applicability of Article 6(3) of the Directive to Projects Initiated Before the Transposition Date*

In Case C-209/04, *Commission v. Austria*, which concerned a motorway project, the Court stated that 'the principle that projects likely to have significant effects on the environment must be subjected to an environmental assessment does not apply where the application for authorisation for a project was formally lodged before the expiry of the time-limit for transposition of a directive'.[381]

The Court clarified that the starting point for the applicability of the directive is the date when a project was formally presented for permitting.[382] In this particular case, the formal application for a permit for the motorway had been lodged before Austria's accession to the EU (when EU law didn't apply), although the permit itself had been delivered after the directive had become applicable.

In order to provide the necessary legal certainty, the Court drew an analogy with the EIA Directive[383] and relevant case-law on the temporal application of the latter.[384] It observed that:

381. C-209/04, *Commission v. Austria*, para. 56.
382. *Ibid.*, para. 54.
383. At the time, Council Directive 85/337/EEC of 27 June 1985 on the assessment of the effects of certain public and private projects on the environment, OJ 1985 L 175, p. 40.
384. C-431/92, *Commission v. Germany*, paras 29 and 32; and C-81/96, *Burgemeester en wethouders van Haarlemmerliede en Spaarnwoude and Others*, para. 23.

> The reason for that is that a directive such as the Habitats Directive is primarily designed to cover large-scale projects which will most often require a long time to complete. It would therefore not be appropriate for the relevant procedures, which are already complex at national level and which were formally initiated prior to the date of the expiry of the period for transposing the directive, to be made more cumbersome and time-consuming by the specific requirements imposed by the directive and for situations already established to be affected by it.[385]

This situation is, of course, to be distinguished from situations where the transposition date has passed but a site has not yet acquired SCI status or been classified as an SPA. The case-law of Case C-117/03, *Dragaggi*, Case C-244/05, *Bund Naturschutz* and Case C-374/98, *Basses-Corbières* will apply to the latter situations (*see* sections §3.01[B] and §3.03[C][1] above).

It is also important to take account of the case-law in Case C-226/08, *Stadt Papenburg* as this shows that obligations may still arise in respect of an activity which benefits from an authorisation dating from before the transposition deadline. Thus, even though the authorisation of the project is granted, its implementation falls under the 'general obligation of protection', flowing from Article 6(2) and 'consisting in avoiding deterioration and disturbance which could have significant effects in the light of the directive's objectives'.[386] This is addressed in more detail in section §3.04[E] below on the relationship between Article 6(2) and Article 6(3).

[4] Wide Spatial Scope of Article 6(3): Plans and Projects Do Not Have to Be Within the Boundaries of a Natura 2000 Site

The main factor triggering the requirement of an Article 6(3) assessment is the probability or the risk that a plan or project will harm a site. The Court has recognised that Article 6(3) has a wide spatial scope, which is not limited to the actual geographical area of the plan or location of the project concerned. Furthermore, the scope is not confined to projects located within a Natura 2000 site or plans whose geographical area is within the boundaries of a Natura 2000 site.

Case C-142/16, *Commission v. Germany* ('Moorburg') involved a Commission legal challenge in respect of the construction of a coal-fired power plant in Moorburg. The project was at 'a considerable distance' from the Natura 2000 areas concerned but the Court found that this 'in no way precludes the applicability of the requirements laid down in Article 6(3)'.[387] More specifically, the impact assessment carried out by the German authorities themselves indicated that the inevitable death of fish species listed in Annex II of the Habitats Directive (caused by the power plant's cooling mechanism, which would draw large quantities of water from the river Elbe) would affect the reproduction of the species within the Natura 2000 areas upstream of the plant.

Case C-254/19, *Friends of the Irish Environment*, concerned a challenge by an Irish environmental association, the Friends of the Irish Environment Ltd, to a permit

385. C-209/04, *Commission v. Austria*, para. 57.
386. C-226/08, *Stadt Papenburg*, paras 48 and 49.
387. C-142/16, *Moorburg*, para. 29.

granted to a liquefied gas regasification terminal which was to be carried out in the vicinity of two Natura 2000 sites, the Lower River Shannon SAC (IE0002165) and the River Shannon and River Fergus Estuaries SPA (IE0004077). Following a preliminary reference, the Court considered that 'it cannot be ruled out that such a project might have a significant effect on those sites'.[388]

[5] The Notion of 'Plan' under Article 6(3)

The wording of Article 6(3) refers to 'any plan or project'. Like 'project', 'plan' is not defined in the Habitats Directive.

The notion of 'plan' featured in Case C-6/04, *Commission v. United Kingdom*. According to the Commission, the United Kingdom's transposing legislation did not 'clearly require land use plans to be subject to appropriate assessment of their implications for SACs in accordance with Article 6(3) and (4) of the Habitats Directive'.[389] The Commission's argument was that, although land use plans do not as such authorise development and a planning permission was still required, they do, nevertheless, influence development decisions. The Commission's plea was upheld by the Court. The latter noted that national provisions require 'applications for planning permission to be determined in the light of the relevant land use plans'.[390] It thus accepted the potential influence of such plans on subsequent permissions.

In the same case, the Court ruled that there was a failure by the United Kingdom to provide for an assessment of water abstraction plans under Article 6(3).[391]

Article 6(3) is not applicable, however, at the stage of preliminary administrative reflections. This was confirmed in Case C-179/06 *Commission v. Italy*. The Court considered that the Commission had failed to demonstrate that the framework agreements approved by the municipality of Altamura, by a series of decisions taken by its municipal council, 'are more than at the stage of preliminary administrative reflection and carry a degree of precision in the planning in question which calls for an environmental assessment of their effects'.[392] Italy had indicated that the existence of such an agreement concerning 100 construction projects did not preclude the application of applicable legal provisions for authorisation at later stages. The Court considered that there were not enough elements to indicate that measures likely to have a significant effect on the site concerned within the meaning of Article 6(3) of the Directive were at issue.

It is worth mentioning that there is a parallel obligation in the SEA Directive to carry out an SEA of a plan requiring an appropriate assessment under Article 6(3) of the Habitats Directive – *see* Chapter 6, §6.02.

388. C-254/19, *Friends of the Irish Environment Ltd*, para. 58.
389. C-6/04, *Commission v. United Kingdom*, para. 51.
390. *Ibid.*, para. 55.
391. *Ibid.*, paras 44, 45 and 46.
392. C-179/06, *Commission v. Italy*, para. 41.

[6] *Transposition of Article 6(3): Notion of 'Project' and Purported Exemptions of General Categories of Project*

[a] *General Waivers Are Likely to Contravene Article 6(3)*

Enacting national legislation which allows the assessment obligation for certain types of plans or projects to benefit from a general waiver can only be acceptable when it is demonstrated, beyond any reasonable doubt, that those activities or projects cause no disturbance likely to significantly affect the objectives of the Directive.[393]

When transposing Article 6(3), Member States must observe a requirement not to automatically exclude certain categories of project from the scope of transposition on the grounds that the projects' damaging potential is insignificant or that pre-existing national law does not require the projects to have a permit.

[b] *Programmatic Legislation with Prior Waiver of Pre-assessed Activities*

In Joined Cases C-293/17 and C-294/17, *PAS* concerning the impact of nitrogen deposition from agricultural activities on Dutch Natura 2000 sites, the Court examined national legislation which, while not excluding the application of Article 6(3) outright, as in the German, French and Belgian examples presented below, nevertheless significantly qualified it. The question arose as to whether Article 6(3) precludes national programmatic legislation allowing the competent authorities to authorise projects on the basis of an 'appropriate assessment', carried out in advance and 'in which a specific overall amount of nitrogen deposition has been deemed compatible with that legislation's objectives of protection'.[394] The Court noted that 'the fact that an assessment at such a level of generality makes it possible to examine better the cumulative effects of various projects does not mean, however, that national legislation such as that at issue in the main proceedings necessarily meets all the requirements stemming from Article 6(3)'.[395] In such cases, the conditions set down in Article 6(3) and notably the obligation to refrain from authorising projects, if there is a risk of adversely affecting the integrity of the Natura 2000 sites concerned, have to be strictly fulfilled. The competent authorities may be entitled to authorise an individual project on the basis of such a prior global assessment only if they are satisfied that the assessment carried out in advance meets those requirements in respect of each specific individual project, under the strict scrutiny of the national judge. In such cases, the Member State must demonstrate 'that the provisions which it has adopted enable it to be excluded, on the basis of objective information, that any plan or project subject to that authorisation scheme will have a significant effect on a Natura 2000 site, whether individually or in combination with other plans or projects'.[396]

393. C-538/09, *Commission v. Belgium*, para. 41 to 43; C-293/17, *PAS*, paras 114 and 115.
394. C-293/17, *PAS*, para. 90.
395. *Ibid.*, para. 97.
396. *Ibid.*, para. 109.

The Court went on to express caution about reliance on an approach to Article 6(3) assessment that is based on averages, noting that:

> An average value is not, in principle, capable of ensuring that there are no significant effects on any single protected site as a result of fertilising or grazing, as such effects seem to depend, *inter alia*, on the extent and, as the case may be, the intensiveness of those activities, the proximity which may exist between the place in which those activities are carried out and the protected site concerned, and specific conditions, for example owing to the interaction of other sources of nitrogen, potentially characterising that site.[397]

In other words, the notion of a 'project' amounts to a 'so-called autonomous definition, not depending on the nature of the administrative decisions'[398] authorising the activities at stake.

[c] *Examples of Waivers That Contravened Article 6(3)*

[i] German Waiver for Agriculture, Forestry, Fishing and Water Use

In Case C-98/03, *Commission v. Germany*, the Commission challenged German legislation which excluded from the term 'project' the use of soil for the purposes of agriculture, forestry and fishing, where that project takes account of the objectives and principles of nature protection and countryside conservation. The text required verification that serious environmental damage is prevented, but the Court did not find this to be sufficient.[399] Also excluded were projects relating to installations for the use of water, on account of the fact that they were not subject to authorisation. But 'the use of small quantities of water does not in itself preclude the possibility that some of those uses are likely to have a significant effect on a protected site'.[400]

[ii] French Waiver for Natura 2000 Contracts and for Activities Not Subject to Authorisation

In Case C-241/08, *Commission v. France*, the Court condemned France for a systematic exemption of works and developments provided for in Natura 2000 contracts. France had sought to justify the exemption on the ground that, in so far as those contracts were intended to achieve conservation and restoration objectives for Natura 2000 sites, they were directly connected with or necessary for site management and, as such, fell outside the obligation of assessment under Article 6(3). The Court did not accept this argument, as it could not be ruled out 'that, while they may have as their objective the conservation or restoration of a site, the works or developments provided for in those

397. *Ibid.*, para. 119.
398. Hendrik Schoukens, *Ongoing Activities and Natura 2000 Biodiversity Protection vs Legitimate Expectations?*, 11 The Journal for European Environmental & Planning Law 1-30 at 20 (2014) DOI: 10.1163/18760104-01101001.
399. C-98/03, *Commission v. Germany*, paras 42-44.
400. *Ibid.*, para. 44.

contracts may, nevertheless, not be directly connected with or necessary for the management of that site'.[401] According to the Court, 'such an exemption is not such as to guarantee that those activities do not adversely affect the integrity of the protected site'.[402]

The Court also condemned France for systematically exempting works and development programmes and projects which were subject to a declaratory system from the Article 6(3) procedure.[403] This infringement was accepted by France.[404]

[iii] Belgian Declaratory Scheme

In Case C-538/09, *Commission v. Belgium*, the Court condemned Belgium for legislation under which certain projects - defined by type and size - were exempted from environmental assessment and only required a declaration to be made by the developer to the local authority. The case arose from the Commission's examination of a complaint about the operation of a cattle shed close to an SAC.[405] This led it to the conclusion that Belgium had not correctly transposed Article 6(3) - a conclusion upheld by the Court in its judgment. Belgium argued that there were comprehensive conditions laid down in national regulations to which these projects were subject, but the Court did not accept that these justified not applying the requirements of Article 6(3).[406]

One of the arguments advanced by Belgium was that the declaratory scheme applied only to installations and activities 'with a low impact on humans and on the environment', for which the Belgian Government had laid down comprehensive conditions. Citing an earlier decision in a case concerning the EIA Directive,[407] the Court observed that 'even a small-scale project can have significant effects on the environment, if it is in a location where the environmental factors, such as fauna and flora, soil, water, climate or cultural heritage, are sensitive to the slightest alteration'.[408] The Court then stated:

> It follows that a Member State cannot assume that categories of plans or projects defined by reference to spheres of activity and special installations will, by definition, have a low impact on humans and on the environment.[409]

[iv] Slovak Waiver for Emergency Tree-Felling

In Case C-661/20, *Commission v. Slovakia*, the Court upheld a Commission complaint that Slovakia had breached Article 6(3) because, amongst other things, it had adopted

401. C-241/08, *Commission v. France*, para. 49-51.
402. *Ibid.*, para. 31.
403. *Ibid.*, para. 62.
404. *Ibid.*, para. 58.
405. C-538/09, *Commission v. Belgium*, para. 14.
406. *Ibid.*, paras 46 to 64.
407. C-392/96, *Commission v. Ireland*, para. 66.
408. C-538/09, *Commission v. Belgium*, para. 55.
409. *Ibid.*, para. 56.

a general exemption for emergency felling operations in forests from having to undergo an appropriate assessment under Article 6(3).[410]

[7] *Notion of 'Project': Influence of the Definition of 'Project' in Article 1(2) of the EIA Directive*

In Case C-127/02, *Waddenzee,* the Court provided valuable clarification on the meaning of 'project' for purposes of Article 6(3). Its judgment was in response to a preliminary reference from the Netherlands on issues related to national licences to engage in mechanical cockle fishing in the Waddenzee SPA for a determined period of time. Mechanical cockle fishing had already been a long-standing activity which was subject to a yearly licensing system, underpinned each time by a fresh assessment as to whether and where the activity could be continued.

One of the issues requiring clarification concerned whether an activity of this kind comes within the notion of 'project' for purposes of Article 6(3). The notion of 'project' had not been defined in the Habitats Directive but there was a very broad definition in Article 1(2) of the EIA Directive (then Directive 85/337/EEC[411]), which included 'other interventions in the natural surroundings and landscape including those involving the extraction of mineral resources'.[412] The Court made reference to this definition.

Referring to the cockle fishing, the Court stated that:

> The fact that the activity has been carried on periodically for several years on the site concerned and that a licence has to be obtained for it every year, each new issuance of which requires an assessment both of the possibility of carrying on that activity and of the site where it may be carried on, does not in itself constitute an obstacle to considering it, at the time of each application, as a distinct plan or project within the meaning of the Habitats Directive.[413]

The national legislation featuring in Case C-127/02, *Waddenzee,* involved a system of licences based on assessment and thus lent itself to adaptation to the requirements of Article 6(3) which also provides for an assessment-based consent system. Subsequent case-law shows, however, that it is not necessary to have such an existing system in order for an activity to constitute a 'project'.[414]

---

410. C-661/20, *Commission v. Slovakia,* paras 66-71.
411. Repealed in the meantime by Directive 2011/92/EU of the European Parliament and of the Council of 13 December 2011 on the assessment of the effects of certain public and private projects on the environment.
412. Article 2(1) of Directive 2011/92/EU reads as follows: 'For the purposes of this Directive, the following definitions shall apply: (a) "project" means – the execution of construction works or of other installations or schemes; – other interventions in the natural surroundings and landscape including those involving the extraction of mineral resources.'
413. C-127/02, *Waddenzee,* para. 28.
414. C-226/08, *Stadt Papenburg.*

[8] Notion of 'Project' under the Habitats Directive Is Wider than under the EIA Directive

While a project falling under the EIA Directive automatically falls under the Habitats Directive, the reverse does not apply, as the wording of Article 6(3) is not limited to a 'physical intervention in the natural surroundings'.[415]

The Court made this point clear in response to another preliminary reference from the Netherlands. In Joined Cases C-293/17 and C-294/17, *PAS*, concerning the impact of nitrogen deposition from agricultural activities, it was specifically asked by a Dutch court whether a project that fell outside the scope of the EIA Directive could nevertheless still come within the scope of the Habitats Directive.

Noting that the definition of a project in the EIA Directive is more restrictive than that stemming from the Habitats Directive, the Court confirmed that 'if an activity is covered by Directive 85/337, it must, a fortiori, be covered by the Habitats Directive'.[416]

However, the notion of 'project' under the Habitats Directive is much wider and is not limited to the definition set out in the EIA Directive. More specifically, the Court took the view that the grazing of cattle and the application of fertilisers on the surface of land or below its surface in the vicinity of Natura 2000 sites may be classified as a 'project' in the meaning of Article 6(3), even if those activities, in so far as they are not a physical intervention in the natural surroundings, do not constitute a 'project' within the meaning of Article 1(2)(a) of the EIA Directive.

This clarification is important. It means that case-law on the limits of the scope of the definition of a 'project' under the EIA Directive will not necessarily be applicable, by analogy, to the Habitats Directive.

[9] Authorisations Granted by a Legislative Authority

In Case C-182/10, *Solvay*, the Court clarified that the Article 6(3) obligations are incumbent on Member States, 'regardless of the nature of the national authority with competence to authorise the plan or project concerned'.[417] The referring court had asked whether Article 6(3) must be interpreted as allowing a legislative authority to authorise a plan or project without it having ascertained that it will not adversely affect the integrity of the site concerned. The question arose in the context of objections by members of the public to the ratification by decree of works related to two airports and a railway in the region of Wallonia in Belgium.

The Court confirmed that decisions of a legislative authority do not enjoy any exemption. Given that Article 6(3) of the Habitats Directive, which refers to the 'competent national authorities', does not lay down any special (derogatory) rule for plans or projects approved by a legislative authority, 'that status consequently has no

415. Article 2(1) of the Directive 2011/92/EU.
416. Joined Cases C-293/17 and C-294/17, *PAS*, para. 65.
417. C-182/10, *Solvay*, para. 69.

effect on the extent or scope of the obligations imposed on the Member States by Article 6(3) of the Habitats Directive'.[418]

A similar issue arose in a later preliminary reference from Belgium, Case C-411/17, *Doel*. This complex case arose from a legal challenge brought by two environmental associations in respect of Belgian legislation which provided for the re-commencement and prolongation of the life of a nuclear power station that had previously been shut down. The Court confirmed that national legislation, such as the law prolonging the life of nuclear plants in Belgium had the characteristics of an agreement given by the authorities in respect of the project concerned.[419] The measures concerned, together with the work of upgrading and ensuring compliance with current safety standards, constituted a project requiring an assessment under Article 6(3). 'Such an assessment should be conducted in respect of those measures before they are adopted by the legislature'.[420]

[10] Notion of 'Project': Recurring Activities, Continuing Activities That Have Received a Previous Authorisation and Lapsed Consents

[a] Recurring Activities May Require Appropriate Assessment

In Case C-226/08, *Stadt Papenburg*, the Court addressed the issue of maintenance of dredging works and took the view that:

> the fact that that activity has been definitively authorised under national law before the expiry of the time limit for transposition of the Habitats Directive does not constitute, in itself, an obstacle to regarding it, at the time of each intervention in the navigable channel, as a distinct project for the purposes of the Habitats Directive.[421]

The case concerned regular dredging of the River Ems in order to allow ships with a draught of 7.3 meters to navigate between a shipyard and the North Sea.[422] Dredging operations had been authorised before the transposition deadline of the Habitats Directive but after its entry into force. The decision to authorise was definitive and meant, in accordance with German law, that future 'required dredging operations' are considered to have been granted permission.[423] According to the Court, however:

> no reason based on the principle of legal certainty or the principle of protection of legitimate expectations precludes the dredging works at issue in the main proceedings, although they have been permanently authorised under national law, from

418. *Ibid.*
419. C-411/17, *Doel*, para. 144.
420. Operative part of judgment.
421. C-226/08, *Stadt Papenburg*, para. 41.
422. Papenburg is a port town in Lower Saxony on the river Ems, hosting a shipyard specialised in the construction of large cruise liners.
423. C-226/08, *Stadt Papenburg*, para. 11.

being subject to the procedure provided for in Article 6(3) and (4) of the Habitats Directive as distinct and successive projects.[424]

The Habitats Directive fulfils all requirements of clearness, preciseness and predictability with regard to individuals[425] and 'the principle of the protection of legitimate expectations cannot be extended to the point of generally preventing new rules from applying to the future effects of situations which arose under the earlier rules'.[426]

The Court did not go so far as to determine whether, in respect of the contested dredging, there was a single project (i.e., a single project involving recurring interventions but covered by a historic authorisation) or a new project (with Article 6(3) being applicable in the case of the latter). 'What exact conditions are to be taken into account to qualify a project as a "single project" remained quite unsettled'[427] and each case would have to be considered on its own merits. Case C-226/08, *Stadt Papenburg* did, however, outline some factors that may be taken into account, such as the regularity or nature of the maintenance works at issue, or the conditions under which they are carried out. In particular, where such works 'are designed to maintain the navigable channel at a certain depth by means of regular dredging necessary for that purpose, those maintenance works can be considered to be one and the same project for the purposes of Article 6(3) of the Habitats Directive'.[428] Perhaps, had the dredging been intensified or designed to achieve further deepening of the existing channel, 'another outcome might have been possible'.[429]

Similar issues arose in Case C-418/04, *Commission v. Ireland*. The Commission successfully argued that Ireland had contravened Article 6(3) by carrying out drainage works without prior appropriate assessment in respect of a wetland SPA, which had been harmed as a result. It was clear that drainage work had been recurrent with previous drainage work having taken place before the Habitats Directive became applicable.[430] There was no evidence, however, that recurring work was covered by any authorisation pre-dating the entry into force of Article 6(3).

[b] Notion of Single Project Covering Recurring Activities

In Joined Cases C-293/17 and C-294/17, *PAS*, the Court was asked whether Article 6(3) must be interpreted as meaning that a recurring activity, such as the application of fertilisers on the surface of land or below its surface, authorised under national law

424. *Ibid.*, para. 44.
425. *Ibid.*, para. 43.
426. *Ibid.*, para. 46.
427. Hendrik Schoukens, *Ongoing Activities and Natura 2000 Biodiversity Protection vs Legitimate Expectations?*, 11 The Journal for European Environmental & Planning Law 1-30 (2014) DOI: 10.1163/18760104-01101001.
428. C-226/08, *Stadt Papenburg*, para. 47.
429. Hendrik Schoukens, *Ongoing Activities and Natura 2000 Biodiversity Protection vs Legitimate Expectations?*, 11 The Journal for European Environmental & Planning Law 1-30 (2014) DOI: 10.1163/18760104-01101001.
430. C-418/04, *Commission v. Ireland*, paras 248 to 265.

before the entry into force of the Habitats Directive, may be regarded as one and the same project for the purposes of that provision, with the result that that activity does not fall within the scope of Article 6(3). The Court allowed for such a possibility but was careful to set out qualifications. The activity could be exempted from a new authorisation procedure 'in so far as it constitutes a single operation characterised by a common purpose, continuity and, *inter alia*, the location and the conditions in which it is carried out being the same'.[431]

In responding to this question, the Court also referred to an additional safeguard to be applied to single projects authorised before Article 6(3) became applicable. It ruled that 'if a single project was authorised before the system of protection laid down by that provision became applicable to the site in question, the carrying out of that project may nevertheless fall within the scope of Article 6(2) of the directive' (*see also* section §3.04[E] below).

In this context, it is worth recalling that, for such single projects, there may also be a period when, before the applicability of Article 6(2) of the Directive, the case-law of Case C-117/03, *Dragaggi* and Case C-244/05, *Bund-Naturschutz* applies (*see* section §3.01[B] above).

[c] Requirement for New Consent

In Case C-411/17, *Doel*, in relation to the reopening of a Belgian nuclear power plant, the Court maintained the approach it took in Case C-226/08, *Stadt Papenburg* that, even where an activity was authorised before the entry into force of the Habitats Directive, this is not in itself an impediment to regarding such an activity as a distinct project for the purposes of Article 6(3). The Court further refined its analytical criteria. In this case, the industrial electricity production by the Doel 1 and Doel 2 power stations was authorised before the entry into force of the Habitats Directive for an unlimited period, but a national law adopted in 2003 had limited the period of activity to 40 years, which ran up to 15 February 2015 for the Doel 1 power station and upto 1 December 2015 for the Doel 2 power station. This earlier legislative choice had created the need for new legislation to restart one of the two power stations.[432] Major upgrading works would be required in light of scientific development and in order to ensure compliance with current safety standards,[433] moreover, 'a production consent was granted to the operator of those power stations after the Habitats Directive had entered into force, following an increase in their capacity'.[434] In this case, the measures to prolong the life duration of the nuclear power plants, together with the work of upgrading and ensuring compliance with current safety standards, constituted 'a project in respect of which an appropriate assessment of its effects on the protected sites concerned should be conducted'.[435]

---

431. C-293/17, *PAS*, para. 86.
432. C-411/17, *Doel*, para. 130.
433. *Ibid.*, para. 145.
434. *Ibid.*, para. 131.
435. *Ibid.*, para. 145.

[d] Lapsed Consent

Another related scenario is one involving an extension to a permit which has lapsed without the permitted activity having ever taken place. This was addressed in Case C-254/19, *Friends of the Irish Environment*. A prior consent had been granted for the construction of a liquefied gas regasification terminal but it was not preceded by an assessment in accordance with Article 6(3).[436] Furthermore, that consent had expired without works actually commencing. There was a decision of Ireland's Planning Appeals Board to grant an additional period of five years to permit works to start. The question arose as to whether this decision to extend the permit by five years represented a new consent or rather a renewal of an existing consent. The Court rejected arguments that only a decision changing the project as originally permitted can constitute 'consent'.[437] It also distinguished the circumstances from those that arose in Case C-226/08, *Stadt Papenburg*. The purpose of the consent at issue (i.e., to extend the permit) was not to renew the consent for a recurrent activity in the course of operation, 'but to allow the execution of a project which, as is apparent from the order for reference, in particular the description of the Irish legal framework, was the subject of a first consent that lapsed without the intended works having even commenced'.[438] The Court stated that:

> The decision extending the ten-year period originally set for carrying out a project for the construction of a liquefied natural gas regasification terminal is to be regarded as an agreement of a project under Article 6(3) of the Habitats Directive where the original consent for that project, having lapsed, ceased to have legal effect on expiry of the period which it had set for those works and the latter have not been undertaken.[439]

With regard to the decision agreeing on the project, in Case C-254/19, *Friends of the Irish Environment*, the Court noted that:

> While the Habitats Directive does not define the conditions governing how the authorities 'agree' to a given project under Article 6(3) of that directive, the definition of 'development consent' in Article 1(2)(c) of the EIA Directive is relevant in defining that term.[440]

Where an 'original consent ceased to have effect on expiry of the ten-year period it had set and work could no longer be carried out',[441] 'it follows that, at the end of that period, the original consent had lapsed and was therefore not altered by the consent at issue in the main proceedings, but replaced by it'[442] and 'the fact that the project at issue in the main proceedings could have proceeded under the original consent is, in

436. C-254/19, *Friends of the Irish Environment*, para. 23.
437. *Ibid.*, para. 44.
438. *Ibid.*, para. 38.
439. *Ibid.*, para. 48.
440. *Ibid.*, para. 42.
441. *Ibid.*, para. 45.
442. *Ibid.*

that regard, irrelevant'.[443] Therefore, such a consent was found to constitute a new consent under the EIA Directive and, consequently, also an 'agreement' under Article 6(3) of the Habitats Directive.

[e] *Single Project May Exist Even if the Original Consent Was Flawed*

In Case C-278/21, *Aquapli,* the Court again considered the situation of a single or ongoing project. The circumstances and resulting case-law are dealt with in detail in section §3.04[G][4] below. As will be seen, the Court was ready to accept that, for purposes of a later authorisation, there was an ongoing project which did not fall within the scope of Article 6(3), although it was evident that an earlier authorisation – which was subject to Article 6(3) – had not fully complied with Article 6(3). The Court was nevertheless able to indicate a number of ways in which the earlier infringement might be addressed.

[11] *Timing of the Appropriate Assessment: Requirement for It to Be Ex Ante*

In order for an assessment to fulfil the requirements of Article 6(3) of the Habitats Directive, it has to be carried out *ex ante* i.e., before the permit is granted.

In Case C-411/17, *Doel,* the Court confirmed that 'the assessment must be conducted before agreement is given'.[444]

In Case C-404/09, *Commission v. Spain,* it found that a study drawn up *after* the authorisation of certain projects could not be regarded 'as relevant in the context of Article 6(3) of the Habitats Directive'.[445]

It is useful to compare this approach with the similar approach taken by the Court in relation to the EIA Directive. The Court had earlier condemned Irish domestic legislation allowing, by way of a procedure for 'retention permission', *ex post* fulfilment of the screening and assessment requirements of the EIA Directive in respect of unlawful developments, i.e., purported fulfilment of these procedural requirements after projects had already been unlawfully executed.[446]

There remains the possibility of – and even requirement for – *ex post* assessment in order to fulfil the ongoing obligation of Article 6(2) or rectify any infringement of Article 6(2) to (4) of the Habitats Directive. This is addressed in more detail in sections §3.04[E] and [G] below.

443. *Ibid.*, para. 46.
444. C-411/17, *Doel,* para. 141.
445. C-404/09, *Commission v. Spain,* para. 104.
446. C-215/06, *Commission v. Ireland.*

[12] *Timing of the Appropriate Assessment: Multi-stage National Permitting Procedures*

As the Habitats Directive does not define the conditions regarding how the authorities agree to a given project, the Court refers by analogy to the relevant case-law on the EIA Directive around the concept of multi-stage 'development consent' and the timing of the assessment.

Thus, where the national law foresees a number of steps in the permitting procedure, 'the assessment under Article 6(3) of the Habitats Directive, should, in principle, be carried out as soon as the effects which the project in question is likely to have on a protected site are sufficiently identifiable'.[447]

In Case C-411/17, *Doel*, the Court found that the national legislation prolonging the life duration of nuclear plants in Belgium, together with the necessary works for upgrading and reaching compliance with safety standards had 'the characteristics of an agreement given by the authorities in respect of the project concerned'.[448] It stated that the Article 6(3) 'assessment should be conducted in respect of those measures before they are adopted by the legislature', adding that:

> The fact that the implementation of those measures involves subsequent acts, such as the issue, for one of the power stations in question, of a new specific consent for the production of electricity for industrial purposes, is not decisive in that respect. Work that is inextricably linked to those measures must also be subject to such an assessment before the adoption of those measures if its nature and potential impact on the protected sites are sufficiently identifiable at that stage, a finding which it is for the referring court to make.[449]

Thus, the Court allowed for the possibility of more than one appropriate assessment, depending on what is identifiable at each stage of a multi-stage process.

[13] *Overview of the Process of Appropriate Assessment under Article 6(3)*

The Court stated in Case C-243/15, Lesoochranárske zoskupenie ('LZ II'), that:

> Article 6(3) of Directive 92/43 establishes a procedure, involving prior examination, that is founded on a stringent authorisation criterion which, incorporating the precautionary principle, makes it possible to prevent in an effective manner adverse effects on the integrity of protected sites due to the plans or projects envisaged.[450]

This stringent authorisation criterion obliges the competent national authorities to refuse authorisation for a plan or project where doubts remain as to the absence of adverse effects of those plans or projects on the integrity of such sites.[451]

447. C-411/17, *Doel*, para. 143.
448. *Ibid.*, para. 144.
449. *Ibid.*, para. 145.
450. C-243/15, *LZ II*, para. 66.
451. C-127/02, *Waddenzee*, paras 57 and 58; and C-399/14, *Grüne Liga Sachsen*, para. 48.

The Article 6(3) assessment procedure encompasses the carrying out of an assessment and the drawing of the necessary inferences from this.

The first part 'requires the Member States to carry out an appropriate assessment of the implications for a protected site of a plan or project when there is a likelihood that the plan or project will have a significant effect on that site'.[452]

The second part, which is envisaged in the second sentence of Article 6(3), 'and occurs following the appropriate assessment of the implications of the plan or project for the site concerned, allows such a plan or project to be authorised *only if it will not* adversely affect the integrity of the site concerned' (emphasis added).[453]

[14] Trigger for an Appropriate Assessment: Notion of 'Likely Significant Effect'

Although, as has been seen, the case-law establishes that the notions of 'plan' and 'project' are broad, not every plan or project falls under the obligation to carry out a fully fledged Article 6(3) assessment.

In Case C-127/02, *Waddenzee*, the Court explained what triggers the appropriate assessment obligation under Article 6(3).

Referring to the wording of Article 6(3), the Court noted that 'a requirement for an appropriate assessment of the implications of a plan or project is thus conditional on its being likely to have a significant effect on the site'.[454]

This does not mean, however, that the authorities must have the certainty that such a significant effect will arise. The triggering of the assessment mechanism does not presume that the plan or project, in question, *definitely* has a significant effect on the site concerned. On the contrary, the Article 6(3) obligation to carry out an appropriate assessment 'follows from the mere probability that such an effect attaches to that plan or project'.[455]

The Court also introduced the notion of *risk*, stating that:

> It follows that the first sentence of Article 6(3) of the Habitats Directive subordinates the requirement for an appropriate assessment of the implications of a plan or project to the condition that there be a probability or *a risk* that the latter will have significant effects on the site concerned (emphasis added).[456]

The Court referred both to the analogous provisions of Article 2(1) of the EIA Directive[457] and to the Guidelines[458] prepared by the services of the Commission –

452. C-293/17, *PAS*, para. 92; C-387/15, *Orleans*, para. 44.
453. C-293/17, *PAS*, para. 99; C-441/17, *Commission v. Poland*, para. 115.
454. C-127/02, *Waddenzee*, para. 40.
455. *Ibid.*, para. 41.
456. *Ibid.*, para. 43.
457. *Ibid.*, paras 24-27 and 42.
458. *Ibid.*, para. 41.

'Managing Natura 2000 Sites: The provisions of Article 6 of the Habitats Directive (92/43/EEC)'.[459]

[15] *Appraising the Probability or Risk of a Significant Effect*

In clarifying in Case C-127/02, *Waddenzee,* what would constitute a risk triggering the need for an appropriate assessment, the Court referred to the precautionary principle[460] – then enshrined in Article 174(2) of the EC Treaty and now found in Article 191, TFEU – and to the objectives of the Habitats Directive. The Court clarified that 'such a risk exists if it cannot be excluded on the basis of objective information that the plan or project will have significant effects on the site concerned'.[461] In case of doubt as to the absence of significant effects, an assessment must be carried out. Such an interpretation 'makes it possible to ensure effectively that plans or projects which adversely affect the integrity of the site concerned are not authorised, and thereby contributes to achieving, in accordance with the third recital in the preamble to the Habitats Directive and Article 2(1) thereof, its main aim, namely, ensuring biodiversity through the conservation of natural habitats and of wild fauna and flora'.[462]

[a] *Importance of Link to Conservation Objectives*

The Court went on to make a link with site conservation objectives, referring to Article 6(3) in combination with Recital 10 of the Habitats Directive. The Court thus related the significance of the impact on a site of a plan or project to the site's conservation objectives.[463]

In Cases C-293/17, PAS, and C-441/17, *Commission v. Poland*, the Court stated:

> Having regard to the precautionary principle, where a plan or project not directly connected with or necessary to the management of a site may undermine the site's conservation objectives, it must be considered likely to have a significant effect on that site.[464]

Conversely, if a plan or project, even when it has an effect on a site, 'is not likely to undermine its conservation objectives, it cannot be considered likely to have a significant effect on the site concerned'.[465]

This shows the fundamental importance of Member States determining the conservation objectives for each Natura 2000 site.

---

459. https://ec.europa.eu/environment/nature/natura2000/management/docs/art6/provision_of_art6_en.pdf An updated document was published under Commission Notice C(2018) 7621 final, Brussels, 21 November 2018, https://ec.europa.eu/environment/nature/natura2000/management/docs/art6/EN_art_6_guide_jun_2019.pdf.
460. C-127/02, *Waddenzee,* para. 44.
461. *Ibid.*
462. *Ibid.*
463. *Ibid.*, para. 46.
464. C-293/17, *PAS,* para. 93; C-441/17, *Commission v. Poland,* para. 112.
465. C-127/02, *Waddenzee,* para. 47.

Furthermore, as conservation objectives can vary depending on the specific characteristics of the sites concerned, the appraisal of risk can only be done on a case-by-case basis. Thus, appraisal of *risk* 'must be made in the light *inter alia* of the characteristics and specific environmental conditions of the site concerned by such a plan or project'.[466]

[16] Appropriate Assessment Cannot Be Avoided by Referring to Mitigation Measures at the Screening Stage

Mitigation measures cannot be considered when screening whether a fully appropriate assessment should be made under Article 6(3).

In Case C-323/17, *People Over Wind and Sweetman*, an Irish court raised the matter with the Court, asking whether mitigation measures can be considered when carrying out screening under Article 6(3) of the Habitats Directive.

The case concerned the laying of a cable to connect a wind farm to the electricity grid, with potential impacts on two Natura 2000 areas and, in particular, on the habitats of freshwater pearl mussels. The population of the Nore pearl mussel was estimated to have fallen from 20,000 individuals in 1991 to 300 individuals at the time of the project proposal. It had also become apparent from the most recent monitoring reports that the species were under threat of extinction on account of a high level of sedimentation of the river. The installation of the wind farm had already been approved. A screening report had concluded that an Article 6(3) assessment was unnecessary but that, in the absence of protective measures, there might occur a release of silt or pollutants such as concrete, with potentially harmful negative impacts on the pearl mussel. Hence, the question of the national judge on whether, if targeted mitigation measures are prescribed, this can exempt the project from undergoing an Article 6(3) assessment.

The Court's reply was negative. In order to determine 'whether it is necessary to carry out, subsequently, an appropriate assessment of the implications, for a site concerned, of a plan or project, it is not appropriate, at the screening stage, to take account of the measures intended to avoid or reduce the harmful effects of the plan or project on that site'.[467]

In Case C-721/21, *Ecoadvocacy*, however, the Court made it clear that its ruling in Case C-323/17, *People Over Wind and Sweetman*:

> Cannot have the effect of precluding the taking into account, during the screening phase of a project, of all the constituent elements of that project inherent in it which have the effect of reducing the harmful effects of the project on the site concerned.[468]

At issue in Case C-721/21, *Ecoadvocacy* was a housing development which included standard arrangements for the treatment of surface-water run-off. The run-off

466. C-293/17, *PAS*, para. 93; C-441/17, *Commission v. Poland*, para. 112.
467. C-323/17, *People Over Wind and Sweetman*, para. 40.
468. *Ibid.*, para. 48.

would be discharged to a tributary of the River Boyne, an SAC as well as an SPA. The authority responsible for the development consent had concluded that neither an EIA nor an appropriate assessment (AA) were necessary. Its decision was challenged.

As far as the Court was concerned, the arrangements for the surface-water run-off did not disclose that there was a likelihood of harm to the Natura 2000 site. It stated that:

> Where such elements are incorporated into the design of a project not with the aim of reducing the negative effects of that project on the site concerned, but as *standard features required for all projects of the same type*, those elements cannot, inter alia, be regarded as indicative of probable significant harm to that site (emphasis added).[469]

[17] Second Part of Assessment Process: Obligation to Refrain from Authorising Plans or Projects if a Reasonable Doubt Persists with Regard to Potential Negative Impacts

The second sentence of Article 6(3) gives rise to a further obligation once the examination required by the first sentence is finalised. This obligation relates to the decision on whether or not to authorise the plan or project concerned. This part of the assessment obligation 'allows such a plan or project to be authorised only if it will not adversely affect the integrity of the site concerned'.[470]

In the view of the Court:

> Article 6(3) of the Habitats Directive thus integrates the precautionary principle and makes it possible to prevent in an effective manner adverse effects on the integrity of protected sites as a result of the plans or projects envisaged. A less stringent authorisation criterion than that in question could not ensure as effectively the fulfilment of the objective of site protection intended under that provision.[471]

[18] The Form and Content of the Appropriate Assessment

The Habitats Directive does not define the concept of 'appropriate assessment' and it 'does not define any particular method for the carrying out of such an assessment'.[472]

Notwithstanding this, there is now extensive case-law on what is required from such an assessment in order for it to be considered compliant with Article 6(3) of the Habitats Directive. In this regard, the Court repeatedly draws on the precautionary principle when examining questions of compliance with Article 6(3).

---

469. C-721/21, *Ecoadvocacy*, para. 49.
470. C-293/17, *PAS*, para. 99; C-441/17, *Commission v. Poland*, para. 115.
471. C-293/17, *PAS*, para. 100; C-441/17, *Commission v. Poland*, para. 118.
472. C-304/05, *Commission v. Italy*, para. 57.

First of all:

> Article 6(3) provides for an assessment procedure intended to ensure, by means of a prior examination, that a plan or project which is not directly connected with or necessary to the management of the site concerned but likely to have a significant effect on it is authorised only to the extent that it will not adversely affect the integrity of that site.[473]

This involves the application of several criteria or parameters on which the Court has taken a firm position:

(1) All aspects of the plan or project which can, by themselves or in combination with other plans or projects, affect a site's conservation objectives and must be identified in light of the 'best scientific knowledge in the field'.[474]
(2) Authorisation can be granted only if 'no reasonable scientific doubt'[475] remains as to the absence of adverse effects. (3) Certainty must be acquired *before* the final decision is made to grant a permit.

[a] Need for Completeness in the Appropriate Assessment and Certainty Before the Final Decision

Parameters or elements important for determining the complete impact on the integrity of the site in question must not be postponed to a later stage, i.e., after the permit is granted. Other studies cannot be considered relevant for the purpose of compliance with Article 6(3) when they are 'prepared during the works or after their completion, that is to say after grant of the authorisation'.[476]

Similarly, a permit which allows the developer to determine, at a later stage, certain parameters relating to the construction phase, such as the location of the construction compound and haul routes, can only be compliant 'if that authority is certain that the development consent granted establishes conditions that are strict enough to guarantee that those parameters will not adversely affect the integrity of the site'.[477] Only those parameters in respect of which there is no scientific doubt that they will not affect the site can be entirely left to be decided later by the developer.

Case C-304/05, *Commission v. Italy,* illustrates the Court's strict approach. Italy was condemned, *inter alia,* for not having sufficiently evaluated the impact entailed by a project designed to modify and enlarge ski runs and construct associated facilities in the Santa Caterina Valfurva skiing area, in the Italian Alps, with a view to the holding of the 2005 World Alpine Ski Championships. The project involved the creation of a corridor in a forest area to make the ski runs and the construction of a cable car.

473. C-127/02, *Waddenzee,* para. 34; C-304/05, *Commission v. Italy,* para. 56.
474. C-127/02, *Waddenzee,* para. 61; and C-239/04, *Castro Verde,* para. 24.
475. C-293/17, *PAS,* paras 106 and 113.
476. C-304/05, *Commission v. Spain,* para. 72.
477. C-461/17, *Holohan,* para. 47.

Additional envisaged works included a departure station, a ski stadium, a car park near to the departure station, a bridge over the Frodolfo stream, a refuge at Valle dell'Alpe and service routes. The protected area was an SPA under the Birds Directive to which Article 6(3) of the Habitats Directive was applicable by virtue of the latter instrument's Article 7 (*see* section §3.04[C][2] above).

The Italian government argued that an Article 6(3) assessment had, in fact, been carried out. It referred, on the one hand, to an environmental impact study drawn up by an architect on behalf of two public works undertakings and, on the other hand, to a report relating to assessment of the environmental impact of the project in question drawn up by Istituto di Ricerca per l'Ecologia e l'Economia Applicate alle Aree Alpine (Research Institute for Applied Ecology and Economics in Alpine Regions - the 'IREALP').

The Court drew on parameters it had developed in its earlier judgments in Case C-127/02, *Waddenzee* and Case C-239/04, *Commission v. Portugal ('Castro Verde')*. It observed that the assessment must be organised in such a manner that the competent national authorities can be certain that a plan or project will *not* have adverse effects on the integrity of the site concerned, given that, where doubt remains as to the absence of such effects, the competent authority will have to refuse the authorisation.[478] The authorities need to rely on the best scientific knowledge in the field.[479]

In light of these parameters, the Court proceeded to examine the two documents concerned, i.e., the environmental impact study and the IREALP report. It noted that the study itself recommended additional environmental assessments and a new examination of the impact of the works[480] on the assumption that more information would come to light, later on, at the implementation stage of the project. The preliminary study clearly indicated that it is to be considered a 'guidance document for decisions, which highlights risks and provides suggestions in order to resolve problems, rather than a precise measurement of the impact'[481] which the proposed works will have on the environment. This was found insufficient by the Court because of the preliminary nature of its findings and the lack of definitive conclusions.[482]

As regards the birds for which the SPA had been classified, the IREALP's report did not, however, contain an exhaustive list of the wild birds present in the area.[483]

The Court observed that the study and the report 'have gaps and lack complete, precise and definitive findings and conclusions capable of removing all scientific doubt as to the effects of the works proposed on the SPAs concerned'.[484] Noting that 'such findings and conclusions were essential in order that the competent authorities might gain the necessary level of certainty to take the decision to authorize the works', the Court found that the authorisation of the works did not, as a consequence, comply with Article 6(3).

478. C-304/05, *Commission v. Italy*, para. 58.
479. *Ibid.*, para. 59.
480. *Ibid.*, para. 63.
481. *Ibid.*, para. 31.
482. *Ibid.*, para. 67.
483. *Ibid.*, para. 66.
484. *Ibid.*, para. 69.

Case, C-461/17, *Holohan,* sheds light on the need for completeness in any appropriate assessment. The Court held that all the habitats and species for which the site is protected must be catalogued and drew a presumption of non-compliance with Article 6(3) if the assessment had not identified 'the entirety of the habitats and species for which the site has been listed' as this 'would not be sufficient to dispel all reasonable scientific doubt as to the absence of adverse effects on the integrity of the protected site'.[485]

It may be sufficient, however, to 'establish that only certain protected habitat types and species are present in the part of the protected area that is affected by the project and that the other protected habitat types and species present on the site are not liable to be affected'.[486]

Furthermore, 'the assessment of that risk must be made in the light of, in particular, the characteristics and specific environmental conditions of the site concerned by such a plan or project'.[487]

[b] Use of Earlier or Parallel Assessments

Earlier assessments which cover the requirements of the Habitats Directive, in the context of earlier consents, may be taken into account, 'in order to avoid the same project being subject to several environmental assessments',[488] on the condition, however, that the preceding assessments contain 'complete, precise and definitive conclusions capable of removing all reasonable scientific doubt as to the effects of the works, and provided that there are no changes in the relevant environmental and scientific data, no changes to the project and no other plans or projects that must be taken into account'.[489]

This topic is also addressed in Case C-278/21, *Aquapli,* in the context of an assessment to remedy an earlier failure to comply with Article 6(3) – *see* section §3.04[G][4][d] below.

[c] Other Species Present on the Site and Habitat Types and Species Outside the Site

An appropriate assessment may need to encompass species present on a Natura 2000 site, but for which that site has not been listed, as well as species and habitats outside the boundaries of the Natura 2000 site.

Case C-461/17, *Holohan,* arose from a legal challenge to the approval of a road project which crossed two Natura 2000 sites and which had been submitted to both an EIA and an appropriate assessment process. The referring court noted, however, that the documents prepared for the EIA and appropriate assessment were limited in their

485. C-461/17, *Holohan,* para. 37.
486. *Ibid.,* para. 38.
487. C-521/12, *Briels,* para. 20; and C-258/11, *Sweetman,* para. 30.
488. C-254/19, *Friends of the Irish Environment,* para. 54.
489. *Ibid.,* para. 55.

coverage of habitats and species. The Court confirmed that, in order to meet the requirements of Article 6(3), the assessment must identify and 'examine both the implications of the proposed project for the species present on that site, and for which that site has not been listed, and the implications for habitat types and species to be found outside the boundaries of that site, provided that those implications are liable to affect the conservation objectives of the site'.[490]

As the Court referred favourably to the Opinion of the Advocate General, it is useful to mention the latter's rationale for covering both these categories in the appropriate assessment.

The Advocate General noted that the conservation status of a habitat type expressly includes the typical species of the habitat concerned. Any adverse effects on those species at the locations occupied by that habitat type would also attach to the habitat type concerned.[491] The Advocate General gave the example of typical plant species of the priority habitat type 'Alluvial forests with *Alnus glutinosa* and *Fraxinus excelsior* (*Alno-Padion, Alnion incanae, Salicion albae*)' (Natura 2000 Code 91E0*) mentioned by the Commission's Interpretation Manual of Habitats, referred to in Annex I to the Habitats Directive.[492] Moreover, typical species of a habitat type were not confined to plant species.[493]

The Advocate General also noted that habitat types and species which are not expressly protected may play an essential role in the conservation of protected habitat types and species.[494] It is essential that rivers and streams are passable if migratory fish such as salmon (*Salmo salar*) are able to reach their spawning grounds.[495] What is more, the life cycle of certain protected species is to some extent also dependent on very specific other species. Thus, the larvae of the freshwater pearl mussel (*Margaritifera margaritifera*) and the endemic River Nore freshwater pearl mussel (*Margaritifera durrovensis*), both of which are present in the future SAC concerned, live for a time as parasites in the gills of river trout (*Salmo trutta fario*) or salmon.[496]

As for habitats and species outside of the protected areas concerned, as Case C-142/16, Moorburg shows, activities carried outside protected areas, which give rise to adverse effects within those areas, must also be assessed under Article 6(3) of the Habitats Directive and:

> Equally important from the point of view of assessment under Article 6(3) of the Habitats Directive are the adverse effects on species outside the future SAC or SPA, where these are either protected species themselves or are species typical of protected habitats, or where they are in some other way necessary to the conservation of protected habitats and species.

490. C-461/17, *Holohan*, para. 40.
491. Opinion of the Advocate General in C-461/17, *Holohan*, para. 35.
492. *Ibid.*, paras 36 to 38.
493. *Ibid.*, paras 39.
494. *Ibid.*, para. 40.
495. *Ibid.*, para. 41.
496. *Ibid.*, para. 42.

> Furthermore, adverse effects on habitats outside protected areas may also be important. This is the case in particular where a protected area, although protecting specific species, does not include all the habitats used by those species. In that event, any degradation of such habitats arising outside the protected areas could adversely affect the protected presence of species within those protected areas.[497]

[19] Public Participation in an Article 6(3) Process

The text of Article 6(3) of the Habitats Directive refers briefly to the possibility of public participation ('… and, if appropriate, after having obtained the opinion of the general public').

The EIA Directive was already in place when the Habitats Directive was adopted and, as can be seen from the case-law, there are projects which fall within the scope of both the Habitats Directive and the EIA Directive. The EIA Directive creates, amongst other things, a framework for public participation[498] and by virtue of its provisions, a project requiring an appropriate assessment under Article 6(3) of the Habitats Directive may require public participation under the EIA Directive. In 1998, the then European Community signed the Aarhus Convention, Article 6 of which provides for public participation in respect of certain projects. In 2003, the EU adopted a directive on public participation to give effect to the Aarhus Convention.[499] This directive did not, however, make any changes to Article 6(3) of the Habitats Directive. In 2005, the EU formally ratified the Aarhus Convention.

Against this background, Case C-243/15, *LZ II*, clarifies the extent to which Article 6(3) of the Habitats Directive itself requires public participation.

The plaintiff, a Slovak environmental association became aware of an administrative procedure initiated by the district authority of Trenčín, concerning an application submitted by a company breeding deer for hunting purposes, 'in order to obtain authorisation of a project relating to the construction of an enclosure, for the purpose of extending a deer reserve'.[500] The construction of the enclosure was to be done on land plots located in a site classified as an SPA and, at the same time, listed as an SCI. The plaintiff sought to participate in the procedure but was denied the status of 'party to the procedure', because, under Slovak law, it could only have the status of 'interested person'.[501] The plaintiff was also denied standing to bring a legal challenge which led to a preliminary reference to the Court. In upholding the plaintiff's entitlement to bring a legal challenge (*see* section §3.04[G][2] below), the Court also

497. *Ibid.*, paras 48 and 49.
498. In 2001, the SEA Directive was adopted and created a similar framework for public consultation in respect of plans and programmes.
499. Directive 2003/35/EC of the European Parliament and of the Council of 26 May 2003 providing for public participation in respect of the drawing up of certain plans and programmes relating to the environment and amending with regard to public participation and access to justice Council Directives 85/337/EEC and 96/61/EC, OJ L 156, 25.6.2003, p. 17-25.
500. C-243/15, *LZ II*, para. 19.
501. *Ibid.*, para. 22.

confirmed that it enjoyed participatory rights under Article 6(3) of the Habitats Directive.

The Court read Article 6(3) of the Directive in conjunction with Article 6(1)(b) of the Aarhus Convention, 'an instrument which forms an integral part of the EU legal order',[502] and which renders the provisions of Article 6[503] of the Convention applicable to decisions on proposed activities not listed in Annex I to the Convention, which may have a significant effect on the environment. The project at stake in the case concerned (enclosure of a plot) does not represent an activity listed in Annex I to the Convention, 'for which public involvement is systematically required'[504] but as the national authorities decided to initiate a fully fledged Article 6(3) procedure, it could be inferred that an assessment was necessary with regard to the significance of the project's effect on the environment, within the meaning of Article 6(1)(b) of the Aarhus Convention.[505]

An environmental association which meets the definition of 'public concerned' set out in Article 2(5)[506] of the Aarhus Convention draws from Article 6(3) of the Habitats Directive, read in conjunction with Article 6(1)(b) of that Convention, a right to participate in an Article 6(3) procedure. Under Article 6 of the Convention, the right to participate is composed, in particular, of a right to participate effectively during the environmental decision-making by submitting, 'in writing or, as appropriate, at a public hearing or inquiry with the applicant, any comments, information, analyses or opinions that it considers relevant to the proposed activity'. There must be 'early public participation, when all options are open and effective public participation can take place'.[507]

502. *Ibid.*, para. 45.
503. *Ibid.*, para. 45. According to Article 6(1)(b) of the Aarhus Convention, 'each Party … (b) shall, in accordance with its national law, also apply the provisions of this article to decisions on proposed activities not listed in Annex I which may have a significant effect on the environment. To this end, Parties shall determine whether such a proposed activity is subject to these provisions.'
504. Matthijs van Wolferen, *University of Groningen, The Netherlands, Case C-243/15 Lesoochranárske zoskupenie vlk v Obvodný úrad Trenčín*, 14 The Journal for European Environmental & Planning Law 136-151 (2017).
505. C-243/15, *LZ II*, para. 47.
506. Article 2(5) of the Aarhus Convention defines the 'the public concerned' to mean 'the public affected or likely to be affected by, or having an interest in, the environmental decision-making; for the purposes of this definition, non-governmental organisations promoting environmental protection and meeting any requirements under national law shall be deemed to have an interest.'
507. C-243/15, *LZ II*, para. 46, and Article 6 of the Aarhus Convention which reads:

> 2. The public concerned shall be informed, either by public notice or individually as appropriate, early in an environmental decision-making procedure, and in an adequate, timely and effective manner …
> 3. The public participation procedures shall include reasonable time-frames for the different phases, allowing sufficient time for informing the public in accordance with paragraph 2 above and for the public to prepare and participate effectively during the environmental decision-making.
> 4. Each Party shall provide for early public participation, when all options are open and effective public participation can take place.

It is worth observing that the Court took note of the possible crucial role that an environmental association might play in a decision-making procedure:

> In this context, the referring court has, moreover, observed that, since only the applicant for the permit is automatically a party to the procedure, it is possible that, without the participation in the administrative procedure of an environmental organisation such as LZ as a party to the procedure, arguments supporting protection of the environment will be neither put forward nor taken into account, so that the fundamental objective of the procedure envisaged in Article 6(3) of Directive 92/43, namely that of ensuring a high level of environmental protection, will not be achieved.[508]

[20] *Impact on Site Integrity: Importance of Ensuring Favourable Conservation Status*

As already noted, the assessment of the implications on the site is closely connected with the conservation objectives of the site. An appropriate assessment 'implies that, before the plan or project is approved, all the aspects of the plan or project which can, either individually or in combination with other plans or projects, affect the conservation objectives of that site must be identified, in the light of the best scientific knowledge in the field'.[509]

[a] Need to Preserve the Site at Favourable Conservation Status

The need to maintain a favourable conservation status is the criterion to be used when assessing the impacts. In order for the integrity of a site as a natural habitat not to be adversely affected for purposes of the second sentence of Article 6(3), 'the site needs to be preserved at a favourable conservation status'.[510] This entails the 'lasting preservation of the constitutive characteristics of the site concerned that are connected to the presence of a natural habitat type whose preservation was the objective justifying the designation'.[511]

---

5. Each Party should, where appropriate, encourage prospective applicants to identify the public concerned, to enter into discussions, and to provide information regarding the objectives of their application before applying for a permit.
6. Each Party shall require the competent public authorities to give the public concerned access for examination, upon request where so required under national law, free of charge and as soon as it becomes available, to all information relevant to the decision-making referred to in this article that is available at the time of the public participation procedure, without prejudice to the right of Parties to refuse to disclose certain information in accordance with Article 4, paragraphs 3 and 4 ...
7. Procedures for public participation shall allow the public to submit, in writing or, as appropriate, at a public hearing or inquiry with the applicant, any comments, information, analyses or opinions that it considers relevant to the proposed activity.

508. C-243/15, *LZ II*, para. 70.
509. C-461/17, *Holohan*, para. 33.
510. *Ibid.*, para. 35.
511. *Ibid.*, para. 35; C-441/17, *Commission v. Poland*, para. 116.

[b] Even Limited Destruction Can Adversely Affect Site Integrity

Case C-258/11, *Sweetman*, illustrates what preservation of conservation status can mean in practice. The case arose from a legal challenge to a road scheme involving the permanent loss within the Lough Corrib SCI in Ireland of approximately 1.47 hectares of limestone pavement, a priority habitat type. Those 1.47 hectares would be lost from a distinct sub-area containing a total of 85 hectares of limestone pavement. That surface of 85 hectares itself formed part of a total of 270 hectares of such limestone pavement in the entire SCI.

The national decision-maker accepted that the road scheme would have a locally significant negative impact on the SCI but decided that such an impact did not adversely affect the integrity of that site.[512] The Commission, which intervened in the proceedings, considered that such an interpretation would fail 'to prevent the "death by a thousand cuts" phenomenon, that is to say, cumulative habitat loss as a result of multiple, or at least a number of, lower level projects being allowed to proceed on the same site'.[513]

The Court took a strict view, observing that the natural habitat affected by the proposed road scheme was amongst the priority natural habitat types, which Article 1(d) of the Habitats Directive defines as 'natural habitat types in danger of disappearance' for whose conservation the EU has 'particular responsibility'.[514]

It noted that the Lough Corrib SCI was designated as a site hosting a priority habitat type because, in particular, of the presence in that site of limestone pavement, a natural resource which, once destroyed, cannot be replaced. The conservation objective thus corresponded to maintenance at a favourable conservation status of that site's constitutive characteristics, namely the presence of limestone pavement.[515]

It held that:

> Consequently, if, after an appropriate assessment of a plan or project's implications for a site, carried out on the basis of the first sentence of Article 6(3) of the Habitats Directive, the competent national authority concludes that that plan or project will lead to *the lasting and irreparable loss of the whole or part* of a priority natural habitat type whose conservation was the objective that justified the designation of the site concerned as an SCI, the view should be taken that such a plan or project will adversely affect the integrity of that site (emphasis added).[516]

[c] Implications of Unfavourable Conservation Status

In the Dutch nitrogen case, C-293/17, *PAS*, the Court referred to Article 1(e) of the Habitats Directive which defines when the conservation status of a natural habitat is 'favourable', noting that this is 'when, *inter alia*, its natural range and the areas it

512. C-258/11, *Sweetman*, para. 26.
513. Opinion of the Advocate General in C-258/11, *Sweetman*, para. 67.
514. C-258/11, *Sweetman*, para. 42.
515. *Ibid.*, para. 45.
516. *Ibid.*, para. 46.

covers within that range are stable or increasing and the specific structure and functions which are necessary for its long-term maintenance exist and are likely to continue to exist for the foreseeable future'.[517]

Logically, where, as in the circumstances of the Dutch case itself, the conservation status of a natural habitat is unfavourable, 'the possibility of authorising activities which may subsequently affect the ecological situation of the sites concerned seems necessarily limited'.[518]

[21] Requirement to Take Account of Protective Measures Without Circumventing Article 6(3) and/or 6(4)

When assessing a proposed plan or project, the competent authorities have a responsibility to take account of protective measures (sometimes referred to as 'mitigation measures' or 'mitigating measures') included in the proposal but, in doing so, they must not circumvent the requirements of Article 6(3) and/or 6(4).

[a] Distinction Between Protective Measures and Compensatory Measures

There is a distinction to be made between protective measures, which are integral to a plan or project but mitigate its effects, and compensatory measures which are regulated under Article 6(4) of the Habitats Directive. The distinction must be made in light of the precautionary principle, and the requirement to refrain from authorising a project which is likely to impact negatively on a Natura 2000 site when the conditions under Article 6(4) are not strictly fulfilled.

[b] Protective Measures Can and Must Be Taken into Account

Protective measures can be taken into account at the time of the appropriate assessment, and it is even the responsibility[519] of the competent authorities to take them into account. In Case C-142/16, *Moorburg*, the Court stated that:

> The application of the precautionary principle in the context of the implementation of Article 6(3) of the Habitats Directive requires the competent national authority to take into account, inter alia, the protective measures forming part of that project aimed at avoiding or reducing any direct adverse effects on the site, in order to ensure that it does not adversely affect the integrity of the protected site.[520]

517. C-293/17, *PAS*, para. 102.
518. *Ibid.*, para. 103.
519. C-142/16, *Moorburg*, para. 34.
520. *Ibid.*; C-521/12, *Briels*, para. 28, and C-387/15 and C-388/15, *Orleans*, para. 54.

[c] *Definitive Data Is Necessary to Justify Reliance on Protective Measures*

If reliance is to be placed on protective measures, however, it needs to be based on definitive data as to their effectiveness.[521] In Case C-142/16, *Moorburg,* for instance, a fish ladder had been installed with the objective of increasing fish stocks by allowing a quicker migration, and thus compensating for the fish deaths near the Moorburg plant, but definitive data on its effectiveness was lacking (future monitoring was proposed) and, even though it was intended to reduce direct significant effects on the Natura 2000 areas situated upstream of the Moorburg plant, the installation of the fish ladder 'could not guarantee beyond all reasonable doubt',[522] that the plant would not adversely affect the integrity of the site.

Case, C-142/16, *Moorburg* thus shows that the Court's case-law sets limits on the extent to which competent authorities can rely on protective measures to satisfy the requirement of the second part of the assessment process.

[d] *Protective Measures Cannot Be Compensatory Measures in Disguise*

Case, C-521/12, *Briels,* further underlines the limits that the Court has applied. In particular, the Court has declined to interpret Article 6(3) as allowing for a plan or project's approval on the basis of measures which purport to be protective but are, in reality, compensatory in nature. It has made clear the need to 'avoid a situation where competent national authorities allow so-called "mitigating" measures - which are in reality compensatory measures - in order to circumvent the specific procedures provided for in Article 6(3) and authorise projects which adversely affect the integrity of the site concerned'.[523]

The circumstances of C-521/12, *Briels* concerned the impacts of a motorway widening project on the Dutch Natura 2000 site Vlijmens Ven, Moerputten & Bossche Broek, which had been designated for the habitat type molinia meadows. An assessment had concluded that there would be negative implications for the existing area comprising the protected habitat type. As part of the project, it was proposed to create an even larger area of molinia meadows of higher quality in the site concerned.

The Court did not accept that these purported mitigation measures could be relied on in order to reach a conclusion that the integrity of the site would not be adversely affected. It was clear that the motorway project would have significant adverse effects and it was also clear that the measures to create new molinia meadows were not aimed either at avoiding or reducing the significant adverse effects for the habitat type; rather, they tended to 'compensate after the fact for those effects'.[524]

Such purported mitigation measures could not open the door to permitting under Article 6(3) if doubts about negative impacts could not be completely dissipated. The

521. C-142/16, *Moorburg,* para. 37.
522. *Ibid.*, para. 38.
523. C-521/12, *Briels,* para. 33.
524. *Ibid.*, para. 31.

Court noted that there was inherent uncertainty surrounding the success of the proposed creation of new meadows, stating:

> It should further be noted that, as a rule, any positive effects of a future creation of new habitat which is aimed at compensating for the loss of area and the quality of that same habitat type on a protected site, even where the new area will be bigger and of higher quality, are highly difficult to forecast with any degree of certainty and, in any event, will be visible only several years in the future.

Consequently, they could not be taken into account in the procedural stage provided for in Article 6(3).[525]

Similar considerations arose in Case C-164/17, *Grace and Sweetman*. The circumstances concerned a proposal to build a wind farm within an SPA which had been classified for the hen harrier, a species listed in Annex I of the Birds Directive. The development proposal included a management plan, which envisaged measures to address the impact of the wind farm project on the hen harrier. It put in place safeguards to ensure that the foraging habitat of the hen harrier was not reduced and *might even be enhanced*. During the lifetime of the contested development, however, some part of the site would lose the potential to provide the hen harrier with an appropriate habitat. In spite of this dynamic management which ensured that any part of the SPA that could provide suitable habitat would not be reduced and might even be enhanced, some parts of the SPA would no longer be able, if the project went ahead, to provide a suitable habitat.[526] The Court observed that:

> Any positive effects of the future creation of a new habitat, which is aimed at compensating for the loss of area and quality of that habitat type in a protected area are highly difficult to forecast with any degree of certainty or will be visible only in the future.[527]

The Court concluded that such management measures may not be taken into account under Article 6(3), when assessing whether the project in question will not adversely affect the integrity of the site concerned. Article 6(4) of the Directive must be therefore considered.[528]

[e] Prior Compensatory Measures Are Still Compensatory Measures

In Joined Cases C-387/15 and C-388/15, *Orleans*,[529] the Court considered another line of argument aimed at justifying an approval under Article 6(3), this time, one based on the creation of positive ecological results *before* any negative effects would manifest themselves. The circumstances concerned a development plan for a large part of the port of Antwerp in Belgium on the left bank of the Scheldt. This was likely to affect the Natura 2000 site known as 'Scheldt and Durme estuary from the Dutch border to

525. *Ibid.*, para. 32.
526. C-164/17, *Grace and Sweetman*, para. 48.
527. *Ibid.*, para. 52.
528. *Ibid.*, para. 57.
529. C-387/15 and Joined Case C-388/15, *Orleans*.

Ghent', designated as an SAC for the habitat type 'estuary'. Purported mitigation measures were foreseen, consisting of the establishment of habitats and habitats of species in ecological core areas. These measures were to be implemented in advance, i.e., before the development of affected areas became possible. The Court was asked to clarify whether 'measures, contained in a plan or project not directly connected with or necessary to the management of a Site of Community Importance, providing, prior to the occurrence of adverse effects on a natural habitat type present thereon, for the future creation of an area of that type, but the completion of which will take place subsequently to the assessment of the significance of any adverse effects on the integrity of that site'[530] are to be considered under Article 6(3) or rather seen as compensatory measures under Article 6(4).

The Court maintained the line taken in Case C-521/12, *Briels* that protective measures which aim at compensating for the negative effects of a plan or project on a Natura 2000 site cannot be taken into account in the Article 6(3) assessment. Such measures should be categorised as 'compensatory measures',[531] within the meaning of Article 6(4), and if the conditions laid down therein are satisfied.

With regard to the circumstances of Cases C-387/15 and C-388/15, *Orleans*, the Court observed that the adverse effects on the Natura 2000 site in question were certain (since the referring court was able to quantify them), while the benefits resulting from the creation of the nature reserves were uncertain (since it was not complete). The circumstances were thus similar to those in *Briels*. Both involved, at the time of assessing the implications of the plan or project, the identical premise that future benefits will mitigate the significant adverse effects on that site, even though the development measures in question had not been completed.[532]

[f] Protective Measures Post-dating a Negative Assessment Cannot Be Taken into Account

In Case C-411/19, *WWF Italia*, the Court considered the application of Article 6(3) and its relationship with Article 6(4) in circumstances that were procedurally especially complex. The case arose as a result of a legal challenge by several Italian environmental associations to the approval of an 18-kilometer stretch of the national route no. 675 in Latium. There were two alternatives for the route and one of them had received a negative opinion from the Ministry of the Environment on the grounds that the project had not undergone a thorough appropriate assessment and because it would negatively impact a Natura 2000 area, Fiume Mignone. The Ministry of Environment issued an opinion to the effect that potential mitigation measures would not reduce the impact on the site. In spite of the negative opinion of the Ministry of Environment, however, the preliminary project had been approved by the Council of Ministers, via a specific procedure. The green light was motivated by a major public interest and was subject to

530. C-387/15, *Orleans*, para. 30.
531. *Ibid.*, para. 64.
532. *Ibid.*, para. 56.

some conditions, including that the appropriate assessment study be completed. Finally, the preliminary project was approved, following which the final project and its EIA were to be drawn up. The Lazio Region was named as the body responsible for verifying that study in order, *inter alia*, to identify any additional mitigating and compensatory measures that might be necessary.[533]

In response to a question from the referring court, the Court stated that Article 6 'must be interpreted as precluding national legislation allowing that plan or project, after its negative assessment under Article 6(3) and before its final adoption pursuant to Article 6(4), to be supplemented by measures mitigating its impact on that area and for the assessment of its impact on that area to continue'.[534]

The judgment in this case again underlines the strictness with which the Court treats the fulfilment of the appropriate assessment requirement under Article 6(3) and the dividing line between Article 6(3) and Article 6(4).

[22] Relevance to an Appropriate Assessment of Conservation Measures under Article 6(1) and Protective Measures under Article 6(2)

In the Dutch nitrogen case, C-293/17,[535] *PAS*, amongst other questions, the referring court asked, in essence, whether, and under what conditions, the assessment under Article 6(3) may take into account the existence of 'conservation measures' within the meaning of Article 6(1) and, 'preventive measures' within the meaning of Article 6(2) of the Habitats Directive. The Court observed that 'in particular, the referring court is uncertain whether such types of measures may be taken into account in an "appropriate assessment" within the meaning of Article 6(3) of the Habitats Directive only if they have already been adopted and have yielded results'.[536]

The Court's reply does not deviate from its already established and firm position on Article 6(3). It would be 'contrary to the effectiveness of Article 6(1) and (2) of the Habitats Directive for the effects of necessary measures under those provisions to be invoked in order to grant, under paragraph 3 of that article, the authorisation of a plan or project which has implications for the site concerned before they are actually implemented'.[537] The Court added that the positive effects of the necessary measures under paragraphs 1 and 2 of Article 6 of the Habitats Directive cannot be invoked in order to grant, under paragraph 3 of that article, authorisation to projects which have an adverse effect on protected sites.[538]

More generally, a measure may be taken into consideration in an appropriate assessment only when it is sufficiently certain that it will make an effective contribution to avoiding harm to the integrity of the site concerned by guaranteeing beyond all

533. C-411/19, *WWF Italia*, para. 23.
534. *Ibid.*, operative part of judgment, para. 2.
535. C-293/17, *PAS*, para. 121.
536. *Ibid.*, para. 122.
537. *Ibid.*, para. 123; *see also* C-441/17, *Commission v. Poland*, para. 213.
538. C-293/17, *PAS*, para. 124.

reasonable doubt that the plan or project at issue will not adversely affect the integrity of that site.[539]

[23] Impermissible to Rely on Future Monitoring Results

Case C-142/16, *Moorburg* shows that, in the absence of definitive data regarding the effectiveness of protective measures proposed, authorities cannot issue an Article 6(3) permit on the basis of an impact assessment that indicates that effectiveness can only be confirmed following several years of monitoring.[540] The Court stated that 'as regards multi-phase monitoring, such monitoring cannot be considered as sufficient to ensure performance of the obligation laid down in Article 6(3) of the Habitats Directive'.[541]

[24] Need to Take Account of the Best Scientific Knowledge Available

In Case C-127/02, *Waddenzee,* the Court confirmed that a compliant Article 6(3) assessment:

> Implies that all the aspects of the plan or project which can, either individually or in combination with other plans or projects, affect those objectives must be identified in the light of the best scientific knowledge in the field. Those objectives may, as is clear from Articles 3 and 4 of the Habitats Directive, in particular Article 4(4), be established on the basis, inter alia, of the importance of the sites for the maintenance or restoration at a favourable conservation status of a natural habitat type in Annex I to that directive or a species in Annex II thereto and for the coherence of Natura 2000, and of the threats of degradation or destruction to which they are exposed.[542]

[25] Authorisation Must Be Refused if Any Scientific Doubt Subsists with Regard to Potential Negative Effects on the Integrity of the Site

Where doubt remains as to the absence of adverse effects on the integrity of the site linked to the plan or project being considered, the competent authority *will have to refuse authorisation.*

In Case C-127/02, *Waddenzee,* the Court stated that:

> In this respect, it is clear that the authorisation criterion laid down in the second sentence of Article 6(3) of the Habitats Directive integrates the precautionary principle (*see* Case C-157/96 *National Farmers' Union and Others* [1998] ECR I2211, paragraph 63) and makes it possible effectively to prevent adverse effects on the integrity of protected sites as the result of the plans or projects being considered. A less stringent authorisation criterion than that in question could not

539. *Ibid.,* para. 126.
540. C-142/16, *Moorburg,* para. 37.
541. *Ibid.,* para. 43.
542. C-127/02, *Waddenzee,* para. 54.

as effectively ensure the fulfilment of the objective of site protection intended under that provision.[543]

[26] Cumulative Effects in Relation to Other Plans or Projects

In Case C-127/02, *Waddenzee*, the Court confirmed that an appropriate assessment must 'take into account the cumulative effects which result from the combination of that plan or project with other plans or projects in view of the site's conservation objectives'.[544]

It is irrelevant, from the perspective of this obligation to assess the cumulative effects, that a project was permitted and built before the period for transposition of the Habitats Directive expired.

Thus, in Case *C-142/16, Moorburg*, the Court upheld a Commission complaint against Germany that the cumulative assessment of the proposed power plant should have taken into consideration a pumped storage power plant dating back to 1958. Projects which 'are likely to cause, as a result of their combination with the project to which the impact assessment relates, deterioration or disturbance likely to affect the migratory fish present in the river and consequently result in the deterioration of the site concerned in the light of the objectives pursued by the Habitats Directive, are not to be excluded from the impact assessment required under Article 6(3) of the Habitats Directive'.[545]

However, the in-combination obligation does not arise in respect of proposed developments that have no prospect of being carried out. Thus, in Case *C-142/16, Moorburg*, the Court rejected a Commission complaint that the in-combination obligation should also have encompassed a proposed run-of-river hydroelectric power plant. Germany convinced the Court that there was no prospect of this project proceeding since it required a right of use of the water and the holder of that right had declared that it would not give consent to the project.

[27] More Stringent Transposition and Application of Article 6(3) than the Habitats Directive Requires

The previously cited case-law on Article 6(3) focuses on circumstances which might disclose that national measures to comply with that provision are insufficiently strict. What of circumstances where the national measures are demonstrably stricter and more restrictive than what Article 6(3) requires?

Such circumstances featured in Case C-2/10, *Azienda Agro-Zootecnica Franchini and Eolica di Altamura*, a preliminary reference submitted by an Italian court with respect to legislation of the Puglia Region prohibiting the location of wind turbines not

543. *Ibid.*, paras 57 and 58.
544. *Ibid.*, para. 53.
545. C-142/16, *Moorburg*, para. 62.

intended for self-consumption in SCIs and SPAs forming part of the Natura 2000 network.

The prohibition had been introduced without the prior assessment provided for in Article 6(3) of the Habitats Directive. The referring court asked whether the Habitats and Birds Directive on the one hand and EU legislation aimed at the promotion of renewable energy (namely, Directives 2001/77/EC[546] and 2009/28/EC[547]) on the other, preclude such legislation, which automatically prohibits the placing of certain types of wind turbines in protected sites without prior assessment of the environmental impact on the sites concerned.

The Court referred to Article 14 of the Birds Directive which specifically allows for more stringent national measures and Article 193 of the TFEU which provides that Member States may adopt more stringent measures. The latter needs to be compatible with the Treaty on European Union (TEU) and the TFEU and communicated to the Commission, although the lack of notification by Member States does not render unlawful the more stringent measures adopted. As the Court remarked, Article 193 TFEU 'does not make implementation of the planned measures conditional upon agreement by the Commission or its failure to object'.[548]

Given the existence of relevant EU renewable energy legislation, the Puglian prohibition also needed to be examined for compliance with a prohibition on discrimination (reflecting a broader EU law requirement of non-discrimination) laid down in Article 6(1) of Directive 2001/77/EC and a requirement of proportionality laid down in Article 13 of Directive 2009/28/EC. It was for the referring court to determine whether the national measure at issue was proportionate and 'whether the difference in treatment between the projects for the construction of wind turbines and projects relating to other industrial activities proposed for sites forming part of the Natura 2000 network may be justified on the basis of objective differences between those two kinds of project'.[549]

In principle, such measures can be seen as pursuing 'the same objectives as the Habitats Directive'[550] and 'the referring court must have regard to the particular features of wind turbines, taking into account in particular the dangers which they may represent for birds, such as the risk of collision, disturbances and displacement, barrier effects forcing birds to change direction and habitat loss or degradation'.[551]

In conclusion, the Habitats and Birds Directives allow for the possibility of more stringent measures that are not preceded by an appropriate assessment under Article 6(3) of the former. The context, however, is important. The measures must be

546. Directive 2001/77/EC of the European Parliament and of the Council of 27 September 2001 on the promotion of electricity produced from renewable energy sources in the internal electricity market, OJ L 283, 27.10.2001, p. 33-40.
547. Directive 2009/28/EC of the European Parliament and of the Council of 23 April 2009 on the promotion of the use of energy from renewable sources and amending and subsequently repealing Directives 2001/77/EC and 2003/30/EC, OJ L 140, 5.6.2009, p. 16-62.
548. C-2/10, *Azienda Agro-Zootecnica Franchini and Eolica di Altamura*, para. 53.
549. *Ibid.*, paras 65 and 74.
550. *Ibid.*, para. 52.
551. *Ibid.*, para. 66.

non-discriminatory and must be reconciled with other EU legislation of specific relevance (here, renewable energy legislation).

[E] The Relationship Between Article 6(2) and Article 6(3) of the Habitats Directive

As already noted, protection objectives are pursued through, amongst others, a set of obligations contained under paragraphs (2) and (3) of Article 6: the non-deterioration obligation; and the obligation to subject all plans or projects likely to have a negative impact on a Natura 2000 site to an assessment of those impacts to which attaches a related obligation to refuse authorisation in case a significant negative impact cannot be ruled out.

On several occasions, the Court has been called upon to examine how these different provisions are intended to interact with each other. The case-law establishes that they need to be read as forming a coherent whole.

[1] Issue of Whether Article 6(2) and 6(3) Require Concomitant Application

In Case C-127/02, *Waddenzee,* the environmental associations who had instituted the national proceedings argued that, while the cockle fishing at issue constituted a 'plan' or 'project' within the meaning of Article 6(3), it nevertheless needed to be examined in light of Article 6(2). It was therefore appropriate to 'consider whether Article 6(3) must be regarded as a specific application of the rules in Article 6(2), so that those two paragraphs must be applied cumulatively, or as a provision with a separate, independent purpose, so that Article 6(2) relates to existing use while Article 6(3) applies to new plans or projects'.[552]

Against this background, the Court considered that, by the second question in its reference, the national court was in essence asking what the relationship is between Article 6(2) and Article 6(3) of the Habitats Directive.

In marking the distinction between Article 6(2) and Article 6(3), the Court stated that:

> Article 6(3) of the Habitats Directive establishes a procedure intended to ensure, by means of a preliminary examination, that a plan or project which is not directly connected with or necessary to the management of the site concerned but likely to have a significant effect on it is authorised only to the extent that it will not adversely affect the integrity of that site, while Article 6(2) of the Habitats Directive establishes an obligation of general protection consisting in avoiding deterioration and disturbances which could have significant effects in the light of the Directive's objectives.[553]

552. C-127/02, *Waddenzee,* para. 16.
553. *Ibid.*, para. 38.

The Court concluded that Article 6(3) and 6(2) serve distinct purposes and cannot be applicable concomitantly. Its reasoning was as follows. If a plan or project has undergone an appropriate assessment and the decision of the authorities is fully compatible with Article 6(3) of the Directive (in the sense that the assessment process has ascertained, or the decision has ensured that the plan or project will not adversely affect the integrity of the site concerned), such an application of Article 6(3) satisfies the purpose of protection and, therefore, a concomitant application of Article 6(2) is superfluous.

Thus:

> The fact that a plan or project has been authorised according to the procedure laid down in Article 6(3) of the Habitats Directive renders superfluous, as regards the action to be taken on the protected site under the plan or project, a concomitant application of the rule of general protection laid down in Article 6(2). Authorisation of a plan or project granted in accordance with Article 6(3) of the Habitats Directive necessarily assumes that it is considered not likely adversely to affect the integrity of the site concerned and, consequently, not likely to give rise to deterioration or significant disturbances within the meaning of Article 6(2).[554]

The Court added an important qualification, however, to address the possibility that, notwithstanding a compliant appropriate assessment and the absence of any error by a competent authority under Article 6(3), a plan or project subsequently proves likely to give rise to habitat deterioration or significant species disturbance. In such circumstances, application of Article 6(2) again comes into play, making it possible to 'satisfy the essential objective of the preservation and protection of the quality of the environment, including the conservation of natural habitats and of wild fauna and flora'.[555]

[2] Concomitant Breaches of Article 6(2) and 6(3)

While Case C-127/02, *Waddenzee* establishes that a Member State is not required to apply Article 6(2) concomitantly with Article 6(3) of the Habitats Directive, it does not follow that there cannot be concomitant breaches of both paragraphs. Commission's direct actions against Member States can result in such a finding where the Commission presents evidence of a contravention of Article 6(2), alongside evidence of a contravention of Article 6(3). In particular, the approval of a plan or project in breach of Article 6(3) may be followed by its execution in breach of Article 6(2).

As the Court stated in Case C-304/05, *Commission v. Italy*:

> Where from examination of the first complaint, authorisation for a plan or project has been granted without complying with Article 6(3) of Directive 92/43, a breach of Article 6(2) in relation to a special area of conservation may be found where

554. *Ibid.*, paras 35 and 36.
555. *Ibid.*, para. 37.

deterioration of a habitat or disturbance of the species for which the area in question was designated has been established.[556]

Case C-304/05, *Commission v. Italy* provides a concrete example of Article 6(2) being breached concomitantly with Article 6(3). Having examined the evidence before it, the Court concluded that a project to modify existing ski runs and construct associated facilities had been authorised in breach of Article 6(3) of the Habitats Directive.[557] Furthermore, works to execute the project had actually resulted in the felling of some 2,500 trees in an afforested part of the area concerned, constituting the habitat of several protected species of birds, such as the goshawk, the ptarmigan, the black woodpecker and the black grouse. As the works had destroyed the breeding sites of these species, the conclusion of the Court was that the 'works and their repercussions on SPA IT 2040044 were incompatible with the protective legal status from which that area should have benefited pursuant to Article 6(2) of Directive 92/43'.[558]

[3] Ongoing Nature of the Obligation under Article 6(2)

Case C-304/05, *Commission v. Italy* illustrates why, notwithstanding the intended self-standing role of Article 6(3), Article 6(2) still needs to be borne in mind in relation to plans and projects falling within the scope of Article 6(3).

Furthermore, as has already been noted, when clarifying in Case C-127/02, *Waddenzee*, the relationship between Article 6(2) and Article 6(3), the Court confirmed that Article 6(2) has continued applicability even where a plan or project has been *duly authorised* under Article 6(3). As already mentioned, the Court's rationale was that, in circumstances where, through no one's fault, the application of Article 6(3) fails to ensure the required protective results, the application of Article 6(2) still makes it possible to meet the essential objective of the Habitats Directive.

The same rationale explains why the Court considered Article 6(2) to apply in circumstances where Article 6(3) was inapplicable and a valid prior authorisation was given for a plan or project. Such circumstances can arise, for example, where a plan or project is approved before, but implemented after, the Habitat's Directive takes effect.

For this reason, Article 6(2) must be applied also where an authorisation has been granted *fully,* in accordance with Article 6(3), *but factors not imputable to the authorising authority cause the project or the plan already permitted to start producing adverse effects on the site.* 'Under those conditions, application of Article 6(2) of the Habitats Directive makes it possible to satisfy the essential objective of the preservation and protection of the quality of the environment, including the conservation of natural habitats and of wild fauna and flora, as stated in the first recital in the preamble to that directive.'[559]The Court's position was made clear in relation to the river dredging that featured in Case C-226/08, *Stadt Papenburg.* It confirmed that Article 6(2) operates at

556. C-304/05, *Commission v. Italy,* para. 94.
557. *Ibid.,* para. 71.
558. *Ibid.,* para. 96.
559. C-127/02, *Waddenzee,* para. 37.

the implementation stage of a project which 'was authorised before the system of protection laid down by the Habitats Directive became applicable to the site in question, and accordingly such a project was not subject to the requirements related to the procedure for prior assessment according to Article 6(3)'.[560] In like vein, it confirmed that Article 6(2) applied to the open-cast mines that featured in Case C-404/09, *Commission v. Spain.*[561]

In such cases, where permits were issued before Article 6(3) requirements became applicable (and hence an authorisation compliant with Article 6(3) has not been granted), the scrutiny applied by the Court in relation to compliance with Article 6(2) is rigorous.

In Case C-404/09, *Commission v. Spain,* Article 6(3) was not applicable at the time when open-cast mining activities had been permitted. The Commission pleaded successfully, however, that there was a breach of Article 6(2) since, after the classification of the site as an SPA, an area of 17.92 hectares of Habitat Type 9230 had been destroyed[562] and this was detrimental to a bird species, the capercaillie, requiring protection in the SPA.[563] The Court also found that Spain was in breach of Article 6(2) in respect of the noise and vibrations which the mining operations continued to produce. These were perceptible within the SPA and were 'likely significantly to disturb the capercaillie population protected by virtue of that SPA'.[564]

In Case *C-141/14, Commission v. Bulgaria,* the Court considered whether Article 6(2) could require its national authorities to oppose the actual implementation of a wind farm project authorised before Bulgaria's accession to the EU.[565] As in Case C-404/09, *Commission v. Spain,* it confirmed that Article 6(2) applies to installations where the project was approved before the protection regime became applicable.[566]

In Case C-504/14, *Commission v. Greece,* there was a question about street lighting from restaurants, hotels and shops close to an SCI in the Kyparissia area which disturbed protected sea turtles during egg-laying and affected the newly hatched turtles as they moved towards the sea. Greece advanced the argument that street lighting was in place before such facilities became subject to an appropriate assessment under Article 6(3) of the Habitats Directive. The Court noted that the prohibition on deterioration laid down in the Habitats Directive 'is not limited to an obligation, on the part of the Member State concerned, to prohibit or bring to an end only "new" harmful activities'.[567] It found that since it failed to take the appropriate protective measures to prevent, as of the date when the Kyparissia area was placed on the list of SCIs, existing street lighting from disturbing the sea turtles, Greece had failed to meet its obligations under Article 6(2) of the Habitats Directive.

560. C-226/08, *Stadt Papenburg,* paras 48 and 49.
561. C-404/09, *Commission v. Spain,* paras 124 and 125.
562. *Ibid.,* para. 131.
563. *Ibid.,* paras 132-134.
564. *Ibid.,* para. 136.
565. C-141/14, *Commission v. Bulgaria,* para. 50.
566. *Ibid.,* para. 51.
567. C-504/14, *Commission v. Greece,* para. 100.

[4] Article 6(2) Requirement to Review Certain Previously Approved Plans or Projects

By confirming that, under certain circumstances, Article 6(2) requires a subsequent review of an earlier plan or project, the Court's judgment in Case C-399/14, *Grüne Liga Sachsen* provides further proof of the Court's cohesive approach to Article 6(2) and Article 6(3). It has been observed that this judgment enhances 'the coherence and effectiveness of the regulatory system envisaged under Article 6 of the Habitats Directive'.[568]

The case concerned the approval by a regional German administration of plans for the construction of a road bridge spanning the Elbe, in the city centre of Dresden, and the meadows along its banks. The approval had been preceded by an impact study which, however, the referring court considered to be merely a 'preliminary risk assessment' which did not fulfil the requirements of Article 6(3) and Article 6(4) of the Habitats Directive. A nature protection organisation challenged the original planning approval. It was only after approval of the bridge that the site in question – 'Elbe Valley between Schoena and Muehlberg' – was included in the list of SCIs adopted by the Commission under Article 4 of the Habitats Directive. Construction work began after the site's listing. The regional authority subsequently carried out a new limited assessment of effects to verify, first, whether the project was likely to impact the site in question within the meaning of Article 6(3) and, second, to verify whether the derogatory conditions set under Article 6(4) were met. This resulted in a fresh decision purporting to satisfy Article 6(4). Construction works on the bridge were completed, and the bridge was opened to traffic.

In short, the project was authorised before inclusion of the areas on the SCI list and without undergoing a proper Article 6(3) assessment and was subsequently executed. In the context of an appeal by a nature protection organization against the dismissal of its action by a lower German court, the referring court asked the Court whether the project must undergo a subsequent review of its implications, under Article 6(2) of the Habitats Directive.

In responding, the Court first confirmed that Article 6(2) was applicable. It further confirmed that, under Article 6(2), there was no absolute requirement to carry out a subsequent review of a plan or project already approved before Article 6(3) became applicable. It recalled, nevertheless, that:

> The very existence of a probability or risk that an economic activity on a protected site might cause significant disturbances for a species, is capable of constituting an infringement of Article 6(2) of the Habitats Directive, without a cause and effect relationship between that activity and significant disturbance to the species having to be proved.[569]

568. Lorenzo Squintani, *Assistant Professor of European and Economic Law, University of Groningen, The Netherlands,* 13 The Journal for European Environmental & Planning Law 239-246 (2016).
569. C-399/14, *Grüne Liga Sachsen*, para. 42.

This meant that the *implementation* of a project may be pursued only if the probability or risk is excluded. In this context, the general obligation of protection under Article 6(2) entailed, in certain circumstances, an obligation to carry out a review.

In a similar vein, in Case C-504/14, *Commission v. Greece*, for some projects referred to in the Commission's action, there was no information that these had been authorised and built after the site was listed as an SCI. Temporal applicability of Article 6(2) and (3) was, therefore, uncertain for the buildings concerned. Even so, the Court found that, after the date when the site was listed as an SCI, 'an infringement of Article 6(2) of Directive 92/43 must be found, as the Advocate General has observed in points 55 and 58 of her Opinion, because the Hellenic Republic has not sufficiently circumscribed the use of those buildings ...'.[570] The use of buildings, potentially causing pollution, vibrations, increased human presence and noise and light pollution was also an important element given the sensitivity of the dune habitat located in the Kyparissia area and the high risk of disturbance of protected sea turtles in the breeding period, especially as the buildings were close to nesting areas.

[5] Relevance of Article 6(3) in Situations Where Article 6(2) Requires a Subsequent Review

In Case C-399/14, *Grüne Liga Sachsen*, the referring court also sought clarification on whether, if required under Article 6(2), a subsequent review is needed to satisfy the requirements applicable to an appropriate assessment under Article 6(3).

The Court concluded that it did. It noted that 'the provisions of Article 6(2) and (3) of the Habitats Directive must be construed as a *coherent whole* in the light of the conservation objectives pursued by the directive and that those provisions are designed to ensure the same level of protection of natural habitats and species (emphasis added)'.[571] Therefore, a review required under Article 6(2) of the Habitats Directive 'must be carried out in accordance with the requirements of Article 6(3) of that directive'.[572]

This means that the review must assess all aspects of the plan or project, which can 'either individually or in combination with other plans or projects'[573] affect the protection objectives of the Directive, and 'in the light of the best scientific knowledge in the field'.[574] It must 'not have lacunae and must contain complete, precise and definitive findings and conclusions capable of removing all reasonable scientific doubt as to the effects of the works proposed on the protected site concerned'[575]

As can be inferred from Case-278/21, *Aquapri*, such a new assessment can also be a means of addressing an insufficient consideration of cumulative impacts, as where

570. C-504/14, *Commission v. Greece*, para. 41.
571. C-399/14, *Grüne Liga Sachsen*, para. 52.
572. *Ibid.*, para. 54.
573. *Ibid.*, para. 49.
574. *Ibid.*
575. *Ibid.*, para. 50.

a previous impact assessment only assessed a project individually, disregarding the in-combination effects with other projects.[576]

It has been observed that, in Case C-399/14, *Grüne Liga Sachsen*, the Court has 'basically ensured the full effectiveness of Article 6(3) of the Habitats Directive by means of Article 6(2) thereof'.[577]

[6] Other Circumstances Where Article 6(3) Exerts an Influence on Article 6(2)

Case C-559/19, *Commission v. Spain* ('*Donana*') provides further useful clarification on the influence of Article 6(3) of the Habitats Directive on the fulfilment of obligations under Article 6(2), this time in the context of a direct action by the Commission concerning an alleged breach of Article 6(2) by a Member State.

In its court application, the Commission maintained that, in allowing the over-exploitation of the Almonte-Marismas aquifer and causing the deterioration of natural areas which depend on that aquifer, Spain had failed to adopt appropriate measures to prevent the deterioration of habitats contrary to Article 6(2).

The Court confirmed that, to establish an infringement of Article 6(2), it is sufficient for the Commission to establish that there is *a probability or risk* that the relevant action or inaction of the Member State might cause significant deterioration or disturbance to the habitats or species concerned.[578] The Court was satisfied that, in relation to the level of exploitation of the aquifer, the Commission had established this probability or risk. Moreover, there was evidence of actual deterioration.[579]

The Court went on to note that, in order to invalidate findings of deterioration, Spain should have submitted evidence to remove any reasonable doubt that, from a scientific point of view, continuation of the current practice of groundwater abstraction had no adverse effects. To that end, the Habitats Directive 'requires an examination as to compatibility *such as that which must be carried out under Article 6(3)* of that directive (emphasis added)'.[580]

Thus, in a direct action where a Member State seeks to rebut Commission evidence of non-compliance with Article 6(2), the Court will expect the Member State to satisfy the requirements that apply to the content of an appropriate assessment under Article 6(3).

Overall, 'it is apparent that Article 6(2) must be construed as a "catch all"-clause, encompassing also potential harmful activities which, as such, do not qualify as a

576. C-278/21, *Aquapri*, paras 40 to 43.
577. Lorenzo Squintani, *Assistant Professor of European and Economic Law, University of Groningen, The Netherlands*, 13 The Journal for European Environmental & Planning Law 239-246 (2016).
578. C-559/19, *Donana*, para. 155.
579. *Ibid.*, para. 169.
580. *Ibid.*, para. 170.

"project" under Article 6(3) of the Habitats Directive'.[581] At the same time, it is evident that, even where it is not formally applicable, Article 6(3) exerts an important influence on Article 6(2).

[F] Derogations and Compensatory Measures under Article 6(4)

Article 6(4) of the Directive provides that:

> If, in spite of a negative assessment of the implications for the site and in the absence of alternative solutions, a plan or project must nevertheless be carried out for imperative reasons of overriding public interest, including those of a social or economic nature, the Member State shall take all compensatory measures necessary to ensure that the overall coherence of Natura 2000 is protected. It shall inform the Commission of the compensatory measures adopted.

Furthermore, if the site concerned hosts a priority natural habitat type and/or a priority species:

> The only considerations which may be raised are those relating to human health or public safety, to beneficial consequences of primary importance for the environment or, further to an opinion from the Commission, to other imperative reasons of overriding public interest.

The Birds Directive had not provided for this measure of flexibility to approve a project which was damaging to an SPA where the imperative overriding interest was of a social or economic nature. Indeed, it was the Court's strict interpretation of Article 4(4), first sentence of the Birds Directive in Case C-57/89, *Leybucht Dykes* which prompted the EU legislature to introduce more flexibility through the wording of the derogation possibilities set out in Article 6(4) of the Habitats Directive. By virtue of Article 7 of the Habitats Directive, the derogation possibilities were extended to sites classified under the Birds Directive.

As the Court remarked in Case C-44/95, *Lappel Bank*:

> Article 6(4) of the Habitats Directive, as inserted in the Birds Directive, has, following *Leybucht Dykes* where the point in issue was the reduction of an area already classified, widened the range of grounds justifying encroachment upon SPAs by expressly including therein reasons of a social or economic nature.[582]

It should be stressed that the case-law of the Court has clarified that Article 6(4) cannot be used in the absence of a compliant application of Article 6(3). The two provisions are intrinsically related.

581. Hendrik Schoukens, *Ongoing Activities and Natura 2000 Biodiversity Protection vs Legitimate Expectations?*, 11 The Journal for European Environmental & Planning Law 1-30 (2014) DOI: 10.1163/18760104-01101001.
582. C-44/95, *Lappel Bank*, para. 37.

[1] *Application of Article 6(3): A Prerequisite for Derogations under Article 6(4)*

The proper application of Article 6(3) is essential for authorities wanting to benefit from the derogations allowed under Article 6(4) of the Directive. It is a *sine qua non* condition.

As the Court has noted, 'Article 6(4) of the directive must, as a derogation from the criterion for authorisation laid down in the second sentence of Article 6(3), be interpreted strictly.'[583] It may be observed that the general approach the Court follows is one of strictness in interpreting such derogations.

Thus, Article 6(4) can apply only after the implications of a plan or project have been studied, in accordance with Article 6(3).

Three reasons justify the Court's insistence on strict prior compliance with Article 6(3). First, if a harmful impact has not been properly assessed, one cannot evaluate the sufficiency of imperative reasons of overriding public interest (IROPI) and the existence of less harmful alternatives, which are conditions set down under Article 6(4). Second, Article 6(4) makes a distinction between acceptable imperative reasons according to the type of habitat affected. For priority natural habitat type and/or a priority species, the only considerations which may be raised are those relating to human health or public safety, beneficial consequences of primary importance for the environment or, further to an opinion from the Commission, to other imperative reasons of overriding public interest. It is, therefore, necessary to know whether priority habitats will be adversely affected. Third, in the absence of a proper identification of the damage a plan or project will cause (e.g., the type and area of habitat that will be destroyed or damaged), one cannot establish the extent of the compensation required.

In the ski-run case, C-304/05, *Commission v. Italy,* the Court stated that:

> Knowledge of those implications in the light of the conservation objectives relating to the site in question is a necessary prerequisite for application of Article 6(4) since, in the absence thereof, no condition for application of that derogating provision can be assessed. The assessment of any imperative reasons of overriding public interest and that of the existence of less harmful alternatives require a weighing up against the damage caused to the site by the plan or project under consideration. In addition, in order to determine the nature of any compensatory measures, the damage to the site must be precisely identified.[584]

This position of the Court underlines the importance of the authorities, having the necessary and complete information, on the impact of the project in order to perform such an analysis and to weigh the project against other considerations.

This information has to be acquired by the authorities *before* the time of the decision to grant the authorisation. Thus, in Case C-239/04, *Commission v. Portugal* ('Castro Verde'), the Court stated that 'the fact that, after its completion, the project

583. C-304/05, *Commission v. Italy,* para. 82; *see also* C-239/04, *Castro Verde,* paras 35 and 36.
584. C-304/05, *Commission v. Italy,* para. 83.

may not have produced such effects is immaterial to that assessment. It is at the time of adoption of the decision authorising implementation of the project that there must be no reasonable scientific doubt remaining as to the absence of adverse effects on the integrity of the site in question'.[585]

In response to questions from the referring court in Case C-411/19, *WWF Italia*, the Court clarified first that Article 6(4) derogations could be applied in this case via the approval by the Italian Council of Ministers, in spite of a negative opinion by the environmental competent authorities under Article 6(3), if there is no alternative solution less harmful to the integrity of the Natura 2000 areas concerned. At the same time, it clarified that even if the Member States have discretion in designating the authorities responsible for the Article 6(3) assessment, the authorities cannot continue supplementing that assessment once performed precisely because the assessment must be complete and precise. The underlying rationale is to isolate obligations under Article 6(3) and 6(4) respectively in such a manner as to ensure that each of the requirements prescribed in these provisions are fully met and not circumvented by procedures that would tend to mix the two processes.

[2] Obligation to Study Alternative Solutions

Satisfying the above conditions concerning Article 6(3) is necessary but not sufficient. By virtue of Article 6(4), competent authorities are also under an obligation to demonstrate the absence of alternative solutions.

The Court has demonstrated that it will strictly scrutinise the fulfilment of this condition.

[a] Requirement May Be Breached if Alternatives Studied Are Geographically Too Restricted

In Case C-239/04, *Castro Verde*, the Commission asked the Court to declare that, by implementing a motorway project from Lisbon to the Algarve Region, whose route crossed the Castro Verde SPA, notwithstanding its negative effects and the existence of alternative solutions, Portugal had infringed Article 6(4) of the Habitats Directive. The Commission considered that there was an alternative route which would have by-passed the SPA and avoided negative impacts. In view of the implications for the SPA, the Court took the view that, if it were to be authorised in accordance with the Habitats Directive, the motorway project needed to satisfy the conditions of Article 6(4), including the condition concerning alternative solutions. In this regard, the Court held that it was not sufficient for the Portuguese authorities to demonstrate that they had studied alternative solutions *within* the boundaries of the site affected.

585. C-239/04, *Castro Verde*, para. 24.

It was not apparent that:

> those authorities examined solutions falling outside that SPA and to the west of the settlements referred to above, although, on the basis of information supplied by the Commission, it cannot be ruled out immediately that such solutions were capable of amounting to alternative solutions within the meaning of Article 6(4) of the Habitats Directive, even if they were, as asserted by the Portuguese Republic, liable to present certain difficulties.[586]

The Court therefore upheld the Commission's action.

[b] Less Disadvantageous Criterion

In Case C-411/19, *WWF Italia,* the Court again looked at the issue of alternative solutions in the context of a road construction project, this time an 18-kilometre road link using a 'green route' between Monte Romano Est and Targuinia Sud in the Lazio Region of Italy. This 'green route' was approved by Italian decision-makers in two different procedural stages in 2017 and 2018, although, previously, the Italian Environment Ministry had approved an alternative 'violet route' and had issued a negative opinion on the 'green route' on account of its negative environmental impact. In national court proceedings, the approvals given to the 'green route' were contested by several environmental associations and the referring court sought guidance from the Court on how to examine the choice made in favour of the 'green route' in light of the Article 6(4) reference to absence of alternative solutions.[587]

The referring court stated that 'the imperative reasons of overriding public interest relied upon in relation to the "green route" concern the lower cost of the works, the fact that it satisfies landscaping, historical, cultural and socio-economic protection considerations and the need to complete the trans-European road network'.

In its response, the Court stated that, account being taken of the strict interpretation of Article 6(4):

> It cannot be accepted that the economic cost alone of the measures capable of being considered in the review of alternatives may be a determining factor in the choice of alternative solutions under that provision.[588]

It was for the referring court to determine whether the 'violet route' should be regarded as an alternative solution which is *less disadvantageous* for the integrity of the SAC concerned than the 'green route'. The notion of a less disadvantageous alternative found its way into the operative part of the ruling in Case 411/19, *WWF Italia,* the Court stating that Article 6 does not preclude a project from continuing for imperative reasons of overriding public interest, when a negative opinion was expressed by the competent

586. *Ibid.*, para. 38.
587. C-411/19, *WWF Italia,* para. 39.
588. C-411/19, *WWF Italia,* para. 41.

authorities, 'unless there is an alternative solution with fewer disadvantages for the integrity of the area concerned, which it falls to the referring court to verify'.[589]

[3] Notion of 'Imperative Reasons of Overriding Public Interest'

The first subparagraph of Article 6(4) of the Habitats Directive allows for the approval of a plan or project if this is necessary for 'imperative reasons of overriding public interest, including those of a social or economic nature'. This is sometimes referred to as 'IROPI'. According to the second subparagraph of Article 6(4), if the site concerned hosts a priority natural habitat type or a priority species, the only considerations which may be raised are those relating to human health or public safety, or beneficial consequences of primary importance for the environment or, further to an opinion from the Commission, to other IROPI.[590]

The Court has clarified the notion of imperative reasons of overriding public interest in light of several specific circumstances.

[a] Interest Must Be Both Public and Overriding

In Case C-43/10, *Acheloos*, the Court stated that an interest capable of justifying proceeding with a plan or project must be both 'public' and 'overriding', 'which means that it must be of such an importance that it can be weighed against that directive's objective of the conservation of natural habitats and wild fauna, including birds, and flora'.[591]

[b] Irrigation and Supply of Drinking Water

That case concerned the proposed diversion of water from the River Acheloos in Greece on grounds linked to irrigation and the supply of drinking water. The Court accepted that both grounds would meet the condition of overriding public interest for purposes of the first subparagraph of Article 6(4).[592] With reference to the second subparagraph, there was no Article 6(4) opinion of the Commission for the Court to consider. In its absence, the Court found that the supply of drinking water would satisfy the criterion of public health. By contrast, irrigation would neither satisfy this criterion nor the criterion of public safety, although it was plausible that it might satisfy the criterion of 'beneficial consequences of primary importance for the environment'.[593]

---

589. C-411/19, *WWF Italia*, operative part of judgment, para. 1.
590. For a detailed account of Commission opinions given under Article 6(4), *see* Agustín García Ureta, *EU Biodiversity Law: Wild Birds and Habitats Directives*, 320-328 (Europa Law Publishing 2020). *See also* Christoph Sobotta, *The Margin of Appreciation When Applying Article 6(3) and (4) of the Habitats Directive*, 85, in *Nature Law and Policy in Europe*, Chapter 5 (Andrew L.R. Jackson ed., Routledge 20).
591. C-43/10, *Acheloos*, para. 121.
592. *Ibid.*, para. 122.
593. *Ibid.*, paras 125 and 126.

[c] *Security of Energy Supply*

In the Belgian nuclear power plant case, C-411/17, *Doel*, the Court considered the question of whether the security of a Member State's electricity supply constitutes an imperative reason of overriding public interest within the meaning of the first subparagraph of Article 6(4) of the Habitats Directive.[594] Its reply was positive. The Court referred to Article 194(1)(b) TFEU which identifies security of energy supply in the EU as one of the fundamental objectives of EU policy in the field of energy[595] to conclude that the objective of ensuring the security of electricity supply in a Member State, at all times, meets the condition set under the first subparagraph of Article 6(4).[596]

In Case C-411/17, *Doel*, however, the Court introduced a qualification in respect of the second subparagraph of Article 6(4). If the protected site likely to be affected by the prolongation of the life duration of the nuclear power plants hosted a priority natural habitat type or species as defined by the Habitats Directive, under the second subparagraph of Article 6(4), the only public security ground that would justify proceeding with the project is 'the need to nullify a genuine and serious threat of rupture of that Member State's electricity supply'.[597]

[d] *Infrastructure for a Private Company*

In Case C-182/10,[598] *Solvay*, the Court was asked to rule on whether the notion of IROPI could permit the creation of infrastructure designed to accommodate the management centre of a private company.[599] The context was one in which the Walloon Region had permitted airport and train infrastructure by decree and the management centre was included in the decree. In response, the Court recalled that, to satisfy Article 6(4), the interest must be both 'public' and 'overriding'. It stated that 'works intended for the location or expansion of an undertaking satisfy those conditions only in exceptional circumstances'.[600] It went on to note that it cannot be ruled out that that is the case where a project, although 'of a private character, in fact by its very nature and by its economic and social context presents an overriding public interest and it has been shown that there are no alternative solutions'.[601]

Applying those criteria, however, it concluded that 'the mere construction of infrastructure designed to accommodate a management centre cannot constitute an imperative reason of overriding public interest within the meaning of Article 6(4) of the Habitats Directive'.[602]

594. Question 8(d) of the referring court.
595. C-411/17, *Doel*, para. 156.
596. *Ibid.*, paras 155 and 157.
597. *Ibid.*, para. 159.
598. C-182/10, para. 76.
599. Question 6 of the referring court.
600. C-182/10, *Solvay*, para. 76.
601. *Ibid.*, para. 77.
602. *Ibid.*, para. 78.

[4] Compensation Measures Within or Outside the Natura 2000 Site Affected

As indicated, under certain conditions, Article 6(4) allows the competent authorities to authorise a plan or project in spite of its negative impact on the Natura 2000 site. They must, however, take all the necessary compensatory measures.

In any determination of what constitutes acceptable compensatory measures, the criterion to be applied is the protection of the overall coherence of the Natura 2000 network, independently of the location. As the Court observed in Case C-521/12, *Briels*:

> Article 6(4) of the Habitats Directive covers any measure liable to protect the overall coherence of Natura 2000, *whether it is implemented within the affected site or in another part of the Natura 2000* network (emphasis added).[603]

[G] Challenging and Rectifying Infringements of Article 6(2), (3) and (4) at National Level

Many of the cases already cited in this and other chapters have related to divergent interpretations - either between those of the Member States and those of the Commission, or between those of Member State authorities and those of third parties, such as environmental associations - on which the Court has been asked to take a position. In many cases too, national decisions will have been taken - and sometimes facts created on the ground - which turn out to be inconsistent with the requirements of the applicable protection regimes as interpreted by the Court. This inevitably raises ancillary issues of how national courts - and national authorities - should address the resulting infringements not only in relation to the environment but also in relation to other interests.

[1] General Role of National Courts

Rules of national law implementing EU environmental law and the rules of EU environmental law having direct effect must be able to be relied upon in legal proceedings.[604]

National judges, as EU law judges[605] must contribute to the control of the exercise of the margin of discretion of national authorities, when applying Article 6(3) of the Habitats Directive, for instance.

Thus, 'Article 6(3) of the Habitats Directive may be taken into account by the national court in determining whether a national authority which has granted an

603. C-521/12, *Briels,* para. 38.
604. C-243/15, *LZ II,* para. 59; and by analogy, in respect of Article 10a of Directive 85/337, C-137/14, *Commission v. Germany*, para. 92.
605. C-70/77, *Simmenthal.*

authorisation relating to a plan or project has kept within the limits of the discretion set by the provision in question.'[606]

This also applies in the context of a lack of/or deficient transposition into national law:

> where a national court is called on to ascertain the lawfulness of an authorisation for a plan or project within the meaning of Article 6(3) of the Habitats Directive, it can determine whether the limits on the discretion of the competent national authorities set by that provision have been complied with, even though it has not been transposed into the legal order of the Member State concerned despite the expiry of the time limit laid down for that purpose.[607]

[2] Entitlement of Environmental Associations to Contest the Application of Article 6(3) of the Habitats Directive

For a national court to exercise a role in relation to infringements of Article 6, it must, of course, be seized with a case. As is also explained in Chapter 8, §8.06, the Court has developed important case-law on access to justice in relation to the nature directives.

It is unsurprising that the nature case-law should feature cases in which landowners and economic operators contest aspects of implementation that they consider detrimental to their property or economic interests. An example is Case C-278/21, *Aquapri*, discussed at §3.04[G][4] below.

Landowners and economic operators may not have an interest in challenging decisions, acts or omissions which are detrimental to nature as such, however. Challenges to these may depend on the willingness and entitlement of environmental associations to intervene. The case-law shows that, in some jurisdictions, it was possible for environmental associations to bring judicial challenges from the outset – *see*, for example, Case C-44/95, *Lappel Bank*, which was initiated by a British environmental association. During this earlier period, however, some Member States had very restrictive rules on standing which made it impossible or excessively difficult for environmental associations to intervene.

[a] Value of the Access-to-Justice Provisions in the EIA Directive

In 2005, new access-to-justice provisions in the EIA Directive took effect and these provided a mechanism for environmental associations to challenge compliance with Article 6(3) of the Habitats Directive, where the project concerned was subject to an EIA under the EIA Directive.

The value of the new provisions was demonstrated in Case C-115/09, *Trianel*. This case arose from a legal challenge made by an environmental association, Friends of the Earth, to a coal-fired power station in Lünen in Germany. Friends of the Earth

606. C-127/02, *Waddenzee*, para. 59.
607. *Ibid.*, para. 70.

argued that the EIA undertaken for the project did not satisfy the requirements of Article 6(3) of the Habitats Directive since it did not show that the power station was unlikely to have a significant effect on nearby SACs. German law presented Friends of the Earth with a procedural barrier, however.

Its action was dismissed as the general rules of administrative procedural law provided that 'an action challenging an administrative measure will be admissible only if the administrative measure affects the claimant's rights, that is to say, his individual public law rights',[608] while the relevant national provisions for the protection of nature primarily concerned the general public and not the protection of individual rights. The fact that this restriction based on the requirement of individual concern was likely to undermine the useful effect of the access-to-justice provision of the EIA Directive – i.e., Article 10a of Directive 85/337 as it then was[609] – led the national court to address a preliminary reference to the Court. The Court's reply was clear: although it is for the Member States to determine what rights can give rise, when infringed, to an action concerning the environment, they cannot deprive environmental associations which fulfil the conditions laid down in Article 1(2) of the EIA Directive of the opportunity of playing the role granted to them both by Directive 85/337/EEC and by the Aarhus Convention.[610]

Thanks to Case C-115/09, *Trianel*, the access-to-justice provisions of the EIA Directive preclude national legislation which does not permit an environmental association from relying in litigation based on the EIA Directive on a rule – such as that enshrined in Article 6(3) of the Habitats Directive – which protects only the interests of the general public and not the interests of individuals.[611]

[b] Access to Justice Rights Based on the Aarhus Convention and Article 47 of the Charter

As previously noted, however, the notion of 'project' under the Habitats Directive is broader than that of 'project' under the EIA Directive, and it took another case to establish an environmental association's entitlement to challenge a project that fell outside the scope of the EIA Directive. This was Case C-243/15, *LZ II*, already referred to above in section §3.04[D][19] in relation to public participation rights linked to Article 6(3).

The plaintiff, a Slovak environmental association, 'LZ' was notified of an administrative procedure initiated by the district authority of Trenčín, concerning an application submitted by a company breeding deer for hunting purposes, 'in order to obtain authorisation of a project relating to the construction of an enclosure, for the purpose of extending a deer reserve'.[612] The construction of the enclosure was to be

608. C-115/09, *Trianel*, para. 29.
609. Repealed in the meantime by Directive 2011/92/EU. Article 10a of Directive 85/337/EEC has become Article 11 of Directive 2011/92/EU.
610. C-115/09, *Trianel*, para. 44.
611. *Ibid.*, para. 50.
612. C-243/15, *LZ II*, para. 19.

done on land plots located in a site classified as an SPA and, at the time, listed as an SCI. LZ made subsequent enquiries in order to obtain information and requested that the procedure be stayed. It was denied the status of 'party to the procedure', however, because, under Slovak law, it could only have the status of 'interested person'.[613] The environmental association challenged this through an administrative appeal, without success, and the permit for the enclosure was granted.

This denial of the status of 'party to the procedure' also had an impact on the ability of LZ to challenge the final decision before a national court, in particular its ability to contest the permit as being contrary to Article 6(3) of the Habitats Directive.[614] Under Slovak law, the action against the decision denying the association the status of party to the procedure did not necessarily have to be examined during the course of the permitting procedure, which could be definitively concluded before a definitive judicial decision on the issue of party status. LZ's action, moreover, was automatically dismissed as soon as the project was authorised, thereby requiring the association to bring 'an action of another type in order to obtain that status and to secure judicial review of compliance by the competent national authorities with their obligations stemming from Article 6(3)'.[615]

The Court ultimately found that EU law precluded an interpretation of rules of national procedural law that resulted in these kinds of barriers to the environmental association concerned being able to effectively invoke Article 6(3) of the Habitats Directive before a national court.

To reach this conclusion, the Court proceeded, step-wise, to establish that LZ had a right to participate in Article 6(3) decision-making and that there were ancillary access to justice rights under EU law:

(1) It would be incompatible with the binding effect attributed to a directive by the Treaty[616] to exclude the possibility for those concerned to rely on the obligations it imposes. The effectiveness of the Habitats Directive and its aim 'require that individuals be able to rely on it in legal proceedings, and that the national courts be able to take that directive into consideration as an element of EU law in order, inter alia, to review whether a national authority which has granted an authorisation relating to a plan or project has complied with its obligations under Article 6(3) of the directive... and has thus kept within the

613. *Ibid.*, para. 22.
614. *Ibid.*, para. 41.
615. *Ibid.*, para. 39.
616. Article 288 TFEU reads as follows: 'To exercise the Union's competences, the institutions shall adopt regulations, directives, decisions, recommendations and opinions. A regulation shall have general application. It shall be binding in its entirety and directly applicable in all Member States. A directive shall be binding, as to the result to be achieved, upon each Member State to which it is addressed, but shall leave to the national authorities the choice of form and methods. A decision shall be binding in its entirety. A decision which specifies those to whom it is addressed shall be binding only on them. Recommendations and opinions shall have no binding force.'

limits of the discretion granted to the competent national authorities by that provision'.[617]

(2) Article 6(3) of the Habitats Directive provides that the competent national authorities, before agreeing to a plan or project as referred to in that provision, must, if appropriate, obtain the opinion of the general public. That provision must be read in conjunction with Article 6(1)(b) of the Aarhus Convention, an instrument which forms an integral part of the EU legal order.[618]

(3) An environmental association which, like LZ, meets the conditions specified in Article 2(5) of the Aarhus Convention derives from Article 6(3) of the Habitats Directive, read in conjunction with Article 6(1)(b) of the Convention, *a right to participate* in a procedure for the adoption of a decision relating to an application for authorisation of a plan or project likely to have a significant effect on the environment in so far as, within the framework of that procedure, one of the decisions envisaged in Article 6(3) of the directive is to be adopted.[619]

(4) Article 47 of the Charter of Fundamental Rights, which enshrines the right to an effective remedy and to a fair hearing, is applicable in this context.[620]

(5) Article 9(2) of the Aarhus Convention grants access to a review procedure to environmental associations, such as LZ which meet the conditions set out in Article 2(5) of the Convention in so far as the review is of a decision which falls within the scope of Article 9(2).[621]

(6) The rights on which an environmental association must be able to rely in an action covered by Article 9(2) of the Aarhus Convention include the rules of national law flowing from Article 6 of the Habitats Directive.[622]

(7) An environmental association must be able to challenge, in such an action, not only a decision not to carry out an appropriate assessment of the implications for the site of the plan or project in question but also, as the case may be, the assessment carried out inasmuch as it is alleged to be vitiated by defects.[623]

617. C-243/15, *LZ II*, para. 44; *see also* C-127/02, *Waddenzee*, paras 66 and 69.
618. C-243/15, *LZ II*, para. 45.
619. *Ibid.*, para. 49.
620. *Ibid.*, paras 51 to 53. *See* in particular para. 51 where the Court states: 'The scope of Article 47 of the Charter, in so far as the action of the Member States is concerned, is defined in Article 51(1) thereof, according to which the provisions of the Charter are addressed to the Member States when they are implementing EU law. That provision confirms the Court's settled case-law, which states that the fundamental rights guaranteed in the legal order of the European Union are applicable in all situations governed by EU law, but not outside such situations (*see*, in particular, judgment of 30 June 2016, Toma and Biroul Executorului Judecatoresc Horaţiu-Vasile Cruduleci, C205/15, EU:C:2016:499, paragraph 23 and the case-law cited).'
621. C-243/15, *LZ II*, para. 55.
622. *Ibid.*, para. 60.
623. *Ibid.*, para. 61.

The Court went on to examine the Slovak procedural rules in light of Article 9(2) of the Aarhus Convention, Article 9(4) of the Aarhus Convention – which requires review procedures under Article 9(2) to provide 'adequate and effective remedies' – and Article 47 of the Charter. It took the view that, in the restrictive way in which they had been interpreted to the disadvantage of LZ, the national procedural rules were indeed unsatisfactory and contrary to EU law.[624]

[c] Legislation on Access to Justice Must Be Clear and Precise

Case C-243/15, *LZ II*, provided national courts with a basis for ensuring that environmental associations could obtain judicial review in respect of Article 6(3) of the Habitats Directive, notwithstanding restrictive national procedural rules on standing. The possibility existed, however, that national courts would still apply such restrictive national rules, denying environmental associations a hearing.

In Case C-432/21, *Commission v. Poland*, the Court took a further step towards ensuring access to justice for environmental associations by ruling that Polish procedural rules denying such access infringed EU law. The Commission had complained that Poland's Law on forests conferred only an internal character on forest management plans. An act approving such a plan did not have the nature of an administrative decision, an interpretation confirmed by Poland's Supreme Administrative Court. The result was that any legal action by an environmental association to challenge such an act was treated as inadmissible by the Polish administrative courts.[625]

The Court found that Article 6(3) of the Habitats Directive, read in conjunction with Article 6(1)(b) and Article 9(2) of the Aarhus Convention, imposed an obligation on Poland to ensure that environmental associations are able to apply to a court for effective review of the substantive and procedural legality of forest management plans, within the meaning of the provisions of the Law on forests, in so far as those plans fall within the scope of Article 6(3) of the Habitats Directive.[626]

Crucially, the Court considered that:

> Legislation providing for such access to a court must satisfy the requirements of *clarity and precision* laid down in the field of environmental law in accordance with the case-law of the Court.[627]

It held that the Polish legislation did not satisfy these requirements.[628]

The Court was not convinced by an argument by Poland that one lower administrative court had ruled that access to justice could be provided under the national procedural rules concerned, observing that:

> Where national legislation has been the subject of different relevant judicial constructions, some leading to the application of that legislation in compliance

624. *Ibid.*, para. 72.
625. C-432/21, *Commission v. Poland*, paras 115 to 117.
626. *Ibid.*, para. 176.
627. *Ibid.*, para. 177.
628. *Ibid.*, para. 178.

> with EU law, others leading to the opposite application, it must be held that, at the very least, such legislation is not sufficiently clear to ensure its application in compliance with EU law.[629]

[3] Obligation on Authorities and Courts to Eliminate the Unlawful Consequences of EU Law Infringements

What ought to be done if a consent process is found to have infringed Article 6(3)? And, by extension, what ought to be done if other infringements of Article 6 arise? The essential obligation is to eliminate ('nullify' is sometimes the expression used) the unlawful consequences of the decision, act or omission concerned.

In the Belgian nuclear power plant case, C-411/17, *Doel,* this obligation was confirmed as applicable in the context of Article 6.

The referring court had asked for clarification on how it should address the possibility that the national legislation at the heart of the case had infringed EU environmental law.[630] The Court treated this as, in essence, a question of whether EU law allows a national court to maintain the effects of the measures at issue (i.e., the national legislation) for the time necessary to remedy any infringement of the EIA Directive and Habitats Directive.

In answering the question, the Court recalled previous case-law on the matter. It noted that, under the principle of sincere cooperation laid down in Article 4(3) TEU, Member States are required to *nullify the unlawful consequences* of an infringement of EU law.[631] The competent national authorities are under an obligation, within the sphere of their competence, to remedy the failure to carry out an assessment [under the EIA Directive] 'for example by revoking or suspending consent already granted in order to carry out such an assessment'.[632]

National courts are also bound by this obligation. Whenever an action against a national measure including such consent has been brought before them, they must adopt measures to *suspend or annul* the project adopted in breach of the obligation to carry out an environmental assessment.[633]

Under the principle of procedural autonomy of the Member States, the detailed procedural rules applicable to such actions are a matter for the domestic legal order of each Member State, 'provided that they are not less favourable than those governing similar domestic situations (the principle of equivalence) and that they do not render impossible in practice or excessively difficult the exercise of rights conferred by the European Union legal order (the principle of effectiveness)'.[634]

'Nullify', i.e., 'eliminate', may imply different remedies depending on consequences that have arisen. The consequences may, for example, include a procedural

629. *Ibid.*, para. 182.
630. Question 9 of the reference.
631. C-411/17, *Doel,* para. 170.
632. *Ibid.*
633. *Ibid.*, para. 172.
634. *Ibid.*, para. 171; C-41/11, *Inter-Environnement Wallonie,* para. 45.

failure to carry out an appropriate assessment to the requisite standard; the grant of a flawed consent; the execution of works which result in detrimental effects on a Natura 2000 site; continuing harmful pollution or damage from an ongoing activity that was not – and is not – made subject to the requirements of Article 6.

This range of circumstances may entail one or more of the following measures having to be considered: the reopening of decisions and the conduct of new assessments; the adoption of new environmental protection measures; and the removal of unlawful works.

There may, at the same time, be issues surrounding the reliance already placed on unlawful decisions by economic operators, and the scope to retain some of the effects of unlawful decisions.

[4] Appropriate Measures to Address an Infringement of Article 6(3)

In Case C-278/21, *Aquapri*, the Court referred to several appropriate measures for addressing an infringement of Article 6(3).

The circumstances concerned a fish-farm, owned by Aquapri, situated near a Danish Natura 2000 site. The fish-farm had been installed and commenced operating under a permit granted in 1999. In 2006, Aquapri sought and was given an authorisation to increase its nitrogen emissions. The competent authority did not consider that any significant effects on the Natura 2000 site were likely. That authorisation was appealed and the review body found that the assessment was flawed because it had not taken account of proposed increased nitrogen emissions from three neighbouring fish-farms. It did not, however, consider that the defect justified annulling the decision.

In 2014, Aquapri required and was given a fresh authorisation on the basis that its nitrogen emissions would remain unchanged compared to 2006 and that, in the meantime, an assessment had found that the fish-farm operation and the three neighbouring operations, considered in combination, were not likely to have a significant effect on the Natura 2000 site. This 2014 authorisation was annulled on appeal. The appeals body found that the 2006 authorisation had not been preceded by an assessment that complied with Article 6(3) of the Habitats Directive. It also concluded that the amount of nitrogen emitted from the four fish-farms was likely to have significant effects on the Natura 2000 site.

Aquapri's appeal against this annulment led to the preliminary reference.

The Court treated the referring court's first question as asking, in essence:

> Whether the first sentence of Article 6(3) of Directive 92/43 must be interpreted as meaning that the continuation, under unchanged conditions, of the activity of an operation which has already been authorised at the planning stage must be subject to the assessment obligation laid down in that provision where, first, the assessment which preceded that authorisation related solely to the impact of that project considered individually, disregarding its combination with other projects, and second, that authorisation makes the continuation of that activity subject to a new authorisation provided or by national law.[635]

635. C-278/21, *Aquapri*, para. 28.

While accepting, subject to verification by the referring court, that the fish-farm operation was continuing and did not constitute a new or separate project requiring a new Article 6(3) assessment, the Court stressed the need to draw legal consequences from any previous infringement of Article 6(3).[636] Recalling, as it had in Case C-411/17, *Doel*, the general obligation of the Member State to eliminate the consequences of any breach 'by taking all measures necessary within the sphere of its competence to remedy it',[637] the Court drew attention to several appropriate measures to address a breach of Article 6(3).

[a] Article 6(2) Review

Where a project has been authorised following an assessment which does not comply with the requirements of the first sentence of Article 6(3), the competent national authority must carry out a subsequent review of the effects of the implementation of that project on the site concerned, on the basis of Article 6(2) of that directive, if that review constitutes the only appropriate measure for avoiding that implementation from leading to deterioration or disturbance that could have had a significant effect on the site concerned.[638]

[b] Revocation or Suspension of an Authorisation

EU law does not preclude a national authority from revoking or suspending the authorisation already granted in order to carry out a new assessment in accordance with the applicable requirements, provided that those measures take place within a reasonable period of time and that account is taken of the extent to which the person concerned may have been able to rely on the lawfulness of that authorisation.[639]

[c] Regularisation

It is also permissible under EU law, in certain exceptional cases provided for by the applicable rules of national law, for the competent authority to regularise a non-compliant situation, which must then not only comply with applicable requirements but also take place under conditions which exclude any risk of circumvention or non-application of the rules of EU law.[640] In this context, the Court cited its EIA case-law on regularisation, set out in Case C-261/18, *Commission v. Ireland* (*'Derrybrien'*).[641]

636. *Ibid.*, para. 38.
637. *Ibid.*, para. 39.
638. *Ibid.*, para. 40.
639. *Ibid.*, para. 42.
640. *Ibid.*
641. C-261/18, *Derrybrien*, paras 75 to 77.

[d] New Authorisation

'Furthermore, where a Member State has provided, either in a measure of general scope, or in a measure of individual scope, that the continuation of an activity already authorised must be the subject of a new authorisation, the competent national authority is required to make that authorisation subject to a new assessment in accordance with the requirements of the first sentence of Article 6(3) of the Habitats Directive, where it appears that that activity has not yet been the subject of such a compliant assessment, in which case that authority will have to draw all the factual and legal consequences which that new assessment entails in the context of the decision which it is called upon to adopt on any new authorisation to be granted.'[642]

The referring court asked whether a national river basin management plan under the Water Framework Directive[643] which had also addressed nitrogen could be taken into account in a new assessment to remedy the failure to comply with Article 6(3). The Court confirmed that account must be taken of the assessments carried out since the flawed Article 6(3) assessment was undertaken, such as those preceding the adoption of a national river basin management plan and a Natura 2000 plan, covering, *inter alia*, the area in which the site likely to be affected by that activity is situated, if those earlier assessments are relevant and if the findings, assessments and conclusions contained therein are complete, accurate and definitive. In reaching this conclusion, the Court was cautious, referring to the need to take account of any possible change in the scientific and environmental data since the previous assessments[644] and also of potential new projects that should be considered in light of potential cumulative effects. The guiding criterion was the need to 'rule out the existence of a likelihood or risk of significant adverse effects'.[645]

[5] *Interaction of Article 6(2), 6(3) and 6(4) of the Habitats Directive: Measures Such as Demolition of a Project*

As already noted, the requirements of Article 6(3) cannot be isolated from those of Article 6(2) and Article 6(4). All need to be read as forming a coherent whole. This has implications where an infringement of Article 6(3) is accompanied by an infringement of Article 6(4) and Article 6(2), in particular, where a project or activity is unlawfully approved and then causes a significant negative effect on a Natura 2000 site without any compensatory measures having been taken.

This scenario was addressed in Case C-399/14, *Grüne Liga Sachsen*, which, as previously noted, concerned the construction of a bridge without a compliant prior Article 6(3) assessment. As is evident from its fourth question to the Court, the

642. C-278/21, *Aquapri*, para. 43.
643. Directive 2000/60/EC of the European Parliament and of the Council of 23 October 2000 establishing a framework for Community action in the field of water policy, OJ L 327, 22.12.2000, p. 1-73.
644. C-278/21, *Aquapri*, para. 52.
645. *Ibid.*

referring court was exercised by the possible radical implications of reopening the consideration of a project which was already built and in use.

With regard to the requirement in Article 6(4) to examine alternative solutions, the referring court wondered whether, in any new assessment [required pursuant to Article 6(2)], it was permissible to incorporate into the examination of alternatives also the costs, ecological implications, particularly for the habitats and species protected under the Habitats Directive, and the economic consequences of removing a structure the construction of which has already been authorised and completed.

In its response, the Court made the following points:

(1) A subsequent review under Article 6(2) of the Habitats Directive must meet the requirements of Article 6(3).[646]
(2) Those requirements may not be amended solely because the structure in question was constructed in accordance with national procedural law.[647]
(3) The effectiveness of the Habitats Directive would be compromised if national procedural law could be used to curtail the need to comply with its requirements.[648]
(4) A new assessment of the implications for the site concerned of a plan or project already implemented must take into account the assumption that the risks of deterioration or disturbance that could be significant, within the meaning of Article 6(2) of the Habitats Directive, have already appeared on account of the completion of the works in question. In addition, that assessment must enable it to be established whether such risks are likely to materialise if those works continue to be used.[649]
(5) Should a new assessment conclude that the construction or entry into service of the bridge has already caused or risks causing deterioration or disturbance, Article 6(4) of the Habitats Directive might still be applied by analogy.[650]

The Court went on to explain how Article 6(4) could be applied by analogy. Its position was strict but it recognised the need to take account of the reality of the bridge that had come into being. The following are key points in its ruling:

(1) The search for an alternative may not disregard any deterioration or disturbance caused by the construction and entry into service of the bridge or any advantages it offers.[651]
(2) The examination of alternative solutions requires weighing the environmental consequences of maintaining or restricting the use of the works at issue,

646. C-399/14, *Grüne Liga Sachsen*, para. 67.
647. *Ibid.*, para. 68.
648. *Ibid.*, para. 69.
649. *Ibid.*, para. 70.
650. *Ibid.*, para. 71.
651. *Ibid.*, para. 74.

including closure or even demolition, on the one hand, against the important public interest that led to their construction, on the other.[652]

(3) If steps such as demolition were considered in the review of alternatives and if those steps themselves were to entail risks of deterioration or disturbance, those steps could not be regarded as an alternative solution within the meaning of Article 6(4).[653]

(4) Should the conclusion be that the works already completed must be demolished, any demolition proposal must itself be considered a 'plan or project' for purposes of Article 6(3) and undergo an appropriate assessment.[654]

As for the economic cost of demolition, that was not of equal importance to the objective of conserving natural habitats and wild fauna and flora pursued by the Habitats Directive. For this reason, the Court did not accept that the economic cost of such measures alone may be a determining factor in the choice of alternative solutions under Article 6(4).[655]

According to Lorenzo Squintani:

> Considering that the demolition of a completed construction is an option according to the Court of Justice, it would be relevant to research whether Member States and undertakings will wait the closure of the judicial review phase before starting implementing a project authorised despite a potential breach of Article 6(3) of the Directive.[656]

[6] The Possibility of Maintaining Some of the Effects of a Permit Issued in Breach of EU Law

As already mentioned, in Case C-411/17, *Doel,* the referring court raised the possibility of maintaining some of the effects of the contested national legislation if it was found to be unlawful. The Court accepted such a possibility.

On a case-by-case basis and by way of exception, a national court can adjust the effects of the annulment of a national provision held to be incompatible with EU law and thus maintain certain effects of the annulled national measure. This has to be done with due consideration for the conditions laid down by the Court's case-law,[657] and it is for the Court alone to determine the conditions and circumstances in which it may be justifiable to maintain the effects of measures taken in breach of EU law.[658]

652. *Ibid.*
653. *Ibid.*, para. 75.
654. *Ibid.*, para. 76.
655. *Ibid.*, para. 77.
656. Lorenzo Squintani, *Assistant Professor of European and Economic Law, University of Groningen, The Netherlands*, 13 The Journal for European Environmental & Planning Law 239-246 (2016).
657. C-379/15, *Association France Nature Environnement,* paras 34 and 37-40.
658. C-411/17, *Doel,* para. 179.

In Case C-411/17, *Doel*, the Court found that the maintenance of effects could be possible in the presence of an 'overriding consideration relating to the protection of the environment',[659] or 'on account of overriding considerations relating to the security of the electricity supply of the Member State concerned'.[660] With regard to the latter, security of energy supply could justify maintaining the effects of national measures adopted in breach of the obligations under the EIA Directive and the Habitats Directive 'only if, in the event that the effects of those measure were annulled or suspended, there was a genuine and serious threat of disruption to the electricity supply of the Member State concerned, which could not be remedied by any other means or alternatives, particularly in the context of the internal market'.[661] Whether the above conditions were fulfilled was for the national judge to assess, in light of the other means and alternatives available to the Member State concerned.

In an earlier case, C-41/11, *Inter-Environnement Wallonie*, the Court had accepted such a possibility in relation to an irregularity under the SEA Directive, since there was a risk of a legal vacuum incompatible with the obligation on Belgium to adopt measures to implement the Nitrates Directive and to comply with an existing judgment against that Member State.[662]

Recourse to maintaining the effects of an annulled authorisation has to remain exceptional[663] and the effects may only be maintained for as long as is strictly necessary to remedy the breach.[664]

[7] Taking Economic Operators into Account

In addressing, in Case C-278/21, *Aquapri*, appropriate measures to eliminate an infringement of Article 6(3) of the Habitats Directive, the Court made important references to the interests of the economic operators affected.

[a] Need to Revoke or Suspend Within a Reasonable Time and Take Account of Reliance on the Impugned Authorisation

In referring to revocation or suspension of an authorisation as appropriate measures in order to carry out a new assessment, the Court made a number of qualifications: 'provided that those measures take place within a reasonable period of time and that account is taken of the extent to which the person concerned may have been able to rely on the lawfulness of that authorisation'.[665] It is important to note, however, that in making these qualifications, the Court also cited paragraph 92 of its judgment in Case C-261/18, *Derrybrien*. It is worth quoting that paragraph in full:

659. C-41/11, *Inter-Environnement Wallonie*, para. 58.
660. C-411/17, *Doel*, para. 179.
661. *Ibid.*
662. C-41/11, *Inter-Environnement Wallonie*, para. 56.
663. C-411/17, *Doel*, paras 179 and 180.
664. *Ibid.*, para. 181.
665. C-278/21, *Aquapri*, para. 42.

> As regards [the] argument based on the contention that the principle of legal certainty and the principle of the protection of legitimate expectations preclude the consents unlawfully granted to the wind farm's operator from being withdrawn, it must be borne in mind, first, that the infringement procedure is based on the objective finding that a Member State has failed to fulfil its obligations under the Treaty or secondary legislation and, secondly, that while the withdrawal of an unlawful measure must occur within a reasonable time and regard must be had to how far the person concerned might have been led to rely on the lawfulness of the measure, the fact remains that such withdrawal is, in principle, permitted (judgment of 4 May 2006, *Commission v United Kingdom*, C-508/03, EU:C:2006:287, paragraphs 67 and 68).[666]

[b] State Liability

In Case C-278/21, *Aquapri*, the Court also found it important to clarify that:

> Whatever measure is used to erase the unlawful consequences of a breach of an assessment obligation such as that provided for in the first sentence of Article 6(3) of Directive 92/43, the Member State responsible for that breach may be held liable, if such a measure results in the revocation or amendment of the authorisation granted as a result of that breach, to *make good any damage* which its conduct may have caused to the economic operator who benefited from that authorisation (emphasis added).[667]

[H] Illegal Developments and Activities

[1] Distinction Between Infringements Resulting from Flawed Procedures and Infringements Resulting from Outright Illegality

An important distinction deserves to be drawn between infringements of Article 6(2) and Article 6(3) that are the result of flawed procedures, such as the ones highlighted in Case C-399/14, Grüne Liga Sachsen and Case C-278/21, *AquaPri*, and infringements of Article 6(2) that result from blatant illegalities and bypassing of any procedures. The obligation to nullify unlawful consequences, described in section §3.04[G][3] above, is applicable to both kinds of infringement, but a number of specific considerations arise in relation to purely illegal developments and activities. First, these fall entirely outside the scope of Article 6(3). Second, as regards Article 6(2), the Member State or a competent authority may argue that, since an illegal development or activity has never been officially approved, no responsibility should be attached to the Member State or the competent authority concerned. The case-law clarifies the circumstances in which a breach of Article 6(2) may be imputed to the Member State. Although limited, the case-law is instructive, providing clarification on how a Member State should take

666. C-261/18, *Derrybrien*, para. 92.
667. C-278/21, *Aquapri*, para. 46.

effective enforcement action to fulfil the requirements of Article 6(2). This topic is further considered in Chapter 7.

[2] Multiple Illegal Developments and Activities at Kyparissia, Greece

Case C-504/14, *Commission v. Greece,* provides an especially good illustration of a protected area being negatively impacted by a range of illegal developments and activities and of a Member State's failure to effectively enforce its own laws. The area concerned was a coastal site, at Kyparissia, with protected dunes, and beaches protected for the sea turtle. The Commission referred Greece to the Court for breaches of, *inter alia*, Article 6(2) and Article 6(3) of the Habitats Directive.

The following illegal developments and activities feature in the case.

[a] Unauthorised Construction Work on Houses

Amongst other matters, the Commission raised a complaint about the commencement of work with a view to implementing a planned property development involving the construction of around 50 dwellings located between Agiannaki and Elaia.[668]

Greece asserted that all construction without a prior building permit was prohibited and that no new permits would be issued until a presidential decree had been adopted.

[b] Unauthorised Road Developments

Amongst other matters, the Commission complained that Greece had *tolerated* the opening up of five new roads to Agiannaki beach.[669] It submitted that, despite the imposition of fines and the rehabilitation called for by the Greek authorities, those roads had remained operational. As a result, vehicles easily gained access to the beach and there was noise and pollution.[670]

Greece submitted that those roads had existed since the early 1970s and that their existence and the fact that they were for common use was confirmed by a court ruling. In any event, since no prior environmental authorisation was obtained either for construction of four of the five roads or for the work carried out on the fifth road, fines were imposed on the construction company in question in 2012. Greece argued that several sets of criminal proceedings had been brought by the authorities and that a number of court cases were also pending which were concerned with those fines and the lawfulness of the roads.[671]

---

668. C-504/14, *Commission v. Greece*, para. 68.
669. *Ibid.*, para. 46.
670. *Ibid.*, para. 47.
671. *Ibid.*, para. 50.

[c] Prohibited Wild Camping

The Commission complained that Greece had tolerated 'wild camping' in a pine forest in the dune land at Elaia beach.[672] It argued that wild camping was problematic from the point of view of dune conservation and the conservation of forest habitats. It also disturbed the sea turtle.[673] While stating that wild camping was prohibited throughout the country, Greece acknowledged that, despite the prohibition and police patrols, the practice still went on. It maintained that there had been wild camping in the Kyparissia area for at least 30 or 40 years but that it had gradually been reduced.[674]

[d] Failure to Enforce a Demolition Order to Remove Beach Platforms

The Commission complained that Greece tolerated, within the Kyparissia area, an excessive amount of beach furniture, namely umbrellas and sunbeds. It maintained that although the Greek authorities issued an order for the demolition of a number of platforms put up on the beaches in that area, that demolition never took place.[675] According to the Commission, these beach facilities, inasmuch as they are fixed on the beach or left there at night, had a negative impact on the breeding areas of the sea turtle, since they reduced the space available for nests and made it difficult for the turtles to move around.[676]

[3] Inapplicability of Article 6(3) of the Habitats Directive to Illegal Developments

In Case, C-504/14, *Commission v. Greece*, the Commission complained that Greece had infringed Article 6(3), *inter alia*, by omitting to undertake an appropriate assessment in respect of the construction of the houses and the opening of the roads mentioned above at section §3.04[H][2][a] and [b]. Greece argued that, where no appropriate assessments were carried out, administrative and criminal proceedings had been commenced.

The Court held that Article 6(3) 'is relevant only when the competent national authorities grant authorisation for a project, as that authorisation must in such a case be preceded by an appropriate assessment of the implications of the project for the site concerned'.[677] It went on to state that:

> Consequently, Article 6(3) of Directive 92/43 does not apply in respect of any action whose implementation was subject to authorisation but which was carried out without authorisation and thus unlawfully. That being the case, there can in

672. *Ibid.*, para. 61.
673. *Ibid.*, para. 62.
674. *Ibid.*, para. 63.
675. *Ibid.*, para. 72.
676. *Ibid.*, para. 73.
677. *Ibid.*, para. 121.

this regard be no finding of failure to fulfil obligations on account of an infringement of Article 6(3).[678]

[4] Need for an Appropriate System of Protection with Enforcement

In Case, C-504/14, *Commission v. Greece*, with regard to the commencement of construction of the houses mentioned above in section §3.04[H][2][a], the Court noted that the Greek authorities had not issued a permit for that purpose. However, it held that:

> There is no merit in the Hellenic Republic's argument that, since that building work was prohibited unless a permit was first obtained, the commencement of the work cannot be attributed to it and does not prove that it has infringed Article 6(2) of Directive 92/43. In fact, as the Commission submits, the Hellenic Republic has not established *an appropriate system of protection* and has not enforced the prohibition on construction, with the result that unregulated, unplanned building works are commenced (emphasis added).[679]

[5] Need for Enforcement Measures to Be Adequate

In Case, C-504/14, *Commission v. Greece*, with regard to the problem of wild camping mentioned above in section §3.04[H][2][c], the Court found that by failing to 'take adequate measures to enforce' the prohibition on wild camping, Greece had failed to fulfil its obligations under Article 6(2) of the Habitats Directive.[680]

[6] Need for Timely and Effective Enforcement Interventions

In Case C-404/09, *Commission v. Spain*, the Court condemned Spain for a breach of Article 6(2) of the Habitats Directive in respect of the illegal 'Ampliación de Feixolín' open-cast mine because, although they had penalised the operator and ordered him to cease that operation, the competent Spanish authorities had only prohibited the operation in November 2009, despite having been informed of its actual operation at least since 2005. By allowing a situation which caused significant disturbances in the 'Alto Sil' SPA to continue for at least four years, Spain had omitted to take, *in good time*, the measures necessary to bring those disturbances to an end.[681]

[7] Possible Insufficiency of Criminal Proceedings and Need for Injunctive Action

In Case, C-504/14, *Commission v. Greece*, with regard to the opening of roads mentioned above in section §3.04[H][2][b], the Court found that the opening up of the

678. *Ibid.*, para. 123.
679. *Ibid.*, para. 43.
680. *Ibid.*, para. 65.
681. C-404/09, *Commission v. Spain*, paras 149 to 152.

roads facilitated vehicle access to the beach. Parking damaged dune habitats and there was an escalation in noise and light which disturbed the sea turtle. It also found that the opening up and construction of those roads was unlawful.[682] It also noted that the roads were operational 'despite the fact that criminal proceedings have been brought and various court cases are pending'.[683]

Against this background, it was not satisfied with the adequacy of the Greek enforcement action, finding that:

> By confining itself (i) to bringing criminal proceedings against the executives of the company that built the roads in question and imposing administrative penalties on that company and (ii) to claiming, before the national courts, that the roads concerned are illegal and must be removed, the Hellenic Republic has failed to fulfil the specific obligation imposed on it by Article 6(2) of Directive 92/43 (see, by analogy, judgment of 9 November 1999, *Commission v Italy*, C-365/97, EU:C:1999:544, paragraph 109).[684]

The Court agreed with the Commission that Greece should have acted to ensure that those thoroughfares *did not remain operational* and that use of them did not significantly disturb the sea turtles or impair the dune habitats.[685]

In finding a breach of Article 6(2), it specifically cited the failure to take *provisional measures* for the protection of the area in order to restrict use of the thoroughfares at issue until the conclusion of the national court proceedings concerning the legality and possible closure of those thoroughfares, when, as the Advocate General had noted at point 77 of her Opinion, there is nothing to suggest that such measures would not be possible either for practical reasons or for reasons relating to EU law.[686]

[8] Need to Make a Necessary Enforcement Order Effective

In Case C-504/14, *Commission v. Greece*, with regard to, *inter alia*, the unimplemented demolition order mentioned above in section §3.04[H][2][d], the Court found that, by failing to take the measures necessary to reduce, within the Kyparissia area, the furniture and various structures on the breeding beaches of the sea turtle, Greece had failed to fulfil its obligations under Article 6(2).

[9] Requirement to Make Reparations

The Opinion of the Advocate General in Case C-434/22, *Latvijas valsts meži*, a preliminary reference from a Latvian court, sheds useful light on the need to make good damage from an illegal development [the Court's judgment had not yet appeared at the

682. C-504/14, *Commission v. Greece*, para. 53.
683. *Ibid.*
684. *Ibid.*, para. 55.
685. *Ibid.*, para. 56.
686. *Ibid.*, para. 57.

time of writing]. The referring court asked, *inter alia*, whether the competent authorities are under a duty to require damage to be made good and to adopt measures if the significance of an impact was not assessed pursuant to Article 6(3) of the Habitats Directive.[687] The circumstances involved the felling of trees in an SAC by a state forestry company without any prior appropriate assessment. As soon as it became aware of the tree-felling, the competent authority ordered the forestry company to leave the dead trees on the ground. For the Advocate General, the order amounted to an intervention to prevent the continuation of a breach of Article 6(3). She nevertheless addressed the issue of reparation, expressing the view that this came within the scope of the duty of sincere co-operation under Article 4(3), TEU, and the requirement to nullify the consequences of a breach of EU law. She considered that rules to guarantee reparation of possible damage resulting from a breach of EU law are necessary, observing that 'the main aim of the respective rules is not to penalise individuals but to establish or maintain a certain status'[688] and that 'the aim of establishing or maintaining a certain status is particularly important in site protection under the Habitats Directive because those rules seek to protect the common natural heritage of the European Union'.[689] She concluded that the Member States must adopt rules under which individuals may be required to make reparation for damage if this has affected Natura 2000 sites in breach of Article 6(3) of the Habitats Directive, noting that, in some cases, the relevant national legal bases may already be derived from the transposition of the Environmental Liability Directive, 'although, because of the various limitations of those rules, it cannot be ruled out that effective transposition of the Habitats Directive requires further rules on reparation to be adopted'.[690]

[10] Notion of Tolerance of Illegal Developments and Activities

The term 'tolerance' figures in Case C-504/14, *Commission v. Greece,* covering situations where the Member State has failed to take necessary and effective enforcement action. The case makes clear that such tolerance can give rise to a breach of Article 6(2).

§3.05 PROPERTY RIGHTS AND FINANCIAL COMPENSATION

[A] Property Rights

It is clear from previous sections that Natura 2000 can entail obligations for private landowners and economic operators. Previously described cases such as C-278/21, *Aquapri,* also illustrate how property rights feature in the case-law.

687. Fifth question of the reference.
688. Opinion of the Advocate General in C-434/22, *Latvijas valsts meži,* para. 77.
689. *Ibid.*, para.78.
690. *Ibid.*, para 79.

In addition, the case-law has specifically considered property rights in the context of the possible entitlement of landowners to financial compensation. In particular, a number of preliminary references from Latvia have shed valuable light on this topic. The resulting case-law confirms the applicability of property rights under the Charter of Fundamental Rights to the issue of financial compensation but does not treat implementation of the Birds and Habitats Directive as giving rise to any automatic entitlement to such compensation. The Court recognises, nevertheless, the discretionary scope for financial compensation while treating this as subject to State aid requirements, where appropriate.

[B] Articles 17(1) and 51(1) of the Charter of Fundamental Rights Are Broadly Applicable

Article 17(1) of the Charter reads as follows:

> Everyone has the right to own, use, dispose of and bequeath his or her lawfully acquired possessions. No one may be deprived of his or her possessions, except in the public interest and in the cases and under the conditions provided for by law, subject to fair compensation being paid in good time for their loss. The use of property may be regulated by law in so far as is necessary for the general interest.

Article 51(1) of the Charter reads as follows:

> The provisions of this Charter are addressed to the institutions, bodies, offices and agencies of the Union with due regard for the principle of subsidiarity and to the Member States only when they are implementing Union law.

In Case C-238/20, *Sātiņi-S,* the Latvian Supreme Court sought a preliminary ruling in proceedings between Sātiņi-S SIA and the Environmental Protection Authority of Latvia concerning the latter's refusal to grant the plaintiff compensation for damage caused to its aquaculture farm by wild birds on a Natura 2000 site on the ground that it had already obtained the maximum amount of money that could be granted to it in light of the *de minimis* rule on State aid.

In 2002, Sātiņi-S purchased two properties, with a total surface area of 687 hectares, including ponds with a surface area of 600.70 hectares, in a protected nature reserve, which was subsequently included, in 2005, in the Natura 2000 network in Latvia. In 2017, Sātiņi-S applied to the Environmental Protection Authority for an award of compensation for the damage caused to aquaculture by birds and other protected animals. That authority refused that request, on the ground that Sātiņi-S had already been awarded a total amount corresponding to the *de minimis* rule of EUR 30,000, over a period of three fiscal years, provided for in Article 3(2) of EU Regulation No. 717/2014. Sātiņi-S brought an action against that decision, claiming that, because it is compensatory in nature, compensation for the damage caused to aquaculture by protected animals was not State aid.[691]

691. C-238/20, *Satiņi-S,* paras 15-17.

The Latvian Supreme Court, amongst other things, asked whether the right to property guaranteed by Article 17 of the Charter does not preclude compensation for the losses caused to aquaculture in a Natura 2000 area by birds protected under the Birds Directive from being significantly less than the losses actually suffered by the applicant.

Article 17 of the Charter was also raised in Case C-234/20, *Sātiņi-S*, another preliminary reference from the Latvian Supreme Court.

In 2002, Sātiņi-S purchased 7.7 hectares of peat bog situated in a nature protection area and in a Natura 2000 conservation area of Community importance in Latvia. Sātiņi-S subsequently sought compensation from the Latvian authorities in view of the prohibition on establishing cranberry plantations on that peatland but was refused on the ground that the applicable national legislation did not provide for such compensation. This refusal was linked to Article 30(1) of EU Regulation No. 1307/2013.[692] With regard to Natura 2000, this provided that:

> Support under this measure shall be granted annually per hectare of agricultural area or per hectare of forest in order to compensate beneficiaries for additional costs and income foregone resulting from disadvantages in the areas concerned, related to the implementation of [the 'Habitats' Directive] and [Directive 2009/147] and [Directive 2000/60].

In this case, the Latvian Supreme Court asked, in essence, whether Article 30(1) of Regulation No. 1305/2013, read in conjunction with Article 17 of the Charter, must be interpreted as meaning that a Natura 2000 payment must be granted to the owner of a peat bog falling within that network on the basis that a restriction was imposed on an economic activity that could be carried out on such a peat bog, such as planting cranberries, where, at the time when he or she acquired the immovable property concerned, the owner was aware of such restriction.

One of the issues which arose in both Cases C-238/20 and C-234/20 was whether Articles 17(1) and 51(1) of the Charter were applicable at all. In each case, the Court followed the same reasoning when rejecting Commission arguments that the Court had no jurisdiction. In Case C-238/20, the Commission argued that payment of the compensation at issue in the main proceedings did not constitute implementation of EU law within the meaning of Article 51(1) of the Charter, since neither the Birds Directive nor the Habitats Directive provides for compensation on the basis of damage caused to private property, in particular aquaculture ponds, when they are implemented. In Case C-234/20, the Commission argued that Article 30 of Regulation No. 1305/2013 does not create any obligation or promise to pay compensation to natural persons on account of all the restrictions allegedly affecting the use of property coming within the Natura 2000 network and, generally, that EU law does not recognise the existence of a general

692. Regulation (EU) No. 1305/2013 of the European Parliament and of the Council of 17 December 2013 on support for rural development by the European Agricultural Fund for Rural Development (EAFRD) and repealing Council Regulation (EC) No. 1698/2005, OJ 2013 L 347, p. 487, and corrigendum OJ 2016 L 130, p. 1, and of Article 17 of the Charter of Fundamental Rights of the European Union ('the Charter').

principle requiring compensation to be granted in all circumstances, that is to say for all those restrictions imposed by way of Natura 2000.

The Court held that the Member States are implementing EU law, within the meaning of Article 51(1) of the Charter, where, in accordance with the requirements of the Birds Directive and the Habitats Directive, they take appropriate steps to avoid in the SACs the deterioration of natural habitats, and the requisite measures to establish a general system of protection for the species of birds covered by the former directive.[693]

First, Article 5 of the Birds Directive requires the Member States to take the requisite measures to establish a general system of protection for all the bird species referred to in Article 1 of that directive.[694]

Second, Article 6(2) of the Habitats Directive provides that Member States are to take appropriate steps to avoid, in the SACs, the deterioration of natural habitats and the habitats of species as well as disturbance of the species for which the areas have been designated, in so far as such disturbance could be significant in relation to the objectives of that directive.[695]

Furthermore, the transposition and implementation by the Member States of those measures, the objective of which is to protect birds and their habitats, inevitably, have repercussions on the right to property of persons to whom immovable property situated in the areas in question belongs, since, at the very least, they are subject to restrictions on the use of that property.[696]

The Court also considered that Article 51(1) of the Charter was applicable in relation to financial compensation, holding that the Member States also implement EU law, within the meaning of Article 51(1) of the Charter, when they establish schemes granting payments under the Birds Directive and the Habitats Directive.[697] It observed that the mere fact that those directives do not provide for a compensation scheme themselves or that they do not impose an obligation on Member States to provide for such a scheme cannot be interpreted as meaning that Article 17 of the Charter is not applicable.[698]

[C] No Automatic Entitlement to Financial Compensation

While accepting the broad applicability of Articles 17(1) and 51(1) of the Charter, the Court did not consider that implementation of the Birds Directive and the Habitats Directive gives rise to any automatic entitlement of landowners or economic operators to financial compensation.

Article 52(1) of the Charter of Fundamental Rights is relevant in this context. It reads as follows:

693. C-238/20, *Satiņi-S*, para. 23.
694. *Ibid.*, para. 24.
695. *Ibid.*, para. 25.
696. *Ibid.*, para. 26.
697. *Ibid.*, para. 27.
698. *Ibid.*, para. 28.

> Any limitation on the exercise of the rights and freedoms recognised by the Charter must be provided for by law and respect the essence of those rights and freedoms.

In Case C-238/20, *Sātiņi-S*, the Court rejected arguments that the limited financial compensation provided to Sātiņi-S, in respect of the aquaculture ponds within Natura 2000, contravened the Charter.

The Court stated that:

> It should be noted at the outset that it is apparent from the wording of Article 17 of the Charter that that article expressly confers a right to compensation only in the event of deprivation of the right to property, such as expropriation, which is clearly not the situation in the present case.[699]

It took the view that:

> In the present case, the regulatory obligations restricting the freedom of owners of property coming within the Natura 2000 network as to the choice and implementation of protective measures for aquaculture, in respect of protected wild birds, do not constitute a deprivation of the right to property of that immovable property, but a restriction on its use, which may be regulated by law to the extent necessary in the public interest, in accordance with the provisions in the third sentence of Article 17(1) of the Charter.

The Court noted that the right to property guaranteed by Article 17 of the Charter is not absolute and that its exercise may be subject to restrictions justified by objectives of general interest pursued by the EU[700] - of which protection of the environment is one.[701] Protection of the environment is capable of justifying a restriction on the use of the right to property, as was confirmed by an earlier judgment in Case C-416/10, *Križan and Others*, paragraph 114.[702]

In reaching this conclusion, the Court cited Article 52(1) of the Charter:

> It is therefore apparent from Article 52(1) of the Charter that restrictions may be imposed on the use of the right to property, provided that the restrictions genuinely meet the objectives of general interest pursued and do not constitute, in relation to the aim pursued, *a disproportionate and intolerable interference, impairing the very substance of the right guaranteed* (emphasis added).[703]

The Court considered that the restrictions on the aquaculture ponds did not contravene these strictures of Article 52(1) of the Charter, observing:

> It does not appear, subject to any review by the referring court in this respect, that measures such as those at issue in the main proceedings, thus taken for the purposes of protecting nature and the environment, under the 'Birds' Directive and the 'Habitats' Directive, and which do not prevent the practice of aquaculture on the plots concerned, but only regulate the conditions of exercise of that activity in order to prevent harm to the environmental interests thus protected, constitute, in

699. *Ibid.*, para. 30.
700. *Ibid.*, para. 32.
701. *Ibid.*, para. 34.
702. *Ibid.*
703. *Ibid.*, para. 33.

> the absence of compensation for affected owners, a disproportionate and intolerable interference impairing the very substance of the right to property.[704]

[D] Scope for Financial Payments under EU Funds and the Relevance of State Aid Rules

[1] Scope for Discretionary Payments

In rejecting the idea of any automatic entitlement of landowners or economic operators to financial compensation for being subject to Natura 2000 restrictions, the Court, nevertheless, recognised the scope for Member States and the EU to provide financial compensation on a discretionary basis.

In Case C-238/20, *Sātiņi-S,* it noted that:

> The Member States may consider, where appropriate, provided that they do so in compliance with EU law, that full or partial compensation is appropriate for owners of plots affected by conservation measures taken under the 'Birds' Directive and the 'Habitats' Directive.[705]

This discretion does not, however, imply the existence of an obligation under EU law to grant such compensation.

This is confirmed by the Court's ruling in Case C-234/20, *Sātiņi-S*. Article 30 of Regulation No. 1305/2013 allowed for payments to landowners within Natura 2000 areas, but the Member States retained a measure of discretion on which areas might benefit. Through its ruling, the Court confirmed that Article 17 of the Charter could not be invoked to qualify that discretion and oblige Latvia to make payments to the plaintiff.

[2] Relevance of State Aid Rules

Any discretionary financial payments made to landowners in Natura 2000 are potentially subject to State aid rules. This is confirmed by the ruling in Case C-238/20, *Sātiņi-S*. As already noted, the plaintiff received EUR 30,000 in respect of the aquaculture ponds which were the subject of the proceedings.

The Latvian Supreme Court asked, in essence, whether Article 107 TFEU [the Treaty provision on State aids] must be interpreted as meaning that compensation granted by a State for the losses suffered by an economic operator as a result of the protective measures applicable in a Natura 2000 network area under the Birds Directive constitutes 'State aid' within the meaning of that provision.

The Court noted that, to classify a measure as a 'State aid' for purposes of Article 107(1), TFEU, several conditions must be fulfilled. First, there must be an intervention by the State or through State resources. Second, the intervention must be liable to affect

704. *Ibid.*, para. 35.
705. *Ibid.*, para. 36.

trade between Member States. Third, it must confer a selective advantage on the recipient. Fourth, it must distort or threaten to distort competition. In addition, Article 107(1) TFEU does not distinguish between measures of State intervention by reference to their causes or their aims but defines them in relation to their effects.[706]

Having analysed the matter, the Court concluded that Article 107(1) TFEU must be interpreted as meaning that compensation granted by a Member State for the losses suffered by an economic operator as a result of the protective measures applicable in a Natura 2000 network area under the Birds Directive confers an advantage capable of constituting 'State aid' for the purposes of that provision, where the other conditions relating to classification as a State aid are satisfied.[707]

[a] The Notion of an Economic Advantage

The Court focused, in particular, on whether the compensatory payment conferred an economic advantage on the recipient.

It observed that 'measures which, whatever their form, are likely directly or indirectly to benefit undertakings or are to be regarded as an economic advantage which the recipient undertaking would not have obtained under normal market conditions are regarded as State aid'.[708]

It added:

> Furthermore, the agreed benefits may include not only positive benefits such as subsidies, loans or direct investment in the capital of undertakings, but also interventions which, in various forms, mitigate the charges which are normally included in the budget of an undertaking and which therefore, without being subsidies in the strict sense of the word, are of the same character and have the same effect.[709]

It confirmed that the existence of an agreed advantage by means of a State measure is not called into question by the compensatory nature of such a measure on the ground that it seeks to remedy the losses incurred by an economic operator following the application of an obligation deriving from EU legislation or, as is the case in the main proceedings, to compensate such an operator for the damage caused to its undertaking by the occurrence of natural events linked with the normal conditions of the exercise of the economic activity.[710]

It concluded this part of its analysis as follows:

> The costs of complying with regulatory obligations for the protection of the environment, in particular that of wild fauna, and responsibility for the damage, which the latter may cause to an undertaking in the aquaculture sector, such as that at issue in the main proceedings, are part of the normal operating costs of such an undertaking. Therefore, the grant of compensation for damage caused to its

706. *Ibid.*, para. 39.
707. *Ibid.*, para. 53.
708. *Ibid.*, para. 41.
709. *Ibid.*, para. 42.
710. *Ibid.*, para. 43.

> undertaking by protected animals constitutes an economic advantage to which the undertaking concerned cannot in principle be entitled under normal market conditions.[711]

[b] *The Notion of Public Interest Obligations*

The Court's analysis then extended to an issue of whether classification as a State aid should be excluded as regards the compensation at issue on the ground that the objective of that compensation is to compensate for damage incurred by the operators concerned because those operators must fulfil *public interest obligations* laid down by their Member State in the context of the implementation of EU environmental protection rules, in this case, the Birds Directive.

The Court was not persuaded by this argument.

The Court recalled that the exception for fulfilment of public interest obligations required four conditions to be satisfied. First, the recipient undertaking must actually have public service obligations to discharge and those obligations must be clearly defined. Second, the parameters on the basis of which the compensation is calculated must be established, in advance, in an objective and transparent manner. Third, the compensation cannot exceed what is necessary to cover all or part of the costs incurred in the discharge of public service obligations, taking into account the relevant revenue and a reasonable profit for discharging those obligations. Fourth and lastly, where the undertaking which is to discharge public service obligations is not chosen pursuant to a public procurement procedure, the level of compensation needed must be determined on the basis of an analysis of the costs which a typical undertaking, well run and adequately equipped so as to be able to meet the necessary public service requirements, would have incurred in discharging those obligations, taking into account the relevant revenue and a reasonable profit for discharging its obligations.[712]

The Court found that the mere fact that an economic operator has to comply with Natura 2000 obligations does not establish that such an operator is tasked with public service obligations.[713] It rejected an argument by Ireland that the compensation paid to the plaintiff related to sums due or paid on the basis of the non-contractual liability of the Member State concerned. Rather, the compensation related to the compensation of costs – arising from regulatory obligations or natural events – is normally borne by the undertakings concerned in the context of their economic activity. In the present case, there was thus no question of compensation for damage caused by the national authorities.[714]

711. *Ibid.*, para. 44.
712. *Ibid.*, para. 47.
713. *Ibid.*, para. 48.
714. *Ibid.*, paras 49 and 50.

CHAPTER 4

Protection of Species

§4.01 PROTECTION OF SPECIES UNDER THE NATURE DIRECTIVES

Each of the Nature Directives provides for the protection of species by way of provisions designed to safeguard them from direct threats or harmful exploitation. These provisions are associated with some of the most emotive nature conservation issues, such as hunting, although they are relevant to a great many other human activities as well.

There are close parallels between the set of species protection provisions in the Birds Directive and the corresponding set of species protection provisions in the Habitats Directive. Each set was conceived according to a similar rationale and, unsurprisingly, the close parallels extend to how the Court has addressed each set in its case-law. There are some significant differences between the directives, however. The Birds Directive provides protection to *all* species of wild birds, whereas the Habitats Directive is much more selective. Compared to wild bird species, however, the animal species that enjoy the highest level of protection under the Habitats Directive arguably enjoy a greater degree of protection of their breeding and resting places[715] – although counterbalancing this, there are more extensive habitat protection provisions in the Birds Directive.[716]

715. *See* Article 12(1)(d) of the Habitats Directive.
716. *See* Article 3 and the second sentence of Article 4(4) of the Birds Directive. In relation to Article 4(4), *see* Case C-507/04, *Commission v. Austria*, para. 206. For species not covered by Article 4, Article 3 will apply, as is demonstrated by Case C-117/00, *Commission v. Ireland* – *See* Chapter 5, §5.02[B].

§4.02 PROTECTION OF SPECIES UNDER THE BIRDS DIRECTIVE

[A] Three Types of Provision

The Birds Directive includes provisions designed for the protection of the species of birds referred to in its Article 1, i.e., 'all species of naturally occurring birds in the wild state in the European territory of the Member States to which the Treaty applies'[717] including their eggs, nests and habitats.[718]

In a nutshell, in order to establish an effective system of protection, the Directive introduced three types of provisions in addition to the habitat provisions already described in Chapters 2 and 3.

The first type consists of *prohibitions*. Article 5 of the Directive requires Member States to prohibit the deliberate killing capture or disturbance of wild birds. It also requires them to prohibit the deliberate destruction of, or damage to, nests and eggs; the taking and keeping of eggs; and the keeping of certain wild bird species. Article 6(1) prohibits the marketing of wild birds and their parts and derivatives. Article 8 prohibits the use of non-selective hunting means.

The second type consists of provisions which, subject to strict conditions, allow *certain activities* which would otherwise infringe the prohibitions of Article 5 and Article 6(1). Article 6(2) and (3) allows marketing of species listed in Annex III of the Birds Directive and Article 7 allows the hunting of species listed in Annex II of the Birds Directive. For species not listed in these annexes, the prohibitions of Article 5 and Article 6(1) apply.

The third type allows for the use, on a case-by-case basis, of *derogations*, i.e., exceptions. Under Article 9, it is possible to grant derogations in respect of the obligations of Articles 5 to 8, but use of derogations is made subject to strict conditions.[719]

In terms of spatial scope, all of these provisions have to be generally applied across the territory of the Member States. They are not, for instance, spatially limited to areas within the boundaries of SPAs.

Reflecting the concerns of the period, the 1973 European Commission Environmental Action Programme that first signalled the possibility of legislation on wild birds pointed to the need for adoption of measures to prevent the 'mass destruction of birds, especially songbirds and migratory birds'. The species protection provisions of the Birds Directive now represent a set of safeguards against such mass destruction.[720]

717. Article 1 of Directive 2009/147/EC of the European Parliament and of the Council of 30 November 2009 on the conservation of wild birds, OJ L20, 26.1.2010, p. 7-25, codifying Council Directive 79/409/EEC of 2 April 1979 on the conservation of wild birds, i.e., 'the Birds Directive'.
718. Article 1(2) of the Birds Directive provides that the directive 'shall apply to birds, their eggs, nests and habitats'.
719. C-262/85, *Commission v. Italy*, para. 7.
720. Agustín García Ureta, *EU Biodiversity Law: Wild Birds and Habitats Directives*, 72-73 (Europa Law Publishing, 2020).

[B] General System of Protection Foreseen under Article 5

Article 5 of the Birds Directive reads as follows:

> Without prejudice to Articles 7 and 9, Member States shall take the requisite measures to establish a general system of protection for all species of birds referred to in Article 1, prohibiting in particular:
>
> (a) deliberate killing or capture by any method; deliberate destruction of, or damage to, their nests and eggs or removal of their nests;
> (b) taking their eggs in the wild and keeping these eggs even if empty;
> (c) deliberate disturbance of these birds particularly during the period of breeding and rearing, in so far as disturbance would be significant having regard to the objectives of this Directive;
> (d) keeping birds of species the hunting and capture of which is prohibited.

Under Article 5, Member States are obliged to take requisite measures to establish a general system of protection for all species of birds naturally occurring in the wild state in their respective territory including eggs, nests and habitats, prohibiting, in particular, the acts listed from letters (a) to (d).

[1] Transposition of Article 5 Must Respect Its Full Scope

[a] Protection Cannot Be Limited in Time

In Case C-252/85, *Commission v. France*, the Commission challenged gaps in France's transposition of Article 5. The Court, *inter alia*, upheld a Commission complaint that the French Government had unjustifiably limited the protection of nests and eggs to the closed season.

The Court stressed that the prohibitions set out in Article 5 (b) and (c) of the Birds Directive must apply without any limitations in time. As some of the species reuse nests built in earlier years, an uninterrupted protection of the nests is necessary.[721]

[b] Protection Cannot Be Limited to Certain Bird Species and Bird Species Cannot Be Excluded for Certain Periods

In Case C-252/85, *Commission v. France*, the Court also confirmed that the scope of the protection regime must not be limited by reference to 'national biological heritage'. The Commission had challenged the French transposition, since it limited the protection regime to 'the preservation of the national biological heritage', thereby reducing the scope of Article 1 of the Birds Directive, which refers clearly to all species of naturally occurring birds in the wild state in the European territory of Member States. The Court found that national legislation limiting the protection of wild birds by reference to the concept of national heritage is incompatible with the Directive. It referred to the third

721. C-252/85, *Commission v. France*, para. 9.

recital of the preamble to the Directive, to underline that the protection of migratory species is typically a transfrontier problem entailing common responsibilities for the Member States. Hence, complete and effective protection of wild birds must be ensured irrespective of the areas they inhabit or pass through.[722]

In a similar vein, in Case C-247/85, *Commission v. Belgium*, Belgium was condemned by the Court because its transposition law, Royal Decree of 20 July 1972, limited the protection required by the Directive to the species of birds living in the wild state in the Benelux countries. The wording of the provision in question did cover birds which were only passing through the Benelux countries, but the Court held that:

> The protective effect of the directive also covers species of naturally occurring birds in the wild state in the European territory of another Member State which are not naturally or usually to be found in the territory of the Benelux countries but which are transported there, kept there or marketed there, whether alive or dead.[723]

As the Belgian law did not extend the protection regime conferred by the Directive to these groups of birds, the Court found it incompatible with the Birds Directive.

As Case C-507/04, *Commission v. Austria* shows, even a temporally limited exclusion of a species will contravene Article 5. In this case, the Court condemned Austria for a breach of Article 5 because, under the legislation of the Province of Burgenland, the European starling was left entirely unprotected in the period between 15 July and 30 November. Austria argued that this exclusion was justified by the derogation possibilities of Article 9(1)(a) of the Birds Directive in respect of crop damage to vines. The Court rejected this argument. It accepted that the prevention of damage to vines can, in principle, justify the taking of derogating measures pursuant to the third indent of Article 9(1)(a) of the Directive[724] but went on to state:

> However, that provision does not provide a legal basis for a species being entirely removed – even if the removal is temporally limited – from the system of protection laid down by the Directive.
>
> Removing a species of bird entirely from the system of protection laid down by the Directive, even for a defined period, could jeopardise the very existence of that species. Thus, the Member States are authorised to derogate from the system of protection for wild birds only if they observe the requirements set out in Article 9(2) of the Directive.[725]

The Court also held that this exclusion amounted to a breach of Article 1 of the Birds Directive,[726] as well as Article 9.

722. *Ibid.*, paras 15 and 16.
723. C-247/85, *Commission v. Belgium*, para. 22.
724. C-507/04, *Commission v. Austria*, para. 113.
725. *Ibid.*, paras 114-115.
726. *Ibid.*, paras 87-94.

[c] Prohibitions Cannot Be Geographically Restricted

In Case C-88/19, *Alianta pentru combatera abuzurilor,* the Advocate General observed that, like those of Article 12 of the Habitats Directive, the prohibitions of Article 5 of the Birds Directive are not geographically restricted.[727] She noted that, in Case C-192/11, *Commission v. Poland,* 'the Court criticised the fact that a Member State had excluded grey herons (*Ardea cinerea*) and cormorants (*Phalacrocorax carbo*) present in fish ponds from protection under Article 5'. [In formal terms, the Commission's claim in Case C-192/11, *Commission v. Poland,* was that Poland had given an invalid derogation for purposes of Article 9(1) and 9(2) of the Birds Directive,[728] but, logically there was a concomitant breach of Article 5, although this was not pleaded].

[d] Permissive Exceptions Are Not Allowed

In Case C-412/85, *Commission v. Germany,* the Court upheld a Commission complaint that the German transposing legislation contravened Article 5 because it provided that the prohibitions foreseen did not apply where the acts concerned take place in the course of 'the normal use of the land for agricultural, forestry or fishing purposes' or in the context of 'the exploitation of the products obtained from such activities'.[729] The Court took the view that the German legislation constituted an unlawful derogation from the general prohibition concerning the protection of birds enshrined in Article 5 because it did not satisfy the derogation conditions foreseen in Article 9 of the Directive.[730]

[2] Impermissible for a National Practice to Limit the Scope of Article 5

Moving forward in time, the Court's judgment in Joined Cases C-473 and C-474/19, *Skydda Skogen* is consistent with the earlier judgments on the scope of Article 5 described above.

In 2019, through a preliminary reference, a Swedish court asked, in essence, whether *a national practice* could limit the scope of the prohibitions in Article 5 to species listed in Annex I of the Birds Directive or to species which find themselves at some level of risk or are suffering a long-term decline in population.

The underlying dispute related to the legality of tree-felling in a Swedish municipality. In the proceedings concerned, Joined Cases C-473 and C-474/19, *Skydda Skogen,* the Court confirmed that Article 5 precluded such a practice. The provision's scope could not be narrowed, as the provision was intended to confer protection on all species of birds naturally occurring in the wild state in the EU's territory.[731] The Court considered that the wording of Article 5 was clear and unambiguous but it also referred

727. Opinion of the Advocate General in C-88/19, *Alianta pentru combatera abuzurilor,* para. 41.
728. C-192/11, *Commission v. Poland,* paras 60-63.
729. C-412/85, *Commission v. Germany,* para. 8.
730. *Ibid.,* paras 17 to 20.
731. Joined Cases C-473 and C-474/19, *Skydda Skogen,* paras 29 and 44.

to other considerations, such as the high level of protection that EU policy on the environment aims at.[732]

[C] General Prohibition on the Marketing of Wild Birds under Article 6(1) and Exceptions to This under Article 6(2) and (3)

According to Article 6(1) of the Birds Directive, as concerns all the bird species referred to under Article 1, Member States have to prohibit 'the sale, the transport for sale, keeping for sale and the offering for sale of live or dead birds and of any readily recognisable parts or derivatives of such birds'.

According to Article 6(2) and (3), however, under certain conditions and within limits, Member States may authorise the marketing of the species listed in Annex III to the Directive. By virtue of Article 6(2), the marketing-related prohibition does not operate for species of birds listed in Annex III, Part A of the Directive where these were legally captured, killed or acquired. As regards species listed in Annex III, Part B to the Directive, Article 6(3) allows some of the prohibited marketing activities to be authorised on a geographically limited basis but prior consultation with the European Commission is obligatory.

[1] Non-european Subspecies of a Protected Species Is Covered

As mentioned above, Article 1 species, are 'all species of naturally occurring birds in the wild state in the European territory of the Member States to which the Treaty applies', including their eggs, nests and habitats.

In Case C-202/94, *van der Feesten*, the Court confirmed that the Birds Directive – and, more specifically, the provisions of Articles 5 and 6 – apply to bird subspecies which occur naturally in the wild only outside the European territory of the Member States if the species to which they belong or other subspecies of that species occur naturally in the wild within the territory in question.

Following the seizure at his home of a number of birds belonging to the subspecies Cardnelis carduelis caniceps, or grey-headed goldfinch, imported into the Netherlands from Denmark, Mr van der Feesten contested that measure with a view to securing their recovery. The referring court sought clarification on whether the subspecies was covered by the Birds Directive. It stated that the *Carduelis*, or black-headed goldfinch is a species of bird occurring naturally in the wild and in several subspecies in the European territory of the Member States to which the Treaty applies. However, the *Carduelis caniceps* was, it stated, a subspecies which occurs naturally in the wild only outside the European territory in question.

In justifying the coverage of the subspecies, the Court noted that, if non-European subspecies could be freely imported into the Community [now the Union], the risk that exotic subspecies might be released into the wild there, leading possibly to artificial alterations of the natural avifauna occurring in the Community, could not be excluded.

732. *Ibid.*, paras 36-38.

This would be incompatible with the objective of safeguarding biological balances mentioned in the second recital in the preamble to the Birds Directive.[733]

[2] *Transposing Legislation Cannot Expand the Scope of the Exceptions in Article 6(2) and (3)*

In Case C-262/85, *Commission v. Italy*, the Court described the provisions of Article 6(1) as imposing 'a general prohibition on the marketing of all the birds covered by the Directive'.[734] In that case, the Commission successfully challenged Italian legislation which allowed the marketing of all of the 72 species of birds which were huntable in Italy. Annex III, Part A[735] of the Directive included only 7 species that could be marketed, however. Therefore, the greater scope for marketing wild birds given by the Italian legislation was found to clearly contravene Article 6.

The Court observed that:

> It is clear from the protection to be afforded under the Directive that it is intended to avoid a situation in which all the species that may be hunted may also be marketed because of the pressure which marketing may exert on hunting and consequently on the population level of the species in question.[736]

[3] *Single Market Limits on Stricter National Marketing Measures*

Case C-169/89, *Gourmetterie Van den Burg* throws an interesting sidelight on the interplay between Article 6(2), Article 7 and Article 14 of the Birds Directive, which allows Member States to introduce 'stricter protective measures' than those foreseen in the Directive.

In this case, Dutch inspectors had instituted criminal proceedings against a Dutch food trader who was selling dead red grouse legally acquired from the United Kingdom. Under Dutch law, this species could not be lawfully marketed. The red grouse was listed in Annex II/A of the Directive as a species which could be hunted in the United Kingdom, however. As such, it could be lawfully marketed under Article 6(2) of the Directive.

As Article 6(2) removes marketing prohibitions for legally acquired birds, the Court looked into the Treaty provisions on the free movement of goods and considered whether the Dutch restrictions could be justified, given that the Birds Directive effects

733. C-202/94, *van der Feesten*, para. 17.
734. C-262/85, *Commission v. Italy*, para. 18.
735. At the time of the case, under the Birds Directive 79/409/EEC, Annex III/A was Annex III/1 and Annex III/B was Annex III/2. The numbering was modified with the codification of the Directive and the adoption of Directive 2009/147/EC.
736. C-262/85, *Commission v. Italy*, para. 18.

full harmonisation. As regards Article 14, the Court found that its scope is circumscribed and limits the possibility that Member States can adopt stricter measures to cases where the species concerned occurs within their territory.[737]

It held that:

> Article 14 of the directive does not empower a Member State to afford a given species which is neither migratory nor endangered stricter protection, by means of a prohibition on importation and marketing, than that provided for by the legislation of the Member State on whose territory the bird in question occurs, where such legislation is in conformity with the provisions of [the Birds Directive].[738]

[4] Specimens Born and Reared in Captivity Are Not Covered

In Case C-149/94, *Didier Vergy*, the Court held that Article 6 does not apply to the specimens of species of wild birds which are born and reared in captivity.[739] For captive-bred specimens of species of wild birds, it may nevertheless be relevant to consider other provisions of EU law. In Case C-510/99, *Tridon*, the Court had to consider the compatibility with CITES Regulations and the internal market of a French prohibition relating to a species of macaw, which, as a non-European species, was not protected by the Birds Directive at all.[740]

[D] Hunting of Wild Birds in Accordance with Article 7

Article 7 of the Birds Directive reads as follows:

> 1. Owing to their population level, geographical distribution and reproductive rate throughout the Community, the species listed in Annex II may be hunted under national legislation. Member States shall ensure that the hunting of these species does not jeopardise conservation efforts in their distribution area.
> 2. The species referred to in Annex II, Part A may be hunted in the geographical sea and land area where this Directive applies.
> 3. The species referred to in Annex II, Part B may be hunted only in the Member States in respect of which they are indicated.
> 4. Member States shall ensure that the practice of hunting, including falconry if practised, as carried on in accordance with the national measures in force, complies with the principles of wise use and ecologically balanced control of the species of birds concerned and that this practice is compatible as regards the population of these species, in particular migratory species, with the measures resulting from Article 2.

737. C-169/89, *Gourmetterie Van den Burg*, para. 12.
738. *Ibid.*, para. 15.
739. C-149/94, *Didier Vergy*, paras 13 to 15.
740. Nicolas de Sadeleer, *EU Environmental Law and the Internal Market*, Chapter 5, 291 and 295 (Oxford University Press, 2014).

> They shall see in particular that the species to which hunting laws apply are not hunted during the rearing season or during the various stages of reproduction.
>
> In the case of migratory species, they shall see in particular that the species to which hunting regulations apply are not hunted during their period of reproduction or during their return to their rearing grounds.
>
> Member States shall send the Commission all relevant information on the practical application of their hunting regulations.

Hunting has proved to be one of the most difficult and divisive topics covered by the Birds Directive, with hunters and members of bird conservation organisations often taking opposing positions on how to regulate it. The Commission has tried to ease tensions by creating, in 2004, a framework for cooperation between the main European organisations representing each side.[741] Having consulted these organisations and the Member States, it also produced, a guidance document on hunting under the Birds Directive, which draws on the case-law but also covers a range of scientific concepts related to the wording of Article 7.[742]

[1] List of Huntable Species Cannot Be Expanded

Under Article 7(1) of the Directive, hunting is possible for the species listed under Annex II of the Directive, provided that the hunting does not jeopardise conservation efforts in their distribution area.

According to Article 7(2), the species referred to in Annex II, Part A may be hunted in all Member States while, according to Article 7(3), the species referred to in Annex II, Part B may be hunted only in the Member States in respect of which they are indicated.

In Case C-247/85, *Commission v. Belgium*, the Court confirmed that the national transposing legislation 'must guarantee that the species of birds not listed in Annex II may not be hunted'.[743] The Commission had challenged the fact that, under the relevant Belgian legislation, species of birds not listed in Annex II to the Directive could be hunted if the competent authorities laid down each year, for each species and for a defined area, the opening and closing dates of the hunting season. Thus, the competent authorities still had the power to authorise the hunting of species not listed in Annex II to the Directive but listed in the national legislation. According to the Court, this created a 'legally ambiguous situation' and it concluded that Belgium had infringed the requirements of Article 7.[744]

---

741. Mícheál Ó Bríain, *Recent Developments in Implementation of EU Nature Legislation*, 12, in *Nature Law and Policy in Europe*, Chapter 2 (Andrew L.R. Jackson ed., Routledge 2023).
742. European Commission, Guidance document on hunting under Council Directive 79/409/EEC on the conservation of wild birds (2008), https://environment.ec.europa.eu/topics/nature-and-biodiversity/birds-directive/sustainable-hunting-under-birds-directive_en For a detailed account of Article 7, *see also* Agustín García Ureta, *EU Biodiversity Law: Wild Birds and Habitats Directives*, 165-181 (Europa Law Publishing 2020).
743. C-247/85, *Commission v. Belgium*, para. 14.
744. *Ibid.*, para. 16.

[2] Closed Season Restrictions under Article 7(4)

Where hunting is, in principle, permissible, i.e., where the species of birds are listed in Annex II, Article 7(4) obliges Member States to respect certain principles and restrictions. According to Article 7(4), second sentence, Member States must ensure that huntable species 'are not hunted during the rearing season or during the various stages of reproduction'. Where the huntable species are also migratory, Article 7(4), third sentence requires Member States to ensure that they 'are not hunted during their period of reproduction or during their return to the rearing grounds'.

The Court has interpreted these closed-season provisions of the second and third sentences of Article 7(4) very strictly.

[a] *Notion of a 'Complete System of Protection' During Vulnerable Periods*

In Case C-157/89, *Commission v. Italy*, the Court held that:

> The second and third sentences of Article 7(4) of the Directive are designed to secure a complete system of protection in the periods during which the survival of wild birds is particularly under threat. Consequently, the protection against hunting activities cannot be confined to the majority of the birds of a given species, as determined by average reproductive cycles and migratory movements.[745]

In this case, the Commission complained that Italy had authorised the hunting of various species of birds during the rearing season and during the various stages of reproduction and the hunting of various migratory species during their return to their rearing grounds.

The Court noted that:

> Birds' reproductive cycles and migratory movements are subject to a degree of variability which, owing to meteorological circumstances, affects in particular the periods during which reproduction and migration take place. Thus, some young birds of a given species may still be in the nest or dependent on their parents for food. Likewise, a number of birds of a given species may begin their return journey to their rearing grounds comparatively early relative to average migratory flows.[746]

Against this background, the Court rejected an interpretation of the required closed season for hunting based on the needs of *a majority* of birds. It stated that 'it would be incompatible with the objectives of the Directive if, in situations characterised by prolonged dependence of the fledglings on the parents and early migration, part of the population of a given species should fall outside the protection laid down'.[747]

In Case C-435/92, *APAS*, the Court reinforced the approach it took in the Italian case, holding that 'methods whose object or effect is to allow a certain percentage of the birds of a species to escape such protection do not comply with that provision'.[748]

745. C-157/89, *Commission v. Italy*, para. 14.
746. *Ibid.*, para. 12.
747. *Ibid.*, para. 14.
748. C-435/92, *APAS*, para. 13.

In Case C-507/04, *Commission v. Austria,* the Court took the view that the mating period is part of the stages of reproduction, thus further underpinning the notion of a complete system of protection.

The Court noted that the Article 7(4) regime is defined broadly, 'by reference to the specific biological characteristics of the species concerned, given that it concerns, in addition to the rearing season, the various stages of reproduction'.[749] It noted that the case-law 'reflects the consideration that any action during the periods that are connected with the reproduction of birds is liable to affect their reproduction, even if only a part of their population is concerned'[750] and held that 'that is also true of the mating season, during which the species concerned are particularly exposed and vulnerable'.[751]

[b] Fixing Dates of Hunting Season

Case C-435/92, *APAS,* arose from a preliminary reference from the Administrative Court of Nantes in France following a challenge by several environmental associations to the fixing of the closing dates for hunting in the departments of Maine-et-Loire and Loire-Atlantique. The national court asked for guidance on three questions: first, the criteria to be applied in fixing the closing date for the hunting of migratory birds, having regard to the fact that 'the commencement of pre-mating migration is liable to vary each year on the basis of a number of factors'; second, the scope for competent authorities to fix closing dates for hunting which vary according to the species concerned; and, third, the scope for fixing different closing dates in different parts of a Member State's territory.

[i] Criteria for Fixing Dates

In responding to the first question, the Court affirmed, as it had in the Italian case, the need for an approach that provided *complete* protection. It stated that:

> The method consisting in fixing the closing date for hunting by reference to the period during which migratory activity reaches its highest level cannot be considered to be compatible with Article 7(4) of the Directive. The same is true of those methods which take into account the moment at which a certain percentage of birds have started to migrate and of those which consist in ascertaining the average date of the commencement of pre-mating migration.[752]

[ii] Scope for Varying Closing Dates by Species ('Staggering')

The Court's response to the second question was that a Member State may not fix closing dates for the hunting season which [in respect of the same location] vary

749. C-507/04, *Commission v. Austria,* para. 192.
750. *Ibid.,* para. 193.
751. *Ibid.,* para. 194.
752. C-435/92, *APAS,* para. 12.

according to the species of bird unless it can 'adduce evidence, based on scientific and technical data relevant to each individual case, that staggering the closing dates for hunting does not impede the complete protection of the species of bird liable to be affected by such staggering'.[753] In this regard, the Court took note of two difficulties that staggered closing dates might present: in the first place, the *disturbances* caused by hunting to other species of bird for which hunting has already closed; in the second place, the risks of *confusion* between different species. Thus, while not excluding the possibility of staggered closing dates, the Court made it clear that, in light of these difficulties, the Member State must be able to demonstrate that staggering does not undermine the complete protection required under Article 7(4).

[iii] Scope for Varying Closing Dates by Region

With regard to the third question, the Court considered that 'the fact that the closing dates for hunting vary from one region to another is in itself compatible with the third sentence of Article 7(4) of the Directive'.[754]

It went on to note that that provision:

> Requires only that the closing date for hunting be set in such a way as to make possible complete protection of migratory birds during their pre-mating migration. If it appears that the pre-mating migration begins at different times in different parts of the territory of a Member State, that Member State is permitted to set different closing dates for hunting.

[c] Example of a Member State in Contravention of Article 7(4)

In upholding a Commission claim in Case C-38/99, *Commission v. France,* that France infringed Article 7(4) of the Birds Directive, the Court drew on its own analysis in C-157/89, *Commission v. Italy* and Case C-435/92, *APAS*. The Court found that, with respect to both the opening and closing dates for hunting, France did not provide the required complete system of protection.

As regards the *opening dates,* it found that the early opening dates for the hunting of waterfowl indicated in the relevant French legislation:

> Do not enable all individuals of species which are rearing their young to be protected. That is tantamount to admitting that, for certain of the species concerned and in certain areas, hunting is opened too early.[755]

It noted a study which showed that, in the case of mallards, in eight departments no more than 80% of young birds were able to fly by the early opening date for hunting; on the same date, in 26 other departments, a maximum of 90% of young birds were able to fly. In the case of the coot, in eight departments, no more than 80% of young

---

753. *Ibid.*, para. 22.
754. *Ibid.*, para. 24.
755. C-38/99, *Commission v. France,* para. 24.

birds were able to fly by the early opening date of hunting; in 15 other departments, no more than 90% of young birds were able to fly by that date.[756]

As regards *closing dates*, the Court noted data showing that, for 29 migratory species which may be hunted in France, the closing dates for hunting were fixed, depending on the species concerned, 10, 20 or even 30 days later than the date of commencement of return migration (also known as 'pre-mating migration') of the species. It observed that:

> It follows that a greater or lesser percentage of birds, depending on the species involved, is not protected against hunting in the pre-mating migration periods, during which the survival of birds is under particular threat.[757]

It also found that France had failed, in line with the case-law in Case C-435/92, *APAS*, to adduce evidence to justify the staggering of closing dates for hunting.[758]

[3] Relationship Between Article 7 and Article 9 of the Birds Directive

As was made clear in Case C-182/02, *Ligue pour la protection des oiseaux*,[759] a derogation from the system of protection laid down by Article 7 of the Directive remains possible but only under the strict conditions provided for in Article 9 of the Directive. In considering national hunting provisions, therefore, it will often be necessary to have regard not only to the case-law on Article 7 but also the case-law on Article 9 of the Directive.

An example is Case C-161/19, *Commission v. Austria*, in which the Court upheld a Commission complaint that Austria infringed Article 7(4) of the Birds Directive by allowing spring hunting of woodcock in Lower Austria. It was undisputed that the Austrian provisions were not consistent with Article 7(4) but Austria argued that the spring hunting was covered by a lawful derogation under Article 9(1)(c) of the Birds Directive. Before making its finding of infringement of Article 7(4), the Court needed to consider – and dismiss – arguments of lawfulness based on Article 9.

[E] Prohibition of Non-selective Means of Hunting, Capture or Killing under Article 8

In respect of hunting, capture or killing of wild birds, Article 8(1) of the Birds Directive requires Member States to prohibit the use of 'all means, arrangements or methods used for the large-scale capture or killing of birds or capable of causing the local disappearance of a species, in particular, the use of those listed in Annex IV, point (a)'.

Article 8(2) requires them to also prohibit hunting from certain modes of transport and under the conditions mentioned in Annex IV, point (b).

756. *Ibid.*, para. 25.
757. *Ibid.*, para. 41.
758. *Ibid.*, paras 43 and 44.
759. C-182/02, *Ligue pour la protection des oiseaux*, operative part of ruling.

[1] *Need for Complete Transposition*

With regard to Article 8(2), in Case C-339/87, *Commission v. Netherlands,* the Court upheld a Commission complaint that the Netherlands had failed to transpose the prohibition on hunting from aircraft. It rejected an argument by the Netherlands that, in the Netherlands, aircraft are not used to pursue games and that it was superfluous to include such a prohibition in the national legislation. It held that the fact that in a Member State, a particular means of hunting is unknown, does not constitute a reason for not transposing that prohibition into the national legal order.[760]

[2] *Limes and Nets*

Annex IV(a) refers, amongst other means, methods or arrangements, to the following: snares, limes, nets, and traps.

In some Member States, use of non-selective means of capture or killing has proved a very contentious issue in the implementation of the Birds Directive. As with extended hunting seasons, the issue typically needs to be examined in combination with Article 9, since Member State authorities have sought to justify such means by reference to the derogation possibilities of Article 9. The following are a number of illustrations of where use of limes and nets were found to contravene Article 8.

[a] *Use of Limed Twigs to Hunt Thrushes in Spain*

In Case C-79/03, *Commission v. Spain,* the Court upheld a Commission complaint that Spain had infringed Article 8(1) of the Birds Directive by allowing hunting of thrush using limed twigs in Valencia by means of the method known as 'parany'. The 'parany' is described as:

> A device used to capture birds. It consists of a structure of limed twigs arranged in a tree to which the hunted birds are lured with decoys. As soon as a bird comes into contact with a limed twig, it generally loses its ability to fly and may be caught and killed by the hunter.[761]

It was common ground that hunting thrush using limed twigs cannot avoid the capture of birds other than thrushes. A report from the Spanish Ornithological Society showed that, amongst the birds captured by that method, the ratio of thrushes to other species is in the range of 1.24 to 4.[762] Before concluding that it fell within the scope of the prohibition in Article 8(1), the Court observed that:

> Hunting by means of the 'parany' is based on a non-selective method of capture. The fact that, when birds other than those covered by the decree are caught in the

760. C-339/87, *Commission v. Netherlands,* para. 32.
761. C-79/03, *Commission v. Spain,* para. 2.
762. *Ibid.*, para. 19.

limed twigs, the hunters are required to clean them and release them is not sufficient to cast doubt on the non-selective nature of that method of capture.[763]

[b] *Use of Clap-Nets to Capture Finch in Malta*

Article 8(1) also featured in Case C-557/15, *Commission v. Malta*. At issue was the live-capturing of seven species of wild finches involving the use of clap-nets, which was authorised by Malta by way of a derogation purporting to comply with Article 9(1)(c) of the Directive. The Commission argued that 'since such nets are, pursuant to Article 8(1) of Directive 2009/147, read in conjunction with point (a) of Annex IV thereto, regarded as a non-selective method, a derogation involving their use cannot be considered to be proportionate'.[764] The Maltese authorities had acknowledged, in a technical memorandum, 'the non-selective nature of such nets since they have admitted the existence of "by-catch" despite the fact that those nets are manually triggered by hunters'.[765] The Court found that the condition 'laid down in Article 9(1)(c) of Directive 2009/147, according to which the live-capturing of finches can only be permitted if it is carried out on a selective basis, is not met in this instance'.[766] As the use of clap-nets was non-selective, it ruled that there was a concomitant infringement of the prohibition in Article 8(1).[767]

[3] *Semi-automatic and Automatic Weapons*

Article 8(1) in conjunction with Annex IV(a) forbids the 'use of semi-automatic or automatic weapons with a magazine capable of holding more than two rounds of ammunition'. In Case C-262/85, *Commission v. Italy*, the Commission unsuccessfully argued that Italian legislation contravened this requirement. The Court was convinced that the technical details of the relevant Italian firearm requirements were within the bounds of what was permissible.[768]

[F] Derogations under Article 9

Article 9(1) of the Directive provides that:

> Member States may derogate from the provisions of Articles 5 to 8, where there is no other satisfactory solution, for the following reasons:
>
> (a) in the interest of public health and safety;
> - in the interest of air safety;
> - to prevent serious damage to crops, livestock, forests, fisheries and water;

763. *Ibid.*, para. 20.
764. C-557/15, *Commission v. Malta*, para. 79.
765. *Ibid.*, para. 84.
766. *Ibid.*, para. 85.
767. *Ibid.*
768. C-262/85, *Commission v. Italy*, para. 29.

- for the protection of flora and fauna.

(b) for the purposes of research and teaching, of repopulation, of reintroduction and for the breeding necessary for those purpose;

(c) to permit, under strictly supervised conditions and on a selective basis, the capture, keeping or other judicious use of certain birds in small numbers.

According to Article 9(2) of the Directive, the derogations referred to in paragraph 1 must specify:

(a) the species which are subject to the derogations;

(b) the means, arrangements or methods authorised for capture or killing;

(c) the conditions of risk and the circumstances of time and place under which such derogations may be granted;

(d) the authority empowered to declare that the required conditions obtain and to decide what means, arrangements or methods may be used, within what limits and by whom;

(e) the controls which will be carried out.

[1] Overview

[a] Three Conditions to Be Satisfied

Article 9 allows Member States to derogate from the general prohibitions and other restrictions contained in Articles 5 to 8 of the Directive, subject to three conditions. The first is that there must be no other satisfactory solution (a condition also found in the species protection provisions of the Habitats Directive). The second requires the derogation to be justified by one of the grounds exhaustively[769] enumerated under Article 9(1) letters (a) to (c). Under the third condition, 'the derogation must comply with the precise formal conditions set out in Article 9(2), which are intended to limit derogations to what is strictly necessary and to enable the Commission to supervise them'.[770]

An analysis of the case-law shows that, in many cases, purported derogations fail by reference to more than one condition. In particular, reliance on grounds provided for in Article 9(1)(c) involves satisfying several requirements.

[b] Scope to Use Derogations

The scope of Article 9 extends to all the protective provisions contained under Articles 5 to 8 of the Directive. Thus, provided its strict conditions are met, Article 9 can enable any of the following: a derogation from the general prohibition on killing wild birds laid

769. C-247/85, *Commission v. Belgium*, para. 58.
770. *Ibid.*, para. 7.

down in Article 5 of the Directive; a derogation allowing the hunting wild bird species other than the ones envisaged under Article 7(1) to (3) in conjunction with Annex II of the Directive;[771] a derogation permitting hunting or capture during the rearing season or the stages of reproduction regulated by Article 7(4);[772] a derogation for the use of non-selective means of hunting, capture or killing.[773]

Member States cannot invoke grounds of derogation other than those set out in Article 9(1) letters (a) to (c). Thus, in Case C-192/11, *Commission v. Poland*, the Court found that Poland had incorrectly transposed Article 9(1) as it had enlarged the grounds for derogation to include imperative reasons of overriding public interest, including those of social and economic nature[774] [in effect, importing the terminology of derogations under Article 6(4) of the Habitats Directive].

The strictness of the applicable conditions needs to be stressed. A derogation which might be possible in principle may not be possible in practice because the required conditions cannot be satisfied.

[c] Derogation System Must Be Interpreted Strictly

The derogation system foreseen by the Directive 'must be interpreted strictly and impose on the authority taking the decision the burden of proving that those conditions are present for each derogation'.[775]

The authorising decisions 'must contain a clear and sufficient statement of reasons which refers to the reasons, conditions and requirements laid down in that article'.[776] Thus, 'Article 9 of the Directive authorises Member States to derogate from the general prohibition on hunting protected species which is laid down in Articles 5 and 7 of the Directive only by measures which refer in sufficient detail to the factors mentioned in Article 9(1) and (2)'.[777]

The concept of local interest does not appear amongst the reasons listed in Article 9, for instance, hence it cannot justify derogation measures.[778]

[d] Transposing Legislation

While the power to grant derogations can be delegated to regional or subordinate[779] authorities, the transposition of Article 9 has to ensure that these strict conditions are properly reflected in the national legislation. Indeed, if the national legislation does not

771. C-262/85, *Commission v. Italy*, para. 13.
772. C-182/02, *Ligue pour la protection des oiseaux*, para. 12: 'Article 9(1)(c) of the Directive permits a Member State to derogate from the opening and closing dates for hunting which follow from consideration of the objectives set out in Article 7(4) of the Directive.'
773. C-252/85, *Commission v. France.*
774. C-192/11, *Commission v. Poland*, paras 36 and 39.
775. C-217/19, *Commission v. Finland*, para. 66.
776. *Ibid.*; C-60/05, *WWF Italia and others*, para. 34.
777. C-182/02, *Ligue pour la protection des oiseaux*, para. 13.
778. C-247/85, *Commission v. Belgium*, para. 58.
779. C-435/92, *APAS*, para. 26.

in itself establish the criteria and conditions provided for in Article 9(2) or require regions to take account of those criteria and conditions, it introduces an element of uncertainty as regards the obligations which the regions must observe when adopting their regulations.[780]

As the Court noted in Case C-507/04, *Commission v. Austria*:

> Any measure that derogates from the Directive's protective provisions must be examined in light of the conditions and criteria set out in Article 9 of the Directive. Consequently, the Member States cannot entitle the authority vested with the power to make regulations to adopt measures derogating from the protective rules prescribed by the Directive without defining in a precise manner the substantive and formal requirements, arising from that article, to which such derogations must be subject (see, to this effect, *WWF Italia and Others*, paragraphs 25 and 28).[781]

[e] Derogations Cannot Be Too General or Unqualified

In one of its earliest judgments in relation to the nature directives, the Court in Case C-247/85, *Commission v. Belgium*, condemned Belgium for derogations that were framed too widely and lacked the required qualifications. The purported derogations gave a very broad scope to destroy birds' nests built against houses[782] and also allowed a very large scope to capture, kill, destroy or drive away house sparrows, tree sparrows and starlings and destroy their eggs nests and broods.[783] The sweeping generality and lack of qualification of these purported derogations were found to contravene Article 9.[784]

[f] Relationship with Other Provisions

The case-law shows that issues concerning compliance with Article 9 will often need to be considered in conjunction with issues concerning compliance with the relevant provisions of Articles 5 to 8 of the Birds Directive. This is because a lack of compliance with Article 9 will typically involve a concomitant breach of one of these provisions. The Commission has not always pleaded concomitant breaches, however, as Case C-192/11, *Commission v. Poland* shows.[785]

[2] Condition Requiring the Absence of Another Satisfactory Solution

The condition that there is no other satisfactory solution must be fulfilled as a *prerequisite* for the use of one of the derogation grounds listed in Article 9(1).

780. C-157/89, *Commission v. Italy*, paras 16 and 17; and C-118/94, *Veneto*, para. 25.
781. C-507/04, *Commission v. Austria*, para. 287.
782. C-247/85, *Commission v. Belgium*, paras 24 to 29.
783. *Ibid.*, paras 30 to 35.
784. *Ibid.*, paras 28 and 34.
785. *See* Chapter 8 §8.03[E].

[a] Need for a Formal Statement of Reasons Based on the Best Available Scientific Knowledge

In Case C-557/15, *Commission v. Malta,* the Court considered the condition of the absence of another satisfactory solution in the context of finch-trapping. While it did not take issue with the Maltese transposing legislation, which required that this condition needed to be addressed when granting a derogation,[786] it found that Maltese declarations authorising autumn trapping of finches during the 2014 and 2015 seasons were non-compliant with Article 9 as they did not contain 'any reference to the absence of another satisfactory solution'.[787] Nor did they contain a reference to technical, legal and scientific reports which, according to the Maltese Government, would have been submitted within the context of a mandatory review by the Maltese Ornis Committee[788] or to the recommendations based on that information. In any case, such derogation decisions must contain 'a clear and sufficient statement of reasons concerning the condition of the absence of another satisfactory solution'.[789]

This point was reinforced in Case C-900/19, *One Voice,* in which the Court made a link with Article 9(2) of the Birds Directive:

> It cannot be considered that national legislation making use of the derogation provided for in Article 9 of the Birds Directive fulfils the conditions relating to the obligation to state reasons, which are laid down in Article 9(2) of that directive where it merely states that there is no other satisfactory solution, that statement not being supported by a detailed statement of reasons based on the best relevant scientific knowledge and setting out the reasons which led the competent authority to conclude that all the conditions capable of permitting a derogation within the meaning of Article 9 of that directive, including the condition relating to the absence of another satisfactory solution, are fulfilled.[790]

[b] Need to Assess and Compare Solutions in the Light of Reasonable Options and Best Available Techniques

In Case C-900/19, *One Voice,* the Court held that:

> It must also be borne in mind that, where the competent authority is called upon to determine that there are no other satisfactory solutions, it must *compare* the various solutions that fulfil the conditions of the derogation laid down in Article

786. C-557/15, *Commission v. Malta,* para. 48.
787. *Ibid.,* paras 49 and 50.
788. The Ornis Committee is a body established under the Maltese legislation to review the derogation decisions. Regulation 9 of the Conservation of Wild Birds Regulations transposing, in essence, Article 9 of Directive 2009/147, made arrangements for a specific decision-making procedure which must be followed during the assessment of such a derogation, and included a mandatory review by the Maltese Ornis Committee.
789. C-557/15, *Commission v. Malta,* para. 51.
790. C-900/19, *One Voice,* para. 32.

> 9(1)(c) of the Birds Directive in order to determine the solution that appeared to be the most satisfactory (emphasis added).[791]

Having noted the relevance of Article 13 TFEU, according to which the EU is to have regard to the welfare requirements of animals, the Court held that:

> The satisfactory nature of the alternative solutions must be assessed in the light of the reasonable options and the best available techniques.[792]

[c] *Traditional Nature of a Non-selective Method Is Insufficient to Show There Is No Other Solution*

In Case C-900/19, *One Voice,* the Court ruled, in a preliminary reference, that the traditional nature of a method of capture of birds is not, in itself, sufficient to establish that another satisfactory solution, within the meaning of Article 9, cannot be substituted for that method. The context was a legal challenge by two environmental associations to a 1989 French Decree authorising the use of a non-selective traditional hunting method, namely *the use of limes,* without the condition concerning the absence of another satisfactory solution having been satisfied. The captured birds were to be used as decoys for hunting other birds. The condition as to absence of another satisfactory solution was one of the issues the referring court raised.

The Court noted that the hunting of wild birds for recreational purposes under the conditions laid down by the Birds Directive may constitute 'judicious use' under Article 9(1)(c) and that traditional methods of hunting may also fall within the concept of 'judicious use', since, as Article 2 of that directive mentions, Member States must take account, when taking the measures referred to in that article of recreational requirements.[793]

It recalled, however, that the preservation of traditional activities does not constitute an autonomous derogation from the system of protection established by the Birds Directive.[794] It noted that:

> Hunting methods often form part of local traditions or use, so that, if the aim of preserving them constituted a ground for an autonomous derogation, that would result in the authorisation of a large number of practices that are contrary to the requirements of Article 9 of the Birds Directive. Such an approach would run counter to the strict interpretation which must obtain in the case of that provision.[795]

---

791. *Ibid.*, para. 37.
792. *Ibid.*, para. 39.
793. *Ibid.*, para. 33.
794. *Ibid.*, para. 35. The Court referred to C-247/85, *Commission v. Belgium,* para. 8; C-57/89, *Commission v. Germany,* para. 22; and C-217/19, *Commission v. Finland,* para. 85.
795. C-900/19, *One Voice,* para. 36.

[d] Capture of Birds to Facilitate Bird Fanciers

In Case C-10/96, *LRPBO and AVES*, a preliminary reference from the Belgian Council of State, the Court considered the condition in relation to *the capture of wild birds for breeding purposes*. A Belgian environmental association had contested the legality of orders of the Walloon Government allowing this practice (which was for the benefit of bird fanciers). The Court pointed out that a derogation from the system of protection established by the Birds Directive and, in particular, from the prohibition of killing or capturing protected species, as laid down in Article 5(a), can be granted only if there is no other satisfactory solution.[796] In this regard, the Court noted that breeding and reproduction of protected birds in captivity may definitely constitute such an alternative solution, where they are scientifically and technically possible. Furthermore, breeding and reproduction in captivity could be regarded as not constituting an 'other satisfactory solution' only if 'it were established that, were it not for the capture of birds in the wild, those activities could not prosper'.[797]

The Court went on to note that:

> The fact that the breeding and reproduction in captivity of the species concerned are not yet feasible on a large scale by reason of the installations and the inveterate habits of bird fanciers, habits which, moreover, have been encouraged by domestic rules derogating from the general scheme of the Directive, is not in itself such as to cast doubt on the satisfactory nature of the alternative solution to capturing birds in the wild.[798]

In light of this analysis, the Court ruled that:

> The Directive, and, in particular Article 9(1)(c) thereof, must be interpreted as meaning that a Member State may not, on a decreasing basis and for a limited period, authorize the capture of certain protected species in order to enable bird fanciers to stock their aviaries, where breeding and reproduction of those species in captivity are possible but are not yet practicable on a large scale by reason of the fact that many fanciers would be compelled to alter their installations and change their habits.

In this case, the Court also examined the condition in relation to another specific issue – that of obviating 'the problems of consanguinity resulting from too many endogenous crossings'. The Court was not convinced that invoking such problems would satisfy the condition as to no other satisfactory solution. It stated that 'that condition would not be met if it were possible to obviate the problems of consanguinity by cooperation and exchanges of specimens between breeding establishments'.[799] The Court did not entirely exclude the possibility that the condition of the absence of a satisfactory alternative solution might be fulfilled in such cases but stressed that strict requirements would apply. Thus, if the obviation of consanguinity which would result

796. C-10/96, *LRPBO and AVES*, para. 17.
797. *Ibid.*, para. 20.
798. *Ibid.*, para. 21.
799. *Ibid.*, para. 25.

from too many endogenous crossings was not possible by other means, 'the number of specimens which may be captured must be fixed at the level of what proves to be objectively necessary to provide a solution for those problems'.[800]

[e] *Use of Non-selective Means Such as Limes and Nets*

[i] Spanish Example

In Case C-79/03, *Commission v. Spain*, the Court was not convinced by arguments by Spain that there was no other satisfactory solution to the use of non-selective limed twigs to hunt thrushes in Valencia. The ground invoked by Spain was Article 9(1)(a), serious damage to crops. The Court noted, however, that, in other Spanish regions where there was large-scale cultivation of olives and grapes and where there were also large populations of thrushes, hunting using limed twigs was not permitted. Instead, thrushes could be shot, which is a selective method of culling. It was not apparent that the olive groves and vineyards in those regions suffered greater damage than the same crops in Valencia.[801]

The Court was also not convinced by Spain's argument that replacing hunting thrushes by means of the 'parany' with shooting because of the increase in the number of guns and hunting days, which it would entail, would cause harassment to other species of game birds to such an extent that their populations would decrease in size. It noted that thrushes were hunted in Valencia at the same time and without problems.[802]

[ii] French Example

Having ruled out in Case C-900/19, *One Voice*, that its traditional nature demonstrated that there was no other satisfactory solution to the use of limes to capture wild birds for use as decoys, the Court observed that there were other options, such as the breeding and reproduction of protected species in captivity.[803]

It made the following specific observations:

> Moreover, although the capture of birds using limes is in itself part of the hunting activity, it is only a step preliminary to other methods of taking birds, since the birds thus caught are intended for use as decoys for the purpose of attracting other birds of the same species, which are then shot at with guns.
>
> The mere fact that another method of capture requires a change and, consequently, a departure from certain characteristics of a tradition cannot suffice for the view to be taken that there is no 'other satisfactory solution' within the meaning of Article 9(1) of the Birds Directive.

800. *Ibid.*, para. 27.
801. C-79/03, *Commission v. Spain*, para. 25.
802. *Ibid.*, para. 26.
803. C-900/19, *One Voice*, paras 40 and 41.

It is worth noting that similar provisions of a French decree had been subject to earlier scrutiny by the Court in Case C-252/85, *Commission v. France*. On the earlier occasion, the Court dismissed a Commission plea that France infringed Article 8(1) of the Birds Directive in relation to the use of lime. At that time, the Commission argued that use of limes could not constitute a 'judicious use' under Article 9(1)(c). Based on the documents before it, the Court held that the use of limes was not incompatible with Article 9(1)(c) of the Birds Directive.[804] In Case C-252/85, *Commission v. France*, however, the Court was not called upon to examine the issue of no other satisfactory solution. In Case C-900/19, *One Voice*, it was therefore examining it for the first time in relation to the practice.

[f] *Extensions to Hunting Seasons*

In Case C-182/02, *Ligue pour la protection des oiseaux*, the Court considered this condition in relation to *hunting seasons*. The Court's ruling followed a preliminary reference from the French Conseil d'Etat in which one of the issues was the legality of a French ministerial decree on hunting dates which purported to validly derogate from the closed-season requirements of Article 7(4) of the Birds Directive.

The Court ruled that the condition of no other alternative:

> Cannot be considered to have been satisfied when the hunting period under a derogation coincides, without need, with periods in which the Directive aims to provide particular protection (see, to that effect, *Commission v. Italy*, paragraph 39). There would be no such need if the sole purpose of the derogation authorising hunting were to extend the hunting periods for certain species of birds in territories which they already frequent during the hunting periods fixed in accordance with Article 7 of the Directive.[805]

Thus, while accepting that Article 9 derogations could be used in relation to hunting, the Court limited the possibility in circumstances where the birds concerned could be hunted in the same territories during the normal hunting period.

The condition featured in a number of subsequent Commission direct actions about spring hunting.

[i] Austrian Example of Spring Hunting

In Case C-161/19, *Commission v. Austria*, the Court did not accept Austria's argument that there was no alternative to spring hunting of woodcock in Lower Austria, citing, amongst other reasons, the possibility of hunting the species in the autumn.[806]

---

804. C-252/85, *Commission v. France*, paras 23 to 32.
805. C-182/02, *Ligue pour la protection des oiseaux*, para. 16.
806. C-161/19, *Commission v. Austria*, para. 51.

[ii] Finnish Example of Spring Hunting

In Case C-344/03, *Commission v. Finland*, the Commission claimed a breach of Article 7(4) of the Directive, as Finland allowed spring hunting of several species of wild aquatic birds listed in Annex II during their rearing season. In the Commission's view, the conditions required for the application of the derogation laid down in Article 9(1)(c) were not met, in particular, the conditions of 'no other satisfactory solution' and of 'small numbers'[807] [This is one of two Commission direct actions on spring hunting, the other being Case C-217/19, *Commission v. Finland*].

The Commission argued that the hunting of the species concerned in the autumn, even if it is in smaller numbers than in the spring, and 'the hunting of other species of aquatic birds present in the autumn' represent another satisfactory solution which can replace spring hunting. In contrast, the Finnish Government contended that there was no other satisfactory solution for replacing spring hunting as it was currently practised in Finland and provided species-specific evidence in support of its contention.

Having reviewed the evidence for all of these species, the Court upheld the Commission's complaint – except in respect of one species, the long-tailed duck. For this species, it ruled that spring hunting fulfilled the condition that there be no other satisfactory solution. It had not been disputed by the parties that this species could not be hunted in autumn in the geographical areas open for spring hunting.

The Court stated that:

> A measure consisting in authorising the hunting in the autumn, or in the spring, of other species of aquatic birds present in those areas by way of replacement for the spring hunting of long-tailed duck cannot be regarded as another satisfactory solution within the meaning of Article 9(1)(c) of the Directive. Such a solution would risk rendering that provision nugatory, at least partially, because it would allow in certain territories for prohibitions on hunting certain species of birds, even though hunting in small numbers might, in theory, not jeopardise the maintenance of their populations at a satisfactory level and, therefore, constitute judicious use of those species. Moreover, unless all bird species are considered to be equivalent for the purposes of hunting, that solution would, in any event, be a source of legal uncertainty, because the basis on which it may be considered that the hunting of a given species can replace the hunting of another species is not clear from the applicable legislation.[808]

Thus, while it is very difficult to justify spring hunting by reference to the condition as to absence of another satisfactory alternative, it is not impossible to do so.

[3] Grounds Based on Article 9(1)(a)

The first and third indents of Article 9(1)(a) enable Member States to grant derogations from the protection regime laid down in the Directive, in the interests of public health and safety and to prevent serious damage to crops, livestock, forests, fisheries and

---

807. C-344/03, *Commission v. Finland*, para. 12.
808. *Ibid.*, para. 44.

water. There is case-law on these. The Court has also shed light on the fourth indent, 'protection of flora and fauna'.

[a] Public Health and Safety

In Case C-247/85, *Commission v. Belgium*, the Commission successfully challenged Belgian legislation which generally authorised the disturbance, removal or destruction of birds' nests built against houses and adjoining buildings. Belgium argued that 'the presence of nests in chimneys and pipes has led on many occasions to fires and floods and they have also caused problems of hygiene, for example in the food industry'.[809] The Court recognised that:

> The prevention of fires, floods and disease, are certainly of such a kind as to justify the removal and destruction of nests under Article 9 of the Directive. However, it is clear from the Belgian Government's own argument that the removal or destruction of nests is necessary only *in specific cases* in which the higher-ranking interests of public health and security must override the protection of birds and their habitats (emphasis added).[810]

The Court noted that 'it cannot be maintained that *all* nests built against houses and adjoining buildings *always* represent a danger to health (emphasis added)'.[811]

[b] Serious Damage to Crops

In like vein, the Court also condemned Belgium in Case C-247/85, *Commission v. Belgium,* for an over-general derogation argued to be justified to prevent serious damage to crops.

The Court found that if certain species cause 'serious damage to crops and orchards or are responsible for pollution and noise in towns or certain regions, Belgium is in principle authorised to provide for a derogation from the general system of protection provided for in Articles 5, 6, and 7'.[812] However, 'a derogation under Article 9 must, according to Article 9(1), cover specific situations'.[813] With regard to the Belgian transposition, the derogation for three species of birds,[814] enshrined in the national legislation, was found by the Court to be too general and therefore not compliant. The Court observed that:

> The Belgian rules do not indicate the reasons regarding the protection of public health or serious damage to crops or other fields mentioned in Article 9(1)(a) of the directive which might necessitate the granting of such a wide category of persons

809. C-247/85, *Commission v. Belgium,* para. 25.
810. *Ibid.*, para. 27.
811. *Ibid.*, para. 28.
812. *Ibid.*, para. 33.
813. *Ibid.*, para. 34.
814. The Belgian Royal Decrees provided for a permission at any time to capture, kill, destroy or drive away the birds, as well as their eggs and broods for three species of birds, namely the house sparrow, the tree sparrow and the starling.

> of a permanent derogation, applying throughout Belgium, from the protection provide for by the directive.[815]

As already noted in section §4.02[B][1][b], in Case C-507/04, *Commission v. Austria*, the Court condemned Austria for a breach of Article 5 in respect of the lack of protection of the European starling between 15 July and 30 November. The Court also found an infringement of Article 9 of the Birds Directive. Austria argued that the removal of protection during this period was justified by the need to protect vines, submitting that flocks of up to 50,000 starlings invaded Burgenland's vineyards each year and that conventional means for driving them away had proved insufficient.[816] The Court observed, however, that the Burgenland legislation neither specified the means, arrangements or methods authorised for capture or killing nor laid down in a binding manner the specific manner in which action might be taken against the starling.[817] Under the Burgenland legislation, it was sufficient for a derogatory regulation to establish the existence of a danger for viticulture resulting from the presence of European starlings. The regulation to be adopted was not required, however, to contain specific particulars having regard to the criteria laid down in Article 9(2) of the Birds Directive.[818] Thus, the Burgenland derogation regime did not satisfy the detailed rules for derogation prescribed in Article 9.[819]

In Case C-79/03, *Commission v. Spain*, the Court was not convinced by Spain's argument that hunting of thrushes using non-selective limed twigs was needed to prevent serious damage to crops. The decree allowing this method had linked it to a 'deeply rooted tradition in the Community of Valencia rather than the prevention of serious damage to crops':[820]

> Moreover, it is not in dispute that 80% of the 'paranys' set up in that Community are to be found in the province of Castellón, 69.5% of which are in areas without olive groves or vineyards. Thus, the justification based on prevention of serious damage to those crops does not appear to be consistent with such a situation.[821]

[c] Protection of Flora and Fauna

Case C-507/04, *Commission v. Austria*, in combination with Case C-344/03, *Commission v. Finland*, sheds some oblique light on the indent of Article 9(1)(a) relating to the protection of flora and fauna. In defending itself against a Commission complaint that the province of Carinthia infringed Article 7(4) in respect of the hunting season for capercaillie and black grouse,[822] Austria argued that the consequence of a general

815. C-247/85, *Commission v. Belgium*, para. 34.
816. C-507/04, *Commission v. Austria*, para. 86.
817. *Ibid.*, para. 288.
818. *Ibid.*, para. 289.
819. *Ibid.*, para. 290.
820. C-79/03, *Commission v. Spain*, para. 27.
821. *Ibid.*, para. 28.
822. The Commission did not raise any plea about a concomitant breach of Article 9 of the Birds Directive.

prohibition on hunting these species during the mating season would be that hunters would lose interest in those species of game birds and abandon efforts to conserve the species' habitat. This would have an immediate effect on the population of the species, which need a specific habitat, namely forest pasture, which had become considerably scarcer.

In the context of the condition of the absence of another satisfactory solution, in Case C-344/03, *Commission v. Finland,* Finland had similarly argued that hunters provided valuable services to help maintain populations of eider, golden-eye and goosander.[823] The Court considered that hunting wasn't necessary for the delivery of such services, however.

Referring to the earlier case, the Court observed that, 'while the protection of flora is admittedly one of the grounds of derogation set out in the fourth indent of Article 9(1)(a) of the Directive, protection of that habitat can be ensured regardless of hunting'.[824] It noted the obligation of Member States under Article 4 of the Birds Directive to ensure habitat protection both within and outside SPAs for birds.[825]

[4] Grounds Based on Article 9(1)(c)

Grounds based on Article 9(1)(c) are particularly important since they provide a broad scope in terms of the purposes that can be served by the derogation. The requirements to be satisfied are, however, exacting and there is now considerable case-law on each of them.

[a] Notion of 'Small Numbers'

If grounds are based on Article 9(1)(c), the derogation must be limited to 'small numbers'.

According to the case-law, the criterion of small numbers 'is not an absolute criterion but rather refers to the maintenance of the level of total population and to the reproductive situation of the species concerned'.[826]

The topic has been addressed in several cases, in considerable detail. Key points in the case-law are the importance of a scientific reference based on a 1% criterion; the need to relate the 'small numbers' requirement to 'the situation of the species at issue';[827] the need to ensure that regional derogations respect national ceilings; the need to use the correct reference population to calculate 'small numbers'; and the need to be able to demonstrate by sound scientific knowledge that relevant bird populations are being maintained at a satisfactory level.

823. C-344/03, *Commission v. Finland,* paras 35-40.
824. C-507/04, *Commission v. Austria,* para. 205.
825. *Ibid.,* para. 206.
826. C-252/85, *Commission v. France,* para. 28.
827. C-60/05, *WWF Italia,* para. 35.

[i] Importance of the ORNIS Committee Criterion of 1%

In Case C-344/03, *Commission v. Finland*, the Court looked at the topic in the context of Finland's use of Article 9 for spring hunting. The Commission submitted that, according to the ORNIS committee, 'small numbers' is to be understood to mean less than 1% of the average annual mortality rate of the species in question as regards the species the hunting of which is prohibited and approximately 1% as regards the species the hunting of which is permitted. It argued that, in light of this understanding, Finland did not satisfy the criterion in relation to the hunting of several bird species.

The ORNIS Committee for the Adaptation to Technical and Scientific Progress under Directive 2009/147[828] is composed of expert representatives of the Member States.

In its findings, the Court noted the details of the ORNIS committee work:

> The Commission's paper, entitled 'Second report on the application of Directive 79/409/EEC on the conservation of wild birds' (COM(93) 572 final of 24 November 1993), indicates that, according to the work of the ORNIS committee, 'small numbers' should be understood to mean any sample of less than 1% of the total annual mortality rate of the population in question (average value) for those species which are not to be hunted and a sample in the order of 1% for those species which may be hunted, with 'population in question' being understood, with regard to migratory species, to mean the population of those regions from which come the main contingents passing through the region to which the derogation applies during its period of application.[829]

The Court approved the use of the ORNIS committee criterion as a scientific reference:

> Although it is true that the criterion of small numbers as defined by the ORNIS committee is not legally binding, in this instance it can, by reason of the acknowledged scientific value of that committee's opinions and the failure to adduce any scientific evidence to the contrary, be used by the Court as a basis of reference for assessing whether the derogation granted by the defendant Member State under Article 9(1)(c) of the Directive fulfils the condition that the capture of the birds in question must be carried out in small numbers.[830]

Applying the small numbers threshold of the ORNIS Committee, the Court found that Finland had not respected the 'small numbers' requirement in respect of several – though not all – species.[831] The Court has continued to refer to the ORNIS Committee criterion in subsequent cases.

---

828. The ORNIS Committee is instituted under Article 16(1) of the Birds Directive which reads as follows: The Commission shall be assisted by the Committee for Adaptation to Technical and Scientific Progress.
829. C-344/03, *Commission v. Finland*, para. 53.
830. *Ibid.*, para. 54.
831. *Ibid.*, paras 55 to 60.

[ii] Application of 'Small Numbers' Requirement at Regional Level in the Context of National Ceilings

One concern that might arise is the application of the 'small numbers' criterion at regional level without sufficient regard to the overall national level. This issue was addressed extensively in Case C-60/05, *WWF Italia*. This case arose from a legal challenge by a number of environmental associations to a decision of the Lombardy Region in Italy on the hunting of certain numbers of wild birds belonging to the finch and brambling species during the 2003/2004 hunting season.

Under Italy's transposition of Article 9 of the Birds Directive, the Italian regions were empowered to grant derogations. At national level, an official institute, the National Institute for Wild Fauna or INFS advised that the maximum quota which may be hunted in the entire territory of Italy for the 2003/04 hunting season was 1,500,000 specimens of the finch species and 52,000 specimens of the brambling species. In the context of interregional agreements, Lombardy was allocated a hunting quota of 360,000 finches and 32,000 bramblings.

The referring court posed several questions with a view to having guidance on how to ensure compliance with the 'small numbers' requirement in such a context.

The Court ruled that:

(1) There needs to be a national ceiling, determined on the basis of strict scientific data and this ceiling cannot be exceeded, whatever the internal arrangements are for granting derogations.[832]
(2) Derogating authorities must be able to rely on criteria which are sufficiently precise as to the quantitative ceilings to be complied with.[833]
(3) Member States must ensure that the amount of authorised hunting derogations, in respect of *each* protected species, granted by the derogating authorities does not exceed the ceiling compatible with the restriction on that hunting to 'small numbers' fixed for that species for the entire national territory.[834]
(4) Both the *decisions* of the competent authorities authorising hunting derogations and *the manner in which those decisions are applied* must be subject to effective control exercised in a timely manner.[835]

[iii] Reference Population for Calculating 1% Cannot Be a Whole Flyway Population

There is a risk that, in calculating the 1% threshold, a Member State will refer to an inappropriately large reference population. The Court addressed this risk in the second

832. C-60/05, *WWF Italia*, para. 29.
833. *Ibid.*, para. 36.
834. *Ibid.*, para. 41.
835. *Ibid.*, para. 47.

Finnish spring hunting case, C-217/19, *Commission v. Finland*, which concerned spring hunting of common eiders on the Åland islands.

In this case, the Court recalled that EU legislation on bird protection is to be interpreted in light of the precautionary principle enshrined in the first paragraph of Article 191(2) TFEU in order to avoid 'an overestimation of the number of birds available for exploitation and using calculation methods that make it possible with certainty to stay below the threshold in the order of 1%'.[836] This led to the conclusion that 'as far as migratory species are stationary during their period of reproduction, they should, during that period and for the purpose of interpreting the exception set out in Article 9(1)(c) of the Birds Directive, be treated in the same way as sedentary species'.[837] In this particular case, Finland had based the calculations of the reference population and hence of the small numbers, on the entire Baltic/Wadden Sea flyway population. This was not found compliant by the Court which indicated that the authorities should have 'used the population of the relevant species breeding in the islands of the province of Åland as a baseline'.[838]

The Court rejected the possibility that a Member State might avail itself of a bigger harvest because no other Member State chose to use the derogation possibility:

> The simple fact that a Member State is the only one to authorise a certain practice provides no ground for inferring that it may take over the entire quota available. For that reason, it is appropriate to contemplate hypothetically which other Member States might wish to use that quota and to reserve a relative portion thereof for each of them.[839]

Against this background, the Court found that Finland has failed to fulfil its obligations under Article 7(4) and Article 9(1)(c) of the Birds Directive by recurrently granting authorisations for spring hunting of male common eiders in the province of Åland since 2011.

[iv] Need to Use Sound Scientific Evidence to Calculate 'Small Numbers' and Demonstrate Maintenance of the Population at a Satisfactory Level

In Case C-557/15, *Commission v. Malta*, the Court upheld a Commission complaint that the calculation of 'small numbers' by the Maltese authorities was scientifically unsound in respect of a derogation for trapping seven species of wild finch.[840]

The Court recalled that the 'small numbers' requirement cannot be met if the trapping of birds authorised by way of derogation does not ensure the maintenance of the population of the species concerned at a satisfactory level.[841]

---

836. C-217/19, *Commission v. Finland*, para. 91.
837. *Ibid.*, para. 92.
838. *Ibid.*, para. 94.
839. *Ibid.*, para. 93.
840. C-557/15, *Commission v. Malta*, paras 62 to 76.
841. *Ibid.*, para. 66.

The Court was critical of the adequacy of the evidence adduced by Malta.[842] It also noted that, according to one of the studies used by Malta:

> In Malta, trapping is so intensive that only a handful of each of the common finch species regularly breed on the islands, whereas they breed in high numbers in other areas of the Mediterranean.[843]

The Court concluded that Malta had not adduced sufficient evidence that its derogation regime for the trapping of the seven finch species in question makes it possible to ensure the maintenance of the populations of those species at a satisfactory level.[844]

[b] Notion of 'Judicious Use'

The Court has accepted that a range of different activities can constitute 'judicial use' but the case-law makes clear that this notion is subject to several restrictive criteria.

[i] Scope Can Include Transport

'Capture' and 'keeping' are specifically mentioned in Article 9(1)(c) as types of 'judicious use'. The Court has held that, if the capture and keeping of certain species were duly authorised under Article 9(1)(c) of the Birds Directive, their 'transport may be authorised as well'[845] and the transport of birds which have been lawfully captured or kept constitutes judicious use allowed under the provisions of the directive.[846] Conversely, if the keeping of the birds 'does not accord with Articles 5 and 6 of the Directive, the transport of these birds, which presupposed that they are kept, does not accord with those Articles either'.[847]

[ii] Compliance with the 'Small Numbers' Requirement Is a Prerequisite

The Court has made a link with the 'small numbers' requirement, stating that 'where the condition that the trapping of protected species must concern only certain birds in small numbers is not met, the exploitation of birds by trapping for recreational purposes cannot, in any event, be considered judicious'.[848]

842. *Ibid.*, paras 67 to 70.
843. C-557/15, *Commission v. Malta.*
844. *Ibid.*, para. 74.
845. C-247/85, *Commission v. Belgium*, para. 48.
846. *Ibid.*
847. *Ibid.*
848. C-182/02, *Ligue pour la protection des oiseaux*, para. 17; C-557/15, *Commission v. Malta*, para. 82.

[iii] Maintaining the Population of a Species at a Satisfactory Level

The Court has developed its analysis of the notion of judicious use by reference to the conservation status of the species concerned in light of the tenth Recital of the Directive where it is stated that 'hunting must be compatible with the maintenance of the population of these species at a satisfactory level'.

There are similarities with the case-law on the derogatory provisions under the Habitats Directive and the taking into account of the notion of 'favourable status' – *see* section §4.03[E][6] below.

In Case C-217/19, *Commission v. Finland,* the Court examined the aspect of population maintenance in relation to a derogation for spring hunting of common eider.

The Court recalled that:

> Derogations under Article 9 of the Birds Directive may be granted only if it is ensured that the population of the species concerned is maintained at a 'satisfactory level' and, if that condition is not fulfilled, hunting of birds cannot, in any event, be considered to be judicious and, accordingly, acceptable.[849]

It also recalled that the conditions to be met to derogate from the system of protection of the Birds Directive 'must be based on well-established scientific knowledge' and that 'the best relevant knowledge must be available to the authorities at the time they grant the authorisations'.[850]

Against this background, the Court was not convinced by scientific documents referred to by Finland in relation to the conservation status of the species.[851] It noted that several important and undisputed – scientific references had placed common eiders in higher-risk categories.[852]

The Court noted that:

> It is true that a declining population trend in respect of the species concerned is not sufficient, in itself, to establish the unsatisfactory conservation status of that population. However, when no supplementary evidence goes to show that, for other reasons, the situation should nevertheless be regarded as favourable, such a declining trend does not permit the inference that the population is maintained at a 'satisfactory level'.[853]

The Court then made a cross-reference to its case-law in Case C-674/17, *Tapiola,* on derogations under Article 16 of the Habitats Directive, in which it had recognised the possibility of granting derogations in cases of unfavourable conservation status, by way of exception and in light of the precautionary principle[854] – *see* section §4.03[E][6][c] below.

849. C-217/19, *Commssion v. Finland,* para. 68.
850. *Ibid.,* para. 70.
851. *Ibid.,* paras 71-82.
852. *Ibid.,* para. 82.
853. *Ibid.,* para. 83.
854. *Ibid.,* para. 84; for the Habitats Directive C-674/17, *Tapiola,* paras 68 and 69.

For the Court, it followed that:

> Even if both directives are to be interpreted in a way that includes their respective specific features, that interpretation cannot be regarded as diverging since, subject to their specific features, that interpretation contains similar considerations relating to, inter alia, their respective protection system.[855]

Having examined all the arguments put forward by Finland, however, the Court found that Finland had not established that the species concerned was being maintained at a 'satisfactory level' and that, accordingly, the exploitation might be considered judicious. This requirement of Article 9(1)(c) was therefore not met.[856]

[c] Notion of 'On a Selective Basis' and By-Catch

The use of non-selective hunting means such as limes and nets raises an issue of how the requirement that the permitted activity be 'on a selective basis' can be satisfied under Article 9(1)(c).

In Case C-557/15, *Commission v. Malta,* the issue arose in relation to the use of nets. The Court held that the requirement that the live-capturing of finches can only be permitted if it is carried out on a 'selective basis' was not met.[857] It noted that the Maltese authorities had acknowledged the non-selective nature of the nets at issue 'since they have admitted the existence of a "by-catch" despite the fact that those nets are manually triggered by hunters'.[858]

The Court returned to the issue in Case C-900/19, *One Voice,* in relation to the use of limes. As previously mentioned, the Court had earlier looked at the use of limes under derogation in Case C-252/85, *Commission v. France,* and found that it was not incompatible with Article 9(1)(c). In the latter case, however, the Court made it clear that the earlier judgment had not settled the matter of selectivity. It stated that it had ruled in the earlier case 'without specifically and expressly examining the content of the rules concerning the capture of birds in light of the selectivity criterion'. Therefore, the earlier judgment could not be understood as having expressly validated the French rules on use of limes in light of that criterion.[859]

In Case C-900/19, *One Voice,* the referring court asked, in essence, whether Article 9(1)(c) of the Birds Directive must be interpreted as precluding national legislation which authorises, by derogation from Article 8 of that directive, the use of a method of capture of birds leading to by-catch in small quantities and for a limited period.

The Court noted that, since Article 9(1)(c) of the Birds Directive does not include any reference to national laws, it must be stated that the concept of 'selectivity'

855. C-217/19, *Commission v. Finland,* para. 84.
856. *Ibid.,* paras 87 and 88.
857. C-557/15, *Commission v. Malta,* para. 85.
858. *Ibid.,* para. 84.
859. C-900/19, *One Voice,* para. 48.

constitutes an autonomous concept of EU law that must be interpreted uniformly throughout the EU territory.[860]

It then used the opportunity to subject the criterion to fine analysis, holding as follows:

(1) The derogation must be proportionate to the needs which justify it.[861]
(2) In the assessment of the selectivity of a method of capture, it is appropriate to consider not only the details of that method and the *size of the catch that it entails for the non-target birds* but also its possible consequences for the species captured in terms of *harm caused.*[862]
(3) A distinction should be drawn as to whether the method of capture is *lethal* or *non-lethal*. In the first case, a rather narrow interpretation of the condition of selectivity must be adopted, whereas, in the second case, that condition may be regarded as satisfied where there is by-catch, provided, however, that the species not targeted by that method are captured in small quantities for a defined period and that they can be released without sustaining harm other than negligible harm.[863]
(4) Although the fact that a method of capture which is, in principle, non-lethal leads to by-catch is not, in itself, sufficient to establish the non-selective nature of that method, the size of that by-catch and the extent of any effects on the target and non-target species are indicative of the degree of selectivity of such a method.[864]
(5) It follows from the wording of Article 9(1)(c) of the Birds Directive, read in light of Article 8(1) of that directive, from the objectives of that directive and from the framework within which it falls, a framework which is based on the provisions of Article 3 TEU, of Article 37 of the Charter, of the first subparagraph of Article 191(2) TFEU and of Article 13 TFEU on animal welfare, that the condition of selectivity laid down in Article 9(1)(c) of that directive must be understood as meaning that it can be satisfied, in the case of a non-lethal method of capture leading to by-catch, only if that by-catch is limited in size, that is to say, it concerns only a very small number of specimens captured accidentally, for a limited period, and only if those specimens can be released without sustaining harm other than negligible harm.

The referring court had noted that the use of limes was 'in principle' non-lethal and led to by-catch only in small quantities and for a very limited period. Furthermore, French law required by-catch to be cleaned and released immediately. The Court observed, however, that:

860. *Ibid.*, para. 53.
861. *Ibid.*, para. 61.
862. *Ibid.*, para. 62.
863. *Ibid.*, para. 63.
864. *Ibid.*, para. 64.

> It is highly likely, subject to the findings ultimately made by the referring court, that, despite being cleaned, the birds captured sustain irreparable harm, since limes are capable, by their very nature, of damaging the feathers of any bird captured.[865]

The Court stressed the need for the competent authorities to have the best scientific knowledge available to them to show that the conditions required for derogation from the system of protection established by the Birds Directive are satisfied. It also stressed that, for any derogations granted, the competent authorities must carry out controls in accordance with Article 9(2)(e).[866]

Following this detailed analysis, the Court responded as follows to the question posed by the referring court:

> In the light of the foregoing considerations, the answer to the first question is that Article 9(1)(c) of the Birds Directive must be interpreted as precluding national legislation which authorises, by derogation from Article 8 of that directive, a method of capture leading to by-catch where that by-catch, even in small quantities and for a limited period, is likely to cause harm other than negligible harm to the non-target species captured.[867]

[d] Notion of 'Strictly Supervised Conditions'

The Court has stressed that where trapping is permitted under Article 9(1)(c), it must be 'carried out under strictly supervised conditions'.[868]

The Court examined this requirement in detail in Case C-557/15, *Commission v. Malta*, in relation to finch-trapping. The Maltese authorities relied on a few methods of supervision, which the Commission considered to be systemically flawed. The first method involved a self-reporting obligation on hunters to report in real time by telephone message their 'bag' of captured birds. According to the Maltese authorities, this 'made it possible to collect and check in real time any individual licence holder's catches as well as the uptake of individual bag limits, and to monitor the uptake of national quotas'.[869] Each derogation-beneficiary was also obliged to 'fit specially marked, single-use rings on every bird captured, immediately upon making a catch'. The Maltese authorities argued that use of the rings was rigorously enforced during spot checks by police officers in the field. At the end of the season, unused rings had to be returned to the authorities.[870] The Maltese authorities routinely deployed over 50 officers in order to oversee compliance. All the registered live-capturing stations were inspected at some point during the derogation and 23% of all the individual licence holders were subject to a thorough spot check inspection.[871]

865. *Ibid.*, para. 67.
866. *Ibid.*, paras 68 and 69.
867. *Ibid.*, para. 71.
868. C-182/02, *Ligue pour la protection des oiseaux*, para. 15.
869. C-557/15, *Commission v. Malta*, para. 90.
870. *Ibid.*
871. *Ibid.*, para. 91.

The Court was not convinced and concluded that Malta had failed to adduce evidence that the derogation at issue was used under strictly controlled conditions.[872] It noted that the accuracy of the self-reported statements by telephone seemed uncertain;[873] that, in the context of Malta, characterised by a very high density of derogation beneficiaries, namely over 4 000 and of registered trapping stations, namely over 6 400, the fact that merely 23 % of hunters had been subject to individual checks seemed inadequate;[874] that there was evidence of rather frequent failure to observe restrictions, such as on trapping inside Natura 2000 sites;[875] and that there were significant discrepancies in relation to statistics on the use and return of the single-use rings.[876]

[5] Formal Conditions Set by Article 9(2)

In order for the derogation to be compliant, the formal conditions prescribed under Article 9(2) must be fulfilled.[877]

Article 9(2) does not feature extensively in the case-law but Case C-247/85, *Commission v. Belgium* demonstrates why it matters. As mentioned above, the Court held that a purported very general derogation to destroy birds' nests built against houses could not be justified by reference to Article 9(1)(a). In addition, the Court found that:

> The derogation does not comply with the formal requirements of Article 9(2) either. The provision does not specify *the conditions of risk* and *the circumstances of time and place* in which the derogations may be granted or *the controls* which will be carried out (emphasis added).[878]

As also mentioned above, in the same case, the Court held that a purported general derogation targeting sparrows and starlings could not be justified by reference to Article 9(1)(a). Once again, the Court found a concomitant breach of Article 9(2):

> The derogations do not comply with the criteria and conditions of Article 9(2) in so far as they mention neither the *circumstances of time and place* in which they may be granted nor the *controls* which will be carried out (emphasis added).[879]

Likewise, in Case C-507/04, *Commission v. Austria*, the Court condemned Austria for a purported derogation under Article 9(1)(a) in Burgenland for crop damage caused by starlings, because it did not satisfy the requirements of Article 9(2) – *see* section §4.02[F][3][b] above.

872. *Ibid.*, para. 97.
873. *Ibid.*, para. 93.
874. *Ibid.*, para. 94.
875. *Ibid.*, para. 95.
876. *Ibid.*, para. 96.
877. C-182/02, *Ligue pour la protection des oiseaux*, para. 18.
878. C-247/85, *Commission v. Belgium*, para. 28.
879. *Ibid.*, para. 34.

It is thus clear from the case-law that Article 9(2) represents an important safeguard against Member State attempts to justify very sweeping exceptions to the prohibitions of the Birds Directive.

As already noted, in Case C-900/19, *One Voice,* the Court made a link between Article 9(1) and Article 9(2) of the Birds Directive when holding that the requirement as to no other satisfactory solution needs to be addressed by a detailed statement of reasons.[880]

In the same case, the Court made the link between the selectivity criterion in Article 9(1)(c) and the provisions for controls in Article 9(2)(e), stating:

> Once the derogations have been granted, the competent authorities must, in accordance with Article 9(2)(e) of that directive, carry out the necessary controls in order to ensure that the by-catch is as close as possible to expected levels and sustains no harm other than negligible harm.[881]

The case-law thus establishes the significant role that Article 9(2) plays in ensuring that derogations are framed with the necessary precision and specificity and are effectively controlled once they are granted.

[G] Access to Justice in Relation to Species Protection under the Birds Directive

The access to justice case-law on the nature directives relates to the Habitats Directive but is relevant by analogy to the Birds Directive. Thus, based on the case-law of C-240/09, *Slovak Brown Bears* [*see* section §4.03[G]], it can be assumed that environmental associations will have standing to contest derogation decisions under Article 9 of the Birds Directive or other species protection decisions, such as those on hunting seasons for purposes of the directive's Article 7. In fact, many of the important preliminary references have originated in legal actions taken by such associations, underscoring their oversight role.

In this context, in Case C-60/05, *WWF Italia,* the Court's response to the fourth question posed by the referring court throws useful light on how decision-making under Article 9 needs to allow for subsequent effective oversight. The context was a concern that national procedural rules would leave too little scope for a national supervising authority to annul a non-compliant regional derogation in time, but similar considerations are likely to arise in relation to access to justice. The Court held that:

> The relevant national procedural framework applicable must guarantee not only that the lawfulness of decisions granting authorisations derogating from the system of protection laid down by the Directive may be verified in a timely manner but also that the conditions attached to those decisions are complied with.[882]
>
> However, a control mechanism under which annulment of a decision authorising a hunting derogation adopted in breach of Article 9 of the Directive or

880. C-900/19, *One Voice,* para. 32.
881. *Ibid.*, para. 69.
882. C-60/05, *WWF Italia,* para. 44.

> declaration of a breach of the conditions attached to a decision authorising such hunting would take effect only on expiry of the period laid down for carrying out that hunting would render redundant the system of protection established by the Directive.[883]

The Court ruled that the obligation relating to 'small numbers' in Article 9(1)(c) of the Directive [the subject of the proceedings], requires that the administrative procedures provided for are organised in such a way that both the decisions of the competent authorities authorising hunting derogations and the manner in which those decisions are applied are subject to effective control exercised in a timely manner.[884]

The aspect of timeliness of necessary intervention is seen in the Court's grant of interim orders to the Commission in respect of direct actions relating to separate Italian hunting decisions made by two Italian regions.[885] Without such interim orders, any final Court judgment would have post-dated the use made of these decisions.

§4.03 PROTECTION OF SPECIES UNDER THE HABITATS DIRECTIVE

[A] Overview

[1] Coherent Body of Provisions

In addition to the Natura 2000 provisions found in Article 6, the Habitats Directive contains provisions expressly designed for the protection of species. These are set out in Articles 12 to 16. The latter form a 'coherent body of provisions which require the Member States to establish strict regimes of protection for the animal and plant species concerned'.[886]

[2] Three Types of Provision

Like the species protection provisions of the Birds Directive, the provisions can be considered to comprise *three* types.

First are provisions containing *prohibitions*. Article 12 introduces an obligation to establish a system of strict protection of animal species listed in Annex IV (a) of the Directive and Article 13 introduces a similar obligation in respect of plant species listed in Annex IV (b) of the Directive. Article 15 sets out a prohibition on indiscriminate means of capture and killing.

The Article 12 obligation addresses the 'most common direct threats for the animal species listed in Annex IV (a) to the Habitats Directive'.[887] Article 12 (1) lists a

883. *Ibid.*, para. 45.
884. *Ibid.*, para. 47.
885. *See* Chapter 8, §8.03[F].
886. *See* C-508/04, *Commission v. Austria*, para. 109; and C-6/04; *Commission v. United Kingdom*, para. 112.
887. *See* Hendrik Schoukens & Kees Bastmeijer, *Species Protection in the European Union: How Strict Is It?*, 13, published in *The Habitats Directive in Its EU Environmental Law Context: European*

set of activities to be prohibited: all of forms of deliberate capture or killing of specimens of these species in the wild;[888] deliberate disturbance especially during periods of breeding, rearing, hibernation and migration;[889] deliberate destruction or taking of eggs from the wild;[890] and deterioration or destruction of breeding sites or resting places.[891] Article 12(2) requires related marketing prohibitions. Article 12(4) introduces an obligation to establish a system to monitor the incidental capture and killing of the animal species concerned.

As concerns plant species listed in Annex IV (b) of the Directive, Article 13(1) requires the following to be prohibited: the deliberate picking, collecting, cutting, uprooting or destruction of such plants in their natural range in the wild;[892] the keeping, transport and sale or exchange, or offering for sale or exchange of specimens of protected species taken from the wild.[893]

The second type of provision – found in Article 14 – is aimed at allowing *managed exploitation* of the species listed in Annex V of the Directive.

The third type – found in Article 16 – allows for the use, on a case-by-case basis, and subject to strict conditions of *derogations*, i.e., exceptions.

[3] Commission Notice on Strict Protection

Before examining the individual species protection provisions of the Habitats Directive, it is worth referring to Commission Notice C(2021)7301, Guidance document on the strict protection of animal species of Community interest under the Habitats Directive.[894] This is an updated version of a guidance document which first appeared in 2007. The fact that it now takes the form of a Commission Notice has significance because a notice is formally endorsed by the College of Commissioners. As will be seen, the earlier version of the guidance has been referred to by the Court.[895] Apart from referring to the case-law, the Notice provides valuable technical and scientific insights.

[B] Strict Protection Obligation of Article 12

Under Article 12 of the Habitats Directive, Member States need to take measures to establish a system of strict protection for the animal species listed in Annex IV(a) in their natural range and to prohibit a series of acts, enumerated under its paragraph 1, letters (a) to (d).

Nature's Best Hope? (Charles-Hubert Born, An Cliquet, Hendrik Schoukens, Delphine Misonne & Geert Van Hoorick eds, Routledge, 2014).

888. Article 12(1)(a) of the Habitats Directive.
889. Article 12(1)(b) of the Habitats Directive.
890. Article 12(1)(c) of the Habitats Directive.
891. *Ibid.*
892. Article 13(1)(a) of the Habitats Directive.
893. Article 12(2) and Article 13(2) of the Habitats Directive.
894. EUR-Lex – C(2021)7301 – EN – EUR-Lex (europa.eu).
895. *See* for example, C-342/05, *Commission v. Finland*, para. 29.

Article 12 reads as follows:

1. Member States shall take the requisite measures to establish a system of strict protection for the animal species listed in Annex IV (a) in their natural range, prohibiting:
   (a) all forms of deliberate capture or killing of specimens of these species in the wild;
   (b) deliberate disturbance of these species, particularly during the period of breeding, rearing, hibernation and migration;
   (c) deliberate destruction or taking of eggs from the wild;
   (d) deterioration or destruction of breeding sites or resting places.
2. For these species, Member States shall prohibit the keeping, transport and sale or exchange, and offering for sale or exchange, of specimens taken from the wild, except for those taken legally before this Directive is implemented.
3. The prohibition referred to in paragraph 1 (a) and (b) and paragraph 2 shall apply to all stages of life of the animals to which this Article applies.
4. Member States shall establish a system to monitor the incidental capture and killing of the animal species listed in Annex IV (a). In the light of the information gathered, Member States shall take further research or conservation measures as required to ensure that incidental capture and killing does not have a significant negative impact on the species concerned.

[1] Territorial Scope

[a] Overlap with Natura 2000 but Not Confined to Natura 2000

The territorial scope of Article 12 goes beyond the confines of the Natura 2000 network. Its provisions apply to all specimens of the species listed in Annex IV(a) to the Directive, irrespective of whether they are found within a Natura 2000 site or outside it. In a few cases, however, Annex IV itself sets a geographical limitation. For example, the protection given to the wolf, *Canis lupus,* does not extend to Spanish populations north of the Duero and Greek populations north of the 39th parallel. The territorial scope of Article 12 is further clarified in Case C-88/19, *Alianta pentru combatera abuzurilor* [discussed in the next section].

[i] Overlap with Natura 2000

Where a species figures in both Annex II and Annex IV(a) of the Habitats Directive, the case-law illustrates how, within Natura 2000 sites, the provisions of Article 12 can apply in conjunction with the provisions of Article 6. In Case C-504/14, *Commission v. Greece,* for example, the Commission raised issues concerning the protection of the Mediterranean sea turtle in the Gulf of Kyparissia under both Article 6 and Article 12, and the case illustrates how Article 12 can address situations which Article 6 cannot.[896]

896. C-504/14, *Commission v. Greece,* para. 158.

The Court also found that a number of specific breaches of Article 6(2) in respect of the sea turtle all constituted prohibited disturbances for purposes of Article 12(1)(b).[897]

[ii] Beyond Natura 2000

Beyond Natura 2000, the application of the Habitats Directive's stringent rules on species protection may impinge on spatial developments and land use,[898] especially the prohibition of deterioration or destruction of breeding sites or resting places. Case C-383/09, *Commission v. France* provides an illustration. Following the judgment of the Court against it, France was obliged to reassess measures taken for the recovery and repopulation of the European hamster, whose decline was decisively caused, on the one hand, by the development of maize crops to the detriment of crop diversity,[899] and, on the other hand, by urbanisation and the infrastructure works associated with it.[900]

[b] Notion of 'Natural Range'

The wording of Article 12 refers to a system of strict protection for the animal species concerned 'in their natural range'.

Case C-383/09, *Commission v. France,* illustrates how the 'natural range' of a species covers the edge of a natural range if national frontiers are disregarded. In this case, the Commission sought a declaration that, by failing to establish a programme of measures to ensure strict protection of the European hamster, France had failed to fulfil its obligations under Article 12(1)(d) of the Habitats Directive. Across its global range, the European hamster is considered of 'least concern'[901] but it has been under significant threat in a number of individual EU Member States, such as France, where its population – limited to the Alsace region – drastically declined between 2001 and 2007,[902] coming close to extinction.[903] None of its populations in Alsace were at the minimum viable population threshold, which was estimated at 1,500 individuals spread over an area of contiguous suitable land of 600 hectares. The number of burrows, serving as a reference for observation of the species' status fell from 1160 to

897. *Ibid.*, para. 157.
898. Hendrik Schoukens & Kees Bastmeijer, *Species Protection in the European Union: How Strict Is It?*, 2, published in *The Habitats Directive in Its EU Environmental Law Context: European Nature's Best Hope?* (Charles-Hubert Born, An Cliquet, Hendrik Schoukens, Delphine Misonne & Geert Van Hoorick eds, Routledge 2014).
899. C-383/09, *Commission v. France,* para. 26.
900. *Ibid.*, para. 32.
901. *See* Hendrik Schoukens & Kees Bastmeijer, *Species Protection in the European Union: How Strict Is It?*, 2, published in *The Habitats Directive in Its EU Environmental Law Context: European Nature's Best Hope?* (Charles-Hubert Born, An Cliquet, Hendrik Schoukens, Delphine Misonne & Geert Van Hoorick eds, Routledge 2014).
902. C-383/09, *Commission v. France,* para. 24.
903. Marc Clement, *Global Objectives and Scope of the Habitats Directive: What Does the Obligation of Result Mean in Practice? The European Hamster in Alsace*, 17, published in *The Habitats Directive in Its EU Environmental Law Context European Nature's Best Hope?* (Charles-Hubert Born, An Cliquet, Hendrik Schoukens, Delphine Misonne & Geert Van Hoorick eds).

less than 180. The species is commonly present in Eastern and Central Europe, where its good conservation status could make up for the bad conservation status in France if one embraced a balancing mechanism used by the International Union for Conservation of Nature (IUCN) for the assessment of whether a species should appear on the IUCN Red List.[904] In Case C-383/09, *Commission v. France*, however, the assessment of the natural range was related to the national level. When the Court had to examine the conservation status of the species in its natural range, it looked at the French data.

In Case C-88/19, *Alianta pentru combatera abuzurilor*, a preliminary reference from a Romanian court, the Court was asked to interpret both the notion of 'natural range' and the related territorial scope of Article 12(1) of the Directive. The circumstances concerned the capture and transport of a lone wolf by representatives of a Romanian government authority, the Directorate for the Observation and Protection of Animals, together with a veterinary surgeon. The wolf had been present for several days on the property of a local resident in a Romanian village. There, the wolf had spent time playing and eating with the resident's dogs. The wolf was anaesthetised and arrangements were made to transport it to a bear reserve which had a fenced enclosure for housing wolves rescued from zoos. No prior derogation, pursuant to Article 16 of the Habitats Directive, had been obtained to authorise these actions. Even though the wolf managed to escape during the journey, the plaintiff association filed a criminal complaint that no authorisation to capture and transport the wolf had been obtained as required by Article 16.

The Court had to examine whether the fact that the wolf was captured in a human settlement had resulted in the inapplicability of Article 12. For multiple reasons, the Court took a broad view of the natural range of the wolf. It affirmed that the wolf needed protection outside of the Natura 2000 network and that it would be contrary to the protection system laid down by Article 12 that wolves be automatically withdrawn from specimens of protected species when their natural distribution area comprises human settlements.[905]

It is useful to point to the extensive analysis by the Advocate General of the notion of 'natural range', in particular, to determine whether it excluded human settlements,[906] and to the following observation:

> Wolves are species of animals that exploit large habitats. In the case of such species, the second sentence of Article 4(1) of the Habitats Directive provides that the protected sites are to be confined to the places within the natural range of such species which present the physical or biological factors essential to their life and reproduction. Those rules thus recognise that the natural range of those species also includes sites situated outside the protected areas.[907]

The Advocate General also noted the regulatory technique of excluding certain wolf populations within the wording of Anne IV(a) itself, observing:

---

904. *Ibid.*
905. C-88/19, *Alianța pentru combaterea abuzurilor* paras 48 and 49.
906. Opinion of the Advocate General in C-88/19, *Alianța pentru combaterea abuzurilor*, paras 32-45.
907. *Ibid.*, para. 42.

> As the entry for the wolf in Annex IV(a) shows, any sites excluded from protection would be clearly designated, as parts of certain Member States – Greece north of the 39th parallel, Spain north of the Duero and the reindeer conservation area in Finland – are.[908]

In this specific case, the authorities should have, therefore, applied the strict derogation mechanism foreseen under Article 16 of the Directive to the capture and relocation of the lone wolf.

[2] Need for a Complete, Precise, Clear and Faithful Transposition

In adjudicating on the adequacy of Member States' transposition of Article 12, the Court has made it clear that it expects transposition to be complete, precise, clear and faithful to the Habitats Directive. This reflects a broader transposition standard that the Court applies to the Habitats Directive.

[a] *Faithful Transposition Particularly Important for Management of the Common Heritage*

As the Court noted in Case C-06/04, *Commission v. United Kingdom*, a case, amongst other things, relating to the transposition of Article 12:

> It is apparent from the 4th and 11th recitals in the preamble to the Habitats Directive that threatened habitats and species form part of the European Community's natural heritage and that the threats to them are often of a transboundary nature, so that the adoption of conservation measures is a common responsibility of all Member States. Consequently, as the Advocate General has observed in point 11 of her Opinion, faithful transposition becomes particularly important in an instance such as the present one, where management of the common heritage is entrusted to the Member States in their respective territories.[909]

[b] *Examples of Incomplete or Imprecise Transposition*

By way of illustration, in Case C-75/01, *Commission v. Luxembourg*, the Court condemned Luxembourg for incomplete transposition of Article 12(1)(b), stating:

> Article 23 of the Nature Protection Law, which the Luxembourg Government regards as conforming to Article 12(1)(b) of the Directive, is incapable of transposing the latter provision fully because, whilst prohibiting the disturbance of fauna during the periods of breeding, rearing and hibernation, the prohibition fails expressly to mention the migration period.

908. *Ibid.*, para. 43.
909. C-6/04, *Commission v. United Kingdom*, para. 25.

In the same case, the Court rejected an argument by Luxembourg that it had transposed Article 12(1)(c) by virtue of a provision of Luxembourg legislation approving the Bern Convention.[910] The Court pointed out that:

> That provision applies only to the species listed in Annex II to the Convention, which does not include certain of the species listed in Annex IV(a) to the Directive, to which Article 12 of the Directive refers.

An illustration of the need for clarity and precision is provided by Case C-98/03, *Commission v. Germany*. The Court found that a national prohibition on using pesticides 'where it is foreseeable that it will produce seriously harmful effects on the balance of nature' was not as clear, precise and strict as the prohibition on the deterioration of breeding sites or resting places of protected animals laid down in Article 12(1)(d) of the Directive.[911]

[c] *Impermissible Qualifications in National Legislation*

The Court has also condemned Member States over transposing legislation that introduces qualifications not found in the text of Article 12. This is illustrated by Cases C-6/04, *Commission v. United Kingdom* and C-98/03, *Commission v. Germany*, discussed below in relation to Article 12(1)(d).

[d] *An Unlawful Derogation Regime May Infringe Article 12*

It is worth noting that a national derogation regime which does not comply with Article 16 of the Habitats Directive may also disclose an infringement of Article 12. This is illustrated by Case C-183/05, *Commission v. Ireland*. The Court found that a 'parallel regime of derogations under Irish legislation' was inconsistent with both Articles 12 and 16.[912]

[e] *No Requirement to Go Beyond the Wording of Article 12*

While the Court has confirmed the need to transpose Article 12 strictly, Case C-166/22, *Hellfire Massey Residents Association* shows that it will not require Member State's legislation to address topics not reflected in the provision's actual wording. As is explained in section §4.03[F] below, Article 12 does not require provision for public participation.

910. C-75/01, *Commission v. Luxembourg*, paras 55-58.
911. C-98/03, *Commission v. Germany*, para. 68.
912. C-183/05, *Commission v. Ireland*, para. 49.

[3] Key Requirements under the Strict Protection Obligation

Thanks to a significant number of direct actions by the Commission and preliminary references, an important body of case-law has developed on Article 12. The cases have focused not only on the formal transposition issues already mentioned above but issues of practical implementation.

Practical implementation was a key focus of a groundbreaking decision in Case C-103/00, *Commission v. Greece,* concerning the Mediterranean sea turtle – and a later decision in Case C-504/14, *Commission v. Greece,* concerning the same species. Practical implementation has also featured in relation to the European hamster, addressed in Cases C-383/09, *Commission v. France* and C-477/19, *Magistrat der Stadt Wien*; the Milos viper, addressed in Case C-518/04, *Commission v. Greece*; the Cypriot grass snake, addressed in Case C-340/10, *Commission v. Cyprus*; species of bats and cetaceans, addressed in Case C-183/05, *Commission v. Ireland*; the Iberian lynx, addressed in Case C-308/08, *Commission v. Spain*; the wolf, addressed in, amongst others, Case C-674/17, *Tapiola*; the moor frog, addressed in Cases C-473/19 and C-474/19, Skydda Skogen; and rare species of beetle, addressed in Case C-441/17, *Białowieżka.*

The case-law thus encompasses a range of marine and terrestrial species with very different distributions and vulnerabilities. In addressing these species, the Court has also taken cognisance of how the species protection provisions can be relevant to a range of human activities and interventions, including the following: recreational activities; agriculture and forestry; construction and extraction of natural resources; use of explosives; road traffic; and illegal activities such as poaching.

The case-law has clarified that, in implementing Article 12, Member States must fulfil several key requirements. Even if the obligations laid down by Article 12 appear to amount, at first sight, to a 'set of negative obligations'[913] rather than 'a set of positive measures',[914] the case-law of the Court goes beyond a 'mere textual reading of the Article 12'[915] to confirm a requirement to implement an effective system of protection.

The strict protection regime implies first of all that a legal framework be adopted,[916] even where the number of specimens of a certain protected species has not suffered any decrease.[917] Measures adopted must be coherent and coordinated and

913. Marc Clement, *Global Objectives and Scope of the Habitats Directive: What Does the Obligation of Result Mean in Practice? The European Hamster in Alsace*, 12, published in *The Habitats Directive in Its EU Environmental Law Context European Nature's Best Hope?* (Charles-Hubert Born, An Cliquet, Hendrik Schoukens, Delphine Misonne & Geert Van Hoorick eds, Routledge, Abingdon, 2015).
914. *Ibid.*
915. Marc Clement, *Global Objectives and Scope of the Habitats Directive: What Does the Obligation of Result Mean in Practice? The European Hamster in Alsace*, 13, published in *The Habitats Directive in Its EU Environmental Law Context European Nature's Best Hope?* (Charles-Hubert Born, An Cliquet, Hendrik Schoukens, Delphine Misonne & Geert Van Hoorick eds, Routledge, Abingdon, 2015).
916. C-103/00, *Commission v. Greece,* para. 30.
917. *Ibid.*, para. 31.

essentially of a preventive nature.[918] The system must ensure in the long term that a sufficiently large natural habitat be maintained for the protected species whose populations must be maintained or restored in the type of natural habitat to which it belongs.[919] The provisions on prohibitions in the national laws are, moreover, not sufficient if there is a failure to duly implement them in practice, the Court stating that 'the transposition of [Article 12] requires the Member States not only to adopt a comprehensive legislative framework but also to implement concrete and specific protection measures'.[920]

[a] Need for a Legal Framework Capable of Ensuring Strict Protection

In Case C-103/00, *Commission v. Greece*, the Court upheld a Commission request for a declaration that, by failing to adopt the requisite measures to establish and implement *an effective system* of strict protection for the sea turtle on the island of Zakynthos so as to avoid any disturbance of the species during its breeding period and any activity which might bring about deterioration or destruction of its breeding sites, Greece had failed to fulfil its obligations under Article 12(1)(b) and (d) of the Habitats Directive.

It ruled that the Greek Government had not adopted *a legal framework* which was capable of ensuring strict protection for the sea turtle against any deliberate disturbance during the breeding period and against any deterioration or destruction of its breeding sites.[921]

[b] Need for Coherent and Coordinated Preventive Measures, Including Measures for Effective Implementation

Having provisions on prohibitions in national legislation is not, in itself, sufficient. Member States must establish and *implement* an *effective* system of protection.

In Case C-518/04, *Commission v. Greece*, the Court condemned Greece for failing to adopt measures necessary to establish and implement an effective system of strict protection for a species of viper on the island of Milos. The island was especially important for the species; the island's western half alone hosts half the world's population. As in Case C-103/00, *Commission v. Greece*, the Court found that the necessary legal framework was not in place with measures to give detailed effect to a framework law not adopted.[922] The Court referred to the need for *coherent and coordinated measures of a preventive nature*.

In subsequent cases, the Court has returned to the formulation 'coherent and coordinated measures of a preventive nature'. For example, it appears in Cases

918. C-518/04, *Commission v. Greece*, para. 16; Opinion of Advocate General Léger, in case C-103/00, *Commission v. Greece*, para. 43; C-183/05, *Commission v. Ireland*, para. 30.
919. Opinion of Advocate General Léger in case C-103/00, *Commission v. Greece*, para. 43.
920. C-183/05, *Commission v. Ireland*, para. 29.
921. C-103/00, *Commission v. Greece*, para. 30.
922. C-518/04, *Commission v. Greece*, para. 17.

C-183/05, *Commission v. Ireland,*[923] C-383/09, *Commission v. France,*[924] C-340/10, *Commission v. Cyprus,*[925] and C-504/14, *Commission v. Greece.*[926]

In Case C-183/05, *Commission v. Ireland,* the Court upheld a Commission complaint that Ireland had failed to adopt specific measures for the *effective implementation* of the system of strict protection in respect of several Annex IV(a) animal species, in particular the otter, the Kerry slug, and various species of bat and cetacean. The Commission referred to several gaps, such as an absence of plans to ensure the monitoring of these species, including their breeding sites and resting places. The Court agreed that there were gaps and also agreed with the Commission's argument that the existence of a network of full-time conservation officials responsible for monitoring and protecting species did not, in itself, demonstrate effective implementation.[927] As the Advocate General had earlier noted, it was not evident that this network of officials was delivering the required actions.

In Case C-340/10, *Commission v. Cyprus,* the Court found that Cyprus infringed Article 12(1) in several respects in relation to the rare Cypriot grass snake in the area of Paralimni Lake: by tolerating an illegal racing circuit for moto-cross racing;[928] by failing to address excessive extraction of water, which amounted to a deliberate disturbance;[929] and by failing to adequately address the possible harmful consequences of property development and construction in the vicinity of the lake, which was likely to lead to disturbance.[930]

In C-504/14, *Commission v. Greece,* the Court returned to the issue of protection of sea turtles, which it had previously addressed in Case C-103/00, *Commission v. Greece*. This time, it focused on the protection of the species in the Gulf of Kyparissia. Against the background of evidence of multiple threats to the species in this area, it upheld a Commission complaint that Greece had failed to establish a comprehensive and coherent legal framework. It stated that:

> A collection of legal instruments does not constitute a comprehensive legislative and regulatory framework when those instruments do not prevent breaches of the prohibition on deterioration laid down in Article 6(2) of Directive 92/43 or when the instruments must regularly be supplemented so that the protection required by Article 12 of the directive can be ensured.[931]

The Court considered that its findings of breaches of the prohibition on deterioration in Article 6(2) of the Habitats Directive gave 'reason to suppose that a comprehensive and coherent legislative framework is lacking so far as protection of the Kyparissia area is concerned'.[932] That supposition was confirmed by the fact that

923. C-183/05, *Commission v. Ireland,* para. 30.
924. C-383/09, *Commission v. France,* para. 20.
925. C-340/10, *Commission v. Cyprus,* para. 61.
926. C-504/14, *Commission v. Greece,* para. 140.
927. C-183/05, *Commission v. Ireland,* para. 31.
928. C-340/10, *Commission v. Cyprus,* para. 63.
929. *Ibid.*, para. 64.
930. *Ibid.*, para. 65.
931. C-504/14, *Commission v. Greece,* para. 141.
932. *Ibid.*, para. 142.

Greece had had to adopt various ad hoc ministerial orders to address problems that had manifested themselves indicating that the national legislative framework was incomplete.[933]

[c] *Need to Collect Sufficient Information on Protected Species, Their Habitats, and Relevant Threats*

A compliant protection system implies the existence and the collection, by the national authorities, of the necessary information with regard to breeding sites and resting places and threats to species listed under Annex IV(a) of the Habitats Directive.

[i] Need for a Monitoring System

In Case 183/05, *Commission v. Ireland*, the Court upheld a complaint of the Commission that the Irish authorities did not possess the necessary information in relation to several of the species listed in Annex IV(a) and that lack of information prevented the effective implementation of the system of strict protection.[934] There was a need to have an appropriate monitoring system in place to cover protected species,[935] which was not the case for Ireland, with the exception of the horseshoe bat, the natterjack toad and the leatherback turtle.

[ii] Role of Ad hoc Assessments

For Natura 2000 sites, the appropriate assessment procedure under Article 6(3) of the Habitats Directive should provide a means for assessing whether plans or projects will affect protected species benefiting from site protection. However, Article 6(3) may be inapplicable – for example, the plan or project, and the populations of species it affects may be located outside of Natura 2000. In such cases, the EIA Directive can, as the Commission submitted in Case C-183/05, *Commission v. Ireland*, represent a useful tool to assess the impact of certain developments on protected species by 'alerting the competent authorities to specific threats to the breeding sites and resting places of the species listed in Annex IV to Directive 92/43'.[936] The possible role of the EIA Directive in relation to species protection is addressed further in Chapter 6, §6.02[B][2][b].

[iii] Need to Monitor Illegal Activities

The importance of monitoring extends to threats from illegal activities. In C-674/17, *Tapiola*, the Court was not convinced by arguments of the Finnish authorities that a problem of poaching wolves justified derogating from the prohibition on killing wolves

933. *Ibid.*, paras 142 and 143.
934. C-183/05, *Commission v. Ireland*, paras 19 and 25.
935. *Ibid.*, para. 32.
936. *Ibid.*, para. 34.

under Article 12(1)(a) of the Habitats Directive in order to allow the legal killing of wolf specimens.

It observed that:

> The mere existence of an illegal activity such as poaching or difficulties associated with its monitoring cannot be sufficient to exempt a Member State from its obligation to ensure the safeguarding of species protected under Annex IV to the Habitats Directive. On the contrary, in such a situation, that Member State must give priority to strict and effective monitoring of that illegal activity and implement methods that do not involve failure to observe the prohibitions laid down in Articles 12 to 14 and Article 15(a) and (b) of that directive.[937]

[d] *Need for Preventive Action to Uphold the Prohibitions*

[i] Need for General Preventive Action

The potential scope of the duty to take preventive action can be seen in the Court's ruling in C-504/14, *Commission v. Greece*. In that case, the Court made findings of extensive breaches of Article 6(2) of the Habitats Directive.[938] The Court held that these also amounted to prohibited disturbances for purposes of Article 12(1)(b) and that, by failing to take all the *specific measures* necessary to *prevent* them, Greece had failed to comply with its obligations under Article 12(1)(b).[939] In addition, the evidence of breaches of Article 6(2) showed that Greece had failed to take the measures necessary

937. C-674/17, *Tapiola*, para. 48.

938. In para. 114, the Court found that Greece infringed Article 6(2):

- by tolerating the construction of houses in Agiannaki in 2010, the use, without a sufficient regulatory framework, of other houses in Agiannaki which were built in 2006 and the commencement of building works relating to around 50 dwellings located between Agiannaki and Elaia, and by authorising in 2012 the construction of three holiday houses in Vounaki;
- by tolerating the development of access routes to the beach in the Kyparissia area, namely the opening up of five new roads to Agiannaki beach and the asphalting of certain existing roads and thoroughfares;
- by failing to take adequate measures to enforce the prohibition on wild camping close to the beaches at Kalo Nero and Elaia;
- by failing to take the measures necessary to restrict the operation of bars between Elaia and Kalo Nero, on the breeding beaches of the Caretta caretta sea turtle, and by failing to ensure that the various forms of pollution caused by those bars do not disturb that species;
- by failing to take the measures necessary to reduce, within the Kyparissia area, the furniture and various structures found on the breeding beaches of the Caretta caretta sea turtle and by authorising the construction of a platform near the Messina Mare Hotel;
- by failing to take the measures necessary so as to ensure that the light pollution affecting the breeding beaches of the Caretta caretta sea turtle in the Kyparissia area is adequately curtailed; and
- by failing to take the measures necessary so as to ensure that fishing in the waters off the breeding beaches of the Caretta caretta sea turtle in the Kyparissia area is adequately curtailed.

939. C-504/14, *Commission v. Greece*, paras 157 and 160.

to enforce the prohibition on deterioration or destruction of breeding sites under Article 12(1)(d).[940]

[ii] Need to Regulate Proposed Interventions Correctly

It is not enough to monitor the presence of protected species. Case C-183/05, *Commission v. Ireland,* illustrates the importance of not only monitoring their presence but of ensuring that the prohibitions are respected where interventions are proposed at locations where they are found. In particular, the Court upheld complaints that Ireland had not complied with Article 12 in respect of three projects, approving the Advocate General's analysis. The first was a hotel development which involved renovation of old buildings and which had been subject to an EIA. Despite the EIA having predicted negative effects on the breeding and resting sites of bat populations, the project was approved and work commenced without any derogation having been obtained under Article 16. The second project was a road development, which also underwent an EIA process. This predicted the destruction of roosts of the lesser horseshoe bat (a particularly rare bat species) but the road was nonetheless approved without any evidence of the authorities having considered that this would require a valid derogation (although an Article 16 derogation was afterwards granted). The third project involved use of explosives to lay an offshore gas pipeline in a known breeding and resting area of cetaceans. It was not disputed that the sound of the explosives would have an adverse effect on the cetaceans but the project was authorised without any Article 16 derogation.[941] Procedurally, the Court's subsequent interpretation in Case C-463/20, *Namur-Est Environnement* helps to avoid such an outcome by requiring the derogation decision to form part of the multi-stage decision-making in an EIA process rather than be treated as something apart – *see* Chapter 6, §6.02[B][2][c].

[iii] Need for Effective Control of Illegal Activities

Case C-103/00, *Commission v. Greece,* dealt with a failure of effective protection of the sea turtle in the bay of Laganas on Zakynthos, a vital breeding region, extremely important in the Mediterranean, for the species.[942] The presence of mopeds, pedalos and small boats, as well as illegal buildings on the beaches, were liable to disturb the reproduction cycle of the species. While the use of mopeds on the breeding beaches was prohibited and notices indicating the presence of turtle nests on the beaches had

940. *Ibid.*, paras 161 and 162.
941. C-183/05, *Commission v. Ireland,* paras 34 to 37.
942. The sea turtle Caretta caretta only lays eggs every two or three years. In Greece, the laying season overlaps with the tourist season. The turtle leaves the sea at night and moves towards the driest area of the beach, where it digs a hole of 40 to 60 centimetres in which it lays an average of 120 eggs. Two months later the eggs hatch and the baby turtles crawl onto the sand and head towards the sea. Baby turtles are very vulnerable at this stage and many die.

been erected,[943] the national authorities could not, in practice, control such disturbances, which moreover, were not isolated occurrences.[944] This situation led the Court to condemn Greece for failing to 'establish and implement an effective system of strict protection for the sea turtle on Zakynthos so as to avoid any disturbance of the species'.[945] Measures have to be preventive, so the argument put forward by Greece, that the number of sea turtle nests had not decreased over the previous 15 years, was not upheld.

Similarly, in Case C-340/10, *Commission v. Cyprus*, the Court found that Cyprus had failed to address the operation of an illegal racing circuit in an area used by the protected Cypriot grass snake.[946] The Commission had observed that 'the organisation of moto-cross racing is particularly harmful to the Cypriot grass snake because of the continuous disturbance caused and is a hazard because it leads to injury and even death of the animals'.[947]

[iv] Need for Reinforced Action to Address an Extinction Risk

The potential extent of the preventive measures required by Article 12 is apparent from the Court's ruling in Case C-383/09, *Commission v. France*. The Court drew on the earlier case-law when it addressed and upheld a Commission request for a declaration that, by failing to establish *a programme of measures* to ensure strict protection of the European hamster, France had failed to fulfil its obligations under Article 12(1)(d) of the Directive. It was not in dispute that numbers of European hamsters had sharply decreased in Alsace, the only French region where the species is found, or that this was linked to pressures resulting from agriculture and urbanisation. In particular, maize production had increased at the expense of the grasslands favoured by the hamster, and urbanisation had led to loss and fragmentation of its habitats. While it was evident that France was taking measures to address these pressures, the Court concluded that these measures did not go far enough.[948]

Case C-383/09, *Commission v. France* confirms that, where the protected species at stake is under threat of extinction within a Member State, and 'whilst the Court of Justice did not explicitly hold that Article 12(1) entails a specific obligation of result',[949] there is a particular onus on the Member States when implementing Article 12 to adopt all effective measures, especially if a species does not benefit from Natura 2000 measures.

943. C-103/00, *Commission v. Greece*, para. 35.
944. *Ibid.*, para. 37.
945. *Ibid.*, para. 40.
946. C-340/10, *Commission v. Cyprus*, para. 63.
947. *Ibid.*, para. 41.
948. C-383/09, *Commission v. France*, paras 26-37.
949. *See* Hendrik Schoukens & Kees Bastmeijer, *Species Protection in the European Union: How Strict Is It?*, 15, published in *The Habitats Directive in Its EU Environmental Law Context: European Nature's Best Hope?* (Charles-Hubert Born, An Cliquet, Hendrik Schoukens, Delphine Misonne & Geert Van Hoorick eds, Routledge 2014).

In this context, it is worth recalling Article 2(2) of the Habitats Directive which provides that measures taken pursuant to it 'shall be designed to maintain or restore, at favourable conservation status, natural habitats and species of wild fauna and flora of Community interest'. Where, as in the case of the Cypriot grass snake or the Milos viper, a species has a very restricted distribution confined to one Member State, the responsibility to protect the common heritage may be considered particularly important, given the risk that, without effective protection, the species may entirely disappear.

It is worth quoting the Opinion of the Advocate General in Case C-383/09, *Commission v. France*:

> The requisite substance of protection measures also depends considerably on the conservation status of the species to be protected. If its conservation status is good, it may be sufficient to make general provision for the prohibitions laid down in Article 12(1) of the Habitats Directive and to monitor the species. An unfavourable conservation status gives rise to more far-reaching obligations for the Member States, however, because the system of protection is intended to help to restore a favourable conservation status. The protection of breeding sites and resting places of a species with a very unfavourable conservation status, as in the case of the European hamster in Alsace, therefore requires a generous delimitation of territory in order to prevent the species from disappearing, and thus the functionality of the sites from being lost. The protection measures must, so far as possible, be adjusted specifically to the circumstances giving rise to the unfavourable conservation status.[950]

[4] *Article 12(1)(a), (b) and (c)*

[a] *Notion of 'Deliberate'*

In the Greek sea turtle case, C-103/00, *Commission v. Greece*, the Court considered as 'deliberate disturbance' within the meaning of Article 12(1)(b), the use of mopeds on a beach that was important for the species. The file before the Court showed that mopeds were being used *notwithstanding* warnings as to the presence of protected sea turtles' nests and the presence of pedalos and small boats in the sea area of the beaches concerned.[951]

The notion of 'deliberate' was also clarified in Case C-221/04, *Commission v. Spain*, in relation to Article 12(a), which refers to 'deliberate capture or killing'. In this case, the Commission contested a Spanish permit allowing, in respect of a defined geographical area of over 10,000 hectares, the use of stopped snares for fox-hunting. The Commission argued that the use of stopped snares contravened Article 12(a) because it caused the deliberate capture or killing of otter, a protected species under

950. Opinion of the Advocate General in C-383/09, *Commission v. France*, para. 37. *See also* Hendrik Shoukens, *Science and the Interpretation of the EU Habitats Directive by the Court of Justice of the EU, 2 + 2 = 5?* 176, in *Nature Law and Policy in Europe*, Chapter 9 (Andrew L.R. Jackson ed., Routledge 2023).
951. C-103/00, *Commission v. Greece*, para. 57.

Annex IV(a). The Court noted that, in the context of Article 12(a), 'deliberate' refers to both the capture and the killing of protected animal species.[952] It stated that, 'it must be proven that the author of the act intended the capture or killing of a specimen belonging to a protected animal species or, at the very least, accepted the possibility of such capture or killing'.[953] For several reasons, the Court found against the Commission. Having looked at the evidence, it was not convinced that otter were present in the area where the permit applied. Furthermore, the permit itself was for fox-hunting – and was not intended to allow the capture of otters. In the absence of convincing evidence on the presence of otter in the area concerned, the Commission had not established that the Spanish authorities knew that they risked endangering otters.[954]

In contrast, in Case C-441/17, *Białowieżka,* the Court was satisfied that, in proving a breach of Article 12(1)(d) in respect of logging operations affecting the breeding and resting places of certain Annex IV(a) species of beetles, the Commission had also proved a breach of Article 12(1)(a) in respect of the same species.[955]

Similarly, as already noted in section §4.03[B][3][d][i] above, in Case C-504/14, *Commission v. Greece,* the Court confirmed that multiple disturbances arising from urbanistic and touristic developments and activities infringed Article 12(1)(b).

[b] Impermissible to Qualify the Prohibitions by Reference to the Conservation Status of a Species

In Joined Cases C-473/19 and C-474/19, Skydda Skogen, which concerned Swedish administrative practice on logging, the Court rejected the proposition that where an activity such as forestry manifestly did not have a purpose of killing or disturbing a protected species, there could be a qualified application of Article 12(1)(a) to (c). In particular, the national Swedish practice at issue in the proceedings provided that, in respect of such activities, the prohibitions laid down in Article 12(a) to (c) applied only in the event of a risk of adverse effects on the conservation status of the species concerned and the protection provided by that provision ceases to apply to species which have achieved a favourable conservation status. Referring to its own earlier ruling on the use of mopeds in the Greek sea turtle case, the Court held that the prohibitions listed in Article 12(1)(a) to (c) of the Habitats Directive are capable of applying to an activity, such as forestry work or land development, the purpose of which is manifestly different from the capture or killing, disturbance of animal species or the deliberate destruction or taking of eggs.[956] Furthermore, the Court ruled that there was no basis for limiting the scope of Article 12(1)(a) to (c) according to the conservation status of the species [conservation status is, however, a relevant factor if it is proposed to derogate under Article 16 of the Directive].[957]

952. C-221/04, *Commission v. Spain,* para. 69.
953. *Ibid.,* para. 71.
954. *Ibid.,* paras 71-74.
955. C-441/17, *Białowieżka,* paras 230-238.
956. Joined Cases C-473/19 and C-474/19, *Skydda Skogen,* para. 53.
957. *Ibid.,* paras 54 to 57.

The Court went on to make a number of pertinent observations on shortcomings in how, for purposes of Article 12(1)(a) to (c), the competent national authorities had addressed the potential impact of logging in the area concerned by the national proceedings. It noted the presence of the *Rana arvalis* species, commonly known as the moor frog, and stressed that the system of strict protection must enable actual harm to the protected species to be avoided.[958]

[5] Article 12(1)(d)

[a] Notions of 'Breeding Sites or Resting Places'

Unlike Article 12(1)(a) to (c) of the Habitats Directive, Article 12(1)(d) does not relate to animal species directly but 'seeks to protect significant parts of their habitats',[959] as it specifically refers to a prohibition of 'deterioration or destruction of breeding sites or resting places'.[960]

The system of protection must be so effective 'to prevent interference with protected animal species and, in particular, their habitats'[961] and, therefore, to ensure that significant parts of the habitats are preserved 'so that those species can enjoy the conditions essential for, *inter alia*, resting in those habitats'.[962]

Article 12(1)(d) of the Habitats Directive refers to 'resting places' but neither Article 1 nor any other provision of the Directive defines the expression. In Case C-477/19, *Magistrat der Stadt Wien*, a preliminary reference from an Austrian court, the Court was called upon to interpret it. Like Case C-383/09, *Commission v. France*, the proceedings concerned the European hamster. They were brought by the employee of a property developer against the City Council of Vienna to contest the imposition of a fine for having caused, during a property re-development, the deterioration or destruction of resting places or breeding sites of the hamster.

The property developer had started work for the construction of a building on land where the European hamster had settled. The developer was aware of the situation and had employed an expert to map hamster burrows and determine whether they were inhabited. Without having obtained any derogation, however, the developer then had topsoil removed, the construction site cleared and a pathway to the construction site built in the immediate vicinity of the entrances to the European hamster burrows. At least two of the burrow entrances were destroyed. The City Council of Vienna held the property developer's employee responsible for the deterioration or destruction of resting places or breeding sites of the European hamster.

The employee challenged the imposition of the fine on the grounds that, *inter alia*, the European hamster burrows were not being used by the hamsters when the

958. *Ibid.*, paras 67 to 75.
959. C-477/19, *Magistrat der Stadt Wien*, para. 28.
960. Article 12(1)(d) of the Habitats Directive; *see also* C-674/17, *Tapiola*, para. 27.
961. C-477/19, *Magistrat der Stadt Wien*, para. 33.
962. *Ibid.*, para. 29.

harmful measures were implemented and those measures did not lead to the deterioration or destruction of resting places or breeding sites of that animal species.

The Court treated the relevant question from the referring court as asking, in essence, whether Article 12(1)(d) of the Habitats Directive is to be interpreted as meaning that the term 'resting place' referred to in that provision also includes resting places which *are no longer occupied* by one of the protected animal species listed in Annex IV(a). It confirmed that the term did include such resting places.

The referring court was thus uncertain as to the interpretation of Article 12(1)(d) of the Habitats Directive. In responding, the Court cited[963] a Commission guidance document[964] which defines resting places as 'areas essential to sustain an animal or group of animals when they are not active'[965] and which also need to be protected when they are not used, but where there is a reasonably high probability that the species concerned will return.[966] So even resting places which are no longer occupied by a protected animal species 'must not be allowed to deteriorate or be destroyed since that species may return to such places'.[967]

Case C-441/17, *Białowieżka,* provides a further interesting illustration of the notions of 'breeding sites or resting places'. The Commission challenged the decision of the Polish national authorities which provided for the felling and removal of spruce trees which were colonised by the spruce bark beetle. There was no restriction relating to the age of the trees so that dead or dying trees a century old or more were included. Dead or dying spruce trees also constituted an important habitat for protected saproxylic beetles, however, in particular, the goldstreifiger beetle, the flat bark beetle, the false darkling beetle and *Pytho kolwensis*, all listed in Annex IV(a) to the Habitats Directive.[968] The removal of that type of tree had been specifically identified as a potential threat to those species of beetle. The Court found that the felling of spruce trees inevitably resulted in the killing, and in the deterioration or destruction of breeding sites and resting places of saproxylic beetles, contrary to both Article 12(1)(a) and Article 12(1)(d) of the Habitats Directive. This was irrespective of whether the species concerned were present in significant numbers, as 'Article 12(1)(d) of the Habitats Directive prescribes a regime providing for strict protection of the breeding sites and resting places of the species listed in Annex IV(a) to the Habitats Directive, regardless of their numbers.'[969]

963. *Ibid.*, para. 30.
964. Guidance document on the strict protection of animal species of Community interest under the Habitats Directive 92/43/EEC, https://ec.europa.eu/environment/nature/conservation/species/guidance/pdf/guidance_en.pdf.
965. *Ibid.*, p. 42.
966. C-477/19, *Magistrat der Stadt Wien*, para. 31.
967. *Ibid.*
968. C-441/17, *Białowieżka*, para. 233.
969. *Ibid.*, para. 237.

[b] Impermissible to Limit the Prohibition to Deliberate or Intentional Acts

Article 12(1)(d) of the Habitats Directive requires the prohibition of activities which will lead to the deterioration or destruction of breeding sites or resting places. The qualification 'deliberate' does not feature in the text, in contrast to the text of Article 12(1)(a) to (c).

Some Member States have, nonetheless, sought to introduce qualifications in order to circumscribe the Article 12(1)(d) prohibition. The Court has rejected these qualifications.

In Case C-6/04, *Commission v. United Kingdom*, the Court found that, by prohibiting only the *deliberate* damaging or destruction of breeding sites or resting places of the species concerned, the legislation applicable in Gibraltar did not satisfy the requirements of Article 12(1)(d).[970]

In Case C-98/03, *Commission v. Germany*, the Court found that the transposition of Article 12(1)(d) of the Directive was flawed as it was limited, over the whole territory of the Member State, to *deliberate* acts.[971] Germany had contended that the wording of Article 12 of the Directive must be interpreted, in line with the principle of proportionality, as not requiring the inclusion of non-deliberate destruction or deterioration of those sites in the system of protection that it establishes. Referring to Case C-6/04, *Commission v. United Kingdom*, the Court dismissed Germany's argument.

It noted that:

> By not limiting the prohibition laid down in Article 12(1)(d) of the Directive to deliberate acts, which it has done in respect of acts referred to in Article 12(1)(a) to (c), the Community legislature has demonstrated its intention to give breeding grounds or resting places increased protection against acts causing their deterioration or destruction. Given the importance of the objectives of protecting biodiversity which the Directive aims to achieve, it is by no means disproportionate that the prohibition laid down in Article 12(1)(d) is not limited to deliberate acts.[972]

In the same vein, in Case C-183/05, *Commission v. Ireland*, the Court found that, by providing that acts which *unintentionally* interfere with or destroy breeding sites or resting places of wild species do not constitute an offence, Irish provisions did not satisfy the requirements of Article 12(1)(d), 'which prohibits such acts, whether they are intentional or not'.[973]

[c] Impermissible to Limit the Prohibition by Reference to Conservation Status

In Joined Cases C-473/19 and C-474/19, Skydda Skogen, the Court held that a national practice could not limit the application of the prohibition in Article 12(1)(d) to

970. C-6/04, *Commission v. United Kingdom*, para. 79.
971. C-98/03, *Commission v. Germany*, paras 54 to 56.
972. *Ibid.*, para. 55.
973. C-183/05, *Commission v. Ireland*, para. 47.

situations where the conservation status of the species concerned is likely to deteriorate. The national practice concerned related to logging and the Court's approach mirrored the approach it took in the same case in relation to Article 12(1)(a) to (c).[974]

[6] Article 12(4) – Incidental Capture or Killing

In Case C-308/08, *Commission v. Spain,* the Commission unsuccessfully claimed that Spain had failed to comply with Article 12(4) in respect of an upgraded country road between Villamanrique de la Condesa, in Seville, and El Rocio, in Huelva.

The Commission's complaint – and a related complaint based on the case-law in Case C-117/03 *Dragaggi* – centred on the impact of the country road on the Iberian lynx, a highly endangered species. With regard to Article 12(4), the Commission was concerned that the Iberian lynx was at risk of being struck and killed by vehicles using the road.

Although the action failed, the Court's decision helps illuminate the requirements of Article 12(4), in particular, with regard to a system of monitoring and conservation measures.

With regard to a system of monitoring, the Court noted that the Spanish authorities had created a database on deaths of Iberian lynx attributable to non-natural causes, such as being struck by a vehicle, which enabled identification of the areas within the natural range of the Iberian lynx where it is most at risk.[975]

With regard to conservation measures, the Spanish authorities referred to 'corrective measures' consisting of 'the adoption of measures to deter speeding; the provision of road signs; the erection of animal fencing; and in the improvement of wildlife crossings, bridges and drainage'.[976] The Court accepted this evidence that Article 12(4) was not contravened.[977]

The Court also found that, even if the Spanish authorities continued to study new measures capable of further improving the conditions for conservation and improvement of the species, this could not in itself lead to a breach of Article 12 (4).[978]

[C] Requirements under Article 14 for the Taking in the Wild of Species Listed in Annex V

Article 14 reads as follows:

> 1. If, in the light of the surveillance provided for in Article 11, Member States deem it necessary, they shall take measures to ensure that the taking in the wild of specimens of species of wild fauna and flora listed in Annex V as well as their exploitation is compatible with their being maintained at a favourable conservation status.

974. Joined Cases C-473/19 and C-474/19, *Skydda Skogen,* operative part of ruling.
975. C-308/08, *Commission v. Spain,* para. 57.
976. *Ibid.,* para. 42.
977. *Ibid.,* para. 58.
978. *Ibid.,* para. 59.

2. Where such measures are deemed necessary, they shall include continuation of the surveillance provided for in Article 11. Such measures may also include in particular:
   - regulations regarding access to certain property;
   - temporary or local prohibition of the taking of specimens in the wild and exploitation of certain populations;
   - regulation of the periods and/or methods of taking specimens;
   - application, when specimens are taken, of hunting and fishing rules which take account of the conservation of such populations;
   - establishment of a system of licences for taking specimens or of quotas;
   - regulation of the purchase, sale, offering for sale, keeping for sale or transport for sale of specimens;
   - breeding in captivity of animal species as well as artificial propagation of plant species, under strictly controlled conditions, with a view to reducing the taking of specimens of the wild;
   - assessment of the effect of the measures adopted.

Article 14 relates to a specific list of species, the list comprised in Annex V. Some of the species listed are also listed in Annex II or Annex IV, but with geographical or other restrictions. It is, therefore, important to understand the relationship between the different annexes.

The species of plants and animals listed under Annex II of the Directive fall under the legal regime that applies to sites included within Natura 2000. Within that framework, there is an obligation on Member States to take the necessary conservation measures that correspond to the ecological requirements of the species concerned. Article 3 of the Habitats Directive provides that 'a coherent European ecological network of special areas of conservation shall be set up under the title Natura 2000' and that 'this network, composed of sites hosting the natural habitat types listed in Annex I and habitats of the species listed in Annex II, shall enable the natural habitat types and the species' habitats concerned to be maintained or, where appropriate, restored at a favourable conservation status in their natural range'. According to Article 6(1) of the Directive, 'for special areas of conservation, Member States shall establish the necessary conservation measures involving, if need be, appropriate management plans specifically designed for the sites or integrated into other development plans, and appropriate statutory, administrative or contractual measures which correspond to the ecological requirements of the natural habitat types in Annex I and the species in Annex II present on the sites'.

Annex IV species, which sometimes overlap with Annex II species, benefit from the prohibitions in Articles 12 and 13. As has been noted, these prohibitions are generally applicable and not confined to areas comprised within the Natura 2000 network.

Article 14 confers on the species – or populations of species – listed in Annex V, a lesser level of protection than Articles 6, 12 or 13 but it is not without consequence. For example, Article 14 needs to be seen in conjunction with Article 15, under which species listed in Annex V(a) benefit from a prohibition on the use of indiscriminate means of capture and killing. This is illustrated by the example of the seals which figured in Case C-6/04, *Commission v. United Kingdom,* described in section [D][2] below.

Different permutations are possible. An Annex V species may also be an Annex II species, for example.

[1] Importance of Surveillance under Article 14(2)

The wording of Article 14 points to the importance of surveillance.

In Case C-6/04, *Commission v. United Kingdom,* the United Kingdom was condemned for failure to transpose Article 14(2) along with Article 11 - *see also* Chapter 5.

The Court held with respect to both Article 11 and Article 14(2) that 'the surveillance obligation is fundamental to the effectiveness of the Habitats Directive and it must be transposed in a detailed, clear and precise manner'.[979] It also found that:

> United Kingdom domestic law does not contain any statutory duty requiring the national authorities to undertake surveillance of the conservation status of natural habitats and species, that domestic law involves an element of legal uncertainty. Hence, it is not guaranteed that surveillance of their conservation status is undertaken systematically and on a permanent basis.[980]

[D] Prohibition on Use of Indiscriminate Means under Article 15

Article 15 of the Habitats Directive reads as follows:

> In respect of the capture or killing of species of wild fauna listed in Annex V(a) and in cases where, in accordance with Article 16, derogations are applied to the taking, capture or killing of species listed in Annex IV (a), Member States shall prohibit the use of all indiscriminate means capable of causing local disappearance of, or serious disturbance to, populations of such species, and in particular:
>
> (a) use of the means of capture and killing listed in Annex VI (a);
> (b) any form of capture and killing from the modes of transport referred to in Annex VI (b).

[1] Need to Enshrine the General Prohibition in National Law

In Case C-6/04, *Commission v. United Kingdom,* the Court upheld a Commission complaint that United Kingdom legislation contained no *general prohibition* on the use of all indiscriminate means capable of causing local disappearance of, or serious disturbance to, populations of the relevant species of wild fauna. According to the Commission 'the national legislation does not therefore preclude the emergence of as yet unknown means of indiscriminate capture and killing'.[981] In its defence, the United

979. C-6/04, *Commission v. United Kingdom,* para. 65.
980. *Ibid.,* para. 68.
981. *Ibid.,* para. 91.

Kingdom stated that its national provisions established lists of every indiscriminate means of capture and killing of the protected species that was currently recorded in the United Kingdom and that the lists were kept under review in order to be updated if necessary.[982]

The Court agreed with the Commission, noting that Article 15, 'as is apparent from its very wording, imposes a general obligation designed to prohibit the use of all indiscriminate means of capture or killing of the species of wild fauna concerned'[983] as 'the possibility of updating a list of prohibited methods is less effective than a general prohibition. Delay in updating the aforementioned lists would necessarily lead to lacunae in protection which are specifically intended to be prevented by means of the general prohibition in Article 15 of the Habitats Directive. This interpretation is all the more justified because domestic law contains no statutory duty to review the lists'.[984]

[2] Seals, an Example of the Protection Given to Annex V Species

In Case C-6/04, *Commission v. United Kingdom,* the Court also found a breach in respect of a category of Annex V species, seals. United Kingdom legislation which covered the species was open to the interpretation that only two methods of killing seals expressly mentioned by it were prohibited.[985] The legislation involved 'an element of legal uncertainty as to the methods of killing seals which are prohibited in the United Kingdom and it therefore does not ensure that Article 15 of the Habitats Directive is transposed correctly'.

As the Advocate General noted:

> It must be stated first that Article 15 of the Habitats Directive is applicable to the hunting of the seal species covered by Annex IV, that is to say the Mediterranean monk seal *Monachus* and the Saimaa ringed seal *Phoca hispida saimensis,* but also, in accordance with Annex V, to the hunting of all other species of 'true seal' or 'earless seal' (the *Phocidae* family). In the United Kingdom, the common or harbour seal (*Phoca vitulina*) and grey seal (*Halichoerus grypus*), for example, are to be found.

This illustrates the sorts of permutations that are possible across the different provisions of the Habitats Directive applicable to species. Some seal species feature in both Annex II and Annex IV, others in both Annex II and Annex V. Article 15 applies to all of them.

[3] Use of Non-selective Means for Unprotected Species

Case C-221/04, *Commission v. Spain,* highlights the fact that, while Article 15 encompasses a general prohibition on the use of non-selective means, it is limited in its coverage to the species listed in Annex IV(a) and V(a). Use of non-selective means to

982. *Ibid.*, para. 92.
983. *Ibid.*, *see* paras 94-96.
984. *Ibid.*, para. 96.
985. *Ibid.*, para. 103.

target other species is not prohibited. Although it is not excluded that such use might contravene Article 12 by also negatively affecting a protected species, Case C-221/04, *Commission v. Spain*, shows that this will require precise and convincing evidence.

In this case, the Commission argued that the use, for the hunting of foxes, of stopped snares, a non-selective hunting method created a risk that otters, a protected species, would be deliberately captured. The hunting method is prohibited under Annex VI of the Habitats Directive but it only applies with respect to the species of wild fauna listed in Annex V(a) and in cases where, in accordance with Article 16, derogations are applied to the taking, capture or killing of species listed in Annex IV(a).[986] The prohibition does not cover hunting of foxes as such, since the fox is not listed in either of these annexes. The Commission saw its action dismissed as it could not prove that the use of non-selective hunting methods led to the killing of otters.

[E] Derogations under Article 16

Article 16 of the Habitats Directive reads as follows:

> 1. Provided that there is no satisfactory alternative and the derogation is not detrimental to the maintenance of the populations of the species concerned at a favourable conservation status in their natural range, Member States may derogate from the provisions of Articles 12, 13, 14 and 15 (a) and (b):
>   (a) in the interest of protecting wild fauna and flora and conserving natural habitats;
>   (b) to prevent serious damage, in particular to crops, livestock, forests, fisheries and water and other types of property;
>   (c) in the interests of public health and public safety, or for other imperative reasons of overriding public interest, including those of a social or economic nature and beneficial consequences of primary importance for the environment;
>   (d) for the purpose of research and education, of repopulating and re-introducing these species and for the breedings operations necessary for these purposes, including the artificial propagation of plants;
>   (e) to allow, under strictly supervised conditions, on a selective basis and to a limited extent, the taking or keeping of certain specimens of the species listed in Annex IV in limited numbers specified by the competent national authorities.

[1] Requirement of Restrictive Interpretation

Article 16 of the Habitats Directive provides for the possibility to derogate from the strict protection obligations enshrined in the Directive. This possibility is, however, limited by the requirement to fulfil two overarching cumulative conditions and by the restricted list of reasons provided for in Article 16.

986. Article 15 of the Directive 92/43/EEC.

The possibility is also constrained by the fact that, since it is an exception to the system of protection which the Directive requires,[987] 'Article 16 must be interpreted restrictively'.[988] This reflects the Court's general approach of interpreting derogation provisions restrictively.

In Case, C-674/17, *Tapiola*, which involved an environmental association's legal challenge to an Article 16 derogation to hunt wolves,[989] the Court stated that Article 16(1) imposes on the authority, taking derogation decisions, the burden of proving that the conditions laid down in Article 16 are present for each derogation.[990]

Moreover, Article 16(1) cannot be seen in isolation. As 'Articles 12, 13 and 16 of the Habitats Directive form a coherent body of provisions',[991] aiming at protecting the population of a certain species, a breach of the derogation conditions set out in Article 16, represents, at the same time, a breach of the strict protection obligations contained under these provisions.

[2] Transposition Needs to Be Complete, Precise and Clear

National legislation used to transpose Article 16 must be complete, precise and clear. It should contain no ambiguities. It must also involve a legal framework. An administrative practice will not be sufficient. Furthermore, a Member State is not entitled to create a legal framework that is less stringent than what Article 16 requires.

In Case C-508/04, *Commission v. Austria*, the Commission challenged transposing legislation for the Habitats Directive adopted by different Austrian regions, including Lower Austria. The Court found that the Lower Austrian legislation did not correctly transpose Article 16. The Court stated that national provisions under which the grant of derogations from the prohibitions established by Articles 12 to 14 and 15(a) and (b) of the Directive is subject not to all the criteria and conditions set out in Article 16 of the Directive but, *incompletely*, to certain elements of them, cannot constitute a regime consistent with Article 16.[992] Amongst other things, the Court considered that the *ambiguity* of the wording of Lower Austrian legislation which purported to transpose the reference in Article 16(1) to 'favourable conservation status' was 'incompatible with the requirement for a *precise and clear* transposition of Article 16(1)'.

[a] Compliant Administrative Practice Cannot Make Up for Incompleteness

An administrative practice cannot make up for a deficient legal transposing framework. In Case C-98/03, *Commission v. Germany*, the Commission argued that German

987. C-508/04, *Commission v. Austria*, para. 110.
988. C-6/04, *Commission v. United Kingdom*, para. 111.
989. For valuable insights into the background to this important case, in particular the role of the environmental association, Tapiola, *see Yaffa Epstein, José Vicente López-Bao and Guillaume Chapron, Strict Protection of Species in the EU, Controversies and Trends*, 208-209, in *Nature Law and Policy in Europe*, Chapter 10 (Andrew L.R. Jackson ed., Routledge 2023).
990. C-674/17, *Tapiola*, para. 30.
991. C-6/04, *Commission v. United Kingdom*, para. 112.
992. C-508/04, *Commission v. Austria*, para. 112.

legislation had not taken sufficient account of the conditions laid down in Article 16. Germany counter-argued that the use of the legislation involved administrative decisions and that officials adopting those decisions were bound to observe the conditions of Article 16. The Court rejected this counter-argument and upheld the Commission's complaint.[993]

In Case C-508/04, *Commission v. Austria,* the Court rejected a similar defence by Austria, stating that 'an administrative practice consistent with a directive's provisions is not sufficient to transpose Community law correctly'.[994]

[b] Unlawful for Transposition to Be Less Strict than Article 16

In Case C-6/04, *Commission v. United Kingdom,* the Commission successfully challenged transposing legislation which narrowed the circumstances in which prohibitions of Article 12 applied. The relevant legislation authorised acts which led to the killing of protected species and the deterioration or destruction of their breeding and resting places, 'where those acts are as such lawful'.[995] The Court ruled that this was 'contrary both to the spirit and purpose of the Habitats Directive and to the wording of Article 16 thereof'.[996]

In Case C-46/11, *Commission v. Poland,* the Court held that Article 16(1)(b) did not allow for derogations from the prohibitions relating to protected species on the basis that compliance with these prohibitions would mean not being able to use technologies normally used in agriculture, forestry or fish-farming.[997]

[c] No Requirement to Go Beyond the Wording of Article 16

While the Court has confirmed the need to transpose Article 16 strictly, Case C-166/22, *Hellfire Massey Residents Association* shows that it will not require Member State's legislation to address topics not reflected in the provision's actual wording. As is explained in section §4.03[F] below, Article 16 does not require provision for public participation.

[3] Impermissible to Have Parallel Regimes and Circumventions

In Case C-183/05, *Commission v. Ireland,* the Court condemned Ireland for maintaining a parallel derogation regime which did not satisfy the requirements of Article 16. While Ireland did adopt regulations in 2005 to give effect to Article 16, in parallel it retained section 23 of its 1976 Wildlife Act, which was less stringent. The Court noted that the derogations laid down in section 23 of the Wildlife Act went beyond what is provided

993. C-98/03, *Commission v. Germany,* para. 61.
994. C-508/04, *Commission v. Austria,* para. 113.
995. C-6/04, *Commission v. United Kingdom,* para. 113.
996. *Ibid.*
997. C-46/11, *Commission v. Poland,* para. 31.

for in Article 16 of the Habitats Directive, since the latter determines, in an exhaustive manner, the conditions under which derogations may be made from Article 12. It concluded that the Commission was correct in law to allege that there was a parallel regime of derogations under Irish legislation which was inconsistent with Articles 12 and 16.

A comparable situation to the Irish one arose in Case C-432/21, *Commission v. Poland*. While Poland adopted transposing legislation for Articles 12 to 16, it also adopted a Law on forests according to which forest management implemented, in accordance with the requirements of good forest management practice, did not infringe the relevant species' protection provisions. The Court found that this amounted to an impermissible general derogation. The Court rejected arguments by Poland that other Polish legislative provisions made it possible to meet the conditions of Article 16 of the Habitats Directive, noting that, even if that were proved, there would, in such a case, be a contradiction between, on the one hand, the general derogation provided for in the Law on forests and, on the other hand, those other legislative provisions allegedly applicable.[998]

It stated that:

> A contradiction between the various national provisions not only undermines the principle of legal certainty, but is also liable to mislead the administrative authorities responsible for implementing the provisions of an EU directive as to the manner in which the protection regime is to be applied.[999]

[4] *Two Overarching Cumulative Conditions*

Two overarching conditions apply to the process of granting derogations under Article 16, and they have to be met cumulatively: first, there must be no satisfactory alternative to the derogation and, second, the derogation must not be detrimental to the maintenance of the populations of the species concerned in a favourable conservation status in their natural range.

[5] *Condition of No Satisfactory Alternative*

The derogation decision must be duly motivated as regards the lack of a satisfactory alternative. In Case C-342/05, *Commission v. Finland*, the Court found that two decisions of the national authorities to issue wolf-hunting permits were contrary to Article 16(1) as, *inter alia*, they did not contain 'a clear and sufficient statement of reasons as to the absence of a satisfactory alternative'.[1000]

In another case concerning wolf-hunting derogations in Finland, Case C-674/17, *Tapiola*, the Court stated that:

998. C-432/21, *Commission v. Poland*, para. 34.
999. *Ibid.*, para. 35.
1000. C-342/05, *Commission v. Finland*, para. 31.

> It is for the competent national authorities, when authorising derogation permits such as those at issue in the main proceedings, to establish, taking account in particular of the best relevant scientific and technical evidence and in the light of the circumstances of the specific situation in question, that there is no satisfactory alternative that can achieve the objective pursued, in compliance with the prohibitions laid down in the Habitats Directive.[1001]

In this case, the Finnish authorities considered that permitting the killing of a small number of wolf individuals was the only satisfactory alternative in order to combat poaching. While not completely excluding such a possibility, the Court was sceptical about the justification, and set stringent requirements, stating:

> It is for the national authority to support, on the basis of rigorous scientific data, including, where appropriate, comparative data on the effects of hunting for population management purposes on the conservation status of wolves, the proposition that hunting for population management purposes is actually capable of reducing illegal hunting to such an extent that it would have a net positive effect on the conservation status of the wolf population, whilst taking account of the number of derogation permits envisaged and the most recent estimates of the number of wolves taken illegally.[1002]

Member States must rather give priority to strict monitoring of poaching activities.[1003]

In the operative part of its ruling, the Court stated that an Article 16 derogation whose objective is to combat poaching will not be valid where, *inter alia*, 'it is not duly established that their objective cannot be attained by means of a satisfactory alternative, the mere existence of an illegal activity or difficulties associated with its monitoring not constituting sufficient evidence in that regard'.

[6] Condition of Not Being Detrimental to Favourable Conservation Status

In Case C-508/04, *Commission v. Austria*, the Court confirmed that the condition on favourable conservation status was a 'necessary precondition' in order for derogations to be granted under Article 16(1).[1004] It must be unambiguously provided for in the national transposing legislation.[1005]

Furthermore, to properly respond to this second overarching condition, the authorities granting the derogation must make a prior assessment of the effect on favourable conservation status. In Case C-342/05, *Commission v. Finland*, the Court referred to two Finnish wolf-hunting derogation decisions, observing that, amongst other things, the authorities had 'permitted the hunting of a fixed number of wolves in a well-defined geographical area, but without relying on an assessment of the

1001. C-674/17, *Tapiola*, para. 51.
1002. *Ibid.*, para. 45.
1003. *Ibid.*, para. 48.
1004. C-508/04, *Commission v. Austria*, para. 115.
1005. *Ibid.*, para. 116.

conservation status of the species'.[1006] It held that such decisions, which are not based on an assessment of the effect of the killing of the wolves that they authorise on the maintenance of a favourable conservation status of the population of that species in its natural range are contrary to Article 16(1) of the Habitats Directive.[1007]

[a] Notion of 'Favourable Conservation Status'

According to Article 1(i) of the Habitats Directive:

> Conservation status of a species means the sum of the influences acting on the species concerned that may affect the long-term distribution and abundance of its populations within the territory referred to in Article 2.

Furthermore, the conservation status will be taken as 'favourable' when:

- population dynamics data on the species concerned indicate that it is maintaining itself on a long-term basis as a viable component of its natural habitats;
- the natural range of the species is neither being reduced nor is likely to be reduced for the foreseeable future; and
- there is, and will probably continue to be, a sufficiently large habitat to maintain its populations on a long-term basis.[1008]

As can be seen, the notion of 'favourable conservation status' encompasses several distinct elements: population dynamics, natural range, and sufficiently large habitat.

In this context, it is useful to refer not only to Commission Notice C(2021)7301, already mentioned at §4.03[A][3] above, but to a Commission-funded expert report entitled 'Guidelines for Population Level Management Plans for Large Carnivores'.[1009] It was published in 2008. The Large Carnivore Guidelines provide a uniform methodology to assess the conservation status of each distinct population. In 2015, the Guidelines were complemented by another technical document prepared for the European Commission, entitled Key actions for Large Carnivore populations in Europe.[1010] The latter outlines several specific key actions to be taken with respect to each distinct European large carnivore population.[1011]

1006. C-342/05, *Commission v. Finland*, para. 30.
1007. *Ibid.*, para. 31.
1008. *See also* C-674/17, *Tapiola*, para. 56.
1009. https://www.auvergne-rhone-alpes.developpement-durable.gouv.fr/IMG/pdf/guidelines_lcie_final2008.pdf.
1010. Arie Trouwborst, Luigi Boitani & John D.C. Linnell, *Interpreting 'Favourable Conservation Status' for Large Carnivores in Europe: How Many Are Needed and How Many Are Wanted?*, Biodivers Conserv (2017) 26:37-61 DOI: 10.1007/s10531-016-1238-z.
1011. https://www.europarc.org/wp-content/uploads/2017/02/key_actions_large_carnivores_2015.pdf For other relevant documentation: https://ec.europa.eu/environment/nature/conservation/species/carnivores/library.htm.

[b] *Assessment of Effects on Conservation Status*

[i] Need to Use the Best Scientific Data Available and Apply the Precautionary Principle

In Case C-674/17, the *Tapiola*, the Court confirmed that the assessment of the impact on the conservation status must be based on the best scientific data available, and where uncertainty subsists as to whether or not a derogation would be 'detrimental to the maintenance or restoration of the populations at a favourable conservation status',[1012] the Member State 'must refrain from granting or implementing that derogation',[1013] according to the precautionary principle enshrined in the Article 191(2) TFEU.

[ii] The Spatial Dimension: The Levels at Which Effects on Favourable Conservation Status Should Be Assessed

The Court's case-law on Article 16 sheds light on whether effects on conservation status must be assessed at the local, national, transboundary or biogeographical levels, or at all these levels.[1014]

Before referring to this case-law, it is worth recalling that 'natural range' is not only an integral element of the notion of 'conservation status'. It is also explicitly referred to in the wording of Article 12 of the Habitats Directive and is relevant to the Article 12 case-law. In Case C-383/09, *Commission v. France*, for instance, the hamster's conservation status within France was 'assessed without considering the contiguous population across the border in Germany and further eastward'.[1015]

Turning to Article 16, in Case C-674/17, *Tapiola*, the referring court specifically asked whether, for purposes of a regionally restricted derogation permit under Article 16, conservation status was to be assessed by reference both to a particular area and to the territory of the Member State as a whole or by reference to an even wider range of the species in question.[1016]

In response, the Court stated that, when assessing the grant of a derogation, it is for the competent national authority to determine:

1012. C-674/17, *Tapiola*, para. 66.
1013. *Ibid.*
1014. Arie Trouwborst, Luigi Boitani & John D.C. Linnell, *Interpreting 'Favourable Conservation Status' for Large Carnivores in Europe: How Many Are Needed and How Many Are Wanted?*, Biodivers Conserv (2017) 26:37-61 DOI: 10.1007/s10531-016-1238-z.
1015. Marc Clement, *Global objectives and scope of the Habitats Directive: What Does the Obligation of Result Mean in Practice? The European Hamster in Alsace*, 9-20 in *The Habitats Directive in Its EU Environmental Law Context: European Nature's Best Hope?* (Charles-Hubert Born, An Cliquet, Hendrik Schoukens, Delphine Misonne & Geert Van Hoorick eds, Routledge 2015), as quoted by Arie Trouwborst, Luigi Boitani & John D.C. Linnell, *Interpreting 'Favourable Conservation Status' for Large Carnivores in Europe: How Many Are Needed and How Many Are Wanted?*, Biodivers Conserv (2017) 26:37-61 DOI 10.1007/s10531-016-1238-z.
1016. Question 3 of the referring court.

> In particular at national level or, where applicable, at the level of the biogeographical region in question where the borders of that Member State straddle several biogeographical regions or if the natural range of the species so requires and, to the extent possible, at a cross-border level, as a first step, the conservation status of the populations of the species in question and, in a second step, the geographical and demographic effects that the envisaged derogations are capable of having on those.[1017]

Thus, assessment at national level is key, but assessment at biogeographical or cross-border levels may also be relevant.

In addition, the Court stressed the likely importance of assessment at the local level, observing that:

> The assessment of the impact of a derogation at the level of the territory of a local population is generally necessary in order to determine its impact on the conservation status of the population concerned on a larger scale. In so far as such a derogation must deal with specific requirements and specific situations, the most direct effects of such a derogation are generally felt in the local area to which it relates. Moreover, the conservation status of a population at national or biogeographical level depends also on the cumulative impact of the various derogations affecting local areas.[1018]

The Court, however, firmly rejected the proposition that assessment should extend to populations situated outside of the EU. The specific context was one in which the Finnish authorities had argued that account should be taken of contiguous wolf populations in Russia. The Court held that it could not be accepted that, for the purpose of the assessment of conservation status, 'account should be taken of the part of the natural range of the population in question extending to certain parts of the territory of a third country which is not bound by an obligation of strict protection of species of interest for the European Union'.[1019]

While the Court's reference to the cross-border level indicates that this level may be relevant in the case of neighbouring EU Member States sharing the same legal obligations, 'clearly, the ruling cannot be interpreted to mean that a Member State can lawfully limit its own population to a handful of wolves based on the mere argument that there is a flourishing population across the border'.[1020]

As for the value of assessment at the scale of a biogeographical region, it is useful to note that the EU has nine terrestrial biogeographical regions and five marine regions, each with its own characteristic blend of vegetation, climate, topography and geology. Some Member States may have several biogeographical regions within their territory (e.g., France has four such regions: Atlantic, Alpine, Continental and Mediterranean) whereas others have only one (e.g., the Netherlands has only the Atlantic region).[1021]

1017. C-674/17, *Tapiola*, para. 58.
1018. *Ibid.*, para. 59.
1019. *Ibid.*, para. 60.
1020. Arie Trouwborst & Floor M. Fleurke, *Killing Wolves Legally: Exploring the Scope for Lethal Wolf Management under European Nature Conservation Law*, 22(3) Journal of International Wildlife Law & Policy 231-273 (2019), DOI: 10.1080/13880292.2019.1686223.
1021. The_state_of_nature_brochure.pdf (europa.eu).

Using biogeographical regions to select sites for the Natura 2000 network and assess the conservation status of species and habitats under the Habitats Directive is very useful from a scientific point of view since it allows the species and habitats to be examined under very similar natural conditions, irrespective of national boundaries.[1022]

[iii] Possible Relevance of National Quotas When Assessing How a Derogation Will Affect Conservation Status

In Case C-674/17, *Tapiola,* the Court considered the possible relevance of national quotas to the conservation status assessment. In this specific case, Finland used management plans and national legislation to fix the maximum number of individual wolves that might be killed for a given hunting year within the national territory. The Court confirmed that such measures might help satisfy the requirement concerning favourable conservation status 'since they could ensure that the annual cumulative effect of the individual derogations is without prejudice to the maintenance or restoration of the populations of the species in question at a favourable conservation status'.[1023]

In the circumstances of Case C-674/17, *Tapiola,* the Court was, however, sceptical of the official Finnish position, observing as follows:

It appears from the figures put forward by Tapiola and the Commission, the accuracy of which is for the referring court to ascertain, that in the 2015-2016 hunting year, out of a national population totalling between 275 and 310 specimens, 43 or 44 wolves were killed in Finland on the basis of derogation permits for hunting for population management purposes, authorised under the national law, half of that number being breeding specimens. Thus, hunting for population management purposes involved the killing of almost 15% of the entire wolf population of Finland, including numerous breeding specimens. Moreover, the management plan estimated the annual number of wolves killed illegally at approximately 30 specimens.[1024]

Further, Tapiola and the Commission claim that hunting for population management purposes led to the killing of 13 or 14 additional specimens as compared with those which, according to the estimates, would have been killed as a result of poaching, thus resulting in a net negative effect on that population.[1025]

In light of this information, the Court stated that it was doubtful whether the management plan and the national law setting the maximum number of specimens which may be killed for a hunting year, of which the derogation permits at issue in the main proceedings form part, made it possible to satisfy the requirement concerning conservation status. That was a matter which was, however, for the referring court to ascertain.[1026]

1022. https://ec.europa.eu/environment/nature/pdf/state_of_nature_en.pdf.
1023. C-674/17, *Tapiola,* para. 62.
1024. *Ibid.*, para. 63.
1025. *Ibid.*, para. 64.
1026. *Ibid.*, para. 65.

[c] Derogations Still Possible Where Conservation Status Is Unfavourable

Case C-342/05, *Commission v. Finland,* sheds light on what should happen when the species concerned has an unfavourable conservation status. At the time of the dispute, the Court determined that the conservation status of the wolf in Finland was unfavourable. The Court confirmed that, none the less, the grant of derogations remained possible by way of exception 'where it is duly established that they are not such as to worsen the unfavourable conservation status of those populations or to prevent their restoration at a favourable conservation status'.[1027] Citing Commission guidance, the Court considered that, in such circumstances, a derogation would be neutral for the species concerned. The Court repeated this position in Case C-674/17, *Tapiola.*[1028]

[7] Objectives That May Justify a Derogation under Article 16

Apart from fulfilling the two overarching conditions described above, derogations under Article 16 must relate to one or more of the categories of objectives listed under letters a) to e) of Article 16(1). The categories of objectives covered by letters a) to d) represent specific interests and purposes described in the text. In contrast, the category of objectives covered by letter e) is left open.[1029]

The Court has not yet pronounced itself on each and every one of these objectives but the case-law provides clarification on Article 16(1)(e), in particular.

[a] Article 16(1)(b) – Objective of Preventing Serious Damage

In Case C-342/05, *Commission v. Finland,* Finland sought to justify wolf-hunting permits on the basis that the hunting was to prevent damage.[1030] The Court followed the Advocate General's Opinion that Article 16(1) does not require serious damage to be sustained before derogations can be adopted.[1031] The contested hunting permits did not identify and target the specimen(s) which caused damage, however, and authorised the killing of one or several wolves in a pack. The Court considered that there was insufficient scientific information to underpin the hypothesis that the killing of one or several wolves in a pack certain of whose members cause or are likely to cause damage would indeed prevent, eliminate or reduce that damage. As a result, the Court upheld the Commission's complaint that the Finnish hunting derogations were incompatible with the Habitats Directive.[1032]

As already noted in §4.03[E][2][b] above, in Case C-46/11, *Commission v. Poland,* the Court ruled that Article 16(1)(b) would not justify derogations simply

1027. C-342/05, *Commission v. Finland,* para. 29.
1028. C-674/17, *Tapiola,* para. 68.
1029. *Ibid.,* para. 34.
1030. C-342/05, *Commission v. Finland,* para. 40.
1031. *Ibid.*
1032. *Ibid.,* paras 40-44.

because complying with relevant prohibitions would not allow the use of technologies normally used in agriculture, forestry or fish farming.[1033]

[b] Article 16(1)(e) – Unspecified Objectives

The literature is divided on whether Article 16(1)(e) should be regarded as providing a 'catch-all'[1034] derogation possibility, including when the specific elements of the objectives referred to under letters a) to d) are not present, or whether it is to be treated as a 'residual category to be relied on for purposes not mentioned under (a)-(d)'.[1035] According to Darpo and Epstein as quoted by Arie Trouwborst & Floor M. Fleurke,[1036] Article 16(1)(e) is a typical 'last resort derogation'[1037] possibility whose utilisation must remain exceptional and only if the other objectives listed under letters a) to d) of Article 16(1) have been exhausted.

[i] Article 16(1)(e) Not a General Legal Basis for Derogations

In Case C-674/17, *Tapiola*, the Court confirmed that Article 16(1)(e) is to be treated as a residual or last resort category and cannot displace the other categories where these are clearly relevant. It stated that:

> Article 16(1)(e) of the Habitats Directive cannot serve as a general legal basis for granting derogations from Article 12(1) of that directive, without depriving the other situations covered by Article 16(1) thereof as well as the system of strict protection of their effectiveness.[1038]
>
> It added that:
>
> The objective of a derogation based on Article 16(1)(e) of the Habitats Directive cannot, in principle, be confused with the objectives of the derogations based on Article 16(1)(a) to (d) of that directive, with the result that the former provision can only serve as a basis for the grant of a derogation in cases where the latter provisions are not relevant.[1039]

1033. C-46/11, *Commission v. Poland*, para. 31.
1034. Arie Trouwborst & Floor M. Fleurke, *Killing Wolves Legally: Exploring the Scope for Lethal Wolf Management under European Nature Conservation Law*, 22(3) Journal of International Wildlife Law & Policy 231-273 (2019), DOI: 10.1080/13880292.2019.1686223 quoting Yaffa Epstein & Guillaume Chapron, *The Hunting of Strictly Protected Species: The Tapiola Case and the Limits of Derogation under Article 16 of the Habitats Directive*, 27 European Energy and Environmental Law Review 78 (2018) DOI: 10.54648/eelr2018009.
1035. Arie Trouwborst & Floor M. Fleurke, *Killing Wolves Legally: Exploring the Scope for Lethal Wolf Management under European Nature Conservation Law*, 22(3) Journal of International Wildlife Law & Policy 231-273 (2019), DOI: 10.1080/13880292.2019.1686223.
1036. *Ibid.*
1037. Jan Darpö & Yaffa Epstein, *Thrown to the Wolves: Sweden Once Again Flouts EU Standards on Species Protection and Access to Justice*, Nordic Environmental Law Journal 7 (July 2015), NMT-12015-DarpoEpstein-6-juli.pdf (jandarpo.se).
1038. C-674/17, *Tapiola*, para. 36.
1039. *Ibid.*, para. 37.

In Case C-674/17, *Tapiola*, the purported objective for which Article 16(1)(e) was invoked was to reduce the illegal killing, i.e., poaching of wolves. The Finnish authorities contended that allowing hunting of a certain number of specimens would increase the general feeling of safety of the people living in areas where wolves are present, which in turn would lead to a certain social tolerance vis-a-vis wolves and to the diminishing of poaching.[1040] The Court accepted that combating poaching could be an objective covered by Article 16(1)(e), but, as has previously been noted, it was not convinced that the Finnish authorities had respected the two overarching conditions set out in Article 16(1).

[ii] Set of Requirements to Be Fulfilled under Article 16(1)(e)

Article 16(1)(e) contains an additional set of requirements to be met, covering the limited and specified nature of the number of specimens of species which may be taken or kept; the selective basis and the limited extent which apply to that taking or keeping; and the strict nature of the supervision to which compliance with those conditions must be subject.

[iii] 'In Limited Numbers Specified by the Competent National Authorities'

With regard to the limited and specified number of certain specimens to be taken or kept, this depends on the population level of the species, its conservation status and its biological characteristics and 'must also be determined on the basis of rigorous scientific data which relate to geographic, climatic, environmental and biological factors as well as those enabling an assessment of the situation regarding the species' reproduction and total annual mortality rate owing to natural causes'.[1041]

In addition to the requirement that the establishment of a small number to be taken not be detrimental to the favourable conservation status, it must also 'not entail the risk of significant impact on the structure of the population in question',[1042] and the number must be clearly indicated in the derogation decisions.[1043]

In Case C-674/17, *Tapiola*, the Court was doubtful that this condition was satisfied.[1044]

[iv] 'On a Selective Basis and to a Limited Extent'

As regards the requirement relating to the selective and limited basis on which certain specimens of species are taken or kept, this 'must be determined in the narrowest, most

1040. *Ibid.*, para. 39.
1041. *Ibid.*, para. 71.
1042. *Ibid.*, para. 72.
1043. *Ibid.*
1044. *Ibid.*, para. 75.

specific and efficient way possible',[1045] and it may be necessary to limit the derogation to types or groups of specimens or even to individually identified specimens.[1046]

[v] 'Under Strictly Supervised Conditions'

As for the requirement that derogations under Article 16(1)(e) of the Habitats Directive be implemented under strictly supervised conditions, this triggers an obligation to monitor the *subsequent* impact of the derogation.[1047] In Case C-674/17, *Tapiola*, in spite of the fact that the derogation decisions contained guidance 'as to the types of specimens targeted, in particular young individuals or those causing nuisance',[1048] these were mere recommendations and did not oblige in fact the permit holders to do so.[1049] Notably, the derogation did not ensure that breeding specimens were not targeted, an aspect of utmost importance in light of the Directive's objectives.[1050] In this particular case, the fact that 20 alpha males had been killed within a hunting year cast serious doubts on the fulfilment of the above conditions.

The Court stated that 'the national legislation must ensure that the lawfulness of the decisions granting derogation permits under that provision and the manner in which those decisions are implemented, including as regards compliance with the accompanying conditions relating to, in particular, places, dates, numbers and types of specimens targeted, *are subject to effective control in a timely manner*'.[1051]

The Court referred by analogy to similar provisions in the Birds Directive and Case C-60/05, *WWF Italia*, [discussed in section §4.02[F], where it stated that:

> The obligation on the Member States to ensure that hunting of birds is carried out only in 'small numbers', in accordance with Article 9(1)(c) of the Directive, requires that the administrative procedures provided for are organised in such a way that both the decisions of the competent authorities authorising hunting derogations and the manner in which those decisions are applied are subject to effective control exercised in a timely manner.[1052]

[F] The Scope for Public Participation in Relation to Decision-Making Concerning Articles 12 and 16

Neither Article 12 nor 16 make any express reference to public participation in relation to decisions which may concern these provisions.

The extent to which public participation might be required was addressed in Case C-166/22, *Hellfire Massey Residents Association*. The case arose from objections to the

1045. *Ibid.*, para. 73.
1046. *Ibid.*
1047. *Ibid.*, para. 74.
1048. *Ibid.*, para. 76.
1049. *Ibid.*, para. 77.
1050. *Ibid.*
1051. *Ibid.*, para. 74. *See*, by analogy, C-60/05, *WWF Italia*, para. 47.
1052. C-60/05, *WWF Italia*, para. 47.

construction of a visitor centre. The plaintiff argued that the system of strict protection provided for in Article 12 of the Habitats Directive, as implemented in Irish law, was invalid in so far as it did not integrate the derogation mechanism laid down in Article 16 of that directive into the procedure for granting development consent to projects and, moreover, did not provide for proper public participation, thereby failing to comply with the Aarhus Convention.

[1] Transposition Does Not Require Public Participation

The referring court asked, in essence, whether Articles 12 and 16 of the Habitats Directive are to be interpreted as requiring a piece of national legislation intended to transpose those provisions of the Habitats Directive into national law to provide for: (i) a development consent procedure which involves a decision by a competent authority determining whether it is necessary to apply for a derogation under Article 16 of that directive because of matters identified following the grant of development consent to a project and/or whether surveys are required to that end; and (ii) public participation in that derogation procedure.[1053]

The Court was very clear that no such requirement could be read into either Article 12 or 16. It stated that these provisions do not require the derogation procedure under Article 16 to be integrated into the procedures for granting development consent to projects; nor do they require provision to be made for public participation in such a derogation procedure.[1054] Nor did the EIA Directive lay down such an obligation.[1055]

[2] But a Duty Exists to Interpret and Apply Articles 12 and 16 in Conformity with Other Requirements

While there was no formal transposition requirement, the Court did, however, point out that Articles 12 and 16 and measures transposing them must be *interpreted and applied* in conformity with the requirements arising from other EU acts and from international conventions which are binding on the EU, in particular, the requirements arising from the EIA Directive and from the Aarhus Convention, as interpreted in the case-law of the Court.[1056]

The Court made it clear that, in the specific case where, first, the execution of a project that is subject to the dual requirement for assessment and development consent laid down in Article 2(1) of the EIA Directive involves the developer applying for and obtaining a derogation from the plant and animal species protection measures prescribed in the provisions of national law transposing Articles 12 and 13 of the Habitats Directive and where, second, a Member State confers power to grant such a derogation on an authority other than the one on which it confers power to give development

1053. C-166/22, *Hellfire Massey Residents Association*, para. 29.
1054. *Ibid.*, para. 30.
1055. *Ibid.*, paras 31 to 33.
1056. *Ibid.*, para. 35.

consent for the project, that potential derogation must necessarily be adopted before development consent is given. If it were otherwise, that development consent would be given on an incomplete basis and would not, therefore, meet the applicable requirements.[1057] This topic is also addressed in Chapter 6, §6.02[B][2].

[G] Access to Justice in Relation to Species Protection under the Habitats Directive

The preliminary references on species protection are dominated by legal proceedings brought by environmental associations against decisions of national authorities, but, as noted in section §4.03[E] above, there is no provision for public participation in respect of Articles 12 and 16 of the Habitats Directive. Furthermore, there are no provisions on access to justice in the Habitats Directive, and, in some jurisdictions, there may be no entitlement in national law for an environmental association to bring a legal challenge against a decision of the competent authorities which contravenes Articles 12 or 16.

In its landmark decision in Case C-240/09, *LZ I* (sometimes referred to as *Slovak Brown Bears*), the Court set out a basis in EU law for an environmental association to challenge compliance with these provisions of the Habitats Directive.

The background was that, under Slovak law, it was possible for hunters and others to seek a derogation pursuant to Article 16 from the system of protection for species such as the brown bear, which is listed in Annex IV. Under Slovak law, however, LZ, an environmental association was denied the status of a 'party' to administrative proceedings relating to the grant of derogations.

In a preliminary reference, the referring court asked essentially whether individuals and, in particular, environmental protection associations, where they wish to challenge a decision to derogate from a system of environmental protection, such as that put in place by the Habitats Directive for a species mentioned in Annex IV, may derive a right to bring proceedings under EU law, having regard, in particular, to the provisions of Article 9(3) of the Aarhus Convention.[1058]

While the Court held that Article 9(3) of the Aarhus Convention does not have direct effect, it stated that the referring court should:

> Interpret, to the fullest extent possible, the procedural rules relating to the conditions to be met in order to bring administrative or judicial proceedings in accordance with the objectives of Article 9(3) of that convention and the objective of effective judicial protection of the rights conferred by EU law, in order to enable an environmental protection organisation, such as the Zoskupenie, to challenge before a court a decision taken following administrative proceedings liable to be contrary to EU environmental law.[1059]

As can be seen from Chapters 3 and 8, C-240/09, *Slovak Brown Bears* now fits within a broader body of access to justice case-law related to the nature directives.

1057. *Ibid.*, para. 36. *See also* C-463/20, *Namur-Est Environnement*, paras 52 and 59.
1058. C-240/09, *Slovak Brown Bears*, para. 28.
1059. *Ibid.*, para. 52.

CHAPTER 5

Protection of Natural Areas Outside of Natura 2000 and Species Protection Areas, and Surveillance of Conservation Status

§5.01 INFLUENCE OF NATURA 2000 AND SPECIES PROTECTION ON THE WIDER TERRITORY

As indicated in Chapter 3, the case-law on Article 6(3) of the Habitats Directive, in particular Cases C-142/16, Moorburg and Case C-461/17, *Holohan*, shows that protecting Natura 2000 sites may, de facto, entail protecting natural areas outside of them.[1060] Although not entitled to protection in their own right, external natural areas may need to be protected because they are inextricably linked to the conservation needs of certain species or habitats protected within Natura 2000. The point can be made by reference to a river used by a protected migratory fish species and the catchments of a protected aquatic species. Case C-142/16, Moorburg, illustrates why stretches of a river outside of a Natura 2000 site need to be kept barrier-free for migratory fish that pass into or out of the protected site. A sedentary aquatic species like the freshwater pearl mussel that featured in Case C-461/17, *Holohan*, illustrates why it is important to properly manage natural areas in the catchments of freshwater pearl mussel Natura 2000 sites, since catchment hydrology may be critical to ensuring a constant supply of well-oxygenated sediment-free water to the streams and rivers where the species lives.

The rationale of this case-law on Article 6(3) is also relevant to Article 6(1) and Article 6(2) of the Habitats Directive.

Furthermore, as Chapter 4 indicates, the provisions of Article 5 of the Birds Directive and Articles 12 and 13 of the Habitats Directive have implications for protection of natural areas wherever there is a presence of wild birds' nests or of protected animal or plant species.

1060. *See* Chapter 3, §3.04[D][18][c].

In addition to these, however, a number of other provisions of the nature directives have relevance[1061] and have been subject to interpretation by the Court. A general provision on surveillance in the Habitats Directive has also been subject to interpretation.

§5.02 PROTECTION OF NATURAL AREAS UNDER ARTICLE 3 OF THE BIRDS DIRECTIVE

[A] General Obligation under Article 3 and Relationship with Article 4 of the Birds Directive

Article 3 of the Birds Directive reads as follows:

> 1. In the light of the requirements referred to in Article 2, Member States shall take the requisite measures to preserve, maintain or re-establish a sufficient diversity and area of habitats for all the species of birds referred to in Article 1.
> 2. The preservation, maintenance and re-establishment of biotopes and habitats shall include primarily the following measures:
>   (a) creation of protected areas;
>   (b) upkeep and management in accordance with the ecological needs of habitats inside and outside the protected zones;
>   (c) re-establishment of destroyed biotopes;
>   (d) creation of biotopes.

Article 3 sits alongside Article 4, the first and second paragraphs of which provide the basis for classification of sites as SPAs and thus for their inclusion in Natura 2000. Initially, it was not clear how Articles 3 and 4 were related to each other and, in Case C-355/90, *Santoña Marshes,* the Commission invoked both provisions when complaining about the lack of protection of a Spanish wetland, the Santoña Marshes.

The Court clarified the nature of the obligations imposed by *both* Articles 3 and 4 as follows:

> Articles 3 and 4 of the directive require Member States to preserve, maintain and re-establish habitats as such, because of their ecological value. Moreover, it follows from the ninth recital in the preamble to the directive that the preservation, maintenance or restoration of a sufficient diversity and area of habitats is essential to the conservation of all species of birds. The obligations on Member States under Articles 3 and 4 of the directive therefore exist before any reduction is observed in the number of birds or any risk of a protected species becoming extinct has materialized.[1062]

1061. For very useful insights into the legislative history of Article 3 and Article 4(4), second sentence of the Birds Directive, as well as Article 10 of the Habitats Directive, *see* Andrew L.R. Jackson, *Conservation of Areas Outside the Natura 2000 Network: An Historical Perspective with an Eye to the Future,* in *Nature Law and Policy in Europe,* Chapter 11 (Andrew L.R. Jackson ed., Routledge 2023).

1062. C-355/90, *Santoña Marshes,* para. 15.

It then clarified the relationship between Articles 3 and 4:

> With respect to the relationship between Articles 3 and 4 of the directive, it must be borne in mind that the first of those provisions imposes obligations of a *general nature*, namely the obligation to ensure a sufficient diversity and area of habitats for all the birds referred to in the directive, while the second contains *specific obligations* with regard to the species of birds listed in Annex I and migratory species not listed in that annex (emphasis added).[1063]

Thus, where bird species come within the scope of Article 4, it is not necessary to rely on Article 3. For this reason, the Court found it sufficient to consider the Commission's complaints about the Santoña marshes in light of Article 4.[1064]

[B] Application of Article 3 Where Article 4 Is Inapplicable

While the Court did not need to rely on Article 3 in Case C-355/90, *Santoña Marshes*, in a subsequent case, C-117/00, *Commission v. Ireland*, it clarified how Article 3 can apply in circumstances where Article 4 is inapplicable. In particular, the Court upheld a Commission plea that Ireland had infringed Article 3 in respect of habitats of the red grouse, a bird species not listed in Annex I of the Birds Directive and resident rather than migratory - which meant that, in the Commission's view, it fell outside the scope of protection of Article 4.

The Commission brought the proceedings because of evidence of widespread vegetation loss and soil erosion caused by sheep overgrazing, particularly in respect of Irish commonages.[1065]

The Court took note of the Commission's submission that:

> The habitat of the red grouse is hill land and bog and that its diet consists principally in common heather, on which it also relies for building its nests and for protection from predators. The range of the red grouse is, therefore, limited in Ireland to areas of bog and moorland where heather is plentiful. However, heather is a species of plant that is particularly vulnerable to overgrazing and in Ireland it is under serious threat from this environmental pressure.[1066]

The Commission adduced evidence of a decline in red grouse populations and a contraction in its range. It also showed that the breeding range of the red grouse coincided, to a large extent, with areas identified by a competent national authority as having been degraded by overgrazing.[1067] Ireland, nonetheless, disputed that areas of heathland necessary to the red grouse were under serious threat, although it acknowledged that overgrazing had a negative effect on the numbers of red grouse and on the

1063. *Ibid.*, para. 23.
1064. *Ibid.*
1065. Commonages are areas shared by several landowners. The problem of overstocking of these commonages was linked to agricultural incentives which paid landowners according to the number of livestock they held.
1066. C-117/00, *Commission v. Ireland*, para. 13.
1067. *Ibid.*, para. 18.

extent of the species' habitat.[1068] The Court rejected Ireland's defence, referring to the preventive purpose of Article 3 already set out in Case C-355/90, *Santoña Marshes*, and ruling that Ireland had not taken all the measures necessary to safeguard a sufficient diversity and area of habitats for the red grouse for the purposes of Article 3.[1069]

§5.03 PROTECTION OF NATURAL AREAS UNDER ARTICLE 4(4), SECOND SENTENCE OF THE BIRDS DIRECTIVE

[A] Article 4(4), Second Sentence of the Birds Directive

Article 4 of the Birds Directive is principally concerned with the classification and protection of SPAs for bird species listed in Annex I and for migratory species. The second sentence of Article 4(4) contains an obligation that applies outside of SPAs, however. The provision reads as follows:

> Outside these protection areas, Member States shall also strive to avoid pollution or deterioration of habitats.

The potential significance of this short provision is evident from the Court's ruling in Case C-418/04, *Commission v. Ireland*.

[B] Need for Transposition to Be Complete and Specific

In Case C-418/04, *Commission v. Ireland*, the Court first upheld a Commission plea that Ireland had failed to transpose the provision. It found that the measures relied on by Ireland were incomplete and lacked the necessary specificity.[1070]

[C] Need for Targeted Action and Measures That Constitute a Coherent Whole

The Court also upheld a Commission plea that Ireland had failed to apply fully and correctly the provision.

This was not the first time the Commission had invoked the provision. It did so in Case C-166/97, *Commission v. France* in relation to the siting of a titanogypsum factory in the Seine Estuary,[1071] but, on that occasion, failed to convince the Court.[1072]

The Commission's plea in Case C-418/04, *Commission v. Ireland*, was much more wide-ranging, extending to the whole Irish countryside. It was motivated by a concern that, on their own, a suite of SPAs would not provide sufficient habitat protection for certain species of wild birds with a very dispersed distribution pattern.

1068. *Ibid.*, para. 14.
1069. *Ibid.*, para. 21.
1070. C-418/04, *Commission v. Ireland*, paras 180-187.
1071. C-166/97, *Commission v. France*, para. 28.
1072. *Ibid.*, para. 48.

The Commission adduced several expert reports showing that species such as the cuckoo, skylark, swallow and sand martin had suffered greatly from changes in agricultural practices.[1073] It also adduced convincing evidence of gaps in the measures Ireland presented in its defence.

The Court stated that:

> Although the second sentence of Article 4(4) of the Birds Directive does not require that certain results be achieved, the Member States must nevertheless make *a serious attempt* at protecting those habitats which lie outside the SPAs. It is thus clear, in the present case, that Ireland must endeavour to take suitable steps to avoid pollution or disturbances of the habitats (emphasis added).[1074]

The Court further clarified what the obligation to make a serious attempt implied. It held that 'serious endeavours, namely the taking of all reasonable measures to achieve the success being sought, require *targeted action* (emphasis added)'.[1075]

The Court found that 'the measures taken by Ireland are partial, isolated measures, only some of which promote conservation of the bird populations concerned, but which do not constitute *a coherent whole* (emphasis added)'.[1076]

The second sentence of Article 4(4) of the Birds Directive is especially important for widely dispersed bird species which are nowhere present in any concentrations.

§5.04 PROTECTION OF LANDSCAPE FEATURES UNDER ARTICLE 10 OF THE HABITATS DIRECTIVE

Article 10 of the Habitats Directive provides as follows:

> Member States shall endeavour, where they consider it necessary, in their land-use planning and development policies and, in particular, with a view to improving the ecological coherence of the Natura 2000 network, to encourage the management of features of the landscape which are of major importance for wild fauna and flora.
>
> Such features are those which, by virtue of their linear and continuous structure (such as rivers with their banks or the traditional systems for marking field boundaries) or their function as stepping stones (such as ponds or small woods), are essential for the migration, dispersal and genetic exchange of wild species.

Case C-251/21, *Piltenes meži,* provides useful clarification on the scope of Article 10. Piltenes meži owned a forest of about 500 hectares which included a micro-reserve created by the Latvian authorities for the conservation of the capercaillie, a wild bird species covered by the Birds Directive. The forest owner was refused financial compensation for restrictions associated with this micro-reserve and sought a judicial review. The case turned in part on the interpretation of Article 30(6)(b) of EU

1073. C-418/04, *Commission v. Ireland,* para. 189.
1074. *Ibid.,* para. 179.
1075. *Ibid.,* para. 190.
1076. *Ibid.,* para. 191.

Regulation 1305 ('the Rural Development Regulation')[1077] which defines certain natural areas as eligible for payments and makes explicit reference to Article 10 of the Habitats Directive.

Article 30(6)(b) of the Rural Development Regulation reads as follows:

> Other delimited nature protection areas with environmental restrictions applicable to farming or forests which contribute to the implementation of Article 10 of Directive 92/43/EEC, provided that, per rural development programme, those areas do not exceed 5% of the designated Natura 2000 areas covered by its territorial scope.

The Court noted that Article 10 of the Habitats Directive referred to the ecological coherence of the Natura 2000 network, which included SPAs as well as SACs.[1078] Measures pursuant to Article 10 of the Habitats Directive could therefore comprise measures relevant to wild birds. In this context, the objective of the restrictions applicable in the capercaillie micro-reserve could be seen as improving the coherence of the Natura 2000 network.[1079]

§5.05 SURVEILLANCE OF CONSERVATION STATUS UNDER ARTICLE 11 OF THE HABITATS DIRECTIVE

Article 11 of the Habitats Directive reads as follows:

> Member States shall undertake surveillance of the conservation status of the natural habitats and species referred to in Article 2 with particular regard to priority natural habitat types and priority species.

In Case C-6/04, *Commission v. United Kingdom,* the Court upheld a Commission complaint that the United Kingdom had failed to transpose Article 11. The Court observed that, 'the surveillance obligation is *fundamental* to the effectiveness of the Habitats Directive and it must be transposed in a detailed, clear and precise manner (emphasis added)'.[1080]

Rejecting a United Kingdom submission that it carried out surveillance in practice, the Court stated:

> Inasmuch as it is common ground that United Kingdom domestic law does not contain any statutory duty requiring the national authorities to undertake surveillance of the conservation status of natural habitats and species, that domestic law involves an element of legal uncertainty. Hence, it is not guaranteed that

1077. Regulation (EU) No. 1305/2013 of the European Parliament and of the Council of 17 December 2013 on support for rural development by the European Agricultural Fund for Rural Development (EAFRD) and repealing Council Regulation (EC) No. 1698/2005, OJ L 347, 20.12.2013, p. 487-548.

1078. C-251/21, *Piltenes meži,* para. 57.

1079. *Ibid.,* para. 59.

1080. C-6/04, *Commission v. United Kingdom,* para. 65.

> surveillance of their conservation status is undertaken *systematically* and on a *permanent basis* (emphasis added).[1081]

C-301/12, *Cascina Tre Pini*, indicates that the results of surveillance may have important consequences where it is found that a site no longer qualifies for inclusion on a list of SCIs:

> It follows that, where the results of the surveillance undertaken by the Member States pursuant to Article 11 of the directive give rise to the conclusion that those criteria can irretrievably no longer be met, the Member States must of necessity, under Article 4(1) of the directive, make a proposal for the adaptation of the list of SCIs seeking to make that list meet those criteria once again.[1082]

1081. *Ibid.*, para. 68.
1082. C-301/12, *Cascina Tre Pini*, para. 27.

CHAPTER 6
Mixed or Related Case-Law

§6.01 CASES CONCERNING BOTH THE NATURE DIRECTIVES AND OTHER LEGAL INSTRUMENTS

The case-law on the nature directives is largely self-standing, but the circumstances of some disputes mean that the Court has occasionally had to address the procedural relationship between these two directives and the SEA Directive[1083] or the EIA Directive[1084] (collectively, 'the environmental impact assessment directives'). The result is a 'mixed' case-law.

In addition, the procedural or substantive requirements of other closely related EU directives sometimes need to be applied alongside those of the nature directives – or need to be applied in circumstances where the nature directives are also relevant. This is the case not only with the environmental impact assessment directives but also the Water Framework Directive,[1085] the Environmental Liability Directive,[1086] and certain funding regulations, which include explicit cross-references to the nature directives. The result is 'related' case-law.

1083. Directive 2001/42/EC of the European Parliament and of the Council of 27 June 2001 on the assessment of the effects of certain plans and programmes on the environment, OJ L 197, 21.7.2001, p. 30-37.

1084. Directive 2011/92/EU of the European Parliament and of the Council of 13 December 2011 on the assessment of the effects of certain public and private projects on the environment (codification) Text with EEA relevance, OJ L 26, 28.1.2012, p. 1-21. This is a codification of the original EIA Directive, 85/337/EEC. An important amendment was adopted in 2014: Directive 2014/52/EU of the European Parliament and of the Council of 16 April 2014 amending Directive 2011/92/EU on the assessment of the effects of certain public and private projects on the environment Text with EEA relevance, OJ L 124, 25.4.2014, p. 1-18.

1085. Directive 2000/60/EC of the European Parliament and of the Council of 23 October 2000 establishing a framework for Community action in the field of water policy, OJ L 327, 22.12.2000, p. 1-73.

1086. Directive 2004/35/CE of the European Parliament and of the Council of 21 April 2004 on environmental liability with regard to the prevention and remedying of environmental damage, OJ L 143, 30.4.2004, p. 56-75.

§6.02 THE ENVIRONMENTAL IMPACT ASSESSMENT DIRECTIVES AND THE NATURE DIRECTIVES

[A] SEA Directive and the Nature Directives

[1] Article 6(3) of the Habitats Directive and the SEA Directive

The SEA Directive and the Habitats Directive overlap in that both provide for the assessment of plans. Furthermore, the SEA Directive expressly provides that an environmental assessment shall be carried out for all plans and programmes 'which, in view of the likely effect on sites, have been determined to require an assessment pursuant to Article 6 or 7 of Directive 92/43/EEC'.[1087] Thus, a plan or programme requiring an assessment under Article 6(3) of the Habitats Directive will also require an SEA under the SEA Directive.

[2] Possible Need for an SEA of Measures Not Requiring an Article 6(3) Appropriate Assessment

The SEA Directive also allows for the possible SEA of other plans or programmes.[1088]

There are grey areas, as Case C-43/18, *CFE*, shows. In this case, following proceedings taken by a landowner, the Belgian Council of State submitted a preliminary reference on the question of whether a decree formally declaring a site to be an SAC should have been preceded by an SEA under the SEA Directive.

The Court ultimately concluded that, subject to verification of certain matters, such a decree did *not* require to be preceded by an SEA but its analysis did not dismiss the possibility out of hand.

It held that Article 6(3) of the Habitats Directive was applicable in such a case.[1089] The wording of Article 6(3) itself, however, did not require an appropriate assessment for a plan directly connected with or necessary to the management of the site – something to be determined on the basis, essentially, of the nature of the intervention at issue.[1090] In this regard, it noted that:

> A measure by which a Member State designates a site as a special area of conservation pursuant to the Habitats Directive is, by its nature, directly connected with or necessary to the management of the site. Article 4(4) of the Habitats Directive requires such designations to be made for the purposes of implementing that directive.[1091]

1087. Article 3(2)(b) of Directive 2001/42/EC.
1088. Article 3(4) of the SEA Directive provides as follows: Member States shall determine whether plans and programmes, other than those referred to in paragraph 2, which set the framework for future development consent of projects, are likely to have significant environmental effects.
1089. C-43/18, *CFE*, para. 46.
1090. *Ibid.*, para. 48.
1091. *Ibid.*, para. 49.

As such, the decree would be exempt from both an appropriate assessment under Article 6(3) of the Habitats Directive and the related SEA requirement of the SEA Directive.[1092]

This did not fully conclude the matter, however, since the Court still needed to consider whether an SEA was required under provisions of the SEA Directive not linked to the Habitats Directive – in particular, a provision for the SEA of plans or programmes setting the framework for further development consent of projects.[1093] In particular, it examined whether the decree in question set a framework for future development consent.

It recalled that, in earlier cases on SEA, it had held that the notion of 'plans and programmes' relates to any measure which establishes, by defining rules and procedures, *a significant body of criteria and detailed rules* for the grant and implementation of one or more projects likely to have significant effects on the environment.[1094] It noted that the decree in question provided for preventive measures and laid down general and specific prohibitions.[1095] It also noted that the concept of 'a significant body of criteria and detailed rules' must be construed qualitatively.[1096] If the prohibitions in the decree applied only to projects not requiring consent, the decree would not require an SEA – a matter for the referring court to verify.[1097]

In its remaining analysis, the Court tried to strike a balance between not completely excluding the possibility that such a decree might require an SEA and, at the same time, not requiring an SEA where impacts have already been otherwise assessed. It held that:

> Provided that the assessment of their effects has already been carried out, a measure does not fall within the meaning of 'plans and programmes' if it is part of a hierarchy of measures which have themselves been the subject of an assessment of their environmental effects and it may reasonably be considered that the interests which the SEA Directive is designed to protect have been taken into account sufficiently within that framework.[1098]

[B] EIA Directive and the Nature Directives

[1] Article 6(3) of the Habitats Directive and the EIA Directive

There is an overlap between Article 6(3) of the Habitats Directive and the EIA Directive in as much as both require an assessment of projects.

There are also important differences, however. As is indicated in Chapter 3, the notion of 'project' under the Habitats Directive is wider than that of 'project' under the

1092. *Ibid.*, para. 50.
1093. Article 3(4) of the SEA Directive.
1094. C-43/18, *CFE*, para. 61.
1095. *Ibid.*, para. 62.
1096. *Ibid.*, para. 64.
1097. *Ibid.*, paras 65 and 66.
1098. *Ibid.*, para. 73.

EIA Directive.[1099] Furthermore, compared to the EIA Directive, Article 6(3) of the Habitats Directive is succinct in laying out its procedural requirements – although, as Chapter 3 shows, these requirements are now clarified by extensive case-law.[1100]

Allowing for these differences, the EIA Directive has exerted a significant influence on the Court's case-law on Article 6(3).

When looking at several issues concerning Article 6(3), the Court has referred to previous case-law on the EIA Directive. Thus, in ruling on the inapplicability of Article 6(3) of the Habitats Directive to projects initiated before the time limit for applying the directive, the Court referred to its earlier case-law on a similar issue under the EIA Directive.[1101] Similarly, the Court has referred to its EIA case-law on regularisation in circumstances where Article 6(3) has not been respected in an authorisation process.[1102]

The Court has also used specific content of the EIA Directive to help interpret Article 6(3) of the Habitats Directive. Thus, in Case C-254/19, *Friends of the Irish Environment,* the Court noted that 'while the Habitats Directive does not define the conditions governing how the authorities "agree" to a given project under Article 6(3) of that directive, the definition of "development consent" in Article 1(2)(c) of the EIA Directive is relevant in defining that term'.[1103]

The influence goes in both directions. Thus, the Court took account of the Habitats Directive in Case C-115/09, *Trianel,* when interpreting the access-to-justice provisions of the EIA Directive.[1104]

[2] Articles 12, 13 and 16 of the Habitats Directive and the EIA Directive

[a] Relevance of the EIA Directive to Articles 12, 13 and 16 of the Habitats Directive

The EIA Directive is potentially relevant to Articles 12, 13 and 16 in at least three respects. First, it can serve as a procedure for describing the presence of protected species in a particular locality, and for describing and assessing the likely significant impacts of a proposed project on these. Unlike Natura 2000 sites, the sites occupied by protected species may not always be known with precision in advance. Second, the EIA Directive may affect the *timing* of a derogation decision and govern its *relationship* with other decisions concerning the same project. Third, an EIA can serve as a procedure for consulting the public on, amongst other things, both the species' presence and the likely impacts on them.

Case C-463/20, *Namur-Est Environnement,* a preliminary reference from Belgium, sheds light on all three aspects.

1099. *See* Chapter 3, §3.04[D][7] and [8].
1100. *See* Chapter 3, §3.04[D].
1101. C-209/04, *Commission v. Austria. See* Chapter 3, §3.04[D][3].
1102. *See* Chapter 3, §3.04[G][4].
1103. C-254/19, *Friends of the Irish Environment,* para. 42.
1104. *See* Chapter 3, §3.04[G][2][a].

The reference was made in the context of a dispute between an environmental association and the Walloon Region concerning a derogation decision by the latter pursuant to Article 16 of the Habitats Directive to enable a developer to operate a limestone quarry of over 50 hectares. The quarry development was also subject to an EIA process and the preliminary reference focused on the procedural relationship between the derogation decision and the EIA process. Under the applicable Belgian legislation, the derogation had to be obtained before the final consent in the EIA process, and the derogation decision did not tie the hands of the decision-maker in respect of that consent.

The referring court posed two questions.

By its first, it asked, in essence:

> whether Directive 2011/92 must be interpreted as meaning that a decision adopted under Article 16(1) of Directive 92/43 and which authorises a developer to derogate from the applicable species protection measures in order to carry out a project within the meaning of Article 1(2)(a) of Directive 2011/92 forms part of the development consent procedure, within the meaning of Article 1(2)(c) of that directive, where, first, the project cannot be carried out without the developer having first obtained that decision and, second, the authority competent for granting development consent for such a project retains the ability to assess the project's environmental impact more strictly than was done in that decision.[1105]

By its second, it asked, in essence:

> whether Directive 2011/92 must be interpreted, having regard in particular to Articles 6 and 8 thereof, as meaning that the adoption of a preliminary decision authorising a developer to derogate from the applicable species protection measures in order to carry out a project, within the meaning of Article 1(2)(a) of that directive, need not necessarily be preceded by public participation, provided that such participation is ensured before the adoption of the decision to be taken by the competent authority for the possible development consent for the project.[1106]

[b] *Role of EIA in Describing the Presence of, and Assessing Impacts on, Protected Species*

In responding to the first question in Case C-463/20, *Namur-Est Environnement*, the Court confirmed the relevance of an EIA process to the species protection provisions of the Habitats Directive. It noted that the EIA decision-making process must address the significant effects a project is likely to have on 'the fauna and flora present' in the various areas which may be affected by it.[1107] Where a project requires a derogation under Article 16 of the Habitats Directive, it held that the EIA process must address impacts on species protected under Article 12 and 13 of that directive:

1105. C-463/20, *Namur-Est Environnement*, para. 34.
1106. *Ibid.*, para. 67.
1107. *Ibid.*, para. 50.

> In the specific case where the execution of a project subject to the dual requirement for assessment and development consent laid down in Article 2(1) of Directive 2011/92 involves the developer applying for and obtaining a derogation from the plant and animal species protection measures prescribed by the provisions of national law transposing Articles 12 and 13 of Directive 92/43 and where, consequently, the project is likely to have an impact on those species, the assessment of the project *must* address, in particular, that impact (emphasis added).[1108]

For the Court, it was irrelevant that the Habitats Directive does not itself lay down any obligation to assess the impact that a derogation is likely to have on the species concerned since that directive was independent in scope from the EIA Directive and applied without prejudice to the EIA Directive's assessment obligation.[1109]

[c] Derogation Decisions under Article 16 of the Habitats Directive Can Form an Integral Part of a Multi-stage EIA Decision-Making Process

As indicated in Chapter 4, in Case C-183/05, *Commission v. Ireland*, the Commission presented evidence of a problematical relationship between certain EIA processes in Ireland and the requirements of Article 16 of the Habitats Directive with projects executed following an EIA without an Article 16 derogation having been obtained.[1110]

The Court's ruling in Case C-463/20, *Namur-Est Environnement*, provides a procedural basis for avoiding such problems. In particular, in terms of *sequence*, the ruling indicates that derogation decisions should precede the final development consent for EIA purposes. Second, the decision on the final development consent should not be bound by the prior derogation decision and the final EIA decision-maker must be capable of taking a stricter approach than the decision-maker on the derogation.[1111]

The Court referred to the flexibility and discretion that Member States enjoy with regard to decision-making covered by the EIA Directive.[1112] It noted that the assessment of the environmental impact of a given project may take place not only in the course of the procedure leading to the development consent decision referred to in Article 1(2)(c) of the EIA Directive but also in the course of a procedure leading to a derogation decision prior to that development consent decision, 'in which case those various decisions may be regarded as forming part of a complex decision-making process in that it is carried out in several stages'.[1113] Thus, the Court referred to a derogation decision in the context of the multi-stage decision-making it had addressed in an earlier case on the EIA Directive, C-201/02, *Wells*.

1108. *Ibid.*, para. 52.
1109. *Ibid.*, para. 54.
1110. C-183/05, *Commission v. Ireland*. *See* Chapter 4, §4.03[B][3][c][ii] and §4.03[B][3][d][ii].
1111. C-463/20, *Namur-Est Environnement*, para. 66.
1112. *Ibid.*, paras 54 to 56.
1113. *Ibid.*, para. 54.

Notwithstanding this Member State decision-making discretion, the Court noted that it must be exercised in accordance with the requirements laid down by the EIA Directive and in full compliance with the directive's aims.[1114]

First, the EIA of a project must be a *full* assessment and must take place *before* a development consent decision is taken with regard to the project.[1115] Where a Member State confers power to assess some of the environmental effects of a project and to take a decision upon the conclusion of that partial assessment on an authority [i.e., the authority with power to grant the Article 16 derogation] other than the one on which it confers power to give development consent for the project, that decision must necessarily be adopted *before* development consent is given. This sequence is important as 'if it were otherwise, the development consent would be given on an incomplete basis and would not, therefore, meet the applicable requirements'.[1116] It may be noted that this approach by the Court avoids the procedural problems evident in Case C-183/05, which revealed a procedural disconnection between the different authorities concerned.

Second, the EIA Directive requires an assessment of inter-actions. It follows expressly from Article 3 of the EIA Directive that the obligation to carry out a full assessment of the environmental effects of a project means that account must be taken not only of each of those effects taken individually but also of the interaction between them and thus of the project's overall impact on the environment.[1117] That overall assessment may lead the competent authority to conclude that, having regard to the interaction or interrelationship between the various environmental effects of a project, those effects must be assessed more strictly or, as the case may be, less strictly than one or other effect, considered in isolation, has been assessed beforehand. It follows that, where a Member State confers the power to assess some of the environmental effects of a project and to take a decision upon the conclusion of that partial assessment on an authority [i.e., the authority with power to grant the Article 16 derogation] other than the one on which it confers the power to give development consent for the project, that partial assessment must not prejudge the overall assessment that the authority competent for granting development consent must in any event carry out and that preliminary decision must not prejudge the decision adopted on the conclusion of the overall assessment.[1118] Thus, the derogation decision must be subordinated to the final development consent. Against this background, the Court signalled its satisfaction with the Belgian arrangements, since the derogation decision was indeed subordinated to the final development consent.[1119]

The Court added a third purposive conclusion to its contextual analysis. As regards the objectives pursued by the EIA Directive, and, in particular, its essential objective of ensuring a high level of protection of the environment and of human health

1114. *Ibid.*, para. 57.
1115. *Ibid.*, para. 58.
1116. *Ibid.*, para. 59.
1117. *Ibid.*, para. 60.
1118. *Ibid.*, para. 62.
1119. *Ibid.*, para. 63.

by laying down minimum requirements for the assessment of the environmental impact of projects, the interpretation which emerges from the contextual elements contributes to the attainment of such an objective, by enabling the Member States to entrust a given authority with the responsibility for adopting a preliminary, *focussed decision* on certain environmental effects of projects subject to assessment [i.e., the derogation], while reserving to the authority competent for granting development consent the task of conducting a full and final assessment of the project.

The Court drew attention to the practical benefits of its interpretation:

> Indeed, if the outcome of that partial assessment is negative, the developer may then either abandon its project, without having to continue with the complex assessment and consent procedure instituted by Directive 2011/92, or modify the project in such a way as to remedy the negative effects highlighted by the partial assessment, leaving it to the competent authority to take the final decision on the modified project. Conversely, if the outcome is positive, the authority will be free to take account of the decision previously taken, even though it does not bind it in its final assessment or with regard to the legal consequences to be drawn from that final assessment. The existence of a partial assessment giving rise to a preliminary decision is thus liable to constitute, in all cases, a factor of quality, effectiveness and increased consistency of the assessment and consent procedure.[1120]

[d] Public Participation

There had been no public participation prior to the grant of the derogation that featured in Case C-463/20, *Namur-Est Environnement*, but there had been provision for public participation in respect of the EIA process that subsequently took place. The Court considered that this was permissible under the EIA Directive, but subject to certain conditions.

The Court recalled the public participation requirements of Articles 6 and 8 of the EIA Directive,[1121] but noted that:

> It may, however, prove more difficult to reconcile those various requirements in the context of a multi-stage decision-making process, depending on the different stages of the process and the distribution of competences among the various authorities called upon to take part in it.[1122]

In light of this, it held that the public participation requirements of the EIA Directive meant that the adoption of a preliminary decision authorising a developer to derogate from the applicable species protection measures in order to carry out a project, within the meaning of Article 1(2)(a) of the EIA Directive, need not necessarily be preceded by public participation, provided that such participation is *effectively ensured before* the adoption of the decision to be taken by the competent authority for the possible development consent for the project.[1123]

1120. *Ibid.*, para. 65.
1121. *Ibid.*, paras 68-73.
1122. *Ibid.*, para. 74.
1123. *Ibid.*, para. 81.

Finally, as noted in Chapter 4, in Case C-166/22, *Hellfire Massey Residents Association*, the Court confirmed that neither Article 12 nor 16 of the Habitats Directive require public participation but it stressed the need to interpret and apply these articles in conformity with the requirements of the EIA Directive and again referred to the need for the derogation decision to precede the development consent in a multi-stage EIA process.[1124]

§6.03 THE WATER FRAMEWORK DIRECTIVE AND THE NATURE DIRECTIVES

[A] References to the Nature Directives in the Water Framework Directive

The Water Framework Directive establishes a general European framework for the protection of surface water and groundwater. It was adopted when the nature directives were already in place, specifically refers to Natura 2000 and contains certain substantive requirements that are closely aligned with the objectives of Natura 2000.

More specifically, under its Article 6, Member States are required to keep a register of the protected areas listed in Annex IV to the Water Framework Directive, which includes 'areas designated for the protection of habitats or species where the maintenance or improvement of the status is an important factor in their protection, including relevant Natura 2000 sites'.[1125]

Under Article 11, Member States are required to prepare programmes of measures. In making these programmes operational, Member States are, *inter alia*, required under Article 4(1)(c) to achieve compliance with any standards and objectives applicable to these Natura 2000 sites at the latest 15 years after the date of entry into force of the Water Framework Directive.

Furthermore, the Water Framework Directive contains a derogation provision in its Article 4(7) which may need to be applied alongside the provisions of Article 6(3) and (4) of the Habitats Directive.

The case-law, which is mainly the outcome of Case C-559/19, *Commission v. Spain* (*'Doñana'*), confirms that the implementation of key parts of the Water Framework Directive needs to be closely aligned with the requirements of the Habitats Directives.

[B] Relationship Between Programme of Measures under Article 11 of the Water Framework Directive and the Non-deterioration Obligation of Article 6(2) of the Habitats Directive

In Case C-559/19, *Doñana*, the Court condemned Spain for, *inter alia*, infringing Article 11 of the Water Framework Directive, read in conjunction with Article 4(1)(c) of that

1124. *See* Chapter 4, §4.03[F].
1125. Annex IV.1(v) of the Water Framework Directive.

directive, by failing to lay down, in the programme of measures established in the context of a river basin management plan, any measure to prevent disturbance of the protected habitat types located within the protected area of Doñana caused by the abstraction of groundwater for the needs of the tourist area of Matalascañas. It also condemned Spain for a separate but related breach of Article 6(2) of the Habitats Directive.[1126]

The Court interpreted the Water Framework Directive in close alignment with its interpretation of Article 6(2) of the Habitats Directive.

The case arose from complaints to the Commission concerning the deterioration of the Doñana, in particular as a result of over-exploitation of the groundwater to which the wetlands are connected.

With regard to Article 11 of the Water Framework Directive, the Commission argued that Spain's measures did not provide any solution to the problem of excessive use of water due to tourism, in particular in the coastal town of Matalascañas, and the impact of water abstraction on the conservation of habitats protected under the Habitats Directive.[1127]

The Court noted that, in accordance, *inter alia*, with Article 4(1)(c) and Article 6 of the Water Framework Directive, and Annex IV thereto, in adopting programmes of measures under Article 11 of that directive, the Member States must not only achieve the environmental objectives relating to water laid down in that directive but also ensure compliance with the European legislation relating to protected areas prior to 2015. Spain was thus obliged to implement the mechanisms provided for in the Water Framework Directive in order to comply with the *objectives* laid down by the Habitats Directive concerning the habitats of the Doñana protected natural area prior to that year.[1128]

The Court referred to the non-deterioration obligation in Article 6(2) of the Habitats Directive and stated that:

> Consequently, the programme of measures provided for in Article 11 of Directive 2000/60 must also have as its object the adoption of the measures necessary to avoid any deterioration of the protected areas covered by Directive 92/43.[1129]

The Court proceeded to align the burden of proof for purposes of this duty under Article 11 of the Water Framework Directive with the burden of proof required to establish an infringement of Article 6(2) of the Habitats Directive. Under the latter, which is based on the precautionary principle, 'it is sufficient for the Commission to establish that there is a probability or risk that that action or inaction might cause a deterioration or significant disturbance to the habitats or species concerned'. It held that, for purposes of the examination of the burden of proof under Article 11 of the Water Framework Directive, 'a higher standard of proof cannot be required'.[1130]

1126. *See* Chapter 3, §3.04[E][6].
1127. C-559/19, *Doñana*, para. 131.
1128. *Ibid.*, para. 132.
1129. *Ibid.*, para. 134.
1130. *Ibid.*, para. 135. *See also* Chapter 3, §3.04[E][6].

The Court considered that there was sufficient evidence to consider that excessive water abstraction for urban supply for the tourist area of Matalascañas had adversely affected the conservation of priority habitats located in the vicinity of that urban centre, and, second, that Spain had not adopted, pursuant to Article 11 of the Water Framework Directive, the measures necessary to avoid possible deterioration of the protected areas located in the vicinity of the tourist area of Matalascañas, as required by Article 4(1)(c) of that directive.[1131]

The Court also made a link with a separate infringement of Article 5 of the Water Framework Directive since this underpinned compliance with Article 11. It considered that, without a more precise and adequate assessment of the extent of the risks arising from the abstraction of drinking water for the tourist area of Matalascañas, Spain could not take necessary and effective measures, as provided for in Article 11, to prevent any disturbance of the protected areas in the vicinity of Matalascañas associated with the abstraction of groundwater.[1132]

[C] Characterisation of a River Basin District under Article 5 of the Water Framework Directive

Article 5 of the Water Framework Directive, *inter alia,* requires Member States to characterise their river basins and review the impacts of human activities. This helps lay the basis for the programme of measures under Article 11 of the Water Framework Directive.

As noted above, in Case C-559/19, *Doñana,* the Court condemned Spain for a breach of Article 5 which was relevant to the implementation of Article 11 – and thus also closely related to the implementation of Article 6(2) of the Habitats Directive.

[D] Article 6(3) and Article 6(4) of the Habitats Directive and Article 4(7) of the Water Framework Directive

In general, the Water Framework Directive requires Member States not only to pursue the objectives of that directive – and related directives such as the nature directives but to also avoid deterioration of water bodies. Article 4(7), however, provides for a derogation from this requirement.

In practice, the need for a derogation under Article 4(7) of the Water Framework Directive may coincide with the need for a derogation under Article 6(4) of the Habitats Directive, as Case C-43/10, *Acheloos,* shows.

This preliminary reference arose from legal proceedings against government ministers seeking the annulment of measures relating to a major – and very controversial[1133] – project for the partial diversion of the upper waters of the river Acheloos, Western Greece, to the river Pinios, in Thessaly. The Greek Council of State posed

1131. C-559/19, *Doñana,* para. 136.
1132. *Ibid.,* para. 140.
1133. The project was subject to successive legal proceedings.

multiple questions to the Court with regard to several EU environmental directives applicable to the project, including the Water Framework Directive and the Habitats Directive.[1134]

Apart from its interest for the interpretation of the derogation provisions of Article 6(4) of the Habitats Directive, the judgment in Case C-43/10, *Acheloos*, sheds light on how a parallel derogation procedure under Article 4(7) should be applied under the Water Framework Directive.[1135] This is relevant because both derogation provisions may need to be applied to the same technically complex water infrastructure project. Like the Habitats Directive, the Water Framework Directive is based on the attainment of objectives – principally the good status of the waters it covers and it also sets duties to avoid deterioration. Article 4(7) allows for a derogation from these requirements but is subject to several conditions. These conditions include a condition similar to the 'IROPI'[1136] test in Article 6(4) of the Habitats Directive.[1137]

§6.04 OTHER INSTRUMENTS

[A] Funding Regulations

EU funding regulations can provide for financial support for the implementation of the nature directives and contain important cross-references to them. In Case C-251/21, *Piltenes meži*, mentioned in Chapter 5, a cross-reference in one such regulation led to an interpretation by the Court of the scope of Article 10 of the Habitats Directive.[1138] Furthermore, the important issue of entitlement to financial compensation in relation to the Habitats Directive has been clarified in the context of EU funding provisions, as explained in Chapter 3.[1139]

[B] Environmental Liability Directive

[1] References to the Nature Directives in the Environmental Liability Directive

Like the Water Framework Directive, the Environmental Liability Directive includes provisions closely aligned with the nature directives.[1140] Its purpose is to establish a framework of environmental liability based on the 'polluter-pays' principle, to prevent

1134. *See* Chapter 3, §3.04[F][3].
1135. C-43/10, *Acheloos*, paras 61-69.
1136. 'imperative reasons of overriding public interest.'
1137. *See* Article 4(7)(c) of the Water Framework Directive.
1138. *See* Chapter 5, §5.04.
1139. *See* Chapter 3, §3.05.
1140. For a valuable account of the Environmental Liability Directive in the context of the nature directives, *see* Agustín García Ureta, *EU Biodiversity Law: Wild Birds and Habitats Directives* Chapter 12 (Europa Law Publishing 2020).

and remedy environmental damage. Under its provisions, 'operators'[1141] of 'occupational activities'[1142] can be held liable for 'environmental damage',[1143] and required to take preventive action[1144] or remedial action.[1145]

'Environmental damage' includes 'damage to protected species and natural habitats', which is any damage that has significant adverse effects on reaching or maintaining the favourable conservation status of such habitats or species. The significance of such effects is to be assessed with reference to 'the baseline condition',[1146] taking account of the criteria set out in Annex I.

Three points underscore the very close relationship with the nature directives.

[a] *Overlap with Natura 2000 and Species Protection*

First, 'protected species and natural habitats' are, *inter alia,* defined by reference to the nature directives, and include: the bird species covered by Article 4 of the Birds Directive; the species listed in Annexes II and IV to the Habitats Directive; the habitats of birds species covered by Article 4 of the Birds Directive (and thus SPAs); the habitats listed in Annex I to the Habitats Directive (and thus Natura 2000 sites recognised under the Habitats Directive); and breeding sites or resting places of the animal species listed in Annex IV to the Habitats Directive.[1147] Thus, there is an overlap between the scope of the Environmental Liability Directive and the nature directives in respect of Natura 2000 and species protection.

[b] *Notion of 'Significant Adverse Effects' Closely Linked to Habitats Directive*

Second, in relation to protected species and natural habitats, the notion of 'damage' is defined in terms of 'significant adverse effects' on reaching or maintaining the 'favourable conservation status' of habitats or species.[1148] 'Favourable conservation status' is defined in a like manner to its definition in the Habitats Directive.[1149] In contrast to the Habitats Directive, however, the Environmental Liability Directive contains detailed criteria for assessing the significance of adverse effects on reaching or maintaining favourable conservation status. These criteria are set out in Annex I to the Environmental Liability Directive. They include optional criteria which allow Member

1141. *See* definition in Article 2(6) of the Environmental Liability Directive.
1142. *See* definition in Article 2(7) of the Environmental Liability Directive.
1143. *See* definition in Article 2(1) of the Environmental Liability Directive.
1144. Article 5 of the Environmental Liability Directive.
1145. Article 6 of the Environmental Liability Directive.
1146. *See* definition in Article 2(14) of the Environmental Liability Directive.
1147. *See* definition in Article 2(3) of the Environmental Liability Directive.
1148. *See* Commission Notice Guidelines providing a common understanding of the term 'environmental damage' as defined in Article 2 of Directive 2004/35/EC of the European Parliament and of the Council on environmental liability with regard to the prevention and remedying of environmental damage 2021/C 118/01, C/2021/1860, OJ C 118, 7.4.2021, p. 1-49.
1149. *See* definition in Article 2(4) of the Environmental Liability Directive.

States not to classify certain changes as significant damage. As will be seen below, the Court in Case C-297/19, Naturschutzbund Deutschland, has interpreted these exclusionary criteria in a manner that ensures consistency with and does not undermine the nature directives.

[c] Relevance to Unforeseen Adverse Effects in Nature Directive Derogations and to Illegal Developments and Activities

Third, the definition of damage to protected species and natural habitats excludes 'previously identified adverse effects which result from an act by an operator which was expressly authorised by the relevant authorities' pursuant to Article 6(3) and (4) or Article 16 of the Habitats Directive or Article 9 of the Birds Directive. Thus, the Environmental Liability Directive is closely aligned with the derogation provisions of the nature directives – although the formulation 'previously identified adverse effects' is noteworthy, since it does not cover adverse effects which were not foreseen. For some operators [those responsible for activities listed in Annex III to the Environmental Liability Directive], liability is strict; for others, it is fault-based.[1150] Given all of these elements, the liability regime of the Environmental Liability Directive may be especially relevant to illegal developments or activities which damage Natura 2000 or contravene species protection provisions of the Nature Directives – *see* Chapter 7, §7.04[F][4].

[2] Relevance of the Nature Directives to the Assessment of the Significance of Damage

Case C-297/19, Naturschutzbund Deutschland, concerned, inter alia, the interpretation of the second indent of the third paragraph of Annex I to the Environmental Liability Directive, which sets out one of the exclusionary criteria that can be used when interpreting environmental damage.

The third paragraph of Annex I to the Environmental Liability Directive reads as follows:

> The following does not have to be classified as significant damage:
>
> - negative variations that are smaller than natural fluctuations regarded as normal for the species or habitat in question;
> - negative variations due to natural causes or resulting from intervention relating to the normal management of sites, as defined in habitat records or target documents or as carried on previously by owners or operators;
> - damage to species or habitats for which it is established that they will recover, within a short time and without intervention, either to the baseline condition or to a condition which leads, solely by virtue of the dynamics of the species or habitat, to a condition deemed equivalent or superior to the baseline condition.

1150. *See* Recital 9 of the Environmental Liability Directive.

The preliminary reference related to an SPA classified on the Eiderstedt peninsula in Schleswig-Holstein on account, *inter alia*, of the presence of the black tern, a protected aquatic bird. According to the SPA's management plan, the protection area with respect to that species remained, for the most part, managed traditionally as grassland over extensive areas and, by reason of its size in particular, was still the most important breeding ground for the black tern in Schleswig-Holstein.[1151] The peninsula had to be drained for the purposes of habitation and agricultural use, however. This took place by means of ditches, located between the plots, which ran into a network of channels and were maintained by the respective users of the adjoining land. Responsibility for maintenance of the channels lies with a corporation entrusted with a public law obligation. This operated a pump station and carried out pumping operations that kept the water level down.[1152]

An environmental association argued that, by operating the pumping station, the corporation was causing 'environmental damage', requested the authorities to act and then took legal proceedings. One of the issues which arose was whether any damage was significant and the referring court sought an interpretation of the exclusionary criterion concerning variations 'resulting from intervention relating to the normal management of sites, as defined in habitat records or target documents or as carried on previously by owners or operators'.

In particular, the referring court wished to ascertain, *first*, whether the concept of 'management' must be understood as corresponding solely to agricultural activities or whether it also covered the operation of a pumping station to irrigate and drain agricultural land, *second*, whether the question whether management is 'normal' must be assessed solely in light of the habitat records and target documents, or may also be assessed in light of other general principles of national law such as good professional practices, *third*, whether, in order for management to be as carried on previously by the owner or operator, such management need only have been carried on at some time before the date for transposing the Environmental Liability Directive, namely 30 April 2007, or whether it must also have continued to be carried on that date, and *fourth*, whether or not such previous management occurs irrespective of the habitat records and target documents.[1153]

The Court noted that any damage caused by the pumping station that was expressly authorised on the basis of the provisions of the Habitats Directive or the Birds Directive was not covered.[1154]

With regard to the provisions on exclusionary criteria in Annex 1 to the Environmental Liability Directive, the Court held that these must be interpreted strictly.[1155] It highlighted the risks, including the risks to the Birds and Habitats Directives, of not interpreting them in this way.[1156]

1151. C-297/19, *Naturschutzbund Deutschland*, para. 19.
1152. *Ibid.*, paras 20 and 21.
1153. *Ibid.*, para. 26.
1154. *Ibid.*, paras 38 and 39.
1155. *Ibid.*, para. 45.
1156. *Ibid.*, paras 46 to 49.

With regard to 'normal management of sites', it noted that:

(1) 'management can be regarded as normal only if it is consistent with good practices such as, *inter alia*, good agricultural practices';[1157]
(2) 'normal management of sites' must be understood as encompassing any measure which enables good administration or organisation of sites hosting protected species or natural habitats that is consistent, *inter alia*, with commonly accepted agricultural practices;[1158]
(3) normal management must be determined in light of the necessary measures that the Member States must adopt under the Habitats Directive and the Birds Directive and, in particular, of the management measures provided for in detail in Articles 6 and 12 to 16 of the Habitats Directive and Articles 3 to 9 of the Birds Directive;[1159]
(4) management of a site covered by the Habitats Directive and the Birds Directive can be regarded as normal only if it complies with the objectives and obligations laid down in those directives;[1160]
(5) the management measures that the Member States must adopt on the basis of the Habitats Directive and the Birds Directive, in order to comply with the objectives and obligations laid down by those directives, must necessarily take into account the characteristic aspects of the site, such as, in particular, the existence of human activity;[1161]
(6) 'normal management' may cover agricultural activities, including activities which may be the essential complement thereof, such as irrigation and drainage and, therefore, the operation of a pumping station.[1162]

Having clarified the concept of 'normal management of sites', the Court looked at the first alternative, 'as defined in habitat records or target documents', holding that:

(1) normal management must be defined in light of all the management measures adopted by the Member States on the basis of the Habitats Directive and the Birds Directive in order to meet their obligations to maintain or restore species and habitats protected by those directives;[1163]
(2) both habitat records and target documents correspond to the documents that the Member States must adopt pursuant to the Habitats Directive and the Birds Directive in order to meet the objectives of those directives and the conservation obligations that they owe under them.[1164]

1157. *Ibid.*, para. 52.
1158. *Ibid.*, para. 53.
1159. *Ibid.*, para. 54.
1160. *Ibid.*, para. 55.
1161. *Ibid.*, para. 56.
1162. *Ibid.*, para. 57.
1163. *Ibid.*, para. 58.
1164. *Ibid.*, para. 59.

The Court also opened the prospect of these documents being assessed critically by a national court, including in light of the objectives and obligations laid down in the Habitats Directive and the Birds Directive.[1165]

The Court then looked at the second alternative, 'as carried on previously by owners or operators'. It considered that:

(1) this 'covers management measures which, because they have been carried out for a certain period of time, may be regarded as usual for the site concerned', provided, however, that they do not call into question compliance with the objectives and obligations laid down in the Habitats Directive and the Birds Directive.[1166]
(2) it can be determined whether a practice constitutes previous practice only in light of the date on which the damage occurs. Thus, it is only if a normal management measure was carried out for a sufficiently long period of time until the occurrence of the damage and is generally recognised and established that that damage can be regarded as not significant.[1167]

It can be seen therefore that, in this interpretation of the Environmental Liability Directive, the Court went to considerable lengths to ensure consistency with the requirements of the nature directives.

1165. *Ibid.*, para. 60.
1166. *Ibid.*, para. 61.
1167. *Ibid.*, para. 65.

CHAPTER 7

Challenges Addressed or Influenced by the Court

§7.01 GENERAL AND SPECIFIC CHALLENGES

Previous chapters have looked at the nature case-law in relation to specific provisions of the nature directives. The Court's interpretations have been presented in 'close up'. The case-law can also be viewed from a wider angle, however, and assessed as to how it has addressed a number of broader challenges. First, the Court has faced the general challenge of how to interpret the directives. Second, it has had to respond to a very varied case-load over a period approaching forty years, while maintaining overall case-law cohesion. Third, it has had to combine the functions of interpreting and applying the law. In addition, it has faced a series of more specific challenges, such as how to interpret the directives' transposition requirements and various deadlines. Most of the kinds of specific challenges concerned are not unique to the nature directives, but the nature directives have precise content which the Court has needed to take into account.

The Court has only been able to pronounce itself on challenges arising from cases submitted by the Commission and national courts. These are wide-ranging but, in terms of the challenges of implementing the nature directives, they are not all-encompassing. For instance, the challenge of how to financially support implementation at European level has had to be addressed within a different inter-institutional context – in particular, in periodic negotiations on the content of the CAP and the extent to which this will support Natura 2000. Yet, even in relation to financial support, the Court has made important pronouncements and exerted indirect influence – as section §7.04[G] below shows.

§7.02 THE GENERAL CHALLENGE OF INTERPRETING THE NATURE DIRECTIVES

The nature directives belong to a common category of EU law instrument, viz. the directive, which presents interpretative challenges independent of the content of any specific directive. Directives need to be carried over into national legislation - i.e., 'transposed' - and the Member State duty of transposition can and does raise a cluster of largely generic interpretative challenges. The nature directives also contain clauses allowing for exceptions or 'derogations'. As a device, derogation clauses are relatively common, and, again, the Court has developed a general approach to interpreting them (while still leaving room for interpreting specific derogation clauses as Chapters 3 and 4 have shown).

As for the precise content of the nature directives, it is worth noting that the Birds Directive, in particular, was a pioneering instrument. Although parallels existed in prior international conventions and domestic legislation, it introduced concepts and requirements not previously found in EU secondary legislation. It was concise in wording, leaving much detail to be worked out in its implementation. From the outset, the scope for interpretation was therefore broad. In its design, the Habitats Directive largely followed the template of the Birds Directive, adding more procedural provisions and including more definitions. It too remained concise, however - again leaving significant scope for interpretation.

The evolving legal and policy context is also worth noting. The Birds Directive was adopted before the Treaties contained any reference to the environment, but an environment chapter with explicit reference to a set of principles such as the precautionary principle was in place by the time the Habitats Directive appeared. In addition, thanks to the EIA Directive, an important role was given to environmental assessments in this intervening period. The context continued to evolve with EU ratification of the Aarhus Convention in 2005 and the Lisbon Treaty's incorporation of the Charter of Fundamental Rights into the EU Treaty framework. These wider developments have exerted an influence on the Court's approach to interpretation.

Although the nature directives have presented novel interpretative challenges, the Court has been able to rely on a range of established interpretation methods and tools.[1168] The main methods are literal (sometimes referred to as 'textual'), contextual (or 'systematic'), purposive (sometimes referred to as 'teleological') and consistent. While one method may determine an outcome, more than one method may be brought to bear and the outcome may reflect the application of several.

1168. *See To Say What the Law of the EU Is: Methods of Interpretation and the European Court of Justice*, Lenaerts and Guttierez-Fons, 2013, European University Institute. Distinguished Lecture delivered on the occasion of the XXIV Law of the European Union course of the Academy of European Law, on 6 July 2013.

[A] Literal Interpretation

Literal or textual interpretation relies on the actual wording of the nature directives. The Court endeavours to be faithful to this, allowing for the qualification that, when it comes to interpreting EU legal texts, the wording of the different language versions is equally valid.[1169]

Case C-297/19, Naturschutzbund Deutschland, provides an example of the care the Court takes with different language versions.[1170] The Court noted that there is a divergence in the wording of the second case referred to in the second indent of the third paragraph of Annex I to the Environmental Liability Directive between the German language version and the other language versions.[1171] The other language versions are more restrictive.

The Court pointed out that:

> According to settled case-law of the Court, the wording used in one language version of a provision of EU law cannot serve as the sole basis for the interpretation of that provision, or be made to override the other language versions in that regard. Such an approach would be incompatible with the requirement that EU law be applied uniformly. Where there is a divergence between the various language versions, the provision in question must thus be interpreted by reference to the general scheme and the purpose of the rules of which it forms part.[1172]

The Court considered that the meaning that resulted from a literal reading of the German language version would compromise both the principles and objectives underlying the Environmental Liability Directive[1173] and also undermine the nature directives.[1174] It proceeded to interpret the provision more stringently and align the meaning of the German language version with that of the other language versions:

> It follows that the German language version of the second indent of the third paragraph of Annex I to Directive 2004/35 must be read as meaning that, *as in the other language versions,* the word 'normal' must relate directly to the word 'management' and that the term 'normal management' must relate to both alternatives of the second case provided for in that indent (emphasis added).[1175]

Literal interpretation is seen in the Court's approach in Case C-374/98, *Basses Corbières,* to the changeover from the protection regime set out in the first sentence of Article 4(4) of the Birds Directive to the protection regime set out in Article 6(2), (3) and (4) of the Habitats Directive. This changeover is governed by the wording of Article 7 of the Habitats Directive.

1169. C-561/19, *Consorzio Italian Management e Catania Multiservizi*, different language versions, paras 42 and 43.
1170. *See also* Chapter 6, §6.04[B][2].
1171. C-297/19, *Naturschutzbund Deutschland*, para. 42.
1172. *Ibid.*, para. 43.
1173. *Ibid.*, para. 47.
1174. *Ibid.*, para. 48.
1175. *Ibid.*, para. 49.

The Court observed that:

> It is important to note that the text of Article 7 of the habitats directive *expressly* states that Article 6(2) to (4) of the directive apply, in substitution for the first sentence of Article 4(4) of the birds directive, to the areas *classified* under Article 4(1) or (2) of the latter directive (emphasis added).[1176]
>
> It follows that, *on a literal interpretation* of that passage of Article 7 of the habitats directive, only areas classified as SPAs fall under the influence of Article 6(2) to (4) of that directive (emphasis added).[1177]

In this case, the Court's literal interpretation was actually at odds with the interpretation favoured by both the Commission and France (which was to allow Article 6(2) to (4) of the Habitats Directive to be applied to areas not yet classified as SPAs).

Sometimes, however, a literal interpretation will need to be seen alongside related purposive interpretations [*see* section §7.02[C] below]. Thus, while the Court's literal interpretation found that Article 6(3) of the Habitats Directive did not apply to projects initiated before a site's formal listing as an SCI,[1178] its purposive interpretation was that, by virtue of the conservation objectives of the Habitats Directive, Member States were obliged to provide sites not yet listed with a measure of interim protection.[1179]

[B] Contextual Interpretation

Literal interpretation of the nature directives is important but frequently not decisive because the wording of the nature directives is often concise and of limited assistance.

Contextual interpretation then becomes important. As the Court noted in Case C-477/19, *Magistrat der Stadt Wien*:

> According to settled case-law, in interpreting a provision of EU law, it is necessary to consider not only its wording but also *the context in which it occurs* and the objectives pursued by the rules of which it is part (emphasis added).[1180]

In this case, the Court's reference to contextual interpretation was in relation to a question about the meaning to be given to 'resting places', a term used in Article 12(1)(d) of the Habitats Directive, in particular whether it should cover unoccupied resting places to which a protected species might return. The Court noted that 'it is clear that the wording of Article 12 of the Habitats Directive provides no indication as to how the term "resting places" is to be defined'.[1181] It went on to observe that as regards 'the *context* in which the provision occurs, it should be noted that neither Article 1 of the Habitats Directive nor any other provision of that directive defines the

1176. C-374/98, *Basses Corbières*, para. 44.
1177. *Ibid.*, para. 45.
1178. C-117/03, *Dragaggi*, para. 25. *See* Chapter 3 §3.01[C][1].
1179. C-117/03, *Dragaggi*, para. 27. *See* Chapter 3 §3.01[C][1].
1180. C-477/19, *Magistrat der Stadt Wien*, para. 23.
1181. *Ibid.*, para. 25.

term "resting places" (emphasis added)'.[1182] The Court proceeded to note that, by not limiting the prohibition concerning breeding and resting places to deliberate acts, 'the EU legislature has demonstrated its intention to give breeding sites or resting places *increased* protection against acts causing their deterioration or destruction (emphasis added)'. It further noted that 'unlike the acts referred to in Article 12(1)(a) to (c) of the Habitats Directive, the acts covered by the prohibition laid down in Article 12(1)(d) do not relate to animal species directly but seeks to protect *significant parts of their habitats* (emphasis added)' and that 'the aim of the strict protection offered by Article 12(1)(d) of the directive is to ensure that significant parts of the habitats of protected animal species are preserved so that those species can enjoy the conditions essential for, *inter alia*, resting in those habitats'.[1183] After explicitly and favourably citing a Commission guidance document, the Court reached its conclusion that 'resting places which are no longer occupied by a protected animal species must not be allowed to deteriorate or be destroyed since that species may return to such places'.[1184]

This example illustrates how, in the absence of any definition, the Court can use contextual analysis to give a very specific meaning to a term used in the nature directives.

[C] Purposive Interpretation

Purposive or teleological interpretation aims to ensure that interpretation reflects the *objectives* of the nature directives. It is closely linked to contextual interpretation, as is shown by the example of the interpretation of 'resting places' in Case C-477/19, *Magistrat der Stadt Wien*. Having by contextual interpretation arrived at the result mentioned in section §7.02[C] above, the Court proceeded to consider the *objective* of the Habitats Directive. Noting that the directive seeks to provide strict protection for animal species, in particular by means of the prohibitions laid down in Article 12(1) of the directive, it stated:

> Therefore, the scheme of protection laid down in Article 12 of the Habitats Directive must be *sufficient effectively to prevent interference* with protected animal species and, in particular, their habitats (emphasis added).[1185]
>
> It would not be compatible with that objective to deny protection for resting places of a protected animal species where they are no longer occupied but where there is a sufficiently high probability that that species will return to such places, which is a matter for the referring court to determine.[1186]

Thus, by purposive interpretation, the Court reached the same conclusion as it had by contextual interpretation.

This is just one illustration of how the Court uses purposive interpretation. Indeed, purposive interpretation is evident throughout the nature case-law from the

1182. *Ibid.*, para. 26.
1183. *Ibid.*, paras 28 and 29.
1184. *Ibid.*, para. 31.
1185. *Ibid.*, para. 33.
1186. *Ibid.*, para. 34.

time of the first court rulings on the Birds Directive. The following are some important examples:

> In Case C-57/89, *Leybucht Dykes*, the Court held that the power of a Member State to reduce the extent of an SPA could be justified only on 'exceptional grounds'[1187] which 'must correspond to a general interest superior to the general interest represented by the *ecological objective* of the directive (emphasis added)'.[1188]
>
> In Case C-355/90, *Santoña Marshes*, the Court held that the *objectives of protection* set out in the directive, as expressed in the ninth recital in its preamble, could not be achieved if Member States had to comply with the obligations arising under Article 4(4) only in cases where a special protection area had previously been established.[1189]

The combination of contextual and purposive interpretation is especially striking in the Court's approach to the interrelationship between Article 6(2) and (3) of the Habitats Directive. In Case C-387/15, *Orleans*, the Court stated:

> The provisions of Article 6 of the Habitats Directive must be construed as *a* coherent whole in light of the *conservation objectives* pursued by that directive. Thus, Article 6(2) and (3) are designed to ensure the same level of protection of natural habitats and habitats of species, whilst Article 6(4) constitutes merely a provision derogating from the second sentence of Article 6(3).[1190]

As Chapter 3 shows,[1191] this combination has ensured not only that these provisions can be read as coherent with each other but that they can provide mutual support and underpinning.

[D] Consistent Interpretation

Consistent interpretation means interpreting the nature directives in a manner consistent with the requirements of international conventions.

The landmark decision in Case C-240/09, *Slovak Brown Bears*, provides the most striking example. In a dispute concerning the species protection provisions of the Habitats Directive, the Court held that, while Article 9(3) of the does not have direct effect, the referring court should interpret, to the fullest extent possible, national procedural rules on access to justice, *in accordance with* the objectives of Article 9(3) of the Aarhus Convention, in order to enable an environmental association to challenge before a court an administrative decision liable to be contrary to EU environmental law.[1192]

On the basis of the Court's decision in Case C-166/22, *Hellfire Massey Residents Association*, it can be argued that, in relation to the nature directives, the principle of consistency is not limited to international conventions. In that case, the Court

1187. C-57/89, *Leybucht Dykes*, para. 21.
1188. Ibid, para.22.
1189. C-355/90, *Santoña Marshes*, para. 22.
1190. C-387/15, *Orleans*, para. 32.
1191. *See* Chapter 3.
1192. C-240/09, *Slovak Brown Bears*, para. 52. *See* Chapter 4, §4.03[G].

interpreted Articles 12 and 16 of the Habitats Directive as not requiring public participation in respect of their transposition. It was clear that there was no basis in literal or contextual interpretation to reach a contrary conclusion. Nevertheless, the Court went on to state that Articles 12 and 16 and measures transposing them must be interpreted and applied *in conformity with* the requirements arising from other EU acts and from international conventions which are binding on the EU, in particular, the requirements arising from the EIA Directive and from the Aarhus Convention as interpreted in the case-law of the Court.[1193] Thus, a requirement of consistency - or conformity - was not confined to the Aarhus Convention but was extended to the EIA Directive.

The Court's consistent interpretation has not been limited to interpreting the nature directives in conformity with the Aarhus Convention and the EIA Directive. As Chapter 6 shows, it has extended to interpreting Article 11 of the Water Framework Directive and Annex I of the Environmental Liability Directive in conformity with the *nature directives*.[1194]

[E] Role of Recitals

The recitals of the nature directives do not create any self-standing legal obligations, but, when interpreting the directives' binding provisions, the Court can make use of them.

For example, in Case C-849/19, *Commission v. Greece*, the Court derived a requirement in Article 4(4) of the Habitats Directive for Member States to set conservation objectives.[1195] In deriving this requirement, the Court observed that 'conservation objectives' were referred to in the Habitats Directive's eight and tenth recitals[1196] and in its Article 6(3).[1197] This is just one of many examples, as case-law quotations in this and other chapters demonstrate.

[F] Importance of Treaty Principles

Principles found in the Treaties have played an important role in interpreting the nature directives. By drawing on these, the Court ensures that interpretation takes account of primary EU law, i.e., the Treaties.

1193. C-166/22, *Hellfire Massey Residents Association*, para. 35. *See* Chapter 4 and Chapter 6.
1194. *See* Chapter 6, §6.03[B] and §6.04[B][2].
1195. C-849/19, *Commission v. Greece*, para. 46. *See* Chapter 2.
1196. The eighth recital reads: 'Whereas it is appropriate, in each area designated, to implement the necessary measures having regard to the conservation objectives pursued'. The tenth recital reads: 'Whereas an appropriate assessment must be made of any plan or programme likely to have a significant effect on the conservation objectives of a site which has been designated or is designated in future'.
1197. C-849/19, *Commission v. Greece*, para. 47.

[1] Principle of Sincere Cooperation

In the context of Article 6 of the Habitats Directive, the Court has noted that, under the principle of sincere cooperation laid down in Article 4(3) TEU, Member States are required to nullify the unlawful consequences of an infringement of EU law.[1198]

Under the principle of procedural autonomy of the Member States, the detailed procedural rules applicable to actions to address such unlawful consequences are a matter for the domestic legal order of each Member State, provided that they are not less favourable than those governing similar domestic situations (the principle of equivalence) and that they do not render impossible in practice or excessively difficult the exercise of rights conferred by the EU legal order (the principle of effectiveness).[1199]

Since the nature directives themselves are silent on the matter, the principle of sincere cooperation is therefore very important when it comes to interpreting how Member States – and national courts – should address infringements of the requirements of the directives.

[2] Precautionary Principle

In the landmark Grand Chamber ruling in Case C-127/02, *Waddenzee,* the Court drew on the precautionary principle to interpret how the requirements of Article 6(3) of the Habitats Directive should be applied.

First, it invoked the principle in relation to the stage of determining whether a plan or project should undergo an appropriate assessment.

It noted that the first sentence of Article 6(3) of the Habitats Directive subordinates the requirement for an appropriate assessment of the implications of a plan or project to the condition that there be a probability or a risk that the latter will have significant effects on the site concerned.[1200] The reference to 'risk' is important, since the precautionary principle provides a means of addressing risk that does not depend on harm having actually manifested itself or being inevitable.

The Court went on to state:

> In the light, in particular, of the precautionary principle, *which is one of the foundations of the high level of protection pursued by Community policy on the environment, in accordance with the first subparagraph of Article 174(2) EC,*[1201] *and by reference to which the Habitats Directive must be interpreted,* such a risk exists if it cannot be excluded on the basis of objective information that the plan or project will have significant effects on the site concerned (see, by analogy, *inter alia,* Case C-180/96 *United Kingdom v. Commission* [1998] ECR I-2265, paragraphs 50, 105 and 107). Such an interpretation of the condition to which the assessment of the implications of a plan or project for a specific site is subject, which implies that in case of doubt as to the absence of significant effects such an assessment must be carried out, makes it possible to ensure effectively that plans or projects

1198. C-411/17, *Doel,* para. 170. *See* Chapter 3, §3.04[G][3].
1199. C-411/17, *Doel,* para. 171; C-41/11, *Inter-Environnement Wallonie,* para. 45.
1200. C-127/02, *Waddenzee,* para. 43.
1201. Now Article 191(2) TFEU.

> which adversely affect the integrity of the site concerned are not authorised, and thereby contributes to achieving, in accordance with the third recital in the preamble to the Habitats Directive and Article 2(1) thereof, its main aim, namely, ensuring biodiversity through the conservation of natural habitats and of wild fauna and flora (emphasis added).[1202]

The Court proceeded to also interpret the second sentence of Article 6(3) of the Habitats Directive in light of the precautionary principle, stating:

> In this respect, it is clear that the authorisation criterion laid down in the second sentence of Article 6(3) of the Habitats Directive integrates the precautionary principle (*see* Case C-157/96 *National Farmers' Union and Others* [1998] ECR I-2211, paragraph 63) and makes it possible effectively to prevent adverse effects -on the- integrity of protected sites as the result of the plans or projects being considered. A less stringent authorisation criterion than that in question could not as effectively ensure the fulfilment of the objective of site protection intended under that provision.[1203]

It is noteworthy that the Court saw the precautionary principle as one of the foundations of the high level of protection pursued by EU environment policy and considered that the Habitats Directive *must* be interpreted by reference to it. As is clear from Chapter 3, the precautionary principle infuses interpretations of Article 6(2) and 6(3) of the Habitats Directive in the case-law that developed after the decision in Case C-127/02, *Waddenzee*.

[3] Principle of Proportionality

The principle of proportionality is laid down in Article 5(4), TEU. It provides that EU measures must be *suitable* to the desired end; *necessary* to the desired end; and must not impose a burden on the individual that is *excessive* in relation to the objective sought to be achieved.

In relation to a Commission challenge to the use of the qualification 'deliberate' in Germany's transposition of Article 12(1)(d) of the Habitats Directive, in Case C-98/03, *Commission v. Germany*, Germany contended that the wording of Article 12 of the Directive must be interpreted, in line with the principle of proportionality, as not requiring the inclusion of non-deliberate destruction or deterioration of those sites in the system of protection that it establishes. The Court rejected Germany's argument, stating that 'it is by no means *disproportionate* that the prohibition laid down in Article 12(1)(d) is not limited to deliberate acts (emphasis added)'.[1204]

[G] Importance of Scientific References and Guidance Documents

As mentioned in section [B] above, in Case C-477/19, *Magistrat der Stadt Wien*, the Court drew on a Commission guidance document to fortify its contextual interpretation

1202. C-127/02, *Waddenzee*, para. 44.
1203. C-127/02, *Waddenzee*, para. 58.
1204. C-98/03, *Commission v. Germany*, para. 55.

of the term 'resting place'.[1205] Guidance documents and scientific references are non-binding but there are other examples of their use in the interpretation of the nature directives. In Case C-344/03, *Commission v. Finland*, for instance, the Court drew on the criterion of small numbers as defined by the ORNIS Committee as a basis for assessing compliance with the condition on small numbers in Article 9(1)(c) of the Birds Directive.[1206]

§7.03 THE GENERAL CHALLENGE OF MANAGING THE CASE-LOAD AND THE EVOLVING CASE-LAW

[A] Varied and Often Complex and Fluid Cases

Cases on the nature directives have arisen in a variety of circumstances including: localised disputes[1207] and disputes of wide territorial scope;[1208] disputes about individual projects[1209] and disputes about whole classes of activity;[1210] disputes centred on a single protected species[1211] or even a single specimen,[1212] and disputes about several species;[1213] disputes about legislation or regulations,[1214] disputes about specific consent procedures,[1215] and disputes about enforcement actions,[1216] including private enforcement action.[1217] Apart from cases instituted by the Commission, cases have been brought by environmental associations and individual environmentalists and have also involved opposing third parties. In proceedings before it, the Court may find many different points of view being legally represented.

Complexity has had many aspects. There have been Commission direct actions with multiple pleas and detailed supporting evidence.[1218] Some cases have involved complex factual issues, sometimes of a detailed scientific nature.[1219] Other cases have highlighted the intricacy of national procedures.[1220] Complex considerations have also arisen from the nature directives themselves when their provisions are overlaid onto the facts of specific cases and onto the details of national procedures.[1221]

1205. C-477/19, *Magistrat der Stadt Wien*, para. 31.
1206. C-344/03, *Commission v. Finland*, para. 53. *See* Chapter 4.
1207. *See* for instance, C-44/95, *Lappel Bank*; C-371/98, *First Corporate Shipping*.
1208. *See* for instance, C-3/96, *Commission v. Netherlands*; C-378/01, *Commission v. Italy*; C-235/04, *Commission v. Spain*.
1209. *See* for instance, C-387/15 and C-388/15 *Orleans;* C-275/09, *Brussels Hoofdstedelijk Gewest*; C-304/05, *Commission v. Italy*; C-254/19, *Friends of the Irish Environment*.
1210. *See* for instance, C-127/02, *Waddenzee*.
1211. *See* for instance, C-103/00, *Commission v. Greece*; C-383/09, *Commission v. France*.
1212. C-88/19. *Alianta pentru combatera abuzurilor*.
1213. C-183/05, *Commission v. Ireland*.
1214. C-411/17, *Doel*; C-900/19, *One Voice*.
1215. C-127/02, *Waddenzee*; C-239/04, *Castro Verde*; C-399/14, *Grüne Liga Sachsen*.
1216. C-477/19, *Stadt Wien*.
1217. C-240/09, *Slovak Brown Bears*; C-243/15, *LZ II*.
1218. C-418/04, *Commission v. Ireland*; C-441/17, *Białowieżka*.
1219. C-10/96 *LRPBO and AVES*; C-344/03, *Commission v. Finland*.
1220. C-60/05, *WWF Italia*; C-411/17, *Doel*; C-226/08, *Stadt Papenburg*.
1221. C-127/02, *Waddenzee*; C-226/08, *Stadt Papenburg*; C-141/14, *Commission v. Bulgaria;* Case C-399/14, *Grüne Liga Sachsen;* C-559/19, *Donana*.

Fluidity has been a feature of some cases, i.e., the cases themselves have evolved in ways that have tested the Court. In particular, in a number of important cases, the Court has had to deal with Commission requests for interim measures - and, in Case C-441/17 R, *Białowieżka*, specifically, the Court found it needed to expand the scope of its general approach to upholding the EU's autonomous legal order by providing for penalty payments in respect of such measures.[1222]

The case-law speaks for itself. Both in individual cases and across the span of cases, the Court has shown its capacity to handle the variety and complexity of the cases that have presented themselves, as well as their fluidity.

Factors that have contributed to the effective handling of variety, complexity and fluidity include the Treaty procedures for applying to the Court [*see* Chapter 8]; the roles of reporting judges and Advocate Generals; and the sophistication of the interpretation methods and tools already described. The Article 258 procedure provides for multiple written exchanges between the parties allowing legal and factual issues to be refined along the way. The orders for reference in Article 267 cases enable referring courts to explain the factual, legal and procedural backgrounds to the questions posed and these are supplemented by the submissions of the parties as well as the Commission. The Court's own resources include reporting judges and Advocates General who may follow the nature cases over extended periods of time, bringing to the analysis of specific cases continuity, experience and a deep understanding of what is at stake. As section §7.02 above indicates, the Court applies a sophisticated array of interpretation methods and tools to its decision-making. The most novel and consequential cases can be referred to the Grand Chamber drawing on the full extent of the Court's jurisprudential wisdom.

[B] Managing the Evolving Case-Law over Time

Aside from the challenge of deciding individual cases, there is the challenge of managing the evolution of the case-law over time. On the one hand, there is a need to ensure consistency; on the other, a need to allow for adaptation and even innovation.

Factors lending themselves to stability and predictability are the stability of the nature directives themselves, which remain unchanged since their adoption (apart from annex revisions to cover additional species and habitat types, and, in the case of the Birds Directive, a codification exercise); the familiarity that comes from many issues having featured in previous cases; and a certain predictability in the Commission's legal actions, at least in terms of 'waves' of cases focused on the same provisions - for example, the recent run of cases on SAC designation under Article 4(4), and adoption of conservation measures under Article 6(1) of the Habitats Directive.[1223]

Nevertheless, aside from the Commission's legal actions, there is nothing programmatic about the cases that reach the court. The content of preliminary references

1222. *See* Chapter 8, §8.03[F].
1223. C-290/18, *Commission v. Portugal*; C-849/19, *Commission v. Greece;* C-444/21, *Commission v. Ireland*.

is unpredictable and new – and sometimes novel – issues arise. When it comes to new legal actions brought by the Commission, the details may present issues not previously encountered. Furthermore, while the nature directives have remained stable, important changes in the wider EU legal landscape have occurred since their adoption. New procedural requirements were adopted under the environmental impact assessment directives; the EU became a party to the Aarhus Convention; the Treaties themselves underwent change.

For the most part, the case-law case has evolved organically and incrementally, with new judgments typically referring to, consolidating and building on previous ones. Occasionally, there have been landmark judgments like Case C-127/02, *Waddenzee*, which have set 'the direction of travel' for a cluster of subsequent case-law.

In terms of innovation, section §7.02[D] shows how consistent interpretation has allowed the Court to adapt the nature case-law to reflect the changing legal landscape.

Furthermore, judgments usually leave enough interstitial scope for the Court to revisit an issue in light of new or better-understood considerations. Thus, in Case C-900/19, *One Voice*, the Court took a more critical look at the use of limes under derogation in France than it had in a much earlier case, C-252/85, *Commission v. France* but it was able to distinguish its analysis by reference to aspects it had not previously considered.[1224]

[C] Applying as Well as Interpreting the Law

One of the salient characteristics of the nature case-law is the extent to which it derives in almost equal measure from direct actions and preliminary references – something not necessarily seen in case-law in other subject areas. If either direct actions or preliminary references had played less of a role, the case-law might have evolved differently.

With preliminary references, the Court can concentrate on interpreting the law, leaving its application to the referring court. In this sharing of tasks, the referring court can and must verify the facts, even if, as in a case like C-674/17, *Tapiola*, the Court considers it necessary and appropriate to express itself cogently on the factual submissions it has received. To a significant extent, however, the interpretations generated by preliminary references focus on *how* national courts should address the facts before them. The landmark judgment in Case C-127/02, *Waddenze*, is probably the most famous example since it requires national courts to examine facts through a precautionary lens.

When it comes to direct actions, the Court must both interpret and apply the law, and that presents it with the same challenge that referring courts face when giving effect to interpretative rulings. If there is to be symmetry, the Court must exercise a standard of scrutiny equivalent to what it expects of national courts.[1225] As Chapter 8

1224. *See* Chapter 4 §4.02[F][2][e][ii].
1225. For a very useful perspective on the standard of judicial scrutiny in relation to Article 6(3) and (4) of the Habitats Directive, *see* Christoph Sobotta, *The Margin of Appreciation When*

indicates, the Court has been conscious of this in the context of the burden of proof in direct actions. This is demonstrated by Case C-559/19, *Doñana*. In this case, the Court defined the burden of proof that the Commission must satisfy in terms of establishing a *probability or risk* of habitat deterioration.[1226] If the Commission satisfied this burden (as it did), the Court could then examine whether the national authorities had applied the requisite precautionary approach to that probability or risk. In this way, the Court took a step enabling it to align its own application of the law with its previous interpretation of it.

§7.04 SPECIFIC CHALLENGES

[A] Transposition

The provisions of the nature directives are not complete in themselves. They need to be rendered effective through provisions of national transposing legislation. It cannot be assumed that such legislation will be fit for purpose, however: a key challenge for the Court has been to ensure that national legislation is complete, clear and precise and not marred by ambiguity or legal uncertainty.

The Court has had to deal with national legislation that narrows the scope of the nature directives;[1227] national legislation that widens the scope of the directives [where this is restrictive, as in regard to derogation provisions] allowing exemptions it does not contemplate[1228] ; national legislation that is incomplete[1229] or ambiguous;[1230] parallel national legislation that allows authorities to apply divergent rules;[1231] and arguments that administrative practices can make up for shortcomings in transposing legislation.[1232]

From the outset, the Court has insisted that the scope of transposition needs to be a 'right fit', i.e., it needs to correspond to the scope of the nature directives. This can mean a Member State having to enlarge the scope of its transposing legislation, as where France and Belgium were required to cover more bird species[1233] and the United Kingdom and Germany were required to remove a national restriction of the prohibition in Article 12(1)(d) of the Habitats Directive to 'deliberate' acts.[1234] It can also mean a Member State having to narrow the scope of some national provisions, as where

Applying Article 6(3) and (4) of the Habitats Directive, in *Nature Law and Policy in Europe*, Chapter 5 (Andrew L.R. Jackson ed., Routledge 2023).

1226. *See* Chapter 3, §3.04[E][6] and Chapter 8, §8.03[G][2][b][i].
1227. C-252/85, *Commission v. France*, and C-247/85, *Commission v. Belgium*. *See* Chapter 4, §4.02[B][1][b].
1228. C-192/11, *Commission v. Poland*.
1229. C-75/01, *Commission v. Luxembourg*.
1230. C-508/04, *Commission v. Austria*.
1231. C-183/05, *Commission v. Ireland* and C-432/21, *Commission v. Poland*. *See* Chapter 4.
1232. C-98/03, *Commission v. Germany* and C-508/04, *Commission v. Austria*. *See* Chapter 4.
1233. C-252/85, *Commission v. France*, and C-247/85, *Commission v. Belgium*. *See* Chapter 4, §4.02[B][1][b].
1234. C-6/04, *Commission v. United Kingdom* and C-98/03, *Commission v. Germany*. *See* Chapter 4.

Germany was obliged, in relation to Article 6(3) of the Habitats Directive, to remove a general waiver for agricultural and forestry activities.[1235]

The Court has also consistently placed an emphasis on the need for precision, clarity and completeness in transposition, as well as the need to avoid creating ambiguity and legal uncertainty. Thus, the United Kingdom was condemned for not transposing Article 15 of the Habitats Directive correctly because its legislation left legal uncertainty as to the prohibited methods of killing seals.[1236] Ireland and Poland were condemned for maintaining parallel divergent legislation that created legal uncertainty about the legislation they held out as transposing the species protection requirements of the Habitats Directive.[1237]

The Court has rejected arguments, such as those put forward by Germany and Austria in, respectively, Cases C-98/03, *Commission v. Germany* and C-508/04, *Commission v. Austria*, that compliant administrative practices can make up for legislative deficiencies.[1238] As the Court stated in the Austrian case, 'an administrative practice consistent with a directive's provisions is not sufficient to transpose Community law correctly'.[1239]

However, the Court will not require Member State's transposing legislation to go beyond what the actual wording of the nature directives supports. Thus, in Case C-166/22, *Hellfire Massey Residents Association*, it held that, when transposing Articles 12 and 16 of the Habitats Directive, Member States are not required to make provision for public participation [it referred to the need to provide for public participation under other legal requirements, however, underlining the importance of consistent interpretation].[1240]

Member States have a broad entitlement to adopt stricter measures, but this is not unqualified, as Case C-169/89, *Gourmetterie Van den Burg* shows.[1241]

[B] Other Formal Requirements

The case-law establishes the importance of formal requirements not only in relation to the transposition of the main provisions of the nature directives but also in relation to national instruments used to recognise Natura 2000 sites and derogation decisions.

Thus, in the context of SPA classification, SPAs must be demarcated in such a manner that they can be relied upon against third parties. The maps demarcating SPAs must be 'invested with unquestionable binding force'[1242] and the classification must be such that it 'automatically and simultaneously entails the application of a system of protection and conservation complying with Community law'.[1243] When it comes to

1235. C-98/03, *Commission v. Germany*.
1236. C-6/04, *Commission v. United Kingdom*. *See* Chapter 4.
1237. C-183/05, *Commission v. Ireland* and C-432/21, *Commission v. Poland*. *See* Chapter 4.
1238. *See* Chapter 4.
1239. C-508/04, *Commission v. Austria*, para. 113.
1240. *See* Chapter 4, §4.03[F].
1241. *See* Chapter 4, §4.02[C][3].
1242. C-415/01, *Commission v. Belgium*, para. 22. *See* Chapter 2, §2.02[I][1].
1243. C-415/01, *Commissoin v. Belgium*, para. 26. *See* Chapter 2, §2.02[I][1].

the precise formal arrangements for ensuring binding force, Member States have a margin of discretion, however.[1244]

Similarly, the Court confirmed that SAC designation under Article 4(4) of the Habitats Directive requires a formal act and that the designation obligation cannot be satisfied through site protection measures alone.[1245] The Court noted that 'the provisions of a directive must be implemented with unquestionable binding force, and the specificity, precision and clarity necessary to satisfy the requirements of legal certainty'.[1246]

In relation to derogations, the Court has ruled on the need to satisfy formal requirements such as inclusion of a statement of reasons. Thus, in Case C-557/15, *Commission v. Malta,* Maltese declarations authorising autumn trapping of finches were deemed non-compliant with Article 9 as they did not contain any reference to the absence of another satisfactory solution.[1247]

[C] Deadlines, Delays and Timelines

The Court has been presented with a range of temporal challenges in relation to the nature directives. These have required it, amongst other tasks, to fix the required deadline for fulfilling classification obligations under the Birds Directive;[1248] clarify the effects of delays in classification under the Birds Directive[1249] and completion of the designation process under the Habitats Directive;[1250] and spell out the legal implications where the timeline of a project or activity partly antedates the directives' deadlines.[1251]

The Court's approach has involved balancing different considerations. It has also involved an interplay of literal and purposive interpretations.

The Court has sought, on the one hand, to uphold the literal wording of the nature directives where these provide for deadlines for Member States. Thus, notwithstanding the clear delays in the formal Commission listing of SCIs [caused by the knock-on effect of Member State delays in transmitting national lists], the Court confirmed that the deadline for applicability of Article 6(2), (3) and (4) was the date of actual adoption of the relevant Community lists [in practice, formal list adoption by the Commission occurred several years after the original envisaged 1998 adoption deadline set out in Article 4(3) of the Habitats Directive].[1252]

On the other hand, the Court has sought, through purposive interpretation, to avoid three temporally-determined outcomes that would undermine the objectives of the nature directives.

1244. C-535/07, *Commission v. Austria,* para. 82. *See* Chapter 2, §2.02[I][1].
1245. C-444/21, *Commission v. Ireland,* paras 46 to 51. *See* Chapter 2, §2.03[D][1].
1246. C-444/21, *Commission v. Ireland,* para. 48. *See* Chapter 2, §2.03[D][1].
1247. C-557/15, *Commission v. Malta,* paras 49 and 50. *See* Chapter 4, §4.02[F][2][a].
1248. C-355/90, *Santoña Marshes, see* Chapter 2, §2.02[C].
1249. C-355/90, *Santoña Marshes,* and C-96/98, *Marais-Poitevin, see* Chapter 3, §3.01[B].
1250. C-117/03, *Dragaggi, see* Chapter 3, §3.01[C].
1251. C-209/04, *Commission v. Austria* and C-226/08, *Stadt Papenburg, see* Chapter 3, §3.04[D][3].
1252. C-117/03, *Dragaggi, see* Chapter 3, §3.01[C].

The first is an absence of site protection as a result of delayed SPA classification or delayed completion of the four-stage SAC designation process.

Thus, in upholding the requirement to protect unclassified areas eligible for SPA classification under the Birds Directive, the Court stated:

> The objectives of protection set out in the directive, as expressed in the ninth recital in its preamble, could not be achieved if Member States had to comply with the obligations arising under Article 4(4) only in cases where a special protection area had previously been established.[1253]

Likewise, in upholding the need to provide a measure of interim protection to sites listed by Member States themselves but not yet formally listed by the Commission as SCIs under the Habitats Directive, it stated:

> If those sites are not appropriately protected from that moment, achievement of the objectives seeking the conservation of natural habitats and wild fauna and flora, as set out in particular in the sixth recital in the preamble to the Directive and Article 3(1) thereof, could well be jeopardised. Such a situation would be particularly serious as priority natural habitat types or priority species would be affected, for which, because of the threats to them, early implementation of conservation measures would be appropriate, as recommended in the fifth recital in the preamble to the Directive.[1254]

The second undesirable outcome that the Court has sought to avoid is the creation of incentives for Member States not to fulfil their obligations. Thus, in Case C-374/98, *Basses Corbières,* the Court stated that:

> A Member State cannot derive an advantage from its failure to comply with its Community obligations.[1255]

An illustration is the Court's confirmation that the lack of designation of SCIs as SACs, as required under Article 4(4), does not relieve Member States from the obligation to establish the necessary conservation measures under Article 6(1) of the Habitats Directive.[1256]

The third undesirable outcome that the Court has addressed is 'grand-fathering', i.e., the exemption of certain activities from having to comply with obligations derived from the nature directives on the ground that they benefit from authorisations or authorisation processes that pre-date the directives' time limits for transposition. Thus, while it confirmed that Article 6(3) did not apply to an Austrian motorway project where the application was lodged before the expiry of the time limit for transposing the Habitats Directive,[1257] it held that Article 6(2) applies to the implementation of such projects.[1258] As far as the Court has been concerned, the Habitats Directive fulfils all

1253. C-355/90, *Santoña Marshes,* para. 22, *see* Chapter 3, §3.01[B][2].
1254. C-117/03, *Dragaggi,* para. 27. *See* Chapter 3, §3.01[C].
1255. C-374/98, *Basses Corbières,* para. 51. *See* Chapter 3, §3.03[C][1].
1256. C-444/21, *Commission v. Ireland,* para. 140. *See* Chapter 3, §3.04[B][4].
1257. C-209/04, *Commission v. Austria, see* Chapter 3, §3.04[D][3].
1258. C-226/08, *Stadt Papenburg, see* Chapter 3, §3.04[D][3].

requirements of clearness, preciseness and predictability with regard to individuals[1259] and 'the principle of the protection of legitimate expectations cannot be extended to the point of generally preventing new rules from applying to the future effects of situations which arose under the earlier rules'.[1260]

[D] Need for Member States to Ensure Implementation

The case-law clearly establishes that it is not sufficient for Member States to fulfil formal requirements. *Implementation* of measures is also necessary, in particular the conservation measures required under Article 4 of the Birds Directive and Article 6(1) of the Habitats Directive, the preventive measures required under Article 6(2) of the Habitats Directive, and the species protection measures required under Article 12 of the Habitats Directive.

Thus, in relation to Article 4(1) of the Birds Directive, the Court has stated:

> That provision requires, if it is not to be rendered redundant, that the conservation measures necessary for maintaining a favourable conservation status of the protected habitats and species within the site concerned not only be adopted, but also, and above all, be *actually implemented* (emphasis added).[1261]

In relation to Article 6(1) of the Habitats Directive, in Case C-849/19, *Commission v. Greece,* the Court held that conservation measures adopted by Greece were too general and needed further concrete steps to ensure their *effective implementation.*[1262]

The case-law provides several examples of Member States being condemned for failing to implement Article 6(2) effectively in practice.[1263]

In Case C-183/05, *Commission v. Ireland,* the Court condemned Ireland for failing to adopt specific measures for the *effective implementation* of the system of strict protection provided for in Article 12 of the Habitats Directive.[1264]

[E] Problems of Monitoring and Enforcing Compliance at National Level

One aspect of implementation of measures as described in section [D] above concerns the role of the competent national authorities in monitoring and enforcing compliance by other legal and natural persons with national implementing rules.

From scattered references across the nature case-law and the wider case-law of the Court, it is possible to put together a picture of the efforts and interventions to be expected from the competent authorities.

1259. *Ibid.*, para. 43.
1260. *Ibid.*, para. 46.
1261. C-661/20, *Commission v. Slovakia*, para. 112. *See* Chapter 3.
1262. C-849/19, *Commission v. Greece,* para. 82. *See* Chapter 3, §3.04[B][2].
1263. *See* Chapter 3, §3.04[C][4].
1264. C-183/05, *Commission v. Ireland, See* Chapter 4.

[1] *Need for Applicable Rules and Powers of Intervention*

There needs to be a foundation of binding rules applicable to landowners, economic operators and others in order to give effect to preventive provisions, such as Article 6(2) of the Habitats Directive, together with a corresponding set of powers for the competent authorities to intervene where necessary.

Thus, in Case C-6/04, *Commission v. United Kingdom*, the Court ruled that the United Kingdom had not adequately transposed Article 6(2) in respect of Gibraltar because transposition was limited to a provision allowing the competent authorities to enter into site management agreements with the owners or occupiers of sites. As the Advocate General observed, there was an absence in the law of 'adequate *powers for intervention* by the competent authorities where there is a lack of cooperation on the part of owners or occupiers (emphasis added)'.[1265]

In commenting favourably on Dutch legislation in Case C-293/17, *PAS*, the Court noted that the legislation allowed the authorities to impose measures *both preventive and corrective* and that there was a *power of coercion*, including the possibility of adopting urgent measures.[1266]

[2] *Concept of 'Compliance Assurance'*

Before looking into the case-law, it is useful to refer to the concept of 'compliance assurance'. The Commission has developed, along with Member States, a number of guidance documents on this concept, which cover the nature directives.[1267]

'Compliance assurance' is a composite expression for interventions by public authorities to promote compliance (and prevent breaches), monitor compliance, and enforce compliance. Compliance promotion, monitoring and enforcement are linked along a 'compliance assurance chain', with compliance monitoring providing evidence for subsequent enforcement or promotion. 'Enforcement' itself is divided between interventions to stop infringements (such as civil injunctions), penalise them (through

1265. Opinion of Advocate General in C-6/04, *Commission v. United Kingdom*, para. 23. *See* Chapter 3.
1266. C-293/17, *PAS*, para. 135. *See* Chapter 3.
1267. *See* Summary Guide on environmental compliance assurance in rural areas, available at: https://op.europa.eu/en/publication-detail/-/publication/236733b9-69c2-11eb-aeb5-01aa75ed71a1#:~:text=Environmental%20compliance%20assurance%20in%20rural%20areas%20A%20summary,other%20rural%20land-managers%20comply%20with%20their%20environmental%20obligations; Vade Mecum on environmental compliance assurance in rural areas, available at: https://op.europa.eu/en/publication-detail/-/publication/278dd7f1-69bb-11eb-aeb5-01aa75ed71a1/language-en/format-PDF/source-search; Summary guide on combating environmental crimes and related infringements, available at: https://op.europa.eu/en/publication-detail/-/publication/ce99f624-5cc2-11ec-91ac-01aa75ed71a1; and Guidance on combating environmental crimes and related infringements, available at: https://op.europa.eu/en/publication-detail/-/publication/e004a9c9-596a-11ec-91ac-01aa75ed71a1.

criminal or administrative sanctions) and remediate the harm that they cause (through use of the Environmental Liability Directive, for example).[1268]

The compliance assurance concept reflects the reality that compliance problems require more than one kind of intervention. Infringements cannot be sanctioned (or stopped or remediated) unless first discovered and characterised, for instance - hence the need for compliance monitoring.[1269]

Without ever having referred to 'compliance assurance' as such, the Court has taken positions in the nature case-law which are consistent with compliance assurance principles.

[3] Compliance Monitoring

In Case C-674/17, *Tapiola,* Finland argued that the problem of poaching wolves justified derogating from the prohibition on killing wolves under Article 12(1)(a) of the Habitats Directive in order to allow the legal killing of wolf specimens. The Court was not convinced, observing that:

> The mere existence of an illegal activity such as poaching or difficulties associated with its monitoring cannot be sufficient to exempt a Member State from its obligation to ensure the safeguarding of species protected under Annex IV to the Habitats Directive. On the contrary, in such a situation, that Member State must give priority to *strict and effective monitoring of that illegal activity and implement methods* that do not involve failure to observe the prohibitions laid down in Articles 12 to 14 and Article 15(a) and (b) of that directive (emphasis added).[1270]

Logically, this pronouncement is not only relevant to Article 12 of the Habitats Directive but also to Articles 5, 6, 7 and 8 of the Birds Directive (since, in some Member States, illegal hunting or other forms of illegal exploitation of wild birds are a problem) and the non-deterioration provision of Article 6(2) of the Habitats Directive (since site deterioration caused by illegal activities is a problem in some Member States). The EIR mentioned in Chapter 1 bears this out.[1271]

In respect of activities covered by derogations under Article 9 of the Birds Directive or Article 16 of the Habitats Directive, compliance monitoring can be related to requirements concerning controls.[1272] By way of illustration, in Case C-557/15, *Commission v. Malta,* the Court concluded that Malta had failed to adduce evidence that a derogation for finch-trapping was used under strictly controlled conditions.[1273]

1268. *See also* Liam Cashman, *Ensuring Compliance, Regulatory Regimes under the EU Nature Directives,* in *Nature Law and Policy in Europe,* Chapter 4 (Andrew L.R. Jackson ed., Routledge 20).
1269. Communication on actions to improve environmental compliance and governance, COM(2018), 10; and Staff Working Document, SWD(2018)10.
1270. C-674/17, *Tapiola,* para. 48.
1271. *See* Chapter 1, §1.07[2].
1272. *See* for example Article 9(2)(e) of the Birds Directive.
1273. C-557/15, *Commission v. Malta,* para. 97. *See* Chapter 4, §4.02[F][4][d].

[4] *Enforcement Interventions*

The nature case-law clearly indicates that it is not enough for authorities to monitor compliance, they must also make appropriate interventions to *enforce* compliance.

[a] *Obligation to Nullify the Unlawful Consequences of Infringements*

The obligation to nullify the unlawful consequences of infringements has general relevance in this context.[1274]

[b] *Enforcement System*

In relation to Article 6(2) of the Habitats Directive, Case C-504/14, *Commission v. Greece*, establishes that Member States must provide for a protective system that includes enforcement.[1275] This case is also relevant to Article 12 of the Habitats Directive, since the Court found parallel breaches of Article 6(2) and Article 12.

[c] *Timely Interventions to End Infringements*

Member States cannot remain inactive when compliance monitoring shows that there are clear violations.

Thus, in Case C-103/00, *Commission v. Greece*, the Court found a failure by Greece to fulfil its obligations under Article 12(1)(b) and (d) of the Habitats Directive on the island of Zakynthos in light of, *inter alia*, evidence that the authorities could not control disturbances caused by the use of mopeds on the breeding beaches of protected sea turtles, even though such use was prohibited and notices indicating the presence of turtle nests on the beaches had been erected.[1276]

Furthermore, where provisions have a preventive purpose, *timely* intervention is necessary.

Thus, as noted in Chapter 3, in Case C-404/09, *Commission v. Spain*, the Court condemned Spain for a breach of Article 6(2) of the Habitats Directive because it had omitted to take, *in good time*, the measures necessary to bring certain disturbances to an end.[1277] The reference to provisional measures in Case C-504/14, *Commission v. Greece*, also points to the need for timely intervention to prevent or stop infringements[1278] as does the Court's case-law on the use of interim measures within its own jurisdiction.[1279]

1274. *See* Chapter 3, §3.04[G][3].
1275. *See* Chapter 3, §3.04[H][4].
1276. C-103/00, *Commission v. Greece*, para. 35. *See* Chapter 4.
1277. C-404/09, *Commission v. Spain*, paras 149 to 152. *See* Chapter 3, §3.04[H][5].
1278. *See* Chapter 3, §3.04[H][6].
1279. *See* Chapter 8, §8.03[F].

[d] Implementation of Enforcement Orders

Case C-504/14, *Commission v. Greece*, indicates that it is not enough for a competent authority to obtain an enforcement order, it must also ensure its implementation.[1280]

[e] Remedial Measures, Including Compensatory Measures

Where habitat deterioration is the result of an ongoing harmful activity, ending or controlling that activity may allow habitats to recover over time. Cases C-117/00, *Commission v. Ireland* and C-293/17, *PAS,* illustrate how Natura 2000 sites can be overburdened as a result of excessive levels of livestock, whether because of their direct, erosive impact, or because of their cumulative harmful emissions. Complying with Article 6(2) of the Habitats Directive, even belatedly, can allow for recovery. This, however, may require use of powers referred to by the Court in Case C-293/17, *PAS* [*see* section §7.04[E][1] above].

There may be a need for additional measures to restore a status quo ante. Thus, in rejecting Ireland's argument that it should not have to classify an SPA that had lost its ornithological interest because of predation, the Court referred to evidence of the potential of the site to recover its ornithological interest *if predation was controlled.*[1281]

It is possible, however, that, as a result of an unlawful or illegal action, an ecological interest will be irretrievably lost. The logic of the Court's ruling in Case C-399/14, *Grüne Liga Sachsen* is that compensatory measures are then required.[1282]

This raises an issue of who should bear the responsibility for remediating damage caused by an illegal action or activity. As noted in Chapter 3, the Advocate General in Case C-434/22, *Latvijas valsts meži,* took the view that, pursuant to the duty of sincere cooperation under Article 4(3), TEU, Member States must adopt rules under which individuals may be required to make reparation for damage if this has affected Natura 2000 sites in breach of Article 6(3) of the Habitats Directive.[1283] In addition, as already seen in Chapter 6, independently of the nature directives, the Environmental Liability Directive[1284] provides for the prevention or remediation of damage to Natura 2000 or other interests protected under the nature directives. In line with the polluter pays principle, the obligation to remediate lies with the operator of the occupational activity concerned.

Given that the Court found Greece to be in breach of Article 6(2) of the Habitats Directive because it *tolerated* damaging illegal developments and activities,[1285] it might be argued that a Member State which tolerates a failure by operators to take the required remedial measures in respect of environmental damage to Natura 2000 sites

1280. *See* Chapter 3, §3.04[H][7].
1281. C-418/04, *Commission v. Ireland,* paras 86 to 88. *See* Chapter 2.
1282. *See* Chapter 3.
1283. *See* Chapter 3, §3.04[H][9].
1284. Directive 2004/35/CE of the European Parliament and of the Council of 21 April 2004 on environmental liability with regard to the prevention and remedying of environmental damage, OJ L 143, 30.4.2004, p. 56-75.
1285. *See* Chapter 3, §3.04[H].

infringes both Article 6(2) of the Habitats Directive and the relevant provisions of the Environmental Liability Directive.

Furthermore, it might be argued that the Member States bear a residual obligation to remediate the environmental damage concerned if it proves impossible to secure remedial action from the polluter. An analogy can be drawn with a case concerning waste in which the Court held that Romania remained responsible for controlling toxic dust emissions from a mining waste facility even though the operator had become insolvent.[1286] In Case C-374/98, *Basses Corbières,* in relation to the applicable protection regime of an SPA, the Court stated that a Member State cannot derive an advantage from its failure to comply with its EU-law obligations.[1287]

[f] Sanctions

Neither of the directives contains a standard penalty clause, i.e., a clause requiring Member States to provide for sanctions for infringements of the directive concerned, and sometimes also referring to the implementation of sanctions. This is indicative of the age of the nature directives since such clauses are found in environmental and other directives adopted during the past twenty-five years. An example is the Water Framework Directive, Article 23 of which requires Member States to provide for penalties which are effective, proportionate and dissuasive.

The absence of a standard penalty clause does not mean, however, that Member States are free to omit provisions for sanctions in respect of the nature directives. This is clear from the Court's decision in Case C-68/88, *Commission v. Greece, ('Greek Maize')*, in which it stated:

> It should be observed that where Community legislation does not specifically provide any penalty for an infringement or refers for that purpose to national laws, regulations and administrative provisions, Article 5 of the Treaty [now Article 4(3), TEU] requires the Member States to take all measures necessary to guarantee the application and effectiveness of Community law.[1288]

Furthermore, the Court set a number of conditions that a Member State's system of sanctions must satisfy:

> For that purpose, whilst the choice of penalties remains within their discretion, they must ensure in particular that infringements of Community law are penalized under conditions, both procedural and substantive, which are analogous to those applicable to infringements of national law of a similar nature and importance and which, in any event, make the penalty effective, proportionate and dissuasive.[1289]

1286. C-104/15, *Commission v. Romania,* paras 99 to 101. This case is cited at para. 39 of Commission Notice Guidelines providing a common understanding of the term 'environmental damage' as defined in Article 2 of Directive 2004/35/EC of the European Parliament and of the Council on environmental liability with regard to the prevention and remedying of environmental damage, OJ C 118, 7.4.2021.
1287. C-374/98, *Basses Corbières*, para. 51.
1288. C-68/88, *Greek Maize,* para. 23.
1289. *Ibid.*, para. 24.

In addition, 'the national authorities must proceed, with respect to infringements of Community law, with the same diligence as that which they bring to bear in implementing corresponding national laws'.[1290]

Part of the nature case-law relates to national enforcement proceedings involving possible sanctions.[1291] The nature case-law does not shed light on the application of penalties as such, however, other than to confirm, as noted in section §7.04[E][4][b] above, the application of penalties is not sufficient in itself to demonstrate compliance with the preventive provisions of the nature directives.[1292]

Independently of the nature directives, the Environmental Crime Directive[1293] provides for the criminalisation of some infringements of the nature directives.

[F] Non-compliant Member State Competent Authorities

Within a Member State, the authorities responsible for implementing the nature directives may fail in their responsibilities. There may be failures by the government itself or failures by public authorities at different levels. Failures may involve direct infringements by public authorities or a tolerance by public authorities of infringements committed by private persons.

There may be no organ of state willing or able to hold a non-compliant authority to account. Where powers and responsibilities lie with central government, it may leave obligations unfulfilled because of perceived obstacles to their fulfilment. Where powers and responsibilities lie at regional level, central government may not wish to disturb how they are exercised or face procedural obstacles to intervening effectively. Case C-60/05, *WWF Italia,* illustrates how a national control mechanism, specifically a national power to annul regional derogations governed by the Birds Directive, might fail, because, in practice, the time required to intervene would allow an illegal derogation to first exhaust its effects.[1294]

Four points deserve mention in relation to how the case-law addresses the challenges presented by non-compliant competent authorities.

The first has to do with a limitation in the Commission's enforcement powers under Article 258, TFEU. Under this procedure, the Commission can only take legal action against a Member State. It cannot directly challenge specific Member State authorities. The counterpart to this, though, is that the Commission can hold the Member State accountable for the infringements of regional authorities or the failures of other national authorities. A striking example is provided by Case C-507/04, *Commission v. Austria.* In Austria, responsibility for nature conservation is devolved to the Austrian provinces, with each province entitled to enact its own legal framework. The case illustrates just how heterogeneous the provincial frameworks were in their

1290. *Ibid.*, para. 25.
1291. *See*, for example, C-504/14, *Commission v. Greece*, presented in Chapter 3, §3.04[H].
1292. *See* for example Case C-404/09, *Commission v. Spain.*
1293. Directive 2008/99/EC of the European Parliament and of the Council of 19 November 2008 on the protection of the environment through criminal law, OJ L 328, 6.12.2008, p. 28-37.
1294. *See* Opinion of the Advocate General in Case C-507/04, *Commission v. Austria,* paras 59-63.

transposition of the Birds Directive. The Commission bundled all of its concerns about individual provincial frameworks into a single, compendious legal action against Austria, however; all of the individual provincial shortcomings upheld by the Court were imputed to that Member State.

The potentially far-reaching implications of this means of holding subnational administrations to account can be seen in the interim orders that the Commission obtained under Article 279 against Italy in Case C-503/06 R, *Commission v. Italy,* requiring it to suspend the application of an illegal hunting law adopted by the Region of Liguria, and in Case C-573/08 R, *Commission v. Italy,* requiring it to suspend a similar illegal hunting law adopted by the Region of Lombardy. Had these regions defied the interim orders, the breach would have been imputed to Italy – and Case C-441/17 R, *Białowieżka*, indicates that this could have opened the way to Italy being required to pay a financial penalty.[1295] The limitation of Article 258, TFEU can therefore prove a strength when it comes to ensuring accountability.

The second point is that the Court has not allowed regional authorities to implement the nature directives in a 'selfish' manner in disregard of the common EU heritage that the nature directives seek to protect. This is especially important in relation to migratory species. Thus, the Court has set strict criteria to govern how, in a devolved system, different regional authorities must apply the 'small numbers' requirement under Article 9(1)(c) of the Birds Directive.[1296] Furthermore, in this context, a single Member State, with respect to a particular region, cannot lay claim to a disproportionately large reference population of wild birds to determine what is a small number.[1297]

The third point is that the Court does not accept that, where the Commission has brought an action for non-fulfilment of obligations, the Member State can validly invoke domestic difficulties in its defence.

Thus, in Case C-67/99, *Commission v. Ireland,* Ireland was found to have failed to transmit the list of sites required under Article 4(1) of the Habitats Directive notwithstanding an argument it raised that delays were attributable to domestic difficulties ('in order to obtain approval of the population for the ambitious objectives of the directive, it was considered necessary to launch a vast programme of public consultation'[1298]). This outcome did not deter Ireland from raising a similar defence in Case C-444/21, *Commission v. Ireland,* in relation to the final stage of the SAC designation process, i.e., formal SAC designation. The result was the same, the Court remarking:

> So far as concerns the complexity of the formal designation procedure highlighted by Ireland, which results in particular from the bringing of appeals by the owners of the sites concerned against such a designation, it should be recalled that Member States cannot plead provisions, practices or situations prevailing in its

1295. *See* Chapter 8, §8.03[F].
1296. Chapter 4, §4.02[F][4][a][ii].
1297. C-217/19, *Commission v. Finland. See* Chapter 4 §4.02[F][4][a][iii].
1298. C-67/99, *Commission v. Ireland,* para. 33.

domestic legal order to justify failure to observe obligations arising under EU law.[1299]

The fourth point is that, even where the Commission does not intervene, the Court's case-law on access to justice has confirmed the existence of an avenue for environmental associations and others to hold Member State authorities to account via national courts.[1300]

This last point is buttressed by further requirements stemming from the case-law. First, under the principle of sincere cooperation laid down in Article 4(3) TEU, all organs of a Member State, including national courts,- are required to nullify the unlawful consequences of an infringement of EU law.[1301] Second, arranging to have decisions made by a national legislative authority will not avoid the procedural requirements of Article 6(3) of the Habitats Directive.[1302]

[G] Harmful Subsidies and Benign Subsidies

The nature directives create a legal framework for dealing with negative pressures on nature, whether these impinge on Natura 2000 sites, species benefiting from strict protection, or the wider countryside.

Chapters 2, 3, 4 and 5 provide many examples of such pressures. The pressures, in particular those involving economic activities, do not exist in isolation, however. The cyclical 'DPSIR' model of environmental policy-making stands for 'driver, pressure, state, impact, and response'.[1303] In this model, the nature directives are a response to the poor and threatened state of nature and the adverse impacts of this. The poor state reflects negative pressures, and these pressures themselves reflect 'drivers', economic and societal forces that incentivise - or disincentivise - economic operators and others to act in particular ways.

Harmful subsidies may be a particularly powerful driver of pressures. Especially relevant in this regard is Case C-96/98, *Marais Poitevin*. As noted in Chapter 3, France laid the principal responsibility for the loss and deterioration of wetlands in the Potevin Marshes on the CAP but the Court did not accept that the CAP excused the failure by France to comply with the Birds Directive.[1304]

The CAP was also relevant in Case C-117/00, *Commission v. Ireland*. Ireland was held to be in breach of Article 3 of the Birds Directive and Article 6(2) of the Habitats Directive because of the habitat damage caused by sheep overstocking of commonages.[1305] The overstocking reflected a system of 'headage payments' under the CAP, i.e., farm supports calculated by reference to the number of sheep a farmer kept. There

1299. C-444/21, *Commission v. Ireland*, para. 55.
1300. *See* Chapter 8, §8.06.
1301. C-411/17, *Doel*, para. 170. *See* Chapter 3, §3.04[G][3].
1302. C-182/10, *Solvay*.
1303. *See* Chapter 3 of the Vade Mecum on environmental compliance assurance in rural areas, available at: https://op.europa.eu/en/publication-detail/-/publication/278dd7f1-69bb-11eb-aeb5-01aa75ed71a1/language-en/format-PDF/source-search.
1304. *See* Chapter 3, §3.03[B][2][b].
1305. *See* Chapter 3 and Chapter 5.

was no upper limit based on the capacity of land to carry the subsidised sheep. This caused a 'tragedy of the commons', with no single livestock owner having a reason to curtail stocking levels. While the harmful subsidy did not feature in the case, the outcome resulted in limits being placed on sheep numbers in the areas affected. Thanks to the judgment, the operation of a harmful subsidy – a driver of pressures – had to be qualified.

These cases have exerted an influence on the evolution of the CAP, which is now more closely aligned with the requirements of the nature directives. For example, under the latest regulation on CAP strategic plans,[1306] farmers and other beneficiaries receiving direct payments from the CAP must comply with statutory management requirements (SMRs) in respect of Articles 3 and 4 of the Birds Directive as well as Article 6(1) and (2) of the Habitats Directive.[1307]

A judgment of the Court may also result in the deployment of more benign subsidies, aimed at reducing the detrimental effects of particular pressures. The outcome of Case C-293/17, *PAS,* which also related to the effects of excessive livestock levels on sensitive habitats, had major implications for the Dutch livestock sector. In May 2023, the Commission announced its approval of Dutch schemes, worth EUR 1.47 billion, to reduce nitrogen deposition on Natura 2000. This was to compensate livestock farmers for the voluntary definitive closure of livestock husbandry sites in overburdened Natura 2000 areas.[1308]

More generally, the case-law has clarified the legal framework within which more benign subsidies may be used. Thus, the Court does not treat implementation of the nature directives as giving rise to any automatic entitlement to financial compensation but it recognises a discretionary scope to provide this, subject to fulfilment of State aid requirements, where these are applicable.[1309]

[H] Accountability of EU Institutions, in Particular EU Commission

The Court has shown that accountability is not restricted to the Member States and their authorities.

The nature directives give the Commission only a limited decision-making role but the case-law demonstrates that the Commission too can be held accountable. In Case C-281/16, *Vereniging Hoekschewaards Landschap*, the Commission found itself, in a validity reference, not merely offering observations but, in effect, [unsuccessfully] defending its own decision-making under Article 4 of the Habitats Directive. The Commission cannot be made a defendant before a national court, but this validity

1306. Regulation (EU) 2021/2115 of the European Parliament and of the Council of 2 December 2021 establishing rules on support for strategic plans to be drawn up by Member States under the common agricultural policy (CAP Strategic Plans) and financed by the European Agricultural Guarantee Fund (EAGF) and by the European Agricultural Fund for Rural Development (EAFRD) and repealing Regulations (EU) No. 1305/2013 and (EU) No. 1307/2013, OJ L 435, 6.12.2021, p. 1-186.
1307. *Ibid.*, Article 12 in combination with Annex III.
1308. https://ec.europa.eu/commission/presscorner/detail/en/IP_23_2507.
1309. Case C-238/20, *Satiņi-S* and Case C-234/20, *Satiņi-S*. *See* Chapter 3, §3.05.

reference demonstrates how the case-law has risen to the challenge of ensuring the institution's accountability.[1310]

[I] Loss of and Threats to Nature

In an abstract sense, the entire nature case-law is about the loss of or threats to habitats and species - since the nature directives aim to conserve nature. But instances of specific loss or specific threats don't necessarily always appear in the foreground - or even in the background. Instead, disputes are often about general legal safeguards and procedures.

Specific losses and specific threats to habitats or species are, however, central to some disputes and the case-law shows how the Court has met the challenge of addressing these at different scales. Chapters 3 to 6 provide examples of how the Court has dealt with cases involving such losses and threats, but it is perhaps useful to mention four ways in which the Court has resisted the siren call of approaches which, while having a superficial appearance of being pragmatic or proportionate, would carry the risk of making losses and threats more difficult to stave off or counter.

The approaches it has resisted relate to reducing the directives' shield of protection by reference to certain species, or the status of species, or specific activities or areas; requiring a threshold of species' harm before protective action will be considered necessary; applying a *de minimis* approach to habitat loss; and allowing for obligations to cease to apply where nature has been lost through a Member State's own lack of compliance.

[1] Maintaining a Shield

The Court has insisted that Member States are not entitled to withhold the directives' shield of legal protection for certain species on unsubstantiated or unjustified grounds. Thus, the Court ruled that Belgium was not entitled to apply a very general derogation to address crop damage or other problems associated with the house sparrow, the tree sparrow and the starling: derogations must relate to specific situations.[1311] Similarly, Spain was not entitled to employ a derogation to use limed twigs to hunt thrushes in order to prevent serious crop damage: evidence of crop damage caused by thrushes was lacking.[1312]

In respect of the strict protection obligations of Article 5, the Court declined to uphold a Swedish practice limiting the scope to Annex I species or bird species considered to be at risk.[1313] Strict protection applies to all wild bird species.

By the same token, the Court has not accepted that the shield should be withheld in the interest of specific human activities. It has rejected legal presumptions or general

1310. *See* Chapters 2 and 8.
1311. C-247/85, *Commission v. Belgium*, para. 34. *See* Chapter 4, §4.02[F][3][b].
1312. C-79/03, *Commission v. Spain*, para. 27. *See* Chapter 4, §4.02[F][3][b].
1313. Joined Cases C-473 and C-474/19, *Skydda Skogen*. *See* Chapter 4, §4.02[B][2].

waivers under national law according to which compliance is assumed regardless of the adverse effects that might arise in practice. Thus, in relation to Article 6(2) of the Habitats Directive, the Court condemned French transposing provisions that created a legal presumption in favour of fishing, aquaculture, and hunting.[1314] Similarly, the Court condemned several Member States in respect of general waivers adopted to avoid appropriate assessments under Article 6(3) of the Habitats Directive.[1315] Likewise, the Court has rejected arguments that the shield should not apply in respect of certain areas. Thus, it ruled that urban areas used by the lesser kestrel could not be excluded for purposes of SPA classification.[1316] Similarly, in the Romanian lone wolf case, it ruled that wolves did not cease to benefit from the strict protection of Article 12 of the Habitats Directive simply because they wandered into an urban area.[1317]

[2] Not Expecting a 'Body Count'

In finding breaches of the nature directives, the Court has not required evidence of an actual decline in the population of protected species – a 'body count' – before certain obligations will be considered applicable. Thus, it held that the obligations of Articles 3 and 4 of the Birds Directive exist 'before *any reduction is observed in the number of birds* or any risk of a protected species becoming extinct has materialized (emphasis added)'.[1318]

Furthermore, in one of its earliest nature rulings, it did not follow the interpretation put forward by the United Kingdom that 'deterioration of a special protection area must be such as to threaten the survival or reproduction of protected species within their area of distribution'.[1319]

In the context of evident threats to the sea turtle in the bay of Laganas on Zakynthos in Greece, the Court did not accept an argument that there had been no failure to implement Article 12 of the Habitats Directive because the number of sea turtle nests had not decreased over the previous 15 years.[1320]

Likewise, continued use by protected wildlife of an area that has suffered deterioration is not necessarily a good defence. The Court rejected an argument that, because red-breasted geese still used an area where wind turbines operated, there was no infringement of Article 4(4) of the Birds Directive in respect of an unclassified bird site. Data indicated a loss of attractiveness: red-breasted geese used the site less often than when peak values were recorded before the building of the turbines.[1321]

1314. Case C-241/08, *Commission v. France*. *See* Chapter 3, §3.04[C][3][d].
1315. *See* Chapter 3, §3.04[D][6].
1316. C-235/04, *Commission v. Spain*, para. 73. *See* Chapter 2.
1317. C-88/19, *Alianta pentru combatera abuzurilor*. *See* Chapter 4, §4.03[B][1].
1318. C-355/90, *Commission v. Spain*, para. 15.
1319. C-57/89, *Leybucht Dykes*, para. 13.
1320. C-103/00, *Commission v. Greece*. *See* Chapter 4, §4.03[B][3][d][iii].
1321. C-141/14, *Commission v. Bulgaria*, paras 76, 77. *See* Chapter 3.

[3] Not Accepting 'Death by a Thousand Cuts'

The expression 'death by a thousand cuts' figures in Case C-258/11, *Sweetman* and relates to the cumulative effects of treating individual localised habitat losses as inconsequential for site integrity. The arguments for treating the localised losses as inconsequential are *de minimis* ones. In Case C-258/11, *Sweetman,* the national decision-maker considered that the permanent loss of 1.47 hectares of a priority habitat type did not affect the integrity of an SCI since it still left a presence of over 268 hectares of habitat type out of a total initial resource of 270 hectares. In the proceedings, the Commission referred to the cumulative risk of treating individual damaging interventions in this way.

Indeed, before the Habitats Directive took effect, this risk had already materialised in relation to the very same priority habitat type elsewhere in Ireland. In a separate case, C-392/96, *Commission v. Ireland,* the Court found that Ireland had not complied with the EIA Directive because its threshold system for EIA did not, with respect to land reclamation, take account of the cumulative effect of small local projects: the Irish legislation treated these as automatically insignificant because of their size. As part of its submission, the Commission adduced evidence of the cumulative destruction by small-scale land reclamation of over 200 hectares of limestone pavement in the Burren, an area since included in Natura 2000.[1322]

In Case C-538/09, *Commission v. Belgium,* the Court rejected arguments to justify a declaratory scheme which, according to the Member State, applied only to installations and activities with a low impact on humans and the environment, and for which comprehensive conditions were laid down in national regulations.[1323] Citing C-392/96, *Commission v. Ireland,* the Court observed that 'even a small-scale project can have significant effects on the environment, if it is in a location where the environmental factors, such as fauna and flora, soil, water, climate or cultural heritage, are sensitive to the slightest alteration'.[1324]

[4] Not Accepting the 'Empty Goldfish Bowl'

The Court has accepted that natural causes may justify the derecognition or modification of a site that was previously recognised as requiring protection.[1325]

The Court has not, however, accepted the logic of the 'empty goldfish bowl', i.e., the proposition that obligations should disappear when nature disappears, even though nature's disappearance is the result of a Member State's failure.

Thus, the Court rejected an argument by Ireland that classification of the Cross Lough Important Bird Area ought not to be required, since the species it hosted, the sandwich tern, had disappeared as a result of predation by escaped American mink. Ireland had failed to take measures to safeguard the area and had not provided proof

1322. C-392/96, *Commission v. Ireland,* para. 33.
1323. C-538/09, *Commission v. Belgium,* para. 54.
1324. *Ibid.,* para. 55.
1325. C-301/12, *Cascina Tre Pini. See* Chapter 2.

that the area would no longer be suitable even if protection measures had been taken. Furthermore, the Court was convinced by evidence that trapping mink could reduce the pressure on sandwich terns and that there was a genuine chance that the tern might resettle in the area.[1326]

In like vein, the Court condemned Spain for infringing Article 6(2) of the Habitats Directive in relation to the destruction as a result of open-cast mining of 17.92 hectares of Galicia-Portuguese oak woods in an SPA classified for the capercaillie species. Spain argued that this destruction was unimportant since the area concerned did not contain any capercaillie breeding ground.[1327] The Court rejected this argument:

> That argument cannot be accepted, because, even if that area were not usable as a breeding ground, it could conceivably be used by that species as a habitat for other purposes, such as a living or hibernating area.
>
> Moreover, if that operation had not taken place in that area, the possibility cannot be excluded that, following measures taken by the authorities for that purpose, that area could have become usable as a breeding ground.
>
> In that respect, it should be recalled that the protection of SPAs is not to be limited to measures intended to avoid external anthropogenic impairment and disturbance but must also, according to the situation that presents itself, include positive measures to preserve or improve the state of the site.[1328]

Thus, in relation to Natura 2000, the Court has resisted the logic of the empty goldfish bowl not only in terms of a site's lost *capacity* but also in terms of its lost *potential* to host a species.

1326. C-418/04, *Commission v. Ireland*, paras 86 to 88. *See* Chapter 2.
1327. C-404/09, *Commission v. Spain*, paras 130-132.
1328. *Ibid.*, paras 133-135.

CHAPTER 8

Procedures for Applying to the CJEU, and Access to Justice

§8.01 IMPORTANCE OF ACCESS TO THE CJEU AND NATIONAL COURTS

The nature case-law could not have arisen without the availability of procedures for applying to the CJEU. Nor would the full body of case-law have emerged in the absence of litigants within Member States - an obvious point but of particular relevance when it comes to nature.

To an important extent, the case-law has depended on environmental access to justice, i.e., the entitlement of natural or legal persons to bring a legal challenge over a contravention of environmental law.

§8.02 THE MAIN PROCEDURES

Procedures for applying to the CJEU are provided for in the TFEU, one of the EU's foundation treaties. The TFEU allows for several means of access. In terms of the nature case-law, the most important are provided for in Articles 258 and 267, TFEU.

Article 258 governs 'direct actions' of the European Commission. It empowers the Commission to seek a Court of Justice declaration that, through its acts or omissions, a Member State has breached specific EU law provisions (which can include provisions of the nature directives). Direct actions can lead to far-reaching outcomes - including a Member State being required by the Court to take interim measures under Article 279, TFEU (under an order not to damage a Natura 2000 site, for instance) or being fined under Article 260 TFEU.

Article 267 enables - and sometimes requires - national courts to refer questions on the interpretation or validity of EU laws to the Court of Justice, which is given jurisdiction to give 'preliminary rulings'. These references arise because, in disputes involving EU law, national courts sometimes consider it necessary to obtain an interpretation from the Court of Justice. In the EU legal order, only the latter can hand down a definitive interpretation of EU law. Cases based on Article 267 are sometimes called 'preliminary references' because the reference to the Court of Justice will precede the national court's own adjudication. The reference will consist of one or more questions that the Court is invited to answer. Most Article 267 cases raise questions of interpretation, but the procedure also allows for a more radical possibility – an adjudication by the Court of Justice on whether a piece of EU law is legally valid (hence the expression 'validity reference'). In such cases, the Court has exclusive jurisdiction: it is not open to a national court to determine whether an EU law is valid or not.

The nature case-law reflects use of both Article 258 and Article 267 in almost equal measure. There are numerous court judgments resulting from direct actions and numerous court judgments resulting from preliminary references. This is atypical in terms of the Court's overall case-load, which is heavily dominated by preliminary references.[1329]

The interpretative purpose of preliminary references means that they often shed more light on the meaning of particular provisions than do direct actions. As for direct actions, their main purpose is to address what the Commission considers to be infringements of EU law. In theory, the Court can declare an infringement without setting out any new or refined interpretation. In practice, direct actions have also enriched the interpretation of the directives. They have sometimes addressed issues not raised in preliminary references and their scope and ramifications for the Member State concerned tend to be more consequential – although, as Joined Cases C-293/17 and C-294/17, *PAS*, show, a preliminary reference can sometimes have equally sweeping effects.

Despite having distinct origins and purposes, in practice, the Article 267 nature case-law and the Article 258 nature case-law derive strength from and reinforce each other. For example, the Court's interpretation in Case C-371/98, *First Corporate Shipping*, of the duty of Member States to propose a list of potential Natura 2000 sites under the Habitats Directive established a rationale later relied on in Court judgments against Germany,[1330] France[1331] and Ireland.[1332]

While the existing case-law can be explained by reference to Articles 258 (sometimes in combination with 279) and 267, other TFEU provisions – set out in Articles 259[1333] and 263(4) – might conceivably contribute to future nature case-law.

1329. Yaffa Epstein, José Vicente López-Bao & Guillaume Chapron, *Strict Protection of Species in the EU, Controversies and Trends*, 208, in *Nature Law and Policy in Europe*, Chapter 10 (Andrew L.R. Jackson ed., Routledge 2023).
1330. C-71/99, *Commission v. Germany.*
1331. C-220/99, *Commission v. France.*
1332. C-67/99, *Commission v. Ireland.*
1333. C-121/21, *Czech Republic v. Poland.*

§8.03 ARTICLES 258 AND 260, TFEU

[A] General Commission Approach to Article 258

Why does the Commission bring direct actions against Member States and what factors explain the cases that it brings? Article 258 does not *require* the Commission to take action. Neither does Article 258 constrain the Commission in the choice of what infringements it decides to pursue. Its use is entirely discretionary. The Commission can, for instance, pursue isolated cases if it so chooses, something illustrated by Case C-57/89, *Leybucht Dykes* and Case C-355/90, *Santoña Marshes* – and, more recently, Case C-441/17, *Białowieżka.*

In practice, the Commission's use of Article 258 is selective and focused. Under Article 17 of the TEU, the Commission is entrusted with the role of 'guardian of the Treaties', i.e., it is required to ensure the application of the Treaties and of measures adopted pursuant to them and to oversee the application of EU law under the control of the CJEU. The EU is a union of law and the Commission has a central role in upholding it, including via Article 258. Second, much EU legislation (nature legislation included) takes the form of directives and much use of Article 258 revolves around ensuring that directives are properly embedded in national law. Three types of Article 258 cases can be distinguished. 'Non-communication' cases focus on the failure of Member States to notify national legislation required to implement a directive. 'Non-conformity' cases address shortcomings in the legislation notified. 'Bad application' cases concern failures in practical implementation. The nature case-law provides many examples of non-conformity and bad application cases. The latter can encompass a wide range of failures, from high-level structural ones, such as the failure to classify a proper network of SPAs, to procedural ones, such as a failure to properly assess a plan or project under the Habitats Directive.

[B] Detection of Infringements and Role of Complaints

[1] Importance of Information Member States Must Communicate

The use of Article 258 is dependent on the Commission being able to detect infringements. Some provisions in the nature directives require Member States to formally transmit to the Commission documents containing specific information. For example, Article 4(1) of the Habitats Directive required Member States to transmit a full list of proposed sites for protection within three years of the Directive's adoption, together with related information on each site – the 'standardised Natura 2000 data form'. The Commission can engage Article 258 where Member States fail to provide these documents or provide documents which are incomplete or deficient.

[2] Importance of Complaints

It is more challenging to mount cases which are not tied to such formal communication obligations, but potential sources of information include its own research and third-party complaints submitted by individuals or environmental associations in the Member States.

Throughout the period covered by the nature case-law, the Commission has operated a complaints system which allows individuals and environmental associations to submit complaints which are registered and examined, and subject to some basic administrative guarantees. Several Commission communications have addressed the handling of complaints[1334] and complaints can now be submitted online.[1335] A 2016 communication acknowledged that 'complaints are an important means of detecting infringements of EU law'.[1336]

The Commission's complaint procedure is not intended to provide a means of redress for complainants' grievances (which, for complainants, can be a source of frustration). It is better seen as a conduit for information on compliance problems which the Commission may or may not follow up through use of Article 258 or Article 279. Access to justice at national level may provide a means of addressing these grievances – *see* section §8.06 below.

Some Commission direct actions make clear that they are complaint-derived. Examples include Case C-221/04, *Commission v. Spain,* on the use of snares;[1337] Case C-141/14, *Commission v. Bulgaria,* on the insufficient size of an SPA in Kaliakra and the adverse effects of developments there, including wind farms;[1338] Case C-461/14, *Commission v. Spain,* on the approval of a high-speed rail project;[1339] and Case C-432/21, *Commission v. Poland,* on forest management operations.[1340]

A particularly striking illustration of the value of complainants' information is provided by the Commission's request for supplementary Article 279 interim measures in Case C-441/17, *Białowieżka.* Having been granted an order by the Court addressed to Poland to halt logging activities, the Commission was alerted by complainants to evidence of non-compliance with the order. In returning to the Court, the Commission adduced a report based on satellite images as well as a report made by the Commission services based on a comparison between photographs from members of Polish civil society and official data regarding the location of protected natural habitats and

---

1334. *See* Communication from the Commission 'Updating the handling of relations with the complainant in respect of the application of Union law', COM(2012) 154 of 2 April 2012; and Communication from the Commission – 'EU law: Better results through better application', C/2016/8600, OJC 18, 19.1.2017, p. 10-20.
1335. https://ec.europa.eu/assets/sg/report-a-breach/complaints_en/.
1336. C/2016/8600.
1337. C-221/04, *Commission v. Spain,* para. 8.
1338. C-141/14, *Commission v. Bulgaria,* para. 11.
1339. C-461/14, *Commission v. Spain,* para. 14.
1340. C-432/21, *Commission v. Poland,* para. 25.

species.[1341] The material in the file was sufficient to raise a doubt in the mind of the Court about Poland's conduct.[1342]

It is possible that Commission officials may make an on-the-spot visit and their findings may be included in the file placed before the Court. Case C-504/14, *Commission v. Greece*, which concerns the application of Articles 6 and 12 of the Habitats Directive in respect of sea turtle habitats in the Gulf of Kyparissia, makes reference to such an on-the-spot visit.[1343]

[C] Commission Enforcement Policy on the Nature Directives

Court judgments resulting from Commission's direct actions on the nature directives extend back to the 1980s, thus spanning a period approaching forty years.

At the outset, the nature *acquis* did not include the Habitats Directive and cases concerned only the Birds Directive. The very first wave addressed the misalignment of certain national legislation with the species protection provisions of the Birds Directive and included Cases C-247/85, *Commission v. Belgium;* C-252/85, *Commission v. France*; C-262/85, *Commission v. Italy*; and C-412/85, *Commission v. Germany*. These early non-conformity cases, which set a strict benchmark in relation to transposition, were followed by two cases concerning SPAs: Case C-57/89, *Leybucht Dykes* and Case C-355/90, *Santoña Marshes*. All of these direct actions were legally groundbreaking, not only because they addressed nature conservation for the first time but because, in this emergent phase, which lasted until circa 1990, preliminary references scarcely featured in the nature case-law.

Case C-355/90, *Santoña Marshes* addressed for the first time the non-classification and lack of protection of a single IBA, a key wetland in the north of Spain. The Court's reasoning was very useful in pointing the Commission to the legal approach it needed to follow and the evidence it needed to adduce if it was to secure an SPA's establishment. The scale of under-classification of SPAs was, however, very significant at the time, running to many hundreds of sites across the then territory of the Member States. It would have been excessively difficult for the Commission to address the problem by focusing on each individual one. As is explained in Chapter 2, §2.02[G], in Case C-3/96, *Commission v. Netherlands*, the Commission tested an approach which involved addressing the overall deficits in a Member State's SPA classifications.

This Dutch case laid the basis for subsequent Article 258 cases addressing, in a strategic way, the need to classify a network of SPAs under the Birds Directive. Examples include Case C-334/04, *Commission v. Greece* and Case C-418/04, *Commission v. Ireland*.

In the second half of the 1990s came the challenge of enforcing the Habitats Directive. As with the Birds Directive, the Commission opened non-conformity cases

1341. *See* para. 89 of Order of 20 November 2017 in Case C-441/17, *Białowieżka*.
1342. *See* para. 109 of Order of 20 November 2017 in Case C-441/17, *Białowieżka*.
1343. C-504/14, *Commission v. Greece*, para. 98.

and, *mutatis mutandis*, it employed a comparable strategic approach to tackling Member State delays in recognising and protecting sites under the new directive.

This legal enforcement work took place in the absence of an express Commission enforcement policy. Although the use of Article 258 is discretionary, the Commission held itself ready to pursue all detected infringements. This generated unrealistic expectations, especially as the number of nature-related and other environmental complaints increased and the EU expanded.

Eventually, in the new millennium, through a number of communications on EU law in general, the Commission chose to embody an expressly selective enforcement policy. The most recent communication is from 2022.[1344]

In 2008, a communication addressed environmental law specifically.[1345]

The 2020 Biodiversity Strategy recognises Commission enforcement as an integral part of the Commission's policy on biodiversity.[1346] It states:

> As regards the Birds and Habitats Directives, enforcement will focus on completing the Natura 2000 network, the effective management of all sites, species-protection provisions, and species and habitats that show declining trends.[1347]

This envisages a broad scope for direct actions on the nature directives, but it is worth observing that, in terms of the Commission's limited resources, nature must compete with other enforcement priorities.

[D] Pre-litigation Stage

Article 258 is designed to allow disputes to be resolved without the need for court action. In practice, the Commission first opens an infringement file, giving it a specific number. Use of Article 258 begins with what is called a 'pre-litigation' stage, involving the issue of warning letters – first a Letter of Formal Notice and then a Reasoned Opinion, all referable to the infringement file. The aim of the correspondence is to draw Member States' attention to, and invite them to resolve, compliance problems the Commission has identified. As long as the procedure is ongoing, it is governed by confidentiality, reflecting a recognised interest in amicable resolution.

The pre-litigation stage is also designed to be the prelude to possible court proceedings, however, which means it is subject to important formal criteria. In particular, the *petitum* (the short, operative part of the Reasoned Opinion) is expected to crystallise the legal dispute and define the period (usually two months) within which the Member State must take appropriate action.

At the expiry of the Reasoned Opinion's time limit, the subject matter of the dispute is 'frozen'. Even if a long period elapses before a subsequent court judgment,

1344. Communication from the Commission – Enforcing EU law for a Europe that delivers, COM(2022) 518.
1345. Communication on implementing European Community environmental law, COM(2008) 773 final.
1346. Communication EU Biodiversity Strategy for 2030, COM(2020) 380 final.
1347. *Ibid.*, section 3.2.

the Court will rule on the legal and factual situation as it stood at this earlier point in time.

A few important procedural points deserve mention.

First, the Reasoned Opinion itself is expected to reflect the earlier Letter of Formal Notice. The Commission can address to the Member State supplementary Reasoned Opinions or supplementary Letters of Formal Notice to cover its concerns more completely or accurately. It needs, however, to ensure overall consistency between the Letter of Formal Notice stage and the Reasoned Opinion stage. In Case C-159/99, *Commission v. Italy,* the Court treated as inadmissible a Commission complaint concerning the transposition of Article 9(1)(a) and (b) of the Birds Directive: it noted that the Commission had added a new complaint in a supplementary Reasoned Opinion without having enlarged the Letter of Formal Notice.[1348]

Second, the Commission cannot enlarge the scope of the Reasoned Opinion in its Court Application. In Case C-661/20, *Commission v. Slovakia,* the Court held that the Commission could not raise subsequent Slovak legislative amendments introduced by Slovakia in the context of a specific complaint about Slovak legislation set out in the Reasoned Opinion. These amendments had significantly altered the legislative framework for the protection of forests in Slovakia and these fell outside the scope of the complaint in the Reasoned Opinion.[1349]

Third, the freezing of the dispute still leaves some latitude, as can be seen in several nature cases. In Case C-67/99, *Commission v. Ireland,* the Court observed that the circumscription of the subject matter of the proceedings in the pre-litigation stage does not prevent the Commission from setting out its initial complaints in greater detail in the Application to the Court on the condition that it does not alter the subject matter of the dispute.[1350]

In Case C-441/17, *Białowieżka,* the Court observed that the subject matter of an action may extend to events which took place after the Reasoned Opinion was delivered, provided that they are of the same kind as the events to which the Opinion referred and constitute the same conduct.[1351]

In the same vein, in Case C-661/20, *Commission v. Slovakia,* the Court referred to settled case-law to the effect that:

> In so far as an action seeks to raise *a systematic and consistent failure* to comply with the provisions of Article 6(2) of the Habitats Directive, *the production of additional evidence* intended, at the stage of the proceedings before the Court, to support the proposition that the failure thus alleged is general and consistent cannot be ruled out in principle (emphasis added).[1352]

In this case, all the facts relied on by the Commission in its application, relating exclusively to the absence of or inadequacy of appropriate measures to protect the capercaillie habitats in the SPAs classified for its conservation, were subsequent to the

1348. C-159/99, *Commission v. Italy,* paras 52 to 55.
1349. C-661/20, *Commission v. Slovakia,* paras 50-53.
1350. C-67/99, *Commission v. Ireland,* para. 23.
1351. *See* para. 67.
1352. C-661/20, *Commission v. Slovakia,* para. 94.

date of the Reasoned Opinion, but the Court held that they 'could legitimately be mentioned by the Commission in support of its application, by way of illustration of the general failure to fulfil obligations of which it complains'.[1353]

[E] Proceedings Before the Court

Article 258 proceedings before the Court can only begin after the expiry of the Reasoned Opinion's time limit. Such proceedings require a formal decision of the College of Commissioners (as does the issue of the Letter of Formal Notice, the first step of the pre-litigation procedure, and the Reasoned Opinion itself). In the case of the nature directives, this will involve a proposal by the lead service, i.e., Directorate-General Environment and approval by the Commission's central Legal Service, which will supply the agents to plead the case before the Court.

The court proceedings involve an exchange of documents, beginning with a formal Commission Application based on the content of the Reasoned Opinion and taking account of any Member State response.

Allowing for limitations defined by the scope of the Reasoned Opinion, the Commission may have a choice in terms of the number of individual pleas it decides to pursue. It may choose to be selective or more expansive. This can be illustrated by reference to pleas concerning species protection prohibitions and pleas concerning unlawful derogations. Sometimes the Commission has focused on the former, sometimes on the latter and sometimes it has presented combined pleas aimed at establishing concomitant breaches. Case C-507/04, *Commission v. Austria* provides an example of an especially thorough pleading in relation to the exclusion of the starling from any legal protection between 15 July and 30 November in the province of Burgenland. The Commission successfully pleaded breaches of Article 1, Article 5 *and* Article 9 of the Birds Directive.[1354] In contrast, in Case C-192/11, *Commission v. Poland*, the Commission limited itself to a plea based on Article 9 of the Birds Directive in respect of an exclusion of grey herons and cormorants present in fish ponds.[1355] Whatever the choice, if successful, the Commission's action will yield the same practical result: following the Court judgment, the withdrawal by the Member State of the non-compliant national rule or practice. More thorough pleading does, however, serve to underscore the legal architecture of the nature directives, and, in particular, the relationship between prohibitions and derogations.

Pleas may not only straddle the different provisions making up the species protection regimes of the nature directives but they may also straddle species protection and habitat protection provisions in respect of the same circumstances. Thus, in Case, C-504/14, *Commission v. Greece*, the Commission successfully pleaded breaches

1353. *Ibid.*, paras 96 and 97.
1354. *See* Chapter 4, §4.02[B][1][b] and Chapter 4, §4.02[F][3][b].
1355. *See* Chapter 4, §4.02[B][1][c].

of both Articles 6(2) and Article 12 of the Habitats Directive in respect of the same developments and activities in the Gulf of Kyparissia.[1356]

A more expansive approach may, of course, result in an individual plea being rejected for formal or other reasons. In Case, C-504/14, *Commission v. Greece*, for example, the Court, while finding breaches of Article 6(2) and Article 12, rejected a Commission plea based on Article 6(3) of the Habitats Directive in respect of certain illegal developments, holding that Article 6(3) was inapplicable in such situations. The rejection of this specific plea, nevertheless, established a very valuable point of law, helping to define how Member States should address compliance assurance.[1357] The Member State has an opportunity to respond through a Defence. Sometimes a Defence will concede the Commission's case in whole or in part. For example, in Case C-508/04, *Commission v. Austria,* which concerned transposing legislation used by several Austrian regions [including the Province of Burgenland mentioned above], Austria conceded 17 of 27 grounds of infringement.[1358]

The Commission can submit a Reply to the Defence. Depending on the content of the latter document (which may refer to the adoption of new measures, for example, or provide other new material), the Commission may sometimes reduce the grounds being pursued. In Case C-508/04, *Commission v. Austria,* for instance, the Commission withdrew two grounds.

The Member State is entitled to submit the last formal pleading, a Rejoinder.

Exceptionally, it may be possible to produce evidence after closure of the written part of the proceedings. In Case C-504/14, *Commission v. Greece,* the Commission obtained permission from the Court to introduce an opinion of the Greek Council of State as evidence in so far as it concerned the factual and legal situation that existed at the time of expiry of the time limit of the reasoned opinion.[1359] However, in Case C-559/19, *Doñana,* the Court declined to allow Spain to introduce a Unesco report. The Court considered that it had most of the information in the Unesco report and sufficient information to give judgment.[1360]

Sometimes other Member States will intervene, submitting for the Court's consideration their own legal analysis of the dispute. Intervener arguments usually support the position of the Member State defending. Commission enforcement policy is 'horizontal', i.e., it uses criteria potentially applicable to all Member States, and several Member States may be in the Commission's 'sights' on similar grounds. Intervening in a dispute may be a means for another Member State to try to pre-emptively address compliance issues in which it too has a stake. By way of example, in Case C-334/04, *Commission v. Greece,* Spain, France, Portugal and Finland all intervened on the side of Greece to argue against the Court using an updated ornithological reference, IBA 2000, to assess how well Greece had fulfilled its obligation to classify SPAs under the Birds Directive - *see* Chapter 2, §2.02[G][1].

1356. *See* Chapter 4, §4.03[B][1][a][i].
1357. *See* Chapter 3 §3.04[H][2].
1358. C-508/04, *Commission v. Austria,* paras 36-38.
1359. C-504/14, *Commission v. Greece,* paras 18 to 26.
1360. C-559/19, *Doñana,* paras 21-23.

The Commission or the respondent Member State may confirm a wish to have an oral hearing before the Court chamber assigned to deal with the case. Sometimes the Court will send an advance written request for clarification of specific points. Hearings tend to be short, with each side's presentations usually lasting less than thirty minutes.

Mostly, cases are assigned to a five-judge or three-judge Chamber, but, occasionally, in light of its importance, a case is assigned to the full court, or 'Grand Chamber'. Case C-441/17, *Białowieżka,* illustrates how the Grand Chamber can be engaged.

[F] Interim Measures, Article 279, TFEU

Article 279 enables the CJEU to prescribe interim measures in any cases before it. The use of Article 279 is thus ancillary to the use of other procedures, in particular – but not only – that of Article 258. The President or Vice-President of the Court grants interim measures by order and, depending on the circumstances, the same case may feature several successive orders.

Article 258 procedures can be lengthy in duration, often extending over several years. Serious harm may go unaddressed before the Court of Justice delivers its judgment. In theory, Article 279 can be used to prevent such harm in situations where the Article 258 procedure relates to an actual or impending ecological threat. Across all domains of EU law, the Commission makes very sparing use of Article 279, but the nature directives have featured in some of the most striking examples.

In 1989, in Case C-57/89 R, *Leybucht Dykes,* the Commission made its first request for interim measures[1361] in a nature case. More specifically, the Commission requested the Court to order Germany to temporarily suspend work on the construction of a sea-dyke in the area of Leybucht within an SPA under the Birds Directive. The application was unsuccessful but the Court's order[1362] – in which it criticises the length of time the Commission took to react – sheds light on the importance of urgency in the use of the procedure.

Nearly twenty years passed before the Commission again sought interim measures in a nature case, but, lessons having been learned, subsequent requests proved more successful. In 2006, in Case C-503/06 R, *Commission v. Italy,* the Commission obtained an order[1363] requiring Italy to suspend, in respect of the hunting season 2006/2007, the application of a law adopted by the Region of Liguria in purported implementation of the derogation provisions of Article 9 of the Birds Directive. In 2008, in Case C-76/08 R, *Commission v. Malta,* Malta was ordered[1364] to refrain from adopting any measures applying the derogation of Article 9 for the hunting of quails and turtle doves on the 2008 spring migration. In 2009, in Case C-573/08 R, *Commission v. Italy,* the Commission obtained an order[1365] requiring Italy to suspend, in respect of the hunting season 2009/2010, the application of part of another law

1361. At the time, interim measures were governed by Article 186 of the EEC Treaty.
1362. Order of 16 August 1989 in Case C-57/89 R, *Leybucht Dykes.*
1363. Order of 19 December 2006 in Case C-503/06 R, *Commission v. Italy.*
1364. Order of 24 April 2008 in Case C-76/08 R, *Commission v. Malta.*
1365. Order of 10 December 2009 in Case C-573/08 R, *Commission v. Italy.*

purporting to implement Article 9, this time one adopted by the Region of Lombardy. The rationale for use of Article 279 in these hunting cases is that, under the Birds Directive, both hunting and derogations are very time sensitive and an acceptance of an unlawful hunting season pending the outcome of the main case would, de facto, defeat the Directive's objectives.

The success of the Ligurian hunting case gave the Commission confidence to mount an interim request in respect of a proposed motorway bypass in Poland. In Case C-193/07 R, *Commission v. Poland ('Rospuda Bypass')*, the Commission obtained a short interim order suspending compensatory interventions related to the project. Further interim measures proved unnecessary, as Poland voluntarily refrained from carrying out works.

The most consequential nature-centred use of Article 279 to date also involved Poland. The Commission's intervention was prompted by a 2016 decision of the Polish authorities to significantly increase logging operations in the Bialowieza Forest, a Natura 2000 site hosting species and habitats that are dependent on old-growth forests, including the availability of dead wood. In Case C-441/17 R, *Białowieżka*, the Commission obtained a first interim order on 27 July 2017 requiring that certain operations be suspended. It obtained a further interim order on 20 November 2017, this time one envisaging the possible payment of a daily penalty of EUR 100,000 per day if the second interim order was found to have been breached. This step to address a contingency broke new legal ground and followed a Commission submission presenting evidence that the original interim order had not been respected. The Court stated that Article 279 confers on it the power to prescribe any interim measures that it deems necessary in order to ensure that the final decision is fully effective; such a measure may entail provision for a penalty payment to be imposed.

In all of these successful cases, the Commission services needed to act quickly – and think ahead from the time of opening the infringement file. Prospective use of Article 279 meant accelerating the pace of the Article 258 pre-litigation stage, with Member States given shorter time delays than usual to respond to the Letter of Formal Notice or the Reasoned Opinion. This showed that the Commission treated the matters in dispute as ones requiring urgency. Apart from urgency, the Court looks at whether the Commission has presented a prima facie case and whether the balance of interests favours those relied on by the Commission or those relied on by the Member State. These conditions are cumulative, i.e., the Commission will not obtain interim measures if it fails to convince the Court on any one condition.

[G] Admissibility, Burden of Proof and Approach to Scientific Information

[1] Admissibility and Scope for Re-litigation

In adjudicating on a direct action brought by the Commission, the Court will first need to address any arguments on admissibility raised by the Member State. This can bring in procedural points concerning the pre-litigation stage, such as those mentioned in section §8.03[D] above.

Even when the Court's findings go against the Commission, there may be an opportunity for the Commission to bring fresh proceedings, using better arguments or evidence.

In Case C-157/89, *Commission v. Italy*, concerning hunting rules, Italy argued that the Commission's complaints had already been rejected in an earlier case, C-262/85, *Commission v. Italy*, 'with the result that they may not be raised for a second time'.[1366] The Court dismissed Italy's argument, stating that the complaint concerning the need to prohibit hunting during certain periods was disregarded in the earlier case on procedural grounds, and that, 'accordingly, the Court did not rule on whether that complaint was well-founded'.[1367] It went on to condemn Italy in the second case.

[2] Burden of Proof

Where Commission pleas are admissible, the Commission bears the burden of proving them to the requisite standard.

Sometimes, in substance, the Commission's direct actions fail in their entirety. Examples are Case C-221/04, *Commission v. Spain*, in which the Commission failed to convince the Court that use of stopped snares contravened the species protection provisions of the Habitats Directive, and Case C-308/08, *Commission v. Spain*, in which the Commission failed to prove an infringement of Articles 6 and 12(4) of the Habitats Directive in respect of a road upgrade in a stronghold of the Iberian lynx. On the whole, however, the Commission's direct actions have enjoyed a high success rate.

[a] Non-conformity Cases

Where pleas relate to the conformity of national legislation, the Court does not expect the Commission to show that the alleged legislative flaws give rise to problems in practice. This doesn't preclude the Commission from providing illustrations of problems caused by non-conformity.

[b] Bad Application Cases

Bad application pleas raised by the Commission have covered quite different subject matter: non-recognition of sites for inclusion in Natura 2000; failure to protect Natura 2000 sites or sites eligible for Natura 2000; non-adherence to requirements relating to plans and projects affecting Natura 2000; and departures from the requirements of strict protection under both nature directives. There are corresponding differences in the way the Court has dealt with the evidence but also some common themes.

1366. C-157/89, *Commission v. Italy*, para. 5.
1367. *Ibid.*, para. 7.

[i] Basic Approach and Influence of Precautionary Principle

Case C-559/19, *Doñana,* provides a classic formulation of the burden of proof which the Commission must satisfy:

> According to settled case-law, in proceedings for failure to fulfil obligations, it is for the Commission to prove the existence of the alleged infringement and to provide the Court with the information necessary for it to determine whether there has indeed been an infringement, and the Commission may not rely on any presumption for that purpose.[1368]
>
> Next, it is only where the Commission has adduced sufficient evidence to establish the existence of the alleged infringement that it is incumbent on the Member State to challenge in substance and in detail the information produced and the inferences drawn.[1369]

In respect of Article 6 of the Habitats Directive, however, the precautionary principle exerts a powerful influence. In Case C-559/19, *Doñana,* the Court noted that the burden of proof required to establish an infringement of Article 6(2) of the Habitats Directive is based on the precautionary principle and that 'it is sufficient for the Commission to establish that there is a probability or risk that that action or inaction might cause a deterioration or significant disturbance to the habitats or species concerned'.[1370]

[ii] Notions of Completeness

Notions of 'completeness' espoused by the Court have played a significant role in Commission cases concerning the establishment of Natura 2000, the adoption of conservation measures, and the practice of hunting.

Thus, as noted in Chapter 2, §2.02[F], the Birds Directive requires Member States to classify as SPAs *all* the sites which, applying ornithological criteria, appear to be the most suitable for conservation of the species in question;[1371] as noted in Chapter 2, §2.02[B], the Habitats Directive requires them to supply the Commission with *an exhaustive list* of sites eligible as SACs; as noted in Chapter 3, §3.04[B][3], the Habitats Directive requires them satisfy the obligation to adopt conservation measures under Article 6(1) by *complete,* clear and precise measures;[1372] as noted in Chapter 4, §4.02[D][2], the Birds Directive requires them to secure a *complete* system of protection of huntable species in the periods during which their survival is particularly under threat.[1373]

1368. C-559/19, *Doñana,* para. 46.
1369. *Ibid.*, para. 47.
1370. *Ibid.*, para. 135. *See also* Chapter 3, §3.04[E][6].
1371. C-3/96, *Commission v. Netherlands*, para. 62.
1372. C-290/18, *Commission v. Portugal*, para. 53.
1373. C-157/89, *Commission v. Italy*, para. 14.

These notions of completeness can, amongst other things, help the Commission to satisfy the burden of proof by allowing it to concentrate on incompleteness in the Member States' fulfilment of their obligations.

[iii] Scientific Knowledge

The way in which the Court treats scientific knowledge is also important.

An early example is seen in Case C-157/89, *Commission v. Italy*. The Court rejected arguments by Italy that scientific information relied on by the Commission was insufficiently precise and local. The Court applied a 'best information available' approach, confirming the role of authoritative scientific literature of a general character in a context where more specific literature is unavailable.[1374]

This best information available approach is seen to striking effect in a string of cases on SPA classification, beginning with Case C-3/96, *Commission v. Netherlands*. As already noted in Chapter 2, §2.02[G], the Court upheld the Commission's reliance on the IBA inventory, stating that, although not legally binding, the inventory 'can, by reason of its acknowledged scientific value'[1375] and in the absence of contrary scientific evidence, be used by the Court as a basis of reference when assessing the extent to which the Member States have fulfilled their classification obligations.

As noted in Chapter 4, §4.02[F][4][a], in Case C-344/03, *Commission v. Finland*, on spring hunting, the Court used a similar formula when referring to the work of the ORNIS Committee on 'small numbers'. The Court held that, although not legally binding, the work could, by reason of *the acknowledged scientific value of that committee's opinions* and *the failure to adduce any scientific evidence to the contrary*, 'be used by the Court as a basis of reference for assessing whether the derogation granted by the defendant Member State under Article 9(1)(c) of the Directive fulfils the condition that the capture of the birds in question must be carried out in small numbers'.[1376]

As can be seen, this formula leaves room for Member States to adduce contrary scientific evidence, but the Member States have mostly either not contested or been unable to adduce better evidence than these authoritative general references.

Where the Commission adduces more location-specific evidence, the Advocate General can play an important role in sifting its probative value. An example is the close scrutiny by the Advocate General in Case C-418/04, *Commission v. Ireland*, of evidence of bird use of two areas of intertidal mudflat which the Commission argued had been wrongly excluded from the Sandymount Strand and Tolka Estuary SPA in Dublin Bay.[1377]

In some location-specific cases, the Court has accepted Member State evidence that rebuts the findings of scientific reports adduced by the Commission. An example is Case C-308/08, *Commission v. Spain*, on the Iberian lynx.

1374. *Ibid.*, para. 15.
1375. C-3/96, *Commission v. Netherlands*, para. 70.
1376. C-344/03, *Commission v. Finland*, para. 54.
1377. Opinion of the Advocate General in Case C-418/04, *Commission v. Ireland*, paras 63 to 75.

It is not only a matter of the relative weight of the authoritative scientific evidence that the Commission adduces. Some decisions of the Court are based on the *inadequacy* of the information on which the Member State has sought to rely and are framed accordingly. In general, the Court has stressed the role of knowledge to underpin Member States' decision-making. If the Commission adduces evidence contesting the Member State's decision, the outcome may be determined by reference to the incompleteness of the knowledge on which the Member State decision rests. By way of illustration, in Case C-557/15, *Commission v. Malta,* on finch-trapping, the Court upheld a Commission complaint that Malta had failed to comply with the condition laid down in Article 9(1)(c) of Directive 2009/147, according to which the permitted derogation must concern only 'small numbers'.[1378] In the analysis leading to this conclusion, the Court found that:

> The Republic of Malta *has not adduced sufficient evidence* that its derogation regime for the trapping of the seven finch species in question makes it possible to ensure the maintenance of the populations of those species at a satisfactory level (emphasis added).[1379]

Thus, in this instance, the Court considered that there was an onus on the Member State to adduce sufficient evidence to justify its derogation decision. In Case C-507/04, *Commission v. Austria,* the Court pointed out that the burden of proof regarding compliance with requirements in respect of individual derogations rested with the national authority taking the decision.[1380]

It is not only a matter of a Member State decision-maker putting itself in possession of the right knowledge. Case C-209/02, *Commission v. Austria,* confirms the importance of using the best information available *correctly*. The Court upheld a Commission complaint that the competent authority had not drawn the correct inferences from a scientific appraisal of the likely effects of a project in a Natura 2000 site.[1381] The case concerned the approval by the Government of the Province of Styria of a golf course extension on an SPA which hosted corncrake. The decision-maker considered that there would be no adverse effects on corncrake despite the existence of expert reports which had reached the opposite conclusion.

[iv] Plea of General and Persistent Failure

In a direct action of broad scope, it is open to the Commission to advance a plea that the Member State's conduct discloses a general and persistent failure - which may be described in other terms such as systematic and generalised failure or general and consistent failure.[1382] As already noted in section §8.03[D], such a plea offers the

1378. C-557/15, *Commission v. Malta,* para. 76.
1379. *Ibid.,* para. 74.
1380. C-507/04, *Commission v. Austria,* para. 198.
1381. C-209/02, *Commission v. Austria,* para. 26.
1382. C-661/20, *Commission v. Slovakia.*

procedural advantage of allowing the Commission to adduce evidence that post-dates the Reasoned Opinion.

As the Court stated in Case C-444/21, *Commission v. Ireland*:

> Without prejudice to the Commission's obligation to satisfy in each and every case the burden of proof which it bears, in principle nothing prevents the Commission from seeking in parallel a finding that provisions of a directive have not been complied with by reason of the conduct of a Member State's authorities with regard to particular specifically identified situations and a finding that those provisions have not been complied with because its authorities have adopted *a general practice* contrary thereto, which the particular situations illustrate where appropriate (emphasis added).[1383]
>
> Where the Commission has adduced sufficient evidence to show that a Member State's authorities have developed a repeated and persistent practice which is contrary to the provisions of a directive, it is incumbent on that Member State to challenge in substance and in detail the information produced and the consequences flowing therefrom.[1384]

The plea is challenging for the Commission in terms of establishing the representativeness of the examples it presents. In Case C-444/21, *Commission v. Ireland,* which concerned conservation measures required under Article 6(1) of the Habitats Directive, the Court was not convinced that the three examples of species and habitats submitted by the Commission in support of its plea were representative for all the SCIs at issue.[1385] It is important, nevertheless, to look at a judgment in its entirety, and while the Commission failed in this particular plea, it succeeded in a closely related one concerning the failure by Ireland to adopt a complete set of conservation measures[1386] [which illustrates the point about completeness made in section §8.03[G][2][b][ii] above]. The Court's finding in relation to the latter was arguably not much less significant for the Member State in terms of required follow-up than a finding of general and persistent failure would have been.

In its deployment of this general plea, the Commission was more successful in Case C-661/20, *Commission v. Slovakia,* where the Court concluded that:

> The Commission has proved, in a sufficiently documented and detailed manner, the *consistent and generalised* absence of appropriate protective measures, consisting in preventing forest management activities from causing deterioration of the capercaillie (*Tetrao urogallus*) habitats and disturbance of that species likely to have significant effects in view of the conservation objective of that species (emphasis added).[1387]

A difference between these cases is that, whereas in Case C-661/20, *Commission v. Slovakia,* the Commission focused on a single interest, i.e., the capercaillie, in Case C-444/21, *Commission v. Ireland,* it sought to extrapolate from evidence concerning three interests in order to cover a much broader set of concerns.

1383. C-444/21, *Commission v. Ireland,* para. 165.
1384. *Ibid.,* para. 166.
1385. *Ibid.,* paras 170-175.
1386. *Ibid.,* paras 153.
1387. C-661/20, *Commission v. Slovakia,* para. 110.

In Case C-116/22, *Commission v. Germany*, the Commission failed in a comparable general plea against Germany in relation to the establishment of conservation objectives, again because the Court was not convinced that the examples the Commission adduced were sufficiently representative.[1388]

[H] Advocate General's Opinion

Usually, an Opinion of the Advocate General will precede the Court's judgment. Although not binding, the Advocate General's analysis will often prefigure the Court's conclusions and it will sometimes be explicitly cited with approval in the judgment. The texts of Advocate Generals' Opinions are often lengthier than those of the final judgments and typically disclose valuable legal research. Sometimes it is necessary to read the Advocate General's opinion in conjunction with the ruling since the Court will explicitly cite the analysis of the former. For example, in Case C-183/05, *Commission v. Ireland,* the Court ruled against Ireland with respect to three projects negatively affecting species protected under Article 12 of the Habitats Directive. It requires a reading of the Advocate General's analysis to understand why the Court ruled as it did. The Court does not always follow the Advocate General's Opinion, however, as Case C-444/21, *Commission v. Ireland,* demonstrates. In that case, the Advocate General was satisfied that the Commission had shown a general and persistent failure by Ireland to establish conservation measures under the Habitats Directive[1389] but the Court was not.[1390]

Advocate Generals' opinions are immediately published on the Court's Curia website, and typically appear some months before the Court judgment, creating a sense of anticipation of what the outcome is likely to be.

Sometimes a case will proceed to judgment without an Advocate General's Opinion, as Case C-432/21, *Commission v. Poland* shows.

[I] Judgments

In form, there is a basic consistency between the earliest nature cases and present-day ones. The Commission's pleas are presented, along with the Member State's counter-arguments, before the Court's findings. The earliest judgments are, nevertheless, very lapidary, and there has been an evolution over time. Present-day judgments tend to be considerably longer, some extending to well over a hundred paragraphs and having a table of contents, Case C-444/21, *Commission v. Ireland,* being an example.[1391] Compared to the past, there is a clearer demarcation of the structural elements, with arguments of the parties more clearly separated from the Court's findings, for instance.

1388. C-116/22, *Commission v. Germany*, para. 125.
1389. Opinion of the Advocate General in Case C-444/21, *Commission v. Ireland,* paras 90 to 112.
1390. C-444/21, *Commission v. Ireland,* paras 173 to 176.
1391. The judgment in this case runs to a hundred and eighty paragraphs. There are lengthier ones. The judgment in C-507/04, *Commission v. Austria* runs to over three hundred paragraphs, for example.

In the Court's findings, formulations from earlier cases are commonly repeated, helping to demonstrate continuity and coherence in the body of cases on a particular topic. For example, the phrase 'coherent and coordinated measures of a preventive nature' recurs like a leitmotif in successive judgments on Article 12 of the Habitats Directive.[1392]

Like Advocate Generals' opinions, judgments are immediately published on the Court's Curia website.

[J] Follow-up under Article 260, TFEU

An Article 258 judgment in favour of the Commission does not of itself result in closure of the infringement file against the Member State. The infringement file remains open but its further handling is governed by the procedure provided for in Article 260, TFEU. The object of the new procedure is no longer the original Article 258 *petitum* but the operative part of the Article 258 judgment. The Commission's aim is to ensure that the Member State takes the necessary measures to satisfy the Article 258 judgment and bring the infringement to an end. Necessary measures can include adoption of new legislation.

Formally, the Commission sends an immediate request to the Member State to notify the required measures. If there is a delay, the Commission will follow a process similar to the Article 258 pre-litigation stage, i.e., it will send the Member State an Article 260 Letter of Formal Notice; before, such procedural steps used to mirror Article 258 ones but the Lisbon Treaty removed the pre-litigation stage of issuing a Reasoned Opinion. Ultimately, the Commission can submit a second Court of Justice application for failure to comply with the first court judgment.

The early case-law provides examples of second court judgments in relation to the nature directives. In Case C-75/91, *Commission v. Netherlands*, the Court condemned the Netherlands for not complying with the Court's earlier judgment on the Birds Directive in Case C-236/85, *Commission v. Netherlands*. In Case C-345/92, *Commission v. Germany*, the Court condemned Germany for a similar failure to implement the Court's judgment in Case C-412/85, *Commission v. Germany*. In Case C-75/91, *Commission v. Netherlands*, the Court stated that:

> It should be noted that, even though Article 171 [now 260] of the Treaty does not specify the period within which a judgment must be complied with, it is clear in view of the interest in the immediate and uniform implementation of Community law that the process of complying with a judgment must be *initiated at once* and must *be completed as soon as possible* (emphasis added).[1393]

In terms of the time frame for implementing a Court judgment, this formulation remains the yardstick. Compared to the early 1990s, however, the consequences of a second court judgment are more serious, since the Treaty now provides for financial penalties. The Commission can request the Court to order the Member State to pay a

1392. *See* Chapter 4, §4.03[B][3][b].
1393. C-75/91, *Commission v. Netherlands*, para. 7.

lump sum penalty and, in the event that non-compliance persists beyond a second judgment, a daily penalty. To date, there is no example of an Article 258 judgment on the nature directives leading to an Article 260 penalty, but, on several occasions, penalties have been imposed for non-compliance with judgments concerning the EIA Directive.[1394]

§8.04 ARTICLE 267, TFEU

The Article 267 process begins with a national court taking the view that a Court of Justice decision on a question of interpretation or validity of EU law is necessary to enable it to give a judgment in a matter before it.

With some exceptions, Article 267 references for a preliminary ruling are compulsory at the level of courts or tribunals of last instance. A lower national instance has discretion to request a Court of Justice ruling.

Case C-283/81, *Cilfit and Others,* sets out the circumstances in which national courts or tribunals of last instance are not obliged to ask the Court for a preliminary ruling, namely when the question is irrelevant for the resolution of the dispute; when the provision of EU law in question has already been interpreted by the Court; and when the correct interpretation of EU law is so obvious as to leave no scope for any reasonable doubt.

Case C-561/19, *Consorzio Italian Management e Catania Mulitservizi and Catania Multiservizi,* clarifies that the existence of a reasonable doubt 'must be assessed in the light of the characteristic features of EU law, the particular difficulties to which the interpretation of the latter gives rise and the risk of divergences in judicial decisions within the European Union'.[1395]

The nature case-law includes examples of references from both lower instances and the highest instances.

[A] Interpretative References

Most interpretative references concerning the nature directives have resulted from litigation undertaken by environmental associations and environmentalists. Hunting and derogations have featured prominently. So have projects and interventions perceived as a threat to Natura 2000 sites. References have sometimes featured 'satellite' topics, i.e., topics indirectly or tangentially linked to the texts of the nature directives, such as access to justice and public participation. References have also arisen, though less commonly, from other kinds of court proceedings - national enforcement proceedings in Cases C-169/89, *Gourmetterie Van den Burg,* C-149/94, *Didier Vergy,* and C-477/19, *Magistrat der Stadt Wien,* for instance.

1394. *See,* for example, Case C-261/18, *Commission v. Ireland.* The Court imposed a lump sum and daily penalty on Ireland for failing to comply with an earlier ruling on non-compliance with the EIA Directive.

1395. C-561/19, *Consorzio Italian Management e Catania Mulitservizi and Catania Multiservizi,* para. 61.

[B] Validity References

These are far rarer than interpretative references, and, in fact, there is only one example to date that involves the nature directives. In 2017, in Case C-281/16, *Vereniging Hoekschewaards Landschap*,[1396] following a validity reference from the Dutch Council of State, the Court found that the Commission had exceeded its discretion when adopting an implementing decision under the Habitats Directive with regard to a Dutch Natura 2000 site. In earlier national litigation, the Council of State had annulled a unilateral government decision to reduce the same site, on the basis that it was inconsistent with a previous Commission implementing decision which had listed a bigger protected site. To overcome this setback, the Netherlands had proposed a revision of the site boundaries, which the Commission had accepted. The plaintiff environmental association challenged the new decision of the Commission before the Dutch Council of State, which then asked the Court whether the Commission's decision was valid. The Court concluded that there was no evidence of a scientific error in the original site listing which would have justified the revision.

[C] Procedural Aspects of Article 267

[1] Reformulation of Questions

The referring court drafts the questions to be presented to the Court of Justice in the order for reference. The Court may choose to reformulate them.

An example is provided by Case C-293/17, *PAS*.

The first question posed by the referring court reads as follows:

> Can an activity which is not covered by the concept of 'project' as referred to in Article 1(2)(a) of [the EIA Directive] because it is not a physical intervention in the natural surroundings be a project as referred to in Article 6(3) of [the Habitats Directive] because the activity may have a significant effect on a Natura 2000 site?

The Court's reformulation reads:

> By the first question in Case C-293/17, the referring court asks, in essence, whether Article 6(3) of the Habitats Directive must be interpreted as meaning that *the grazing of cattle and the application of fertilisers on the surface of land or below its surface in the vicinity of Natura 2000 sites* may be classified as a 'project' within the meaning of that provision, on the ground that they are likely to have significant consequences for those sites, even if those activities, in so far as they are not a physical intervention in the natural surroundings, do not constitute a 'project' within the meaning of Article 1(2)(a) of the EIA Directive (emphasis added).[1397]

By this reformulation, the Court rendered the question more targeted and case-specific, facilitating the Court's subsequent analysis.

1396. *See* Chapter 2.
1397. C-293/17, *PAS*, para. 59.

[2] *Inadmissibility of Some Questions*

The Court gives national courts broad latitude. Questions posed enjoy a presumption of relevance. As noted in Case C-477/19, *Magistrat der Stadt Wien*:

> The Court may refuse to rule on a question referred for a preliminary ruling by a national court only where it is quite obvious that the interpretation of EU law that is sought bears no relation to the actual facts of the main action or its purpose, where the problem is hypothetical, or where the Court does not have before it the factual or legal material necessary to give a useful answer to the questions submitted to it.[1398]

Case C-477/19, *Magistrat der Stadt Wien* nevertheless provides a good illustration of circumstances in which the Court will refuse (in part) a request for a preliminary ruling. The referring court raised several questions of interpretation with regard to the term 'breeding site' used in Article 12(1)(d) of the Habitats Directive, which the Court treated as inadmissible. It observed that the request for a preliminary ruling did not provide any explanation as to why the term 'breeding site' was relevant to the resolution of the main proceedings[1399] (the Court accepted that the term 'resting place' was relevant and provided an interpretation of this) and that 'the order for reference contains no matters of fact or law which make it possible to determine whether, and to what extent, in addition to classifying part of the European hamster's natural habitat as a "resting place", designating that habitat as a "breeding site" would have any bearing on the outcome of the main proceedings'.[1400] The prohibition of Article 12(1)(d) applied 'regardless of the part of the natural habitat concerned'.[1401]

[3] *Court Process*

Once the questions reach the Court, the Commission and Member States are informed and provided with an opportunity to submit observations. It is standard practice for the Commission to submit these: they represent an important – though sometimes overlooked – aspect of the Commission's legal work. Typically, Commission observations will involve collaboration between lawyers working in the Commission Legal Service and lawyers and nature experts working in the lead service, Directorate General Environment. Usually, the different parties to the national proceedings will also submit observations. For example, the Port of Sheerness – which had benefited from the exclusion of a contentious area of mudflat from an SPA – was an intervener in Case C-44/95, *Lappel Bank*. Taken together, the submissions typically provide the Court with a multifaceted appraisal of the questions posed.

1398. C-477/19, *Magistrat der Stadt Wien*, para. 40.
1399. *Ibid.*, para. 41.
1400. *Ibid.*, para. 43.
1401. *Ibid.*, para. 44.

There is usually an oral stage, in which all those who submitted observations have an opportunity to address the relevant Court chamber. As in Article 258 proceedings, there will generally also be an Advocate General's Opinion.

As in direct actions, the Opinion of the Advocate General plays an important role and, generally speaking, serves as a good indication of the likely outcome. It will also often provide invaluable insights into the basis for the Court's ultimate conclusions. As noted in Chapter 3, §3.04[D][18][a], for instance, the Opinion in Case C-461/17, *Holohan*, provides considerable clarification on the legal and scientific basis for an appropriate assessment to encompass non-listed species, as well as species and habitats outside the boundaries of a Natura 2000 site.

[4] Subsequent Role of the Referring Court

The Court's ruling does not bring matters to an end. The case will return to the referring court for final adjudication in light of the Court's interpretative ruling.

Even when the Court seems very clear in its conclusions, it will allow for a further review by the referring court. An example is provided by Case C-238/20, *Sātiņi-S*. The wording of the Court's decision leaves little doubt that the Court found that Latvian implementing rules for the nature directives did not amount to a disproportionate interference with property rights in respect of an aquaculture activity, but it nevertheless makes provision for a review by the referring court:

> It does not appear, *subject to any review by the referring court in this respect*, that measures such as those at issue in the main proceedings, thus taken for the purposes of protecting nature and the environment, under the 'Birds' Directive and the 'Habitats' Directive, and which do not prevent the practice of aquaculture on the plots concerned, but only regulate the conditions of exercise of that activity in order to prevent harm to the environmental interests thus protected, constitute, in the absence of compensation for affected owners, a disproportionate and intolerable interference impairing the very substance of the right to property (emphasis added).[1402]

The Court may invite the referring Court to verify factual submissions made during the course of the proceedings before it. Thus, in Case C-674/17, *Tapiola*, the Court, in light of evidence provided by the plaintiff and the Commission, considered it doubtful whether measures taken by Finland made it possible to satisfy a requirement under Article 16 of the Habitats Directive, but it went on to state that was a matter for the referring court to ascertain.[1403]

The return to the referring court may lead to a consequential chain of events. As Hendrik Shoukens observes in relation to Case C-293/17, *PAS*, on nitrogen deposition:

> The Dutch Council of State found it unnecessary to appoint further experts in order to review the evidence regarding the potential impact of elevated levels of nitrogen deposition on Dutch Natura 2000 sites. It simply used the conflicting scientific

1402. C-238/20, *Satiņi-S*, para. 35.
1403. C-674/17, *Tapiola*, para. 65.

outputs, the lack of implementation of the recovery actions prior to the permit procedure and the unclear relationship between existing conservation duties and the compensatory actions as arguments to quash the Dutch programmatic approach to nitrogen deposition.[1404]

Part of the further sequel involved the state aid decision mentioned in Chapter 7.[1405]

§8.05 OTHER TREATY PROCEDURES

[A] Article 259, TFEU

Article 259 enables one Member State to bring another Member State before the CJEU.

Article 259 is seldom used – and it has never yet led to a court judgment concerning the nature directives. Nevertheless, the circumstances of Case C-121/21 R, *Czech Republic v. Poland,* illustrate, in rather dramatic fashion, how the directives might conceivably feature in the use of the procedure. Concerned about Polish lignite mining at Turow close to its frontier, the Czech Republic lodged a Court of Justice application charging Poland with infringements of the EIA Directive and the Water Framework Directive. It also successfully sought interim measures under Article 279, obtaining a Court order requiring Poland to cease lignite mining pending the outcome of the main proceedings,[1406] and, in echoes of Case C-441/17, *Białowieżka*, a further order[1407] imposing a financial penalty on Poland for failing to comply with the previous order. The rapidity of the process is striking. As mentioned in Chapter 7, there is a close relationship between the nature directives, on the hand, and the EIA Directive and the Water Framework Directive, on the other; it is therefore not difficult to envisage how Turow-like circumstances might bring the nature directives into play.[1408]

[B] Article 263(4), TFEU and the Aarhus Regulation

Article 263(4) allows natural or legal persons to institute proceedings directly before the CJEU (the General Court) against an act addressed to them (first limb) or an act which is of direct and individual concern to them (second limb) or a regulatory act which is of direct concern to them and does not entail implementing measures (third limb).

1404. Hendrik Shoukens, *Science and the Interpretation of the EU Habitats Directive by the Court of Justice of the EU, 2 + 2 = 5?* 191, in *Nature Law and Policy in Europe,* Chapter 10 (Andrew L.R. Jackson ed., Routledge 2023).
1405. Chapter 7, §7.04[G].
1406. Order of 21 May 2021.
1407. Order of 20 September 2021.
1408. As Agustín García Ureta has noted in relation to appropriate assessment under Article 6(3), the Habitats Directive leaves undefined the cross-border perspective – *see EU Biodiversity Law: Wild Birds and Habitats Directives,* 296 (Europa Law Publishing 2020).There are important cross-border Natura 2000 sites; furthermore, impacts may arise at a considerable distance from where a plan or project is executed. The EIA, SEA and Water Framework Directives all provide mechanisms for cross-border consultation or cooperation and these may prove important in combination with the nature directives.

The nature directives primarily relate to decision-making at national level, but, as can be seen in Case C-281/16, *Vereniging Hoekschewaards Landschap*, some decisions are entrusted to the Commission. Case C-281/16 illustrates how, via a national court, Article 267 can be used to challenge the validity of these.

[1] The Limits of Article 263(4), TFEU

In theory, Article 263(4) might offer an alternative route to challenging such decisions. The CJEU has interpreted legal standing very strictly in respect of the second and third limbs of Article 263(4), however. In practice, these limbs are unavailable to environmental litigants and most individual litigants.[1409]

This is illustrated by Case T-150/05, *Markku Sahlsted*, already outlined in Chapter 2, §2.03[C][3]. An action by a Finnish landowner was declared inadmissible on the basis that the plaintiff did not meet the criteria set by Article 263(4). As mentioned in Chapter 2, however, the Court of First Instance [now the General Court] did refer to the possibility of a preliminary reference.

Related Cases T-100/05, *CFE*, and C-43/18 *CFE*, provide a real – and it seems unique – example of a litigant who, having failed in respect of Article 263(4), was able to have the Court provide an interpretative ruling under Article 267 in respect of the nature directives. In the later procedure, the plaintiff, CFE, a landowner, challenged a decree by the Brussels Region declaring the Sonian Forest an SAC. The plaintiff argued that the process should have been subject to an SEA and there was a preliminary reference on this point under Article 267 – *see* Chapter 6, §6.02[A].

It is interesting to note that, more than a decade previously, the same plaintiff had unsuccessfully tried to challenge before the General Court the Commission Decision in which the site in question was listed as an SCI. As the Court of Justice recalled in its judgment in Case C-43/18, *CFE*:

> By application of 21 February 2005, CFE brought an action for annulment of that decision before the General Court of the European Union. By order of 19 September 2006, *CFE v Commission* (T-100/05, not published, EU:T:2006:260), the General Court declared the action to be inadmissible -on the- ground that CFE was not directly concerned by that decision, in view of the discretion left to the Member States as regards the measures to be taken in relation to designated SCIs. That order has become final.[1410]

[2] 2021 Revision of the Aarhus Regulation

Thanks to a 2021 amendment to the Aarhus Regulation, 1367/2006,[1411] a door has been opened to use of the first limb of Article 263(4) as a means of indirectly challenging

1409. For a recent critical analysis of the Court's approach to Article 263(4), *see* Gerd Winter, *Plaumann Withering: Standing Before the EU General Court Underway from Distinctive to Substantial Concern*, European Journal of Legal Studies, 2023.

1410. C-43/18 *CFE*, para. 21.

1411. Regulation (EC) No. 1367/2006 of the European Parliament and of the Council of 6 September 2006 on the application of the provisions of the Aarhus Convention on Access to Information,

implementing decisions of the kind that featured in Case C-281/16, *Vereniging Hoekschewaards Landschap*. This would avoid the need to apply to a national court.

The adoption of the original Aarhus Regulation followed the EU ratification of the Convention in 2005.[1412] The Regulation was intended to apply the Aarhus Convention's provisions to the EU institutions and bodies and it set out provisions on access to information, public participation and access to justice. The access-to-justice provisions consisted of an entitlement of certain environmental associations to request an EU institution to carry out an administrative review of certain decisions of that institution. The administrative review generated a decision of the Commission addressed to the applicant, which enabled the applicant to invoke the first limb of Article 263 before the General Court of the CJEU. The decisions for which requests could be made were defined very narrowly, however (they did not cover the kind of decision that featured in C-281/16 *Vereniging Hoekschewaards Landschap*), and, in practice, almost all judicial reviews were deemed inadmissible.

In 2017, in a case before it,[1413] the Aarhus Convention Compliance Committee (ACCC), which verifies whether Parties correctly implement the Convention, adopted findings to the effect that, in respect of Article 9(3) and (4) of the Convention, neither the case-law of the CJEU, nor the Aarhus Regulation provide adequate administrative or judicial review of non-legislative environmental acts.[1414] The Committee recommended that the CJEU modify its case-law or that the EU amend the Aarhus Regulation or adopt new legislation. The outcome was the EU's amendment in 2021 of the Aarhus Regulation.[1415] The amendment, amongst other things, expanded the kinds of decisions that could be the subject of a request for administrative review, thus enlarging the potential scope for using of the first limb of Article 263(4). It is the institution's decision on the administrative review rather than the non-legislative act itself that can be appealed to the General Court. Nevertheless, provided the applicant submits grounds addressing the substantive and procedural legality of the contested non-legislative act, any subsequent Article 263(4) judicial review will look in probing detail at how the institution concerned addressed those grounds.[1416]

The revision of the Aarhus Regulation is an instance of the expansion of access to justice in environmental matters, a phenomenon also driven by the Court's case-law in respect of the Member States, including in relation to the nature directives.

Public Participation in Decision-making and Access to Justice in Environmental Matters to Community institutions and bodies, OJ L 264, 25.9.2006, p. 13-19.

1412. Council Decision 2005/370/EC of 17 February 2005 on the conclusion, on behalf of the European Community, of the Convention on access to information, public participation in decision-making and access to justice in environmental matters, OJ L 124, 17.5.2005, p. 1.

1413. Case ACCC/2008/32. The ACCC examines communications from individuals and environmental associations on alleged non-compliance with the Convention.

1414. The Convention excludes legislation from its scope.

1415. Regulation (EU) 2021/1767 of the European Parliament and of the Council of 6 October 2021 amending Regulation (EC) No. 1367/2006 on the application of the provisions of the Aarhus Convention on Access to Information, Public Participation in Decision-making and Access to Justice in Environmental Matters to Community institutions and bodies, OJ L 356, 8.10.2021, p. 1-7.

1416. T-108/17, *ClientEarth*, paras 55-58.

§8.06 ACCESS TO JUSTICE AT MEMBER STATE LEVEL

[A] Importance of Access to Justice to the Nature Case-Law and the Nature Directives

There are several reasons why access to justice at Member State level is important for the nature case-law. First, preliminary references depend on litigation before the national courts. The role of Article 267 in ensuring the uniform interpretation and application of the nature directives may be put in doubt if access to national courts is rendered either impossible or excessively difficult. Second, the nature case-law has a specific access to justice dimension, i.e., the nature case-law itself provides important clarification on access to justice. Third, national courts are 'the ordinary courts' for implementing EU law within the legal systems of the Member States. The nature case-law forms part of EU law and, where relevant to subsequent national disputes, Court interpretations of the nature directives ought to be adhered to by national administrations and national courts. Restrictive national approaches to access to justice may result in national courts being unable to review national administrative decisions that are inconsistent with the nature case-law. This will undermine the uniform application of the directives.

Independently of these specific links to the nature case-law, access to justice at Member State level matters for the nature directives, because it serves as a means of holding public authorities to account for their implementation. It is also a means of ensuring that grievances concerning the directives are addressed.

[B] Access to Justice: A Set of Guarantees

But what does access to justice in environmental matters actually comprise? A European Commission Citizen's Guide[1417] describes access to justice in environmental matters as 'a set of guarantees that allows members of the public to challenge the legality of decisions, acts or omissions of public authorities of the Member States before a national judge'. 'Members of the public' means individuals and their associations. The set of guarantees covers what should happen before, during and after the bringing of a challenge and comprises: a right to bring a challenge, called 'standing'; a sufficient examination of the challenge by a national judge; steps by the judge to put matters right if they agree with the challenge, called 'effective remedies' or 'reliefs'; protection of the claimant from facing prohibitive costs for bringing the challenge, in particular if the judge rejects it; timeliness in the handling of the challenge; and practical information on how to bring a challenge.

1417. Citizen's Guide to Access to Justice in Environmental Matters, Publications Office of the European Union 2018, ISBN: 978-92-79-89648-4, DOI:10.2779/62435. This is available at: https://op.europa.eu/en/publication-detail/-/publication/2b362f0a-bfe4-11e8-99ee-01aa75ed71a1/language-en/format-PDF.

[C] Challengeable Decisions, Acts and Omissions

The notion of challengeable decisions, acts and omissions may concern many different decision-making levels, institutions and decision-makers: national parliaments, regional assemblies and governments responsible for adopting legislation and regulatory acts; nature conservation authorities responsible for site management; ministries and local authorities responsible for adopting plans and programmes; authorities responsible for authorising individual activities, including derogations, or enforcing requirements and prohibitions. As Chapters 2, 3 and 4 show, the nature case-law provides illustrations of national legal challenges to decisions made at very different levels by different kinds of authority.

[D] Sources of Access to Justice Guarantees

The guarantees are grounded in several legal texts, some general and others environmental, and, crucially, in the case-law of the Court – including the nature case-law. As has already been observed, the ACCC has also played a role in shaping access to justice.

[1] Treaty and Charter of Fundamental Rights

Article 19(1) of the TEU requires Member States to provide remedies sufficient to ensure effective legal protection in the fields covered by EU law. When they are implementing EU law, Member States are bound by Article 47 of the Charter of Fundamental Rights[1418] which enshrines in its first paragraph the right to an effective remedy. Article 47 of the Charter corresponds to Article 6 and Article 13 of the European Convention on Human Rights (ECHR) which enshrine, respectively, the right to a fair trial and the right to an effective remedy.

[2] Aarhus Convention

To these general provisions can be added environmental access to justice provisions set out in Article 9 of the Aarhus Convention, which was signed in 1998 and ratified by the EU in 2005.

Article 9(2) requires contracting parties to provide access to a review procedure before a court of law and/or another independent and impartial body established by law, to challenge the substantive and procedural legality of any decision, act or omission subject to the provisions of Article 6 of the Convention, which governs public participation in relation to decisions on specific activities. Article 9(2) is limited to decisions, acts and omissions of public authorities and is for the benefit of the '*public concerned*'.

1418. Inserted into the EU treaty framework by the Lisbon Treaty in 2009.

Article 9(3) requires contracting parties to provide broader access to justice. More specifically, it requires contracting parties to ensure that, where they meet the criteria, if any, laid down in its national law, members of the public have access to administrative or judicial procedures to challenge acts and omissions by private persons and public authorities which contravene provisions of its national law relating to the environment. In this context, 'national law' includes EU law and the definition of '*the public*' includes environmental associations.

Articles 9(4) and (5) provide for a set of overarching ancillary guarantees. Parties are required to ensure that their review procedures provide 'adequate and effective remedies, including injunctive relief as appropriate'. Procedures are required to be 'fair, equitable, timely and not prohibitively expensive.'

[3] EU Legislation

As part of the process of adhering to the Convention, the EU inserted access to justice clauses corresponding to the relevant provisions of Article 9 into a number of pieces of EU environmental legislation, notably the EIA Directive (the nature directives were not, however, included). The Commission also proposed a general directive on access to justice to mirror the broad provisions of Article 9(3) of the Convention.[1419] This did not win enough support from Member States, however, and the proposal was ultimately withdrawn.

[a] EIA Directive

Article 11 of its codified version, Directive 2011/92/EU, gives effect to Article 9(2) of the Aarhus Convention. The access- to- justice provision was inserted into the original EIA Directive by Directive 2003/35/EC and took effect in 2005.

[b] Environmental Liability Directive

The Environmental Liability Directive, 2004/35/EC, has a tailored access to justice provision[1420] linked to an entitlement to make submissions relating to instances of environmental damage and to request action from the competent authorities.[1421] Environmental associations are amongst the persons included in this entitlement. The access to justice provision allows those entitled to request action to also seek a review of the procedural and substantive legality of the decisions, acts or failure to act of the competent authority. Case C-297/19, Naturschutzbund Deutschland, presented in Chapter 6 is an example of use of this provision by an environmental association.[1422]

1419. Proposal for a Directive of the European Parliament and of the Council on access to justice in environmental matters, COM/2003/0624 final.
1420. Article 13, Directive 2004/35/EC.
1421. Article 12, Directive 2004/35/EC.
1422. *See* Chapter 6, §6.04[B][2].

[4] *Case-Law*

Despite the setback of rejection of the Commission's general proposal on access to justice, access to justice in environmental matters made advances. In particular, through a succession of preliminary references, a significant body of Court of Justice case-law was built up. The extent and far-reaching implications of this case-law were already apparent when the Commission decided to adopt a Notice (interpretative communication) on access to justice in environmental matters in 2017.[1423] This mapped the access- to- justice case-law as it then stood. The case-law has since continued to develop.

[E] Commission Policy on Access to Justice

Commission policy recognises the general importance of access to justice, as is clear from the Commission's standard complaint form, which draws attention to the crucial role of national courts in providing remedies for grievances.[1424]

Commission policy also specifically acknowledges the importance of access to justice in environmental matters, as the 2017 Notice and a 2020 Communication on improving access to justice in environmental matters in the EU and its Member States testify.[1425] The Commission's E-Justice Portal contains a fact sheet for each Member State, describing how access to justice in environmental matters works there.[1426]

The 2020 Biodiversity Strategy specifically mentions access to justice, stating:

> In addition, the Commission will support civil society's role as a compliance watchdog and will engage with Member States to improve access to justice in national courts in environmental matters for individuals and NGOs .[1427]

[F] Standing

Individuals or environmental associations can only be heard by a national court if they have recognised legal standing. Standing is fundamental to access to justice. Without it, it will not be possible to mount a successful legal challenge before a national court.

A general right to be heard (the so-called actio popularis) does not exist in EU law. Instead, standing is linked to the existence of procedural or substantive rights conferred by EU law. Standing is for the purpose of protecting these.

This creates an obvious difficulty for nature. As the Advocate General observed in Case C-664/15, *Protect*:

1423. Commission Notice on access to justice in environmental matters, C/2017/2616, OJ C 275, 18.8.2017, p. 1-39.
1424. https://ec.europa.eu/assets/sg/report-a-breach/complaints_en/.
1425. Communication on improving access to justice in environmental matters in the EU and its Member States, COM(2020) 643 final.
1426. https://e-justice.europa.eu/300/EN/access_to_justice_in_environmental_matters.
1427. Communication EU Biodiversity Strategy for 2030, COM(2020) 380 final, section 3.2.

> Neither water nor the fish swimming in it can go to court. Trees likewise have no legal standing.[1428]

It is legally possible to give nature or parts of nature independent legal standing. This possibility comes within the scope of the so-called rights of nature concept. The possibility has been explored in a legal study commissioned by the European Parliament.[1429]

Under current EU law, nature itself does not enjoy standing, however. How then has it been possible for individuals and environmental associations to invoke the nature directives before national courts? To understand how, one needs to consider Member States' legal systems, the kinds of rights that EU law confers, the Aarhus Convention and a series of landmark Court of Justice decisions.

Member States' legal systems vary in their approach to standing. Some require claimants to demonstrate a sufficient interest in the decision, act or omission being contested. Others require claimants to show that the decision, act or omission has impaired or could impair rights that they enjoy. Some systems are more generous than others. For example, in Case C-44/95, *Lappel Bank*, a British environmental association, the Royal Society for the Protection of Birds, was able to challenge a ministerial decision to exclude an area of coastal wetland from an SPA. This shows that, from the earliest days of preliminary references on the nature directives, some national jurisdictions allowed litigants to represent the interests of nature in a legal challenge, taking a broad view of what a sufficient interest could cover. Such standing could not be taken for granted across all national jurisdictions, however. In these circumstances, access to justice derived from EU law became important.

In terms of the rights conferred by EU law, one can distinguish between procedural rights and substantive rights.

Procedural rights usually relate to public participation. They typically have to do with the practical arrangements whereby a public authority informs the public of a proposed decision, receives any submissions, takes these into account and publicly announces its decision. In 1985, the EIA Directive introduced express public participation provisions and these have since been joined by participation provisions in other directives, notably the SEA Directive. The Habitats Directive contains a brief reference to public consultation in its Article 6(3). In Case C-72/95, *Kraaijeveld*, the Court confirmed that the public participation provisions of the EIA Directive could be relied on by individuals before a national court. This was before a specific access-to-justice clause was introduced into that directive. The Court observed:

> In particular, where the Community authorities have, by directive, imposed on Member States the obligation to pursue a particular course of conduct, the useful effect of such an act would be weakened if individuals were prevented from relying on it before their national courts.[1430]

1428. Opinion of the Advocate General in C-664/15, *Protect*, para. 77.
1429. Jan Darpö, *Can Nature Get It Right? A Study on Rights of Nature in the European Context* (European Parliament, Policy Department for Citizens' Rights and Constitutional Affairs Directorate-General for Internal Policies PE 689.328, March 2021).
1430. C-72/95 *Kraaijeveld*, para. 56.

In addition to procedural rights, the Court has recognised that certain EU environmental provisions confer substantive rights on individuals and their associations. These may relate to property ownership or human health, for example.

Procedural and substantive rights are not mutually exclusive. A decision, act or omission of a public authority may have implications for both.

Apart from providing for access to justice, the Aarhus Convention gave a boost to procedural rights and also underscored the role of civic engagement in environmental protection, in particular via the role of environmental associations. The Convention envisages public participation in decisions on specific activities;[1431] plans, programmes and policies relating to the environment;[1432] and executive regulations and/or generally applicable legally binding normative instruments.[1433] The Convention embraces the role of associations, organisations and groups as part of 'the public' and of 'non-governmental organisations promoting environmental protection' as part of the 'public concerned'.[1434]

The foregoing set the scene for the emergence of specific case-law of the Court on access to justice in relation to the nature directives. The access-to-justice case-law is broader than the nature case-law but, in several important judgments, they overlap.

Four cases, in particular, deserve mention: Case C-240/09, Slovak Brown Bears; Case C-115/09, *Trianel*; Case C-243/15, *LZ II*, and Case C-432/21, *Commission v. Poland.*

Chronologically, Case C-240/09, *Slovak Brown Bears*, was decided first, in March 2011. The Court broke new ground in laying out a basis in Article 9(3) of the Aarhus Convention in combination with Article 47 of the Charter of Fundamental Rights for providing an environmental association with access to judicial review in relation to derogation decisions under the Habitats Directive. This landmark decision is presented in more detail in Chapter 4.[1435]

In Case C-115/09, *Trianel*, decided shortly afterwards, in May 2011, the Court found another means of supporting access to justice in relation to the nature directives, this time via the explicit access-to-justice provisions of the EIA Directive. The case is presented in more detail in Chapter 3.[1436]

Case C-243/15, *LZ II*, presented in Chapter 3,[1437] constituted another important step forward, with the Court deriving important participatory and access-to-justice rights from a combination of Article 6(3) of the Habitats Directive, Articles 6(1)(b) and 9(2) of the Aarhus Convention and Article 47 of the Charter of Fundamental Rights.

The added value of Case C-240/09, *Slovak Brown Bears*, and Case C-243/15, *LZ II*, depended on national courts being willing to interpret restrictive national procedural rules in a manner that gave effect to the Court's own broad interpretation of access to

1431. Article 6 of the Aarhus Convention.
1432. Article 7 of the Aarhus Convention.
1433. Article 8 of the Aarhus Convention.
1434. *See* definitions of 'the public' and 'the public concerned' in the Convention's Article 2(4) and its Article 2(5) respectively.
1435. Chapter 4, §4.03[G].
1436. Chapter 3, §3.04[G][2][a].
1437. Chapter 3, §3.04[G][2][b].

justice rights under EU law – 'jurisprudential' access to justice, i.e., access to justice affirmed by the Court's case-law rather than enshrined in secondary EU legislation. This left an open question as to how the Court would deal with a situation where national courts were not prepared to deviate from restrictive national procedural rules.

The answer came with the Court's judgment in Case C-432/21, *Commission v. Poland,* in which it held that certain Polish legislation was contrary to EU law because it did not ensure access to justice in respect of forestry-related decisions concerning the Habitats Directive. As indicated in Chapter 3,[1438] the Polish Supreme Court had previously declined, on procedural grounds, to allow legal challenges to these decisions. The position of the Supreme Court showed that that EU jurisprudential case-law could not always be relied on as an 'open sesame' to judicial review. The Court was thus obliged to take a further step to uphold its own case-law.

Case C-432/21, *Commission v. Poland,* also demonstrates the crucial role of the Commission as a guarantor of jurisprudential access to justice. Without the Commission's direct action, access to the Polish courts might have remained blocked. In terms of securing national judicial oversight of the nature directives, this underscores the inter-institutional importance of the Commission acting as 'guardian' of the Treaties.

[G] Examination of the Case by the National Court

The purpose of a judicial review is to determine the procedural or substantive legality of a decision, act or omission. This requires the national judge to examine the facts behind a public authority's action or inaction and to examine what obligations the authority was required to fulfil under any applicable EU law.

Assuming that the national proceedings are admissible, what intensity of scrutiny or standard of review is required of the national judge, in particular, given that the Treaties and the Aarhus Convention are not explicit on this?

The Court has held that, in the absence of EU rules, it is for the legal system of each Member State to lay down the detailed procedural rules governing actions for safeguarding rights derived from EU law. Approaches may and do differ. As in many other contexts, however, the principle of effectiveness comes into play, i.e., the rules must not make it impossible in practice or excessively difficult to exercise the rights concerned.[1439] Also important are the specific requirements of individual pieces of EU legislation and how the Court has interpreted these.

In respect of the nature directives, the Court's interpretation of Article 6(3) of the Habitats Directive in Case C-127/02 *Waddenzee,* is especially significant, in particular the Court's ruling that the competent authorities may only authorise an activity in a protected Natura 2000 site where, taking into account the conclusions of an appropriate assessment, no reasonable scientific doubt remains that, in light of the site's conservation objectives, the activity will not adversely affect the integrity of the site.[1440]

1438. Chapter 3, §3.04[G][2][c].
1439. C-71/14 *East Sussex,* para. 52.
1440. C-127/02 *Waddenzee,* para. 59.

In examining any case in which Article 6(3) figures, a national judge will need to ensure adherence to this precautionary approach. In particular, the judge will need to determine whether the available scientific evidence relied on by the public authority left any reasonable doubt. This will mean looking at the relevant scientific evidence. The test of whether there is no reasonable doubt is an objective one and cannot be treated as a subjective one lying within the competent authority's sole discretion. This is confirmed by Case C-209/02, *Commission v. Austria* [*see* section §8.03[G][2][b][iii] above].

More generally, to the extent that it arises from preliminary references, the case-law presented in Chapters 3, 4, 5 and 6 provides many examples of how national courts ought to scrutinise actions or inactions of competent authorities.

[H] Effective Remedies

In general, it will not be sufficient for a national court to determine whether a particular decision, act or omission was lawful. If it finds that a public authority has acted unlawfully in relation to the nature directives as interpreted by the case-law, it will need to put matters right, i.e., it will need to order effective remedies or 'reliefs'.

What should it do? The nature directives are silent on the matter. Article 9(4) of the Aarhus Convention requires judicial review procedures to provide adequate and effective remedies, including *injunctive relief* as appropriate. It does not, however, go into detail.

The kinds of relief that a national court can provide are governed by national procedural autonomy. Member States themselves set out the detailed procedural rules to be followed. Different legal systems and traditions have, in practice, provided for a similar range of reliefs, i.e., they allow courts to select from a range of orders that tend to be broadly comparable. The case-law of the Court also provides significant clarification on the appropriateness of different reliefs.

[1] Relationship with Obligation to Nullify Unlawful Consequences of a Breach and Obligation to Prevent Breaches

There is significant overlap with the requirement that every organ of a Member State, including its courts, must nullify the unlawful consequences of a breach of EU law. This requirement, which the Court has derived from Article 4(3) of the TEU, is explained in detail in relation to Article 6 of the Habitats Directive in Chapter 3,§3.04[F][3].

The duty of cooperation in Article 4(3) also requires that breaches be prevented before they occur, with Member States being obliged to refrain from taking any measures that can seriously compromise the attainment of a result prescribed by EU environmental law.[1441] National legal systems must provide for reliefs that comply with these requirements.

1441. *See* Case C-129/96 *Inter-Environnement Wallonie*, para. 45.

[2] Principles of Equivalence and Effectiveness

Member States have discretion with regard to reliefs, provided these are consistent with the principles of equivalence and effectiveness. According to the former, reliefs for a breach of EU law should be no less favourable than those governing similar domestic situations. According to the latter, reliefs should not render it impossible in practice or excessively difficult to exercise rights conferred by EU law.

[3] Range of Possibilities

Against this background, the appropriateness of using a particular kind of national court order will depend on the context and whether a breach has caused actual harm.

[a] Injunctive Relief

With regard to injunctive relief, the Article 279 nature case-law mentioned above is instructive by analogy. Also instructive by analogy is a preliminary reference on injunctive relief related to the permitting of a landfill, Case C-416/10 *Križan*. In that case, the Court recalled that the possibility of interim measures is a general requirement of the EU legal order. In the absence of EU rules, and in line with the principle of procedural autonomy, it is up to Member States to lay down the detailed conditions for granting interim measures. Case C-504/14, *Commission v. Greece*, is also relevant by analogy, since the Court expressly referred to the appropriateness of provisional measures in the context of Article 6(2) of the Habitats Directive and of proceedings by the competent authorities aimed at addressing illegal road developments.[1442] Where disputes concern a failure to act or to take appropriate measures, it will be appropriate for the national court by order to direct the responsible authority to take specific action.

[b] Suspending, Revoking or Annulling Decisions, and Disapplying Conflicting Provisions

As indicated in Chapter 3, §3.04[F][4] in the coverage of Case C-278/21, *Aquapri*, orders to suspend, revoke or annul may be appropriate in respect of unlawful decisions or acts, for example, the approval of a project or plan in contravention of the procedural requirements of Article 6(3) of the Habitats Directive. Sometimes, a national court may need to disapply national legislation or regulatory acts which are in conflict with the nature directives.

[c] Remedial Measures for Harm Caused

What should happen if an unlawful decision, act or omission has already caused environmental harm? How should the harm be made good? This eventuality is addressed in Case C-399/14, *Grüne Liga Sachsen*, covered in detail in Chapter 3,

1442. *See* Chapter 3 §3.04[H][7].

§3.04[G][5]. As noted, the Court did not exclude that the required outcome might involve removal of infrastructure works completed under an impugned national procedure.

From the Court's reasoning, it can also be inferred that compensatory measures might be required. Otherwise, an irregular procedure might confer an advantage.

The Environmental Liability Directive is potentially relevant in such a situation since it provides for remedial measures for 'damage to protected species and natural habitats', a concept closely aligned with the content of the nature directives.[1443]

[d] Contempt of Court

The Court's access-to-justice case-law confronts a possibility which might conceivably arise in relation to the nature directives. This is the possibility of a public authority being unwilling to adhere to a court order. As already indicated in section §8.03[F] above, the Court itself was convinced that it might face such a prospect in relation to its own first interim order in Case C-441/17 R, *Białowieżka*. Hence its anticipation of the possible need to impose a penalty. But what might happen if such a situation arose in national proceedings? What options would a national court have? There is no explicit guidance in the nature case-law, except perhaps Case C-441/17 R, *Białowieżka*, by analogy, but in a preliminary reference on air pollution, Case C-752/18, *Deutsche Umwelthilfe*, the Court sheds light on how a national court should respond if a national authority refuses to comply with a judicial decision.

§8.07 CONCLUSIONS

The nature case-law is a reflection of the scope and effectiveness of the Article 258 and Article 267 procedures. Each procedure has proved its worth.

Because of its pre-litigation stage, use of the Article 258 procedure may not always lead to a case or case-law. Disputes between the Commission and a Member State may be resolved early on, removing any need to involve the Court. Indeed, a great many Article 258 procedures are shelved without any Court application. Useful outcomes are achieved but these rarely attract notice. If evaluated simply as a means of allowing the Court to pass judgment on a Member State's implementation of the nature directives, the procedure nevertheless shows its effectiveness. It has allowed the Commission to litigate a very wide range of conformity and bad application disputes. Individual cases can be quite narrow in scope, focusing on a single problem or location, or they can be extremely wide-ranging. They can be solely about conformity or solely about bad application or a complex combination of each, with multiple separate pleas. They can address one or both of the nature directives or address one or both of these

1443. *See* Commission Notice on Guidelines providing a common understanding of the term 'environmental damage' as defined in Article 2 of Directive 2004/35/EC of the European Parliament and of the Council on environmental liability with regard to the prevention and remedying of environmental damage (2021/C 118/01).

in combination with another instrument, such as the EIA Directive. Provided the Commission can satisfy the burden of proof, the Court never questions the Commission's choice of claims to put forward.

The procedure tends to be slow-moving, usually lasting several years, but, as section §8.03[H] above demonstrates, the Court has responded positively to requests for interim measures under Article 279. It has also made clear that it will uphold its own authority during the litigation process itself, as Case C-441/17, *Białowieżka* shows.

In terms of follow-up, the penalty provisions of Article 260 have, on the whole, proved effective in incentivising Member States to comply with Court judgments.

For its part, Article 267 has allowed many important issues of implementation to benefit from the Court of Justice's interpretation. It has allowed questions to be raised which the Commission might have hesitated to test in a direct action. As a result, references have sometimes played a 'path-finding' role, clarifying provisions in a manner that has helped the Commission to define its grounds in subsequent Article 258 cases.

Both in relation to the nature directives and more generally, Article 267 has clarified requirements to provide access to justice in the Member States. Rulings on standing have opened possibilities for environmental associations where national courts might previously have been closed to them. Rulings on other aspects of access to justice provide considerable clarity on how national courts should use or adapt national procedural autonomy to address issues of compliance with the nature directives in proceedings before them. This has served to buttress the role of national courts in overseeing implementation of the directives.

The interplay of Article 267 and Article 258 is seen in the evolution of the nature case-law. This is not only to the advantage of the Commission in its use of Article 258. As Case C-432/21, *Commission v. Poland,* shows, the Commission's use of Article 258 can serve to secure possible future use of Article 267 by removing an obstacle to access to national courts.

Finally, while the procedures of Article 259 and Article 263(4) have not yet made any impact in relation to the nature directives, recent use of the former and adaptations relevant to the latter suggest how they might play a role under certain circumstances.

Bibliography

1972 Declaration of the United Nations Conference on the Human Environment, https://www.un.org/en/conferences/environment/stockholm1972.

Bern Convention on the conservation of European wildlife and natural habitats, OJ L 38, 10.2.1982, p. 3-32. https://eur-lex.europa.eu/legal-content/EN/TXT/?uri=celex%3A21979A0919%2801%29.

Jean-François Brakeland, *Access to Justice in Environmental Matters: Developments at EU Level* (published in the Gyoseiho-kenkyu, 2014, No. 5), untitled (osaka-u.ac.jp).

Mícheál Ó Bríain, *Recent Developments in Implementation of EU Nature Legislation,* in *Nature Law and Policy in Europe,* Chapter 2 (Andrew L.R. Jackson ed., Routledge 2023).

Briefing – Protected areas in the Eastern Partnership countries, https://www.eea.europa.eu/highlights/europes-eastern-partnership-countries-make.

Liam Cashman, *Ensuring Compliance, Regulatory Regimes under the EU Nature Directives,* in *Nature Law and Policy in Europe,* Chapter 4 (Andrew L.R. Jackson ed., Routledge 20).

Citizen's Guide to Access to Justice in Environmental Matters, Publications Office of the European Union 2018, ISBN: 978-92-79-89648-4, DOI:10.2779/62435.

Marc Clément (2010), Droit européen de l'environnement, Jurisprudence commentée, Editions Larcier.

Marc Clement, Global Objectives and Scope of the Habitats Directive: What Does the Obligation of Result Mean in Practice? The European Hamster in Alsace, published in The Habitats Directive in Its EU Environmental Law Context European Nature's Best Hope?, Charles-Hubert Born, An Cliquet, Hendrik Schoukens, Delphine Misonne & Geert Van Hoorick eds (Routledge, Abingdon, 2015).

Commission Notice Guidelines providing a common understanding of the term 'environmental damage' as defined in Article 2 of Directive 2004/35/EC of the European Parliament and of the Council on environmental liability with regard to the prevention and remedying of environmental damage 2021/C 118/01, C/2021/1860, OJ C 118, 7.4.2021, p. 1-49.

Commission Notice on access to justice in environmental matters, C/2017/2616, OJ C 275, 18.8.2017, pp. 1-39.

Commission Notice C(2018) 7621 final, Brussels, 21.11.2018 https://ec.europa.eu/environment/nature/natura2000/management/docs/art6/EN_art_6_guide_jun_2019.pdf.

Commission Notice on Guidelines providing a common understanding of the term 'environmental damage' as defined in Article 2 of Directive 2004/35/EC of the European Parliament and of the Council on environmental liability with regard to the prevention and remedying of environmental damage (2021/C 118/01).

Commission Notice Guidance document on the strict protection of animal species of Community interest under the Habitats Directive, C/2021/7301 final, EUR-Lex - C(2021)7301 - EN - EUR-Lex (europa.eu).

Communication 'Updating the handling of relations with the complainant in respect of the application of Union law', COM(2012) 154 of 2.4.2012; and Communication from the Commission - EU law: Better results through better application, C/2016/8600.

Communication EU Biodiversity Strategy for 2030, COM(2020) 380 final.

Communication from the Commission - Enforcing EU law for a Europe that delivers, COM(2022) 518.

Communication from the Commission to the European Parliament, the Council, the European Economic and Social Committee and the Committee of the Regions - EU Biodiversity Strategy for 2030, Bringing nature back into our lives, 20.05.2020, COM/2020/380 final, https://op.europa.eu/en/publication-detail/-/publication/a3c806a6-9ab3-11ea-9d2d-01aa75ed71a1/language-en.

Communication on actions to improve environmental compliance and governance, COM(2018)10; and Staff Working Document, SWD(2018)10.

Communication on implementing European Community environmental law, COM(2008) 773 final.

Communication on improving access to justice in environmental matters in the EU and its Member States, COM(2020) 643 final.

Communication on the Environmental Implementation Review 2022, Turning the tide through environmental compliance, COM/2022/438 final.

Council Decision 2005/370/EC of 17 February 2005 on the conclusion, on behalf of the European Community, of the Convention on access to information, public participation in decision-making and access to justice in environmental matters, OJL 124, 17.5.2005, p. 1.

Council Directive 79/409/EEC of 2 April 1979 on the conservation of wild birds, OJ L 103, 25.4.1979, p. 1.

Council Directive 85/337/EEC of 27 June 1985 on the assessment of the effects of certain public and private projects on the environment (OJ 1985 L 175, p. 40).

Council Directive 92/43/EEC of 21 May 1992 on the conservation of natural habitats and of wild fauna and flora, OJ L 206, 22.7.1992, p. 7-50.

Jan Darpö, *Can Nature Get It Right? A Study on Rights of Nature in the European Context* (European Parliament, Policy Department for Citizens' Rights and Constitutional Affairs Directorate-General for Internal Policies PE 689.328, March 2021).

Jan Darpö & Yaffa Epstein, Thrown to the Wolves: Sweden Once Again Flouts EU Standards on Species Protection and Access to Justice, Nordic Environmental Law Journal 7 (July 2015), NMT-12015-DarpoEpstein-6-juli.pdf (jandarpo.se)

Directive 2000/60/EC of the European Parliament and of the Council of 23 October 2000 establishing a framework for Community action in the field of water policy, OJ L 327, 22.12.2000, p. 1-73.

Directive 2001/42/EC of the European Parliament and of the Council of 27 June 2001 on the assessment of the effects of certain plans and programmes on the environment, OJ L 197, 21.7.2001, p. 30-37.

Directive 2001/77/EC of the European Parliament and of the Council of 27 September 2001 on the promotion of electricity produced from renewable energy sources in the internal electricity market, OJ L 283, 27.10.2001, p. 33-40.

Directive 2004/35/CE of the European Parliament and of the Council of 21 April 2004 on environmental liability with regard to the prevention and remedying of environmental damage, OJ L 143, 30.4.2004, p. 56-75.

Directive 2008/56/EC of the European Parliament and of the Council of 17 June 2008 establishing a framework for community action in the field of marine environmental policy, OJ L 164, 25.6.2008, p. 19-40.

Directive 2008/99/EC of the European Parliament and of the Council of 19 November 2008 on the protection of the environment through criminal law, OJ L 328, 6.12.2008, pp. 28-37.

Directive 2009/147/EC of the European Parliament and of the Council of 30 November 2009 on the conservation of wild birds, OJ L 20, 26.1.2010, p. 7-25, codifying Council Directive 79/409/EEC of 2 April 1979 on the conservation of wild birds.

Directive 2009/28/EC of the European Parliament and of the Council of 23 April 2009 on the promotion of the use of energy from renewable sources and amending and subsequently repealing Directives 2001/77/EC and 2003/30/EC, OJ L 140, 5.6.2009, p. 16-62.

Directive 2011/92/EU of the European Parliament and of the Council of 13 December 2011 on the assessment of the effects of certain public and private projects on the environment (codification) Text with EEA relevance, OJ L 26, 28.1.2012, p. 1-21.

Directive 2014/52/EU of the European Parliament and of the Council of 16 April 2014 amending Directive 2011/92/EU on the assessment of the effects of certain public and private projects on the environment, OJ L 124, 25.4.2014, p. 1-18.

Yaffa Epstein, *The Habitats Directive and Bern Convention: Synergy and Dysfunction in Public International and EU Law*, 26(2) Georgetown International Environmental Law Review (GIELR), 145-173 (2014), quoting Jean Pierre-Ribaut, How the Bern Convention Came into Being, Naturopa, 101/2004 https://rm.coe.int/090000168093e8a8.

Yaffa Epstein, José Vicente López-Bao & Guillaume Chapron, *Strict Protection of Species in the EU, Controversies and Trends*, in *Nature Law and Policy in Europe,* Chapter 10 (Andrew L.R. Jackson ed., Routledge 2023).

EU Biodiversity Strategy for 2030 (COM/2020/380 final), https://eur-lex.europa.eu/legal-content/EN/TXT/?qid=1590574123338&uri=CELEX:52020DC0380.

European Commission's Guidance document on the strict protection of animal species of Community interest under the Habitats Directive 92/43/EEC (final version of February 2007), https://ec.europa.eu/environment/nature/conservation/species/guidance/pdf/guidance_en.pdf.

European Commission's reporting under the EU Habitats and Birds Directives 2007–2012, 'The State of Nature in the EU'. State of nature in the EU – European Environment Agency (europa.eu).

European Environment Agency (EEA)'s Report No 10/2020, State of Nature in the EU, page 5, https://www.eea.europa.eu/publications/state-of-nature-in-the-eu-2020.

Eladio Fernández-Galiano, *A Laboratory of Ideas, 'The 25 years of the Bern Convention'*, Naturopa, 101/2004 https://rm.coe.int/090000168093e8a8.

Guidance document on hunting under the Birds Directive https://www.unece.org/fileadmin/DAM/env/pp/compliance/C2007-18/Communication/SupportingDocumentation2006.12.04/EUKommissionenGuidance_birdsdirect_en.pdf, the document was updated in 2008, *see* Circabc (europa.eu).and the European Commission's page Sustainable hunting under the Birds Directive (europa.eu).Guidelines for Population Level Management Plans for Large Carnivores, published by the European Commission in 2008 https://ec.europa.eu/environment/nature/conservation/species/carnivores/pdf/guidelines_for_population_level_management.pdf.

IPBES (Intergovernmental Science-Policy Platform on Biodiversity and Ecosystem Services) – The global assessment report on Biodiversity and Ecosystem Services (2019) – Summary for policymakers.

Andrew L.R. Jackson, *Conserving Europe's Wildlife: Law and Policy of the Natura 2000 Network of Protected Areas* (Routledge, 2018).

Andrew L.R. Jackson, *Conservation of Areas Outside the Natura 2000 Network: An Historical Perspective with an Eye to the Future,* in *Nature Law and Policy in Europe,* Chapter 11 (Andrew L.R. Jackson ed., Routledge 2023).

Ludwig Kramer, *EC Environmental Law, Sixth Edition,* 202 (Sweet and Maxwell, 2007).

John Temple Lang, *The Requirements for an Effective International Nature Conservation System, and the EU Birds and Habitats Directives,* 33, in *Nature Law and Policy in Europe,* Chapter 3 (Andrew L.R. Jackson ed., Routledge 2023).

Graham Machin, *Protecting Bird Habitat of European Importance: The View from Basses Corbières*, 6 Environmental Law Review 175-189 (2004).

Managing Natura 2000 Sites – The provisions of Article 6 of the 'Habitats' Directive 92/43/EEC, 2000 edition https://ec.europa.eu/environment/nature/natura2000/management/docs/art6/provision_of_art6_en.pdf.

Proposal for a Directive of the European Parliament and of the Council on access to justice in environmental matters, COM/2003/0624 final.

Proposal for a Regulation of the European Parliament and of the Council on nature restoration, 22.06.2022, COM/2022/304 final.

Regulation (EC) No 1367/2006 of the European Parliament and of the Council of 6 September 2006 on the application of the provisions of the Aarhus Convention on Access to Information, Public Participation in Decision-making and Access to Justice in Environmental Matters to Community institutions and bodies, OJ L 264, 25.9.2006, pp. 13-19.

Regulation (EU) 2021/1767 of the European Parliament and of the Council of 6 October 2021 amending Regulation (EC) No. 1367/2006 on the application of the provisions of the Aarhus Convention on Access to Information, Public Participation in Decision-making and Access to Justice in Environmental Matters to Community institutions and bodies, OJ L 356, 8.10.2021, pp. 1-7.

Regulation (EU) 2021/783 of the European Parliament and of the Council of 29 April 2021 establishing a Programme for the Environment and Climate Action (LIFE), and repealing Regulation (EU) No. 1293/2013, OJ L 172, 17.5.2021, p. 53-78.

Regulation (EU) No. 1143/2014 of the European Parliament and of the Council of 22 October 2014 on the prevention and management of the introduction and spread of invasive alien species, OJ L 317, 4.11.2014, p. 35-55.

Regulation (EU) No. 1305/2013 of the European Parliament and of the Council of 17 December 2013 on support for rural development by the European Agricultural Fund for Rural Development (EAFRD) and repealing Council Regulation (EC) No. 1698/2005, OJ L 347, 20.12.2013, p. 487-548.

Regulation (EU) 2021/2115 of the European Parliament and of the Council of 2 December 2021 establishing rules on support for strategic plans to be drawn up by Member States under the common agricultural policy (CAP Strategic Plans) and financed by the European Agricultural Guarantee Fund (EAGF) and by the European Agricultural Fund for Rural Development (EAFRD) and repealing Regulations (EU) No 1305/2013 and (EU) No 1307/2013, OJ L 435, 6.12.2021, pp. 1-186.

'Resolution on Institutional and Financial Arrangements' – Chapter III of the Report of the United Nations Conference on the Human environment, https://undocs.org/en/A/CONF.48/14/Rev.1

Revised Resolution No. 2 (1993) of the Standing Committee on the scope of Articles 8 and 9 of the Bern Convention, Strasbourg, 2 December 2011 https://rm.coe.int/16807461dd.

Nicolas de Sadeleer, *EU Environmental Law and the Internal Market,* Chapter 5, 291 and 295 (Oxford University Press, 2014).

Hendrik Schoukens, Ongoing Activities and Natura 2000, Biodiversity Protection vs Legitimate Expectations?, 11 Journal for European Environmental & Planning Law 1-30 (2014).

Hendrik Schoukens & Kees Bastmeijer, Species Protection in the European Union: How Strict Is It?, in The Habitats Directive in Its EU Environmental Law Context:

European Nature's Best Hope?', 13 (Charles-Hubert Born, An Cliquet, Hendrik Schoukens, Delphine Misonne & Geert Van Hoorick eds Routledge, Abingdon, Oxford 2014).

Single European Act, OJ L 169, 29.6.1987, pp. 1-28, ELI: http://data.europa.eu/eli/treaty/sea/sign.

Hendrik Shoukens, *Science and the Interpretation of the EU Habitats Directive by the Court of Justice of the EU, 2 + 2 = 5?*, in *Nature Law and Policy in Europe,* Chapter 10 (Andrew L.R. Jackson ed., Routledge 2023).

Christoph Sobotta, *The Margin of Appreciation When Applying Article 6(3) and (4) of the Habitats Directive*, in *Nature Law and Policy in Europe,* Chapter 5 (Andrew L.R. Jackson ed., Routledge 20.

Lorenzo Squintani, Assistant Professor of European and Economic Law, University of Groningen, The Netherlands, 13 The Journal for European Environmental & Planning Law 239-246 (2016).

Summary Guide on combating environmental crimes and related infringements, available at: https://op.europa.eu/en/publication-detail/-/publication/ce99f624-5cc2-11ec-91ac-01aa75ed71a1; and Guidance on combating environmental crimes and related infringements, available at: https://op.europa.eu/en/publication-detail/-/publication/e004a9c9-596a-11ec-91ac-01aa75ed71a1.

Summary Guide on environmental compliance assurance in rural areas, available at: https://op.europa.eu/en/publication-detail/-/publication/236733b9-69c2-11eb-aeb5-01aa75ed71a1#:~:text=Environmental%20compliance%20assurance%20in%20rural%20areas%20A%20summary,other%20rural%20land-managers%20comply%20with%20their%20environmental%20obligations.

Technical document published by the European Commission, on large carnivores, https://ec.europa.eu/environment/nature/conservation/species/carnivores/pdf/key_actions_large_carnivores_2015.pdf, visited on 11 March 2021.

'The Birds Directive: 40 years conserving our shared natural heritage', publication of the European Commission, https://ec.europa.eu/environment/nature/conservation/wildbirds/40%20yrs%20Birds%20Brochure%20WEB.pdf.

'The Contributions of the EU Nature Directives to the CBD and Other Multilateral Environmental Agreements', Alison E. Beresford, Graeme M. Buchanan, Fiona J. Sanderson, Rebecca Jefferson, & Paul F. Donald, in Conservation Letters, A Journal for the Society for Conservation Biology, DOI: 10.1111/conl. 12259. https://conbio.onlinelibrary.wiley.com/doi/pdf/10.1111/conl.12259.

The Global Risks Report 2020, p. 7, http://www3.weforum.org/docs/WEF_Global_Risk_Report_2020.pdf, visited on 15/03/2021.

To Say What the Law of the EU Is: Methods of Interpretation and the European Court of Justice, Lenaerts and Guttierez-Fons, 2013, European University Institute. Distinguished Lecture delivered on the occasion of the XXIV Law of the European Union course of the Academy of European Law, on 6 July 2013.

Arie Trouwborst & Floor M. Fleurke, *Killing Wolves Legally: Exploring the Scope for Lethal Wolf Management under European Nature Conservation Law*, 22(3)

Journal of International Wildlife Law & Policy, 231-273 (2019) DOI: 10.1080/13880292.2019.1686223.

UNECE Convention on Access to Information, Public Participation in Decision-making and Access to Justice in Environmental Matters (Aarhus Convention) in the appropriate language adopted on 25 June 1998, https://unece.org/environment-policy/public-participation/aarhus-convention/text.

Agustín García Ureta, *EU Biodiversity Law: Wild Birds and Habitats Directives* (Europa Law Publishing 2020).

Vade Mecum on environmental compliance assurance in rural areas, available at: https://op.europa.eu/en/publication-detail/-/publication/278dd7f1-69bb-11eb-aeb5-01aa75ed71a1/language-en/format-PDF/source-search.

Matthijs van Wolferen, *University of Groningen, The Netherlands, Case C-243/15 Lesoochranárske zoskupenie vlk v. Obvodný úrad Trenčín*, 14 The Journal for European Environmental & Planning Law 136-151 (2017).

Web page of the Bonn Convention of the Conservation of Migratory Species of Wild Animals, www.cms.int/en/convention-text.

Web page of the European Commission, Environment, on the Birds Directive, https://ec.europa.eu/environment/nature/legislation/birdsdirective/index_en.htm.

Web page of the European Commission, Environment, on the Habitats Directive, https://ec.europa.eu/environment/nature/legislation/habitatsdirective/index_en.htm.

Web page of the Ramsar Convention on Wetlands, https://www.ramsar.org/fr.

World Wildlife Fund (2018), Living Planet Report – 2018: Aiming Higher, https://www.wwf.org.uk/sites/default/files/2018-10/wwfintl_livingplanet_full.pdf.

Gerd Winter, *Plaumann Withering: Standing Before the EU General Court Underway from Distinctive to Substantial Concern,* European Journal of Legal Studies, 2023.

Table of Cases

Index

D

E

G

H

I

J

K

L

M

N

O

P

Q

R

S

T

U

W

ENERGY AND ENVIRONMENTAL LAW & POLICY SERIES

1. Stephen J. Turner, *A Substantive Environmental Right: An Examination of the Legal Obligations of Decision-makers towards the Environment*, 2009 (ISBN 978-90-411-2815-7).
2. Helle Tegner Anker, Birgitte Egelund Olsen & Anita Rønne (eds), *Legal Systems and Wind Energy: A Comparative Perspective*, 2009 (ISBN 978-90-411-2831-7).
3. David Langlet, *Prior Informed Consent and Hazardous Trade: Regulating Trade in Hazardous Goods at the Intersection of Sovereignty, Free Trade and Environmental Protection*, 2009 (ISBN 978-90-411-2821-8).
4. Louis J. Kotzé and Alexander R. Paterson (eds), *The Role of the Judiciary in Environmental Governance: Comparative Perspectives*, 2009 (ISBN 978-90-411-2708-2).
5. Tuula Honkonen, *The Common but Differentiated Responsibility Principle in Multilateral Environmental Agreement's: Regulatory and Policy Aspects*, 2009 (ISBN 978-90-411-3153-9).
6. Barbara Pozzo (ed.), *The Implementation of the Seveso Directives in an Enlarged Europe: A Look into the Past and a challenge for the Future*, 2009 (ISBN 978-90-411-2854-6).
7. Henrik M. Inadomi, *Independent Power Projects in Developing Countries: Legal Investment Protection and Consequences for Development*, 2010 (ISBN 978-90-411-3178-2).
8. Nahid Islam, *The Law of Non-Navigational Uses of International Watercourses: Options for Regional Regime-Building in Asia*, 2010 (ISBN 978-90-411-3196-6).
9. Yasuhiro Shigeta, *International Judicial Control of Environmental Protection: Standard Setting, Compliance Control and the Development of International Environmental Law by the International Judiciary*, 2010 (ISBN 978-90-411-3151-5).
10. Katleen Janssen, *The Availability of Spatial and Environmental Data in the European Union: At the Crossroads between Public and Economic Interests*, 2010 (ISBN 978-90-411-3287-1).
11. Henrik Bjørnebye, *Investing in EU Energy Security: Exploring the Regulatory Approach to Tomorrow's Electricity Production*, 2010 (ISBN 978-90-411-3118-8).
12. Véronique Bruggeman, *Compensating catastrophe victims: A Comparative Law and Economics Approach*, 2010 (ISBN 978-90-411-3263-5).
13. Michael G. Faure, Han Lixin & Shan Hongjun, *Maritime Pollution Liability and Policy: China, Europe and the US*, 2010 (ISBN 978-90-411-2869-0).

14. Anton Ming-Zhi Gao, *Regulating Gas Liberalization: A Comparative Study on Unbundling and Open Access Regimes in the US, Europe, Japan, South Korea and Taiwan*, 2010 (ISBN 978-90-411-3347-2).
15. Mustafa Erkan, *International Energy Investment Law: Stability through Contractual Clauses*, 2011 (ISBN 978-90-411-3411-0).
16. Levente Borzsa´k, *The Impact of Environmental Concerns on the Public Enforcement Mechanism under EU law: Environmental protection in the 25th hour*, 2011 (ISBN 978-90-411-3408-0).
17. Tarcísio Hardman Reis, *Compensation for Environmental Damages under International Law: The Role of the International Judge*, 2011 (ISBN 978-90-411-3437-0).
18. Kim Talus, *Vertical Natural Gas Transportation Capacity, Upstream Commodity Contracts and EU Competition Law*, 2011 (ISBN 978-90-411-3407-3).
19. WangHui, *Civil Liability for Marine Oil Pollution Damage: A Comparative and Economic Study of the International, US and Chinese Compensation Regime*, 2011 (ISBN 978-90-411-3672-5).
20. Chowdhury Ishrak Ahmed Siddiky, *Cross-Border Pipeline Arrangements: What Would a Single Regulatory Framework Look Like?*, 2012 (ISBN 978-90-411-3844-6).
21. Rozeta Karova, *Liberalization of Electricity Markets and Public Service Obligations in the Energy Community*, 2012 (ISBN 978-90-411-3849-1).
22. Sandra Cassotta, *Environmental Damage and Liability Problems in a Multilevel Context: The Case of the Environmental Liability Directive*, 2012 (ISBN 978-90-411-3830-9).
23. Mark Wilde, *Civil Liability for Environmental Damage: Comparative Analysis of Law and Policy in Europe and US*, 2013 (ISBN 978-90-411-3233-8).
24. Bernard Taverne, *Petroleum, Industry and Governments: A Study of the Involvement of Industry and Governments in Exploring for and Producing Petroleum*, Fourth Edition, 2022 (ISBN 978-94-035-3230-1).
25. Anton Ming-Zhi Gao & Chien Te Fan (eds), *Legal Issues of Renewable Energy in the Asia Region: Recent Developments in a Post-Fukushima and Post-Kyoto Protocol Era*, 2014 (ISBN 978-90-411-4856-8).
26. Sabina Manea, *The Instrumentalization of Property: Legal Interests in the EU Emissions Trading System*, 2014 (ISBN 978-90-411-5420-0).
27. Joseph A. Tolorunse, *Protection of Property Rights in Discovered Petroleum Reservoirs*, 2014 (ISBN 978-90-411-5604-4).
28. Katelijn Van Hende, *Offshore Wind in the European Union: Towards Integrated Management of Our Marine Waters*, 2015 (ISBN 978-90-411-5613-6).
29. Ken'ichi Matsumoto & Anton Ming-Zhi Gao (eds), *Economic Instruments to Combat Climate Change in Asian Countries*, 2015 (ISBN 978-90-411-5408-8).

30. Eduardo G. Pereira & Damilola S. Olawuyi (eds), *Practical Considerations to Negotiate an Enforceable Joint Operating Agreement under Civil Law Jurisdictions*, Second Edition, 2020 (ISBN 978-94-035-0664-7).
31. Ying Shen, *China's Way to Carbon Emissions Reduction: The Choice of Regulatory Instruments and Its Legal Challenges*, 2015 (ISBN 978-90-411-6049-2).
32. Roy Andrew Partain, *Environmental Hazards from Offshore Methane Hydrate Operations: Civil Liability and Regulations for Efficient Governance*, 2017 (ISBN 978-90-411-8730-7).
33. Anton Ming-Zhi Gao & Chien-Te Fan (eds), *The Development of a Comprehensive Legal Framework for the Promotion of Offshore Wind Power: The Lessons from Europe and Pacific Asia*, 2017 (ISBN 978-90-411-8397-2).
34. Tade Oyewunmi, *Regulating Gas Supply to Power Markets: Transnational Approaches to Competitiveness and Security of Supply*, 2018 (ISBN 978-90-411-9869-3).
35. Huseyin Cagri Corlu, *Application of Anti-manipulation Law to EU Wholesale Energy Markets and Its Interplay with EU Competition Law*, 2018 (ISBN 978-90-411-9603-3).
36. Kaisa Huhta, *Capacity Mechanisms in EU Energy Law: Ensuring Security of Supply in the Energy Transition*, 2019 (ISBN 978-94-035-1451-2).
37. Maria João C. Pereira Rolim, *Reconciling Energy, the Environment and Sustainable Development: The Role of Law and Regulation*, 2019 (ISBN 978-94-035-1461-1).
38. Eduardo G. Pereira, Alexandra Wawryk, Heike Trischmann, Catherine Banet & Keith B. Hall (eds), *The Regulation of Decommissioning, Abandonment and Reuse Initiatives in the Oil and Gas Industry: From Obligation to Opportunities*, 2020 (ISBN 978-94-035-0693-7).
39. Rasa Engstedt, *Handbook on European Nuclear Law: Competences of the Euratom Community under the Euratom Treaty*, 2021 (ISBN 978-94-035-2830-4).
40. Cinzia Caporale, Ilja Richard Pavone & Maria Pia Ragionieri (eds), *International Food Law: How Food Law can Balance Health, Environment and Animal Welfare*, 2021 (978-94-035-1761-2).
41. Rafael Leal-Arcas, *Climate Clubs for a Sustainable Future: The Role of International Trade and Investment Law*, 2021 (ISBN 978-94-035-3715-3).
42. Wang Xi & Richard Ottinger, *A Tale of Two Cities: A Comparison of Air Pollution Governance in the Los Angeles Area of the USA and the Beijing-Tianjin-Hebei Area of China*, 2024 (ISBN 978-94-035-4237-9).
43. Nina Claudia Miron & Liam Cashman, *European Union Case Law on the Birds and Habitats Directives*, 2024 (978-94-035-2557-0).